The Road to Crécy

The Road to Crécy
The English Invasion
of France, 1346

Marilyn Livingstone and Morgen Witzel

Harlow, England • London • New York • Boston • San Francisco • Toronto
Sydney • Tokyo • Singapore • Hong Kong • Seoul • Taipei • New Delhi
Cape Town • Madrid • Mexico City • Amsterdam • Munich • Paris • Milan

PEARSON EDUCATION LIMITED

Edinburgh Gate
Harlow CM20 2JE
United Kingdom
Tel: +44 (0)1279 623623
Fax: +44 (0)1279 431059
Website: www.pearsoned.co.uk

First edition published in Great Britain in 2005

© Pearson Education Limited 2005

The rights of Marilyn Livingstone and Morgen Witzel to be identified as authors
of this work have been asserted by them in accordance with the Copyright,
Designs and Patents Act 1988.

ISBN 0 582 78420 4

British Library Cataloguing in Publication Data
A CIP catalogue record for this book can be obtained from the British Library

Library of Congress Cataloging in Publication Data
Livingstone, Marilyn.
    The road to Crécy : the English invasion of France, 1346 / Marilyn
Livingstone and Morgen Witzel.
        p. cm.
    Includes bibliographical references and index.
    ISBN 0–582–78420–4
    1. Hundred Years' War, 1339–1453—Campaigns—France. 2. Crécy,
Battle of, Crécy-en-Ponthieu, France, 1346. 3. Great Britain—History,
Military—1066–1485. 4. France—History, Military—1328–1589. 5. Great
Britain—Foreign relations—France. 6. France—Foreign relations—Great
Britain. I. Witzel, Morgen. II. Title.

DC98.5.C8L58 2005
944'.02542'0944262—dc22

                                                            2004053470

10 9 8 7 6 5 4 3 2 1
09 08 07 06 05

Set by 35 in 10/14pt Galliard
Printed by Biddles Ltd, King's Lynn

The Publishers' policy is to use paper manufactured from sustainable forests.

Contents

List of illustrations

Maps

Acknowledgements

We are grateful to the following for permission to reproduce copyright material:

Plate 6 from the National Archives (ref. E101/390/11 m. 58); plate 10 from the Bibliothèque Royale de Belgique.

In some instances we have been unable to trace the owners of copyright material, and we would appreciate any information that would enable us to do so.

Authors' preface

This book has been some twenty-five years in the making. Throughout this time, the campaign of 1346 and the climactic battle of Crécy have interested us, in part because of the events themselves, which are as fascinating and dramatic and tragic as any reader of history could wish. But we also became interested in the wide variety of sources, including eyewitness accounts, second-hand reports in chronicles and administrative records, which, taken together, make it possible to study the Crécy campaign and many of its participants in great detail.

What we set out to do, therefore, was to reconstruct the campaign of the summer of 1346, shedding as much light as possible on the events and the people who took part in them. This is, unashamedly, a work of narrative history, focused on a single set of events. We make no claims for the relative importance of the Crécy campaign. We do not get involved in the debate over whether there was a military revolution in the fourteenth century; indeed, we do not believe it is possible to draw conclusions on this issue from the study of a single campaign. Nor do we feel the need to contribute to the already large literature on arrays, retinues, war finance and other similar subjects. This is a book about events; events, and the people who made them happen, or to whom they happened.

Any doubts we might have had about the validity of this approach were swiftly dispelled when we began retracing the steps of the English army on campaign. Time and time again, at St-Vaast, Valognes, St-Mère-Église, Carentan, Cheux, Caen, Lisieux, Poix, Airaines, Abbeville, we were reminded of a much more recent and more violent conflict, the memories of which were so strong as to be almost tangible. Somehow, this made the violence that had racked these same places six centuries earlier seem much more real and immediate. We realised that these events and people deserved to be remembered for their own sake, not just because we found them personally interesting or because the sources were particularly good. The tale became worth telling, not as an exercise in historical anslysis, but in its own right.

We owe thanks to a great many people who over the years have influenced our thinking and provided information, including students and friends at the University of Victoria and The Queen's University Belfast. More immediately, we would like to thank Heather McCallum at Longman's for commissioning this project and her continued support for it, Melanie Carter for sorting out production problems and Dorothy McCarthy for her able and rapid copy-editing. Thanks are also due to Professor Anne Curry and the Graduate Seminar at the Centre for Medieval Studies at the University of Reading, for the opportunity to air some ideas. Special thanks must also go to Margot Hone who not only translated correspondence but provided welcome accommodation during research visits to London.

Finally, a word about measurements. Throughout this book, measurements of distance are given in units of feet, yards and miles, measurements of area in acres, measurements of volume in gallons and so on. This was the system in operation throughout Europe at the time, and we feel it would be wrong to superimpose a modern system over the top of it. Medieval men and women thought in terms of miles and acres and bushels – even if they did not always agree on the precise size of these units of measurement – and in the spirit of authenticity we have retained these terms. Readers who wish to convert units of measure to the metric system are of course welcome to do so.

Chapter 1

The Road to War

Here [King Edward] gathered a famous and unconquered army of nobles, knights and commons and a fleet of ships terrible to both the eye and mind of the enemy . . .

Acta Bellicosa[1]

The village of Quettehou sits on a hill in western Normandy, a cluster of houses near the small stone church of St-Vigor. To the east of the village, the hillside leads down to the sea. Here lies the bay of St-Vaast, a horseshoe-shaped bay enclosed by land on two sides and by a long spit of land leading to a rocky islet known as La Hougue on the third. Today the village is small and quiet, and the bay below is usually empty but for a few small fishing boats; the small town of St-Vaast sits on the coastal plain below, beside a modern yacht haven. But on a summer morning more than six centuries ago, the bay was filled with ships, the beach and hillside were alive with thousands of men and horses, and the rumour of war filled the air.

Inside the church of St-Vigor a group of armed men had gathered, glittering in chainmail and plate armour, the bright colours of their coats of arms shining on surcoats and shields. The centre of all attention was the tall man who stood before the altar, a handsome, vigorous man in his mid-thirties, wearing a surcoat with two devices, three golden leopards on a field of red, and a scattering of golden lilies on a field of blue. This was Edward III, king of England and, so he claimed, of France. His stated purpose in bringing his army to France was to wrest the French crown from his adversary, Philippe VI. He himself had landed on the beach below Quettehou not long before, and had come straight to the church with his nobles and commanders. Before the fighting began there were symbolic duties to be performed, duties that would remind his followers once again of their purpose and their goals.

At the king's feet knelt his son. Edward of Woodstock, Prince of Wales, was also armoured and in the same livery as the king, save for the white label on his surcoat that marked him as the eldest son.[2] In his hands he held a drawn sword, the hilt upright so as to form a cross. Sixteen years old, he was already recognised as the heir to the throne; now he was to be confirmed as a war leader in his own right. The king leaned forward and laid his hands on his son's bare head, and spoke a few brief words charging his son to behave with honour and to be true always to his liege lord. The Prince of Wales accepted the charge laid upon him, and rose to his feet, a newly made knight.[3] His transition from boyhood to manhood was now complete.

Others then came forward to receive the same accolade. Following the prince came young William Montacute, Earl of Salisbury. Also just sixteen, he was the son of one of the king's oldest friends and closest companions. His father, also called William, had been at Edward's side on a night in 1330 when the young king and his companions had made their way through Nottingham castle to arrest his own mother and her lover Roger Mortimer, Earl of March, who together had overthrown and murdered Edward's father. The elder Salisbury had died in an accident during a tournament at Windsor two years earlier, but his son was now high in royal favour, and had recently married the king's cousin, Princess Joan of Kent. Now he knelt to receive his knighthood, another mark of favour. Among those watching, a few may have looked sideways at the one-eyed knight Thomas Holland. A few years before, Holland too had married Joan of Kent in a secret ceremony; when her marriage to Montacute was announced, he had then revealed his own claim to her hand. The matter had gone to court, and lawyers for both sides had begun to argue the case before Pope Clement VI, but Holland lacked the money to fight a long and complex battle.[4] Was this knighting now a signal that the king favoured young Salisbury and that Holland was to lose his claim? He must have wondered; yet here he was, preparing to fight in the same ranks as the man ostensibly married to his wife.

After Salisbury came Roger Mortimer, and here everyone present would have appreciated the situation, for Mortimer was the son of the man whom

Edward and Salisbury's father had arrested, and who had been executed for treason shortly after. As yet, the younger Mortimer had not yet been granted his father's title of Earl of March; he was still on probation. But by knighting him, Edward was sending yet another signal. During Edward II's reign, England had been torn apart by civil strife that had claimed the lives of his uncle the Earl of Kent, his cousin the Earl of Lancaster and hundreds of his subjects. That time was now over. Old rivalries, and new ones, were to be put aside. At stake was something much larger than petty disputes over patronage and wives. A great venture lay ahead, and all his knights and nobles were united behind him.

Other young men now came forward, William Ros, Richard de la Bere, Roger de la Warre and others to receive their knighthoods from the king. The prince himself, as was his right, knighted some of his own followers; the Staffordshire man-at-arms Edward atte Wode may have been one of these, but the names of the others are not known.[5] This was a customary act at the beginning of a campaign; the new knights, conscious of the honour that had been done to them, would fight more bravely and serve more conscientiously in order to prove themselves worthy, while other young men would be inspired to emulate them and earn honour of their own.

Another ceremony now followed. Out of the ranks of watching nobles came an armoured man in a surcoat decorated with red and gold horizontal bars. He walked with a limp, having been lame since birth.[6] His name was Godefroi d'Harcourt, and until recently he had been one of the most powerful barons of Normandy and a subject of the king of France. But in 1342 he had fallen out with his neighbour and rival Robert Bertrand, Seigneur de Bricquebec and Marshal of France. A personal quarrel over a dynastic marriage had escalated into full-scale rebellion in the following year. Defeated, Harcourt had been forced to flee from France; some of his friends were caught and executed. For two years Harcourt had remained in exile among the towns of Brabant and Flanders, which were also in revolt against their French overlords, and then in 1345 he crossed to England, where he was received by Edward and laden with honours. It was undoubtedly due to Harcourt, as all present would have known, that the army was landing here in the Bay of St-Vaast. Now Harcourt knelt and, recognising Edward as king of France, formally did homage for his lands and properties in Normandy. More symbolism, equally potent: eight years earlier, Harcourt had signed a document agreeing to provide troops and take part in an invasion of England, and now here he was leading the English into France.[7]

At a command from the king, his own standard was now unfurled, again displaying the twin devices of the leopards of England and the lilies of France. Another symbolic act: the making of new knights on French soil and the homage of a great Norman lord were followed now by the raising of the standard, as the king signified his intent to his 'adversary', as he always referred to Philippe of France. It was then around midday on 12 July 1346. The invasion of France had begun.

*   *   *

An army landing on a beach in Normandy; it is a familiar scene across the centuries, one which is etched in the memories of many since the middle of the twentieth century. It is easy to overstress the parallels, of course; Edward's army was minute by comparison with the vast forces that landed during Operation Overlord in 1944, and his army landed virtually unopposed, without having to fight its way ashore. Most important of all, of course, while the landings in 1944 were intended to liberate France from her conqueror, only the most wide-eyed innocent in the English ranks could have believed that the landings in 1346 were anything other than an outright invasion. Edward may have claimed the throne of France, but that throne, and the country, were in the hands of a determined and powerful enemy.

To understand how and why this invasion came about, it is necessary to step back for a moment and look at the chain of events that led not only to this invasion, but to the bloody and dreadful conflict which later came to be known as the Hundred Years War. When he came to the throne in 1327 following the overthrow and murder of his father, Edward inherited not only the crown but a legacy of conflict, including an ongoing war with Scotland and a history of thirty years of intermittent hostility with the French. The wars with Scotland had begun with Edward I's military inter-vention in the country in the mid-1290s, and had been pretty much con-tinuous ever since. Following Edward II's defeat at Bannockburn in 1314, the balance of the war had tilted against the English, and by the time Edward III came to the throne, the Scots had re-established their old border with England and were raiding repeatedly into the northern English counties. Following Edward II's overthrow, the Scots invaded northern England in force. A counter-offensive led by Roger Mortimer and the boy king Edward III nearly ended in disaster, and a humiliating peace treaty followed in 1328.[8] But as soon as he had overthrown Mortimer and taken power, Edward set about reversing the situation.

By the early 1330s, the Scots were growing weaker as England gained in strength. The great Scottish king Robert Bruce was dead, and his young son David was now king, with government in the hands of regents. Initially Edward left the prosecution of the war in the hands of a group of nobles and knights known as the 'disinherited' – that is, men who had been granted lands in Scotland during the English occupation but had these confiscated by the Bruces – under the leadership of Edward Balliol, a claimant to the Scottish throne.[9] This hands-off approach to Scotland lasted only as long as the 'disinherited' were making progress against the enemy. In 1332 Balliol with a small force of men-at-arms and English archers invaded Scotland and defeated the much larger army of the Scottish regents at the battle of Dupplin Moor. Importantly, the victory was largely achieved by the archers, who shot down the attacking Scots in great numbers while the men-at-arms stood firm and dealt with the remainder. A few months later, however, the situation was reversed; Balliol was defeated at Annan and driven out of Scotland. Edward now resolved to take a hand in events directly. Early in 1333 he raised an army and led it north to besiege the border town of Berwick-on-Tweed. A large Scots army which advanced to relieve the siege was met by the English at Halidon Hill, just north-west of the city. Here the English used the same tactics as at Dupplin Moor, posting their men-at-arms on high ground and flanking them with large bodies of archers who shot the enemy to pieces as they advanced. Scottish casualties were very high and included many important nobles. Much of lowland Scotland was subsequently occupied by the English, and the young King David was sent into exile in France.

Ominously for English fortunes, Philippe VI of France welcomed David in May 1334, and from this point the confluence of French and Scottish policies against the English was to cause Edward serious problems. Scotland and France had strengthened their alliance in 1326 with the Treaty of Corbeil, which guaranteed the support of each for the other in the event of war with England.[10] The presence of King David in France ensured Scottish influence on Anglo-French relations and French influence on

Anglo-Scottish relations, as is evident from the attempts of Philippe VI to put diplomatic pressure on England to try to force Edward to abandon his tenuous hold on Scotland.[11] Writing on these events, the historian Mark Ormrod concludes: 'Every warlike move made by Edward III towards Scotland now brought his country one step closer to open hostilities with France.'[12]

The victory at Halidon Hill was undoubtedly a boost in confidence for the English king, for with this battle he laid to rest, for the moment, the memory of the military incompetence of his father. But the benefits were alarmingly short-term. Despite the ease with which English armies entered Scotland and captured towns and castles, they had as ever great difficulty in obtaining any lasting control. The result was a gradual erosion of English power in lowland Scotland.[13] The occupying forces were unable to control the countryside outside their strongholds; local sympathies were against them, and guerrilla attacks and raids across the border into northern England were a constant problem. Although another large army invaded Scotland in 1337, thereafter the English position became increasingly defensive; the territories seized in lowland Scotland were gradually abandoned apart from Berwick, and the emphasis increasingly was on defending the border and preventing damaging Scottish raids on Cumberland, Westmorland and Northumberland. By 1337, virtually the whole of English attention had turned to France.

* * *

The Scottish war undoubtedly played a major role in drawing France and England into renewed conflict. Viewed from a very simple perspective, by going to war with England, France was honouring its treaty commitments to Scotland in much the same way that Britain honoured its commitments to Belgium in 1914 or to Poland in 1939. There is, however, much more to the matter than treaties and alliances. The roots of the Anglo-French conflict went back a long time, at least to the 1290s, and according to the historian John Le Patourel, back as far as the Norman conquest.[14] As Duke of Normandy, William the Conqueror had held Normandy as a vassal of the French crown; but when he conquered England he was a free agent, and thus held the kingdom of England free of any overlord. This created the paradox of an independent sovereign owning part of another country, a paradox that was heightened in the following century when Henry II of England married Eleanor, Duchess of Aquitaine and brought another huge swathe of continental territory into the hands of the English crown. Through the centuries that followed, the English monarchs dreamed of holding their continental possessions free of obligations to France, while the French kings equally dreamed of wrenching back these 'lost' lands and re-attaching them to the crown of France. In the early thirteenth century the French king Philippe Augustus solved part of the problem by conquering Normandy by force, but Aquitaine remained a subject of dispute.

For much of the middle of the thirteenth century England and France were ruled by pious men, Henry III and Louis IX respectively, who had other agenda and agreed to put the issue to one side. But with the accession of their more bellicose offspring, Edward I and Philippe IV, the problem resurfaced once more. By the early fourteenth century, the French crown was making little secret of its desire to expel the English from Gascony, the wine-rich region that formed the heart of the Duchy of Aquitaine and was still in English hands. Gradually the French were nibbling away at English possessions, suborning and bribing some lords, arranging favourable dynastic marriages with the families of others, planting new towns in what was ostensibly English territory and slowly expanding French influence in the region. The English for their part tried to evade the obligation to do homage, and occasionally resorted to more forceful measures. In October 1323 English and Gascon troops seized the new French *bastide* town of St-Sardos and burned it; in response, the French king Charles IV, son of Philippe IV, declared Gascony forfeit to the French crown and in 1324 mustered an army and prepared to invade the province. On this occasion the English capitulated. Queen Isabella of England, herself the sister of Charles IV, arrived in France to negotiate a peace; she also brought her son Edward, Prince of Wales, to Paris, who did homage to the French crown for English possessions in Gascony.[15] Peace had been restored by 1325, but there was little doubt that the initiative now lay with France, and the slow erosion of English territory and influence continued.

There then occurred a seismic shift in power in both England and France. Queen Isabella did not return to England at once. Instead, still accompanied by her son, she went to Hainault in the Low Countries, where she gathered a force of English exiles and continental mercenaries. She was supported by John, Count of Hainault, whose allegiance was secured by a marriage contract between the Prince Edward and the Count's daughter Philippa. In 1327 Isabella returned in force to England, over-threw her husband – his murder took place soon after – and ruled England in her son's name along with her lover the Earl of March. As related above, their ascendancy was short-lived, and at Nottingham in 1330 Edward launched a *coup d'état* of his own, overthrowing the regents and executing Mortimer. His mother he treated with honour, and although she never again held a position of power, she continued in possession of her lands and properties and frequently attended court. But from that moment onward, Edward was firmly on the throne and determined to consolidate his power at home and abroad.

The year after the death of Edward II, Charles IV of France also died. He was the last male heir of the house of Capet, which had ruled France for almost four hundred years. The sole remaining direct heir to the throne of France was Isabella, Queen of England. This meant that if she became queen of France, upon her death the French crown would pass to her son Edward, who would then be king of both England and France. The French nobles would have none of this, and in fairness it seems difficult to see how both England and France could have been governed together by a single mon-arch. Pragmatism as well as chauvinism probably led the French nobles to set aside Isabella's claim to the French throne on behalf of her son, on the rather dubious legal grounds that the crown could not be inherited through the female line, and to choose instead Isabella's cousin Philippe, Comte de Valois.[16] He was duly crowned Philippe VI in 1328, but like so many men who begin a dynasty, he never really wore the crown easily and throughout his reign remained – perhaps justifiably – unsure of his own legitimacy and suspicious of potential plotters against his reign.

Yet he was an able and active monarch, and one of his first acts was to draw up plans for the final invasion and annexation of Gascony in 1329. Edward III, still under the influence of Isabella and Mortimer, initially dropped the English claim to the French crown and did homage for Gascony a second time. But the threat remained. Gascony was valuable to both sides, and not only for prestige. The wine trade was extremely valuable to the English economy and exchequer; crown revenues from the duchy could be as much as £13,000 per annum.[17]

By the early 1330s it was becoming obvious that a major clash could not be long deferred. Mediation by Pope Clement VI succeeded in postponing matters for a while, and it was proposed that, rather than fighting each other, the two kings should lead their forces jointly on a crusade against the Mamlûk sultans of Egypt to recover the Holy Land. Edward agreed, on condition that the French stopped their incursions into Gascony and ceased their support for Scotland; reluctantly, Philippe did likewise, and public preparations for a crusade began. In reality, both sides used this interval to prepare for war, Edward to deal with the Scots – he hoped – once and for all, and Philippe to prepare a large fleet in the Mediterranean, ostensibly for the purpose of transporting the combined army to the Holy Land.

Late in 1336, the crusading project finally collapsed. Philippe's response was to move his fleet from the Mediterranean to the English Channel, where its presence threatened the English coast and shipping. Already throughout the 1320s and early 1330s, Norman ships had been preying on English merchant shipping in the Channel, leading to retaliatory attacks by English seamen. At first the French had tried half-heartedly to curb these attacks, but had been unable to do so, Charles IV admitting shortly before his death that he could not prosecute Norman pirates because, thanks to the independence of its judicial system, the French crown had no jurisdiction in Norman courts. This sounds like prevarication, but may well be true; the Normans were renowned as the most litigious people in Europe, and guarded their legal rights and privileges very jealously.[18] Now, though, the gloves were coming off, and the French royal fleet joined in attacks on the Suffolk coast and the Isle of Wight in 1336 along with attacks on shipping in various harbours. A defence force was raised to protect the southern and eastern coasts of England, but it had mixed success.[19] Over the next two years, Southampton,[20] Portsmouth, Plymouth and other coastal towns and districts were attacked.[21]

In May 1337 matters came to a head. Three years earlier, Philippe VI's brother-in-law, Robert d'Artois, had sought sanctuary in England. Robert had laid claim to the title and lands of Comte d'Artois, and had relied on Philippe to help him attain them. When the latter failed to do so, Robert first rebelled ineffectually and then went into exile. He had been in England for three years, fighting in the Scots wars and letting off occasional salvos of abuse at Philippe, but posed no particular threat. Nevertheless, in late 1336 Philippe suddenly demanded that Edward return Robert to France to stand trial, and when the king of England refused, in May 1337 Philippe declared him a 'contumacious vassal' and ordered that all his lands on the continent were forfeit to the French crown. This included not only Gascony but also the county of Ponthieu on the Channel coast and along the lower reaches of the river Somme, which had been an English possession since the late thirteenth century (it had been inherited by Edward I's wife, Eleanor of Castile, through her mother). The *baili* of Amiens, Pierre le Courant, was ordered to seize Ponthieu; this order was carried out almost at once, apparently without resistance.[22] At the same time, French forces under the command of the Constable of France, the Comte d'Eu, began the invasion of Gascony.

Edward has sometimes been painted as the aggressor in these proceedings, but there seems little doubt that Philippe wanted war as badly as did Edward; indeed, having massed his fleet in the Channel, he was probably the better prepared of the two. Edward's sheltering of Robert d'Artois was clearly only a pretext for Philippe's action,[23] which in turn formalised a war that had already been going on at sea for some months. The French forces in Gascony initially made little headway, their advance held up by a series of castles and fortified *bastide* towns. Thinking the southern flank secure, Edward and his advisors resolved to launch an offensive campaign of their own on the continent with a view to defeating the French as quickly and decisively as possible. To this end, it was thought necessary to acquire allies on the continent. The first obvious choices were to be found among the cities of Flanders. The Counts of Flanders were vassals of the French crown, but the powerful cloth cities of the north and west were famously restive and had a history of revolt; they were also economically dependent on England, requiring English wool to keep their weavers and dyers and fullers in work. It would take very little to make them rise again. Further east, Edward's brother-in-law William, Count of Hainault could be relied upon for support, and there were already a number of Hainaulters in English service, having come over with Queen Philippa.

Although English forces launched a few hit-and-run raids on the continent, notably at Cadzand, near Sluys in 1337, the initial effort was diplomatic rather than military. In the summer of 1337 Edward's representatives began talks with prospective allies. Such talks were accompanied by promises of large sums of money to ensure support, and it has been estimated that Edward had already promised some £124,000 in subsidies even before his diplomatic mission (headed by Bishop Burghersh of Lincoln) departed for the continent late in 1337. The Burghersh mission promised another £132,000 before Easter of the following year. In total, Edward was over £400,000 in debt by late 1340, most of the money having been spent trying to buy allies on the continent.[24]

Edward himself left for the continent in July 1338 in order to cement the alliances embarked upon in the previous year. Initially his strategy seemed to be working. He gained the support of the Holy Roman Emperor, Ludwig of Bavaria, and a number of other continental rulers, mostly of minor states. The financial pressure of maintaining these alliances was immense, however, and this hindered Edward's ability to launch an offensive campaign against the French; indeed, he was forced to spend much of his time fighting off his creditors. An abortive campaign against Cambrai in 1339 ended in a frustrating stand-off between the English and French forces and an English retreat to Brussels; another campaign in 1340 saw an unsuccessful siege of Tournai by the English and the destruction of a Flemish allied army at the battle of St-Omer.

The only military bright spot in some two and a half years was the defeat of the main body of the French navy at Sluys in June 1340, but even after this victory the English were unable to make any advance on land. Nor did this victory bring much relief by sea, for French ships continued to ravage the English coast from Suffolk around to Dorset, and to prey on English shipping in the Channel. By the autumn of 1340 financial pressures were such that Edward was forced to return to England.[25] His continental allies, never more than lukewarm, abandoned him once it was seen that he was unable to pay the sums promised for their support. The historian E.B. Fryde sums up the effects of this episode thus: 'This costly failure appears to have taught Edward III a lesson for he henceforth never attempted to invade France with the help of a large continental coalition, but adopted a policy of direct invasions from the sea or from bases on French territory, carried out exclusively by English troops.'[26]

Edward's financial position was now one of acute distress. He was borrowing money from both foreign bankers such as the Society of the Bardi from Florence, and from his own merchants, notably William de la Pole and John Pulteney; these were short-term loans to be paid out of the receipts of the taxes and customs. Fryde estimates that Edward's indebtedness before his arrival in the Netherlands in March 1338 was over £276,000.[27] By 1339 he had borrowed money from Italian bankers,

English merchants, continental princes, English clergy and his own magnates. He had pawned the crown jewels, and several of his retinue were hostages for his debts. He could no longer raise credit on the continent and could not pursue his military objectives without restoring his credit rating. The heavy taxes already levied were not enough to allow him to keep up with the demands of his allies, the cost of the Scots war, and the cost of maintaining a court abroad. He was also having difficulty in collecting those taxes that had been levied.[28]

The extent of Edward's indebtedness effectively ruled out any large-scale invasion of French territory. In contrast to the lack of any major English successes, the French had managed to inflict substantial damage on several towns on the south coast of England, including a major attack on Southampton and Portsmouth and smaller raids on the Channel Islands, Dover, Folkestone, Hastings, the Isle of Thanet, the Isle of Wight, Plymouth, Swanage (and environs) and Winchester. Attempts were also made to attack Harwich and Orford, but failed due to poor weather. Meanwhile in Gascony the English seneschal, Oliver Ingham, starved of men and money, could do little to prevent the steady French advance. Although his adversary, Philippe VI, had his own acute financial and administrative problems, Edward's crippling debts made it almost impossible for him to fight an offensive war, and for a time it looked as though his financial crisis would hand victory to the French.

* * *

A truce had been negotiated in Flanders at the end of the 1340 campaign, leaving the Flemish cities still in a state of revolt but otherwise the situation much as it had been before the war. Edward returned to England, to sack his ministers and attempt to reform his finances. He was partially successful in both cases, and certainly felt able to act when the next crisis came, in Brittany. The death of Jean, Duc de Bretagne in April 1341 presented a succession crisis, with both his daughter by his second marriage, Jeanne de Penthièvre, and his son by his third marriage, Jean de Montfort, claiming the title. Jeanne had married Charles de Châtillon, more usually known as Charles de Blois, nephew of Philippe VI, and lost little time in calling on her husband's uncle for support.[29] The French were delighted to assist, their scruples about allowing a woman to inherit a title being conveniently forgotten, and French troops under Philippe's son Jean, Duc de Normandie joined Charles's Breton forces. Jean de Montfort in turn requested English aid, but too late to prevent his capture by Charles at Nantes in 1341. Jean was sent to Paris as a prisoner, but his wife, Jeanne of Flanders, continued the resistance.

Belatedly, English troops finally arrived in Brittany in May 1342 to find Jeanne of Flanders and the remaining loyalists besieged in the castle of Hennebont, on the south coast of Brittany about midway between Vannes and Quimper. A detachment under Walter Mauny (one of the Hainaulters who had come to England with Queen Philippa) relieved the siege and went on to defeat French forces at Auray and Quimperlé. In August the English opened up another front in Brittany with the despatch of a force of 3,000 men under the Earl of Northampton to the port of Brest, also under siege by Charles de Blois and the French. Again the siege was broken, and Northampton drove Charles back on his base at Guingamp and settled down to besiege the town of Morlaix.

On Michaelmas Day 1342, Northampton received word that Charles was approaching with a force of between 10,000 and 15,000 men. He at once took up a position near the village of Lanmeur, about seven miles north-east of Morlaix. On 30 September 1342 the two forces met. Charles drew his army up in conventional style in three large divisions and sent them into the attack one after another. The first two were shot apart by Northampton's English archers and retreated with heavy casualties. But by now Northampton's men were running short of arrows, and he ordered them to fall back into a woodland to the rear of his position. As the third French division attacked, the mounted men-at-arms found themselves unable to ride into the dense woodland, and were shot down at close range by the English archers, who were conserving their arrows but still able to maintain a telling rate of fire. Eventually Charles retreated, having lost around 200 men-at-arms and an unknown number of foot soldiers. Northampton's casualties were minimal.[30]

This victory took much of the heart out of Charles's supporters, and they were disheartened still more in October when King Edward himself landed at Brest with a force of around 10,000. Charles's men, who had expected the fighting to stop for the winter, were caught off guard, and Edward and Northampton drove them eastward. There was one reverse when Robert of Artois, in an attempt to take Vannes in a sudden rush, was defeated by a pro-French force under Olivier de Clisson; Artois himself was mortally wounded in the fighting. But elsewhere the English made steady progress, and around two-thirds of the duchy had been reconquered by the end of the year. The appearance of a large French royal army under Philippe in person put an end to further progress, and, just as in Flanders in 1339 and 1340, the two kings faced off against each other. But once again the English were too weak to attack the French and the French reluctant to attack the English. In January 1343 papal mediators negotiated the truce of Malestroit and both sides returned home.

Another stalemate, though the English had come out of this one marginally better off than in Flanders; much of Brittany was now in the hands of the Montfort faction, which remained allied to them. But in the south the situation had gone from bad to worse. The French now occupied all the north bank of the Gironde, including the two important ports of Bourg and Blaye, and on the south bank were creeping forward almost to within sight of Libourne, twenty-five miles from Bordeaux. Many Gascon nobles had gone over to the French. The English were now restricted to Bordeaux itself and the Medoc and some other parts of the coastal strip; all else was in French hands. For the English, the time had come to rectify the situation in the south. The first step was to find a scapegoat; the seneschal, Oliver Ingham, was recalled and removed from his post in 1343, and died shortly thereafter.[31]

King Philippe of France, however, had his own problems. Always scenting conspiracies, in 1343 he found two exploding simultaneously in his face. The first was among his own allies in Brittany and centred around the powerful baron Olivier de Clisson, the victor at Vannes. Soon after – possibly even before – that battle, Clisson entered into correspondence with King Edward, and late in 1342 he revolted, bringing with him many barons of southern Brittany and western Poitou. The latter were particularly significant, for if they had joined Edward, they would have offered him an open passage from southern Brittany to Gascony. But Clisson made the mistake of travelling to Paris in July 1343, believing that he was covered by a safe conduct under the terms of the truce of Malestroit. The error was fatal; he was arrested at once and executed the following month. His widow, Jeanne, escaped prosecution and launched a campaign of banditry and guerrilla warfare in Poitou, but without Clisson's guiding presence the revolt quickly fell apart.

In Normandy the powerful baron Godefroi d'Harcourt's revolt began as a falling out with his neighbour, Robert Bertrand of Bricquebec. Both desired the hand of a wealthy local heiress for their families. The quarrel rapidly reached such a pitch that in 1341 both parties summoned their armed retainers to do battle, until expressly forbidden to do so by King Philippe. Bertrand obeyed, but Harcourt continued secretly to make preparations for armed conflict. Late in 1342 his retainers attacked the lands of Bertrand's brother Guillaume, Bishop of Bayeux, and destroyed several of his manors. Robert Bertrand, now acting in the king's name, sacked Harcourt's castle of St-Sauveur-le-Vicomte, and several of his supporters were arrested. Harcourt and a few of his followers, including the brothers Nicholas and Guillaume de Groussy and probably also Raoul de Verdun, fled to Brabant in March 1343, where they remained for another two years. Initially Philippe did not regard this as a conspiracy against the throne, but when late in 1343 rumours – almost certainly untrue – began to spread that Harcourt had been acting in conjunction with the English, the charges against him were changed from *lèse-majesté* to treason. Three of his supporters, Jean de la Roche-Tesson, Richard de Percy and Guillaume Bacon, were arrested and executed; their severed heads were hung over the main gate of the Norman town of St-Lô as a warning to others.[32]

*   *   *

Apart from these incidents, 1343 and 1344 passed comparatively quietly, with both sides generally observing the truce – though with exceptions – and strengthening their positions at home while plotting how best to renew the war. Peace talks were held at Avignon in 1344 but, with no real will for peace on either side, these came to nothing. Edward continued with the struggle to get his finances under control and stabilise his government to allow him to prosecute the war without further distractions, and also to continue to prop up his main ally, the Flemish rebel leader van Artevelde in Ghent. Philippe had to deal with the two conspiracies and also with delicate negotiations with Humbert of Dauphiné, the semi-independent lord of a large state east of the Rhône, which he appeared to be ready to sell to France in exchange for a sum of money that would enable him to live the rest of his life in luxury. The purchase of Dauphiné, when eventually completed, greatly extended French influence in the south-east.

Many French nobles took the opportunity of the truce to go crusading in Prussia or Spain. Others joined Edouard de Beaujeu, who took a squadron of galleys to assist in the defence of Smyrna (modern Izmir) against the Turks. Some Englishmen went to Prussia too, notably Thomas Holland, where he met such notables as Raoul de Brienne, shortly to succeed his father as Comte d'Eu and Constable of France, and also the blind King Jean of Bohemia, one of Europe's most famous warriors. Other English knights went off to Spain to join the Castilian forces besieging the Moorish city of Algeçiras. This little band was led by Henry of Grosmont, Earl of Derby, a cousin of the king; Richard Fitzalan, Earl of Arundel, arguably the wealthiest man in Britain; and Derby's sister Eleanor of Lancaster, who was openly living with Arundel as his mistress, despite the latter's having a wife in England. Lancaster tried and failed to persuade King Alfonso XI of Castile to desert his French alliance, while the English men-at-arms caught dysentery and made reckless assaults on the Moorish positions, leaving them in need of rescue by the irritated Castilians. Thus did the men of war of both sides pass the time during the truce.

The year 1345, however, brought a sense of renewed vigour to the war. The truce, which had been supposed to last three years, was tacitly abandoned by both sides. The French resumed operations in Gascony, and Edward raised an army and fleet to go to the Low Countries to support van Artevelde and threaten northern France. A much smaller force, only about 500 men-at-arms and 2,500 archers, was sent to Gascony under the command of the Earl of Derby and Walter Mauny, to attempt to at least stabilise the situation there.

The Flemish campaign was a failure. Edward arrived in Flanders to find that political unrest in Flanders had reached new heights. Van Artevelde was assassinated in July during riots in Ghent, and the Flemish alliance was now in danger of falling apart. Perturbed by this, Edward ordered his army back to England, but poor summer weather delayed the crossing and it was late July before the disordered fleet straggled back into east coast ports. The summer campaigning season had effectively been lost, and Edward pondered his next move. As a sop, Northampton was sent with a small force to north Brittany to push Charles de Blois out of his fortified position at Guingamp, but lacking siege engines he was unable to make headway, although Northampton's lieutenant Thomas Dagworth inflicted another defeat on Charles near Josselin in central Brittany. Northampton was ordered back to England in January 1346, but Dagworth remained behind with a small English force. The only other achievement was the final expulsion of the French from the Channel Islands. These had been occupied by French troops in 1338, but they had been expelled again in 1340 from everywhere but the fortress of Castle Cornet on Guernsey, which had defied the English for a further five years. Now, an expedition led by Thomas Ferrers and including a mixed force of Norman exiles and Gascon sailors laid siege to the castle and finally stormed it, slaughtering the French garrison.

In the south, however, Derby had succeeded beyond anyone's wildest expectations. Upon landing, he had augmented his tiny army with some loyal Gascon troops, and soon had a respectable force at his disposal. Sensing that the French commanders in the area were inactive (probably suffering from an acute shortage of money), he resolved on a counter-attack. Striking into the valley of the Dordogne, Derby arrived before the town of Bergerac on 24 August, and in two days of fighting took the town and routed the main French field army in Gascony, killing or capturing most of its leaders. Barely pausing, Derby moved north and took several key places in Périgord, including the important castle of Auberoche to the east of the city of Périgueux. This threatened Périgueux itself, and in response a second French army under Louis, Comte de Poitiers and Bertrand, Comte de l'Isle advanced from the east in October and laid siege to Auberoche. But on 21 October, Derby (now Earl of Lancaster following the death of his father in September) launched a surprise attack that destroyed this army as well; Poitiers was mortally wounded and l'Isle captured along with many other knights and nobles.

The year 1345 ended with both sides going into winter quarters in the south, with Lancaster settling down at La Réole on the Garonne south-east of Bordeaux. In little more than two months, he had recaptured a sizeable portion of the territory lost to the French over the previous eight years, and had altered the strategic balance in the south.[33] The victories of Bergerac and Auberoche had given the English their best opportunity of the war so far. It remained to be seen whether and how they would exploit it.

Notes

1 *Acta Bellicosa*, translated in Richard Barber (ed.), *The Life and Campaigns of the Black Prince*, Woodbridge, 1986, p. 27.

2 The label was a horizontal line with three short vertical lines below it. An example of the Prince's arms can be seen on his funeral effigy in Canterbury Cathedral.

3 The ceremony of knighthood in the mid-fourteenth century was still a fairly simple one, and usually involved the laying on of hands rather than the later dubbing with a sword. In theory, any knight could make a knight of another, but by this time the dubbing of knights was usually reserved for kings and senior nobles and was becoming more ceremonial. However, knighthoods for bravery in battle, the equivalent to modern battlefield promotions, were still sometimes given. For the sword as symbol of the cross, see Chapter 2.

4 Karl P. Wentersdorf, 'The Clandestine Marriages of the Fair Maid of Kent', *Journal of Medieval History*, vol. 5 (1979), pp. 203–31.

5 Ros, de la Warre and de la Bere are mentioned in *Acta Bellicosa*, in Barber, *Life and Campaigns*, p. 27. The further knighting of the Prince's followers is mentioned by Thomas Bradwardine in a letter dated four days later, translated in Barber, p. 14.

6 Harcourt was known as 'le boiteux', the lame. His father had born the same nickname, which suggests a genetic defect of some sort. This seems to have escaped Harcourt's elder brother Jean.

7 *Acta Bellicosa*, in Barber, *Life and Campaigns*, p. 29. It is not absolutely clear that the act of homage took place at the same time as the knightings, but in symbolic terms this would have been the most appropriate time.

8 For more detail on this and the Anglo-Scottish wars in general, see Colm McNamee, *Wars of the Bruces*, East Linton, 1997.

9 Edward did not publicly support the campaign, and in March 1332 forbade assemblies of men-at-arms in the North and wrote to the pope denying any involvement: M. McKisack, *The Fourteenth Century 1307–1399*, Oxford, 1959, p. 117; A. Tuck, *Crown and Nobility 1272–1461*, Oxford, 1985, p. 108.

10 Tuck, p. 109.

11 This succeeded in effecting a short truce in mid-1335, though this was of limited value as it offered the English a chance to gather their forces for a stronger invasion later in the year.

12 W.M. Ormrod, *The Reign of Edward III*, London, 1990, p. 13.

13 Michael Prestwich, *The Three Edwards: War and State in England 1272–1377*, London, 1980, p. 60.

14 John Le Patourel, 'The Origins of the Hundred Years War', in K. Fowler (ed.), *The Hundred Years War*, London, 1971, p. 38.

15 Pierre Chaplais (ed.), *The War of Saint-Sardos (1323–1325)*, London, 1954.

16 Most historians suggest that this first English claim was not meant seriously, but Le Patourel states that during discussions about the French succession in Paris in 1328, Edward was represented and had some support in the assembly: J. Le Patourel, 'Edward III and the Kingdom of France', *History*, 1958, pp. 174–5.

17 Prestwich, *The Three Edwards*, p. 167.
18 W.M. Ormrod, 'England, Normandy and the Beginnings of the Hundred Years War, 1259–1360', in David Bates and Anne Curry (eds), *England and Normandy in the Middle Ages*, London, 1994, pp. 197–214; Philippe Contamine, 'The Norman "Nation" and the French "Nation" in the Fourteenth and Fifteenth Centuries', in Bates and Curry, pp. 215–34.
19 W.L. Clowes, *The Royal Navy: A History from the Earliest Times to the Present*, London, 1897, vol. 1, pp. 236–7.
20 Colin Platt, *Medieval Southampton*, London, 1973, pp. 107–18.
21 Clowes, pp. 236–9. See Jonathan Sumption, *The Hundred Years War*, London, 1990, vol. 1, *Trial by Battle*, pp. 100–22, for a more detailed chronology of the raids.
22 M.H. Duseval, *Histoire de la Ville d'Amiens*, Amiens, 1848, p. 153. There is some question as to whether the English crown was in effective control of Ponthieu by this date; accounts for the county cease in the early 1330s.
23 Maurice Keen, *England in the Later Middle Ages*, London, 1973, p. 119.
24 E.B. Fryde, 'Financial Resources of Edward III in the Netherlands, 1337–40', *Revue Belge de Philologie et d'Histoire*, XLV (1967), pp. 146–7, 180–1, reprinted in *Studies in Medieval Trade and Finance*, London, 1983.
25 For a full discussion of the circumstances of Edward's return to England in December 1340, see N. Fryde, 'Edward III's Removal of his Ministers and Judges, 1340–1', *Bulletin of the Institute of Historical Research*, 47 (1975), pp. 149–61.
26 E.B. Fryde, 'Edward III's War Finance 1337–41: Transactions in Wool and Credit Operations', unpublished Oxford University D.Phil. thesis, 1947, p. 28.
27 Ibid., p. 27 and Appendix A.
28 M.R. Livingstone, 'The *Nonae*: The Records of the Taxation of the Ninth in England 1340–41', unpublished Ph.D. thesis, The Queen's University of Belfast, 2003, Chapter 2.
29 Charles is sometimes referred to as the Comte de Blois, but this title properly belonged to his brother Louis.
30 For more details of Morlaix and the Breton campaign generally, see Sumption, pp. 370–410; Richard Barber, *Edward, Prince of Wales and Aquitaine: A Biography of the Black Prince*, London, 1978, p. 40; Alfred H. Burne, *The Crécy War*, London, 1955, pp. 68–86.
31 Sumption, p. 421.
32 For a concise view of both plots see Sumption, pp. 411–15. For the aftermath of the affair, see Chapter 5 of this book.
33 For more detailed accounts of this campaign see Sumption, pp. 457–76; Burne, pp. 100–35.

Chapter 2

The Antagonists

The king at that time was in the flower of his youth, and desired nothing better than to combat his enemies.

Jean Froissart

The kings

In 1346, Edward III of England was thirty-four years old, at the peak of his physical and intellectual powers. The historian Mark Ormrod has summed up his character as 'bluff, brave, generous, slightly boorish, heartily heterosexual, fair-minded and, on the whole, even-tempered'.[1] He was tall and robustly built and was said to be a handsome man, as were many of the Plantagenet family. He was not an outstanding intellectual, and Professor Ormrod believes him to have been more interested in the practicalities of kingship than in any of the theories of governance that were fashionable at the time. When he married Philippa, daughter of the Count of Hainault, in 1326 he received as a gift several volumes of advice for young rulers, or 'mirrors for princes' as they were sometimes known, but it is doubtful if he ever opened any of them.[2] He was, however, an avid reader of histories, and collected chronicles of English history in particular, and there seems little doubt that he sought consciously to emulate the achievements of past monarchs such as Henry II and Edward I.[3]

Edward had come to the throne in 1327 at the age of fifteen in difficult circumstances, succeeding his father, who, by almost any measure, was a weak king, and whose reign had been characterised by military defeats abroad and near-continuous unrest at home. Three years later, he had seized power from his father's murderer and became king in fact as well as in name. Since then, his stock had been steadily rising. There had been failures, however. His attempt to finish the work of his grandfather by conquering Scotland had not succeeded, despite several military victories. The war with France had not so far achieved its objectives, or shown much sign of doing so. At home, there were severe financial problems which the war was exacerbating. The old noble houses, which had become alienated from Edward II by his habit of promoting his favourites to positions of authority, watched with suspicion as his son showed signs of doing the same. In 1337, for example, Edward had appointed seven new earls; some were from senior families like the Bohuns and the Courtenays, but others were men of relatively lowly backgrounds such as William Montacute and William Clinton.[4]

However, Edward had managed to make his authority felt, in part because, as Professor Ormrod says, 'above all, he fitted the contemporary image of kingship'.[5] Medieval English kings were not autocrats; as the death of Edward's father had clearly shown, they governed with the consent of their people, especially their earls and barons. They carried on their shoulders a weight of expectations and hopes. They were expected to exhibit personal courage, generosity and magnanimity, to be equally successful as war leaders, statesmen and law-givers; but above all, they were required to embody national pride and self-image. Edward II met a shameful death not because of his homosexual proclivities, not even because he shamelessly promoted his favourites to places of power, but because his actions – his military defeats, his weak foreign policy, the extra-judicial murder of the Earl of Lancaster – were seen as bringing shame on himself and on his subjects.[6]

Accordingly, throughout his reign Edward III strove not only to rule his kingdom, but also to be seen to rule it in a befitting manner. He was generous, even at times when his purse was empty; titles and lands were freely given as rewards for good service, thus fulfilling one of the requirements of the truly chivalrous man, largesse. He was lavish in display; to use a modern term, he was a crowd-pleaser, but he and Queen Philippa also shared a genuine love of luxury and seldom hesitated to buy the best of everything. It is estimated that during his fifty-year reign Edward spent £130,000 on building works alone,[7] plus countless thousands on personal items, furnishings and the like. He gave splendid feasts and sponsored even more magnificent tournaments.

Edward's pragmatism showed itself in other ways. Although he personally led most of the major campaigns of the first twenty years of his reign, he usually played the role of commander-in-chief, delegating authority to his captains, only rarely plunging himself into the thick of the fighting. Later, when his sons were old enough to take the field as commanders in their own right, he handed more control to them. Not the least of the achievements of 1346 was the establishment of the authority of the sixteen-year-old Edward of Woodstock, Prince of Wales, although it would be some years yet before the prince would hold an independent command. The king also seems to have been – on the whole, and with exceptions – an astute judge of people. The men he gathered around him may have been his personal friends, but they also served him well. The creation of the earls in 1337 was not just about rewarding friends for past services, but also a matter of binding men of talent more closely to him. By 1346, Edward's court contained a hard core of experienced captains and administrators, probably the equal of any in Europe.

Edward was also capable of learning from his mistakes, and adapting both his policies and his strategies. At the beginning of the war he had hoped to create an alliance capable of defeating France, and had naively doled out lavish sums as bribes to the counts, dukes and margraves of the Low Countries and Germany. This had failed; the local rulers accepted the bribes but had quickly deserted the alliance when things began to go wrong. Rather than repeating the experiment, Edward vowed that in future he would rely on his own resources, keeping only a few allies for pragmatic reasons such as the Flemings and Bretons (see Chapter 1). In battle, too, he was a quick learner, understanding at once the significance of the tactical formation used at Dupplin Moor (see below) and adopting it for more widespread use.

Pragmatic when it came to government and the leadership of armies, Edward III nonetheless had lofty ambitions. In his passion for history we can discern his wish not only to re-create the empire of Henry II, or something like it, but a deeper desire to find some sort of guiding ideal or inspiration that would unite his realm and people in pursuit of that goal. Like Edward I and the latter's great-uncle Richard of Cornwall, he initially sought this inspiration in the myths (which people of the time regarded as genuine history) of King Arthur, and deliberately encouraged comparisons between his own military successes and those of Arthur.[8] In January 1344 he organised a tournament at Windsor full of Arthurian allusions, complete with a replica Round Table; the event was marred when his closest friend, William Montacute, Earl of Salisbury, was mortally wounded on the tournament field. Edward also began to encourage the cult of St George, the warrior saint who had been much patronised by the Normans in the tenth and eleventh centuries. An undated document describes thousands of pennons and banners bearing the cross of St George, some also showing the arms of the king.[9] And just a few years after the events of this book would come the foundation of the Order of the Garter.

It would be easy to dismiss all these efforts as propaganda. Of course there was an element of propaganda about them, and among his other skills Edward became a master at manipulating public opinion.[10] Professor Ormrod assesses Edward as 'one of the most image-conscious kings of the later Middle Ages',[11] but in all these activities Edward was doing more than just conducting an exercise in public relations. Out of the divisions and chaos of his father's reign, he was seeking to reunite and strengthen the kingdom. And interestingly, he was not doing so simply by ensuring personal loyalty to himself alone, though that was part of it. Among his knights and barons, at least, he was trying to fashion a more general unity; a feeling, perhaps, of 'Englishness'. It is probably no accident that from the mid-fourteenth century there appears an increasing volume of literature written in English, rather than French,[12] and we can assume that the transition from spoken French to spoken English among the knightly and noble classes occurred about the same time.

Brave, generous, ambitious, fond of pageantry and display, Edward III embodied many of the qualities of a successful medieval king. But although he had had his successes on the battlefield, at Halidon Hill and Sluys, his victories had not been decisive ones. Despite Derby's successes in Gascony, the war as a whole had cost much money and lives, and had brought Edward little closer to his professed goals. Despite his personal qualities, in 1346 it remained to be seen whether he would prove in the end to be a successful king.

* * *

Few such doubts should have existed on the other side of the Channel, where the French nobles should have had every reason to be satisfied with their choice of Philippe de Valois as king following the extinction of the Capet dynasty. In 1346, Philippe was fifty-three years old; he had been on the throne for eighteen years, just one year less than his adversary. His reign so far had been undramatic, but quietly competent.

For all that he founded one of France's most important and long-lasting royal dynasties, Philippe de Valois remains an enigmatic figure. He has had no major biographer. Later French historians have condemned him as incompetent and brushed him aside.[13] This is unfair. Philippe had his faults and weaknesses, as did Edward, but he was not so much of a blunderer as is sometimes supposed. Philippe's reign did end in failure, but that does not mean his entire reign was a failure; far from it. By 1346, he had done pretty much everything that could reasonably be required of him. He had opened his reign with a military victory, thrashing the rebellious Flemings at Cassel. He had continued the centralising policies of Philippe IV, slowly strengthening the central administration and looking to extend French influence on the periphery, notably in Dauphiné but also in the south and south-west. Despite losing part of his fleet at Sluys, he had maintained the upper hand in the war with England, had contained if not suppressed the renewed rebellion in Flanders, and had conquered Ponthieu and much of Gascony while continuing to vigorously raid English shipping and ports. He had shown himself to be easily Edward's superior in the diplomatic arena, winning many of the rulers of the Low Countries to his side and maintaining strong alliances with Castile and Savoy; the current pope, a Frenchman, was in his control, and by the end of 1345 he knew he had every chance of seeing his son's brother-in-law on the throne of the Holy Roman Empire.

Yet for all his achievements, it is clear that contemporaries had their reservations about Philippe. Even those chroniclers who supported him and were hostile to the English, such as the authors of the *Grandes Chroniques* and the *Chronique des Quatre Premiers Valois*, were often grudging in their praise and quick to point out his faults. In part, criticisms of Philippe need to be seen against the political climate in France at the time. Much of the history of the preceding dynasty concerns the interminable struggle between the crown and the great nobles, the latter determined to preserve their independence, the former equally determined to assert central control and strengthen the power of the crown. Vast parts of what we now call France, including Brittany, Lorraine, Provence and, of course, Gascony, were nominally fiefs of France but were in practice independent. Others were more strongly linked to the crown but still guarded their own privileges jealously. Nowhere was this problem no more apparent than in Normandy. Although it had been reunited with France in 1204, the Duchy of Normandy still maintained its own legal code, its own courts and its own administration, and was quick to defend these against central authority in Paris. Philippe's own predecessor had complained shortly before his death that he was completely unable to enforce the decisions of his own courts in Normandy without consent of the local authorities.[14] So, the centralising measures taken by Philippe, which with hindsight seem perfectly logical to us, were watched with suspicion by many of his nobles. Mistrust coloured much of the king's relations with his nobles throughout his reign.[15]

This mistrust was wholly returned by the king. One of his less attractive features seems to have been a suspicious nature, at times bordering on the paranoid. As we shall see in later chapters of this book, he was prone to suspect treason even where none existed. Any reverse, even a slight one, was at once blamed on traitors. In fact, serious acts of treason were a relative rarity in France during Philippe's reign. Brittany had attempted secession, and some of his Gascon allies were none too reliable, but on the other hand two potentially serious revolts, those of Clisson and Harcourt mentioned in Chapter 1, were in fact snuffed out fairly promptly by loyal nobles and officials. There were occasional minor acts of sedition, such as the case of Simon Pouillet, a merchant of Compiègne, who reportedly told friends that it would be better to be governed well by an Englishman than badly by a Frenchman, but nothing out of the ordinary. Certainly Philippe's reign was domestically much more tranquil than that of his son. But for all that he never seems to have worn the crown easily, and his reaction to even minor incidents was often brutal; the unfortunate Pouillet, denounced to the authorities, was hanged and quartered in Paris in June 1346. The *Grandes Chroniques* suggests there was some public disquiet at this punishment, which was out of proportion to the crime.[16] More generally, relations with the nobles remained difficult. On the eve of the climactic battle of the 1346 campaign we find Philippe dining with his commanders and pleading with them to set aside old quarrels and unite against the common foe.[17] It is hard to imagine Edward making a similar speech; by 1346, he could count on the unity and support of his nobles.

Another noticeable character trait of Philippe, which could be either a strength or a weakness depending on circumstances, was his tendency to caution. His actions in 1346 are often those of a man who likes to be sure of his facts before he makes a move. This was particularly true of warfare. His one major military victory, Cassel, had been a muddled affair which had turned out right in the end, but this may have left him with a dislike of pitched battles unless he was sure of victory. In 1340 he had faced Edward's smaller army at La Flamengerie, but refused to give battle as he did not believe the odds were in his favour. On that occasion a convenient horoscope was found which advised the French not to give battle, and the French nobles, who had been clamouring for a fight, were forced to give way to this superior authority. But in 1342 in Brittany, Philippe had again refused to attack the English, and by 1346 there were obvious question marks over his taste for battle. In fact his caution in both cases was fully justified, but his attitude did not sit well with his aggressive subordinates. Philippe himself was aware of these criticisms, which would be repeated several times during the campaign to come.

Men-at-arms

The primary fighting force of the great majority of medieval armies was the mounted, armoured horseman. He was known by a variety of names in many languages, but we will use the generic term 'man-at-arms' to encompass the whole range from dukes, counts and earls down to lowly knights bachelor, esquires and mounted serjeants.

On the whole, the knightly and noble classes of England and France had much in common, and shared many features of upbringing, education and outlook. They listened to similar music and poetry, danced the same dances, wore very similar fashions in clothing, and subscribed – or at least paid lip service to – the code of chivalry, which the historian Maurice Keen has described as a kind of 'universal currency' or shared culture in which most of the upper classes of Europe participated.[18] They were also, and this may come as something of a surprise, literate and well-educated; they had to be, for many of them served as officials and bureaucrats as well as soldiers. This was particularly true of England, where members of the

knightly class were for most of the year more likely to be found behind a
desk than in the saddle, serving as sheriffs, escheators, commissioners of
array, commissioners of oyer and terminer or any one of a number of roles
in the complex administration of the realm.

The medieval man-at-arms was a fighting man, but he was also very
much more than that. From time to time, depending on his rank and as
the situation demanded, he was also a tax collector, a judge, a regional
administrator, a coroner, a collector of customs and a law enforcement
officer. In addition, of course, most had landed estates of their own which
had to be managed, rents collected, crops harvested and taken to market,
buildings maintained and so on. It is small wonder that many, feeling that
they already had quite enough tasks and chores, either requested exemption from military service or paid others to go in their place. Some regarded military service as an onerous obligation, to be avoided if possible;
others saw it as a duty that they were willing to perform; still others saw it
as a chance to better themselves, to win riches, honour and glory; some
went because they liked fighting. They were not a homogenous group;
their motives and attitudes were as diverse as their characters.

The central guiding ethos of this class was supposed to be the code of
chivalry, a complex, unwritten set of social values and mores that had
developed in France but spread to most corners of Europe by the fourteenth century.[19] The epic poems of the day, the *chansons de geste*, described the exploits of great chivalric heroes, the paladins of Charlemagne
or the knights of King Arthur's Round Table; other heroes feature occasionally, such as Aeneas, the founder of Rome, or the leaders of the First
Crusade, Bohemond of Antioch and Godfrey de Bouillon, but always with
the same chivalric values grafted onto their characters. Duty to one's overlord, valour and skill in battle, protection of the weak and the innocent,
courtesy to women, devotion to God; these are the values that the culture
of the day held the knight ought to have.[20] The heroes and role models
were men like Roland, who gave his life to stop the Saracen army at
Roncesvalles, or Tristan, who died rather than bring dishonour on his lover
Isolde, or, most of all, Parsifal, who remained pure in body and mind and
devoted his life to the quest for the Holy Grail.

Of course no mere mortal could live up to the idea of Parsifal, and
satirists such as the Frenchman Jean de Meung were quick to point this
out. In Meung's *Roman de la Rose*, the hero embarks on an epic quest not

for the Grail but for a rose, which turns out to be a rather crude metaphor for the female genitalia. But equally it would be a mistake to think that no one took the idea of chivalry seriously. Many took it very seriously indeed. The French knight Geoffrey de Charny, who had fought in Brittany in 1342 and was now serving with the French army in Gascony, set down his thoughts in a work usually known as the *Livre de Chevalerie* some time in the late 1340s. For Charny, the ultimate goal of the knight is honour; all his actions, thoughts and words should be honourable ones. He acknowledges that men will go to war to gain riches and does not condemn this; but those who fight for honour alone, he says, are more to be praised.[21] Charny, it should be added, extends the code of chivalry beyond knights to encompass all men-at-arms of whatever rank; thus the esquires and serjeants are expected to live by the same code as the knight.

Even this ideal could not always be lived up to, and men who were trained to warfare often had trouble separating the horrible necessities of war from the values by which they were expected to live. It should come as no surprise that in medieval warfare, prisoners were massacred, women were raped and religious houses were plundered and burned, sometimes with official sanction. Inevitably too, some of the men of war had trouble making the transition to peacetime, or were simply brutal by nature. Eustace Folville, son of John Folville of Ashby Folville in Leicestershire, embarked on a life of crime along with his brothers Robert and Richard – the latter a clergyman – during the troubled late years of Edward II's reign, and despite being indicted for a series of robberies, rapes and murders, died of natural causes in 1347; he served in the army at least twice, though not apparently in 1346.[22] John Molyns of Stoke Poges, Buckinghamshire was indicted for murdering his wife's son and uncle and for a series of thefts, robberies and beatings; at one point he was forced to go into hiding, but in 1345 he received a full pardon. He did serve with the army in 1346, rose in royal favour and became steward of Queen Philippa's household in the 1350s, but in 1357 was finally convicted of theft and died in prison.[23]

Shortly before dawn on Good Friday, 1347, a gang of men including six knights – several of whom, including John Dalton and William Trussel, were veterans of the 1346 campaign – broke into the manor house of Beaumes near Reading. The manor was owned by Margery de la Beche, the wife of Gerard Delisle, and among those staying there were several of the king's children, including the eight-year-old Lionel of Antwerp and some of his younger siblings. The rampage that followed was shocking even by the standards of the time. Before the eyes of the terrified royal children, the gang stormed through the house, raped Margery de la Beche, killed her uncle, Michael Poynings (another veteran of 1346) and another man, Thomas Clerk, and injured a number of others. The king, furious, declared the perpetrators outlaws and ordered their arrest, but they fled to Scotland before they could be caught.[24] Incidents such as this led the actor and historian Terry Jones to question whether chivalry was ever more than a myth; in his view, Chaucer's 'parfit gentil knyght' was a mercenary who sold his sword for hire and turned a blind eye to atrocities, or even participated in them.[25] In fact, as ever, human nature resists generalisations; those who aspired to Charny's high ideals existed alongside the likes of Folville and Molyns, just as they have done in armies since the beginning of time.

Below the knight in rank came the esquire or *escuyer*, which generally meant a man of good family who had not – or not yet – been dubbed a knight. Some might be young knights in training, waiting to be dubbed; others were older men who had refused knighthood; still others were too poor or had simply been overlooked by the authorities. In practice they were virtually indistinguishable from the knights. Most had landed estates, often quite extensive ones; a wealthy esquire might be considerably richer than a poor knight. In England the esquires were also extensively involved in public service, on various commissions or as deputy escheators or deputy sheriffs; some, such as the Northumberland man John Copeland, even served as sheriffs. Their outlook and attitudes were very much those of the knights, and often little distinction can be made between the two groups. The lowest rank of all were the mounted serjeants, men of common origin but with enough money – or with a patron who had enough money – to equip them with armour, weapons and horses. In the mid-fourteenth century the numbers of these were diminishing as mounted warfare became progressively more expensive, but both armies still included substantial numbers of them.

Despite this common milieu, however, there were differences in attitudes and outlook among the men-at-arms on opposite sides of the English Channel, and to get some idea of the diversity among them, let us look at some examples from each army.

* * *

The dominant figures in any French army of the early part of the four-teenth century were the *grands seigneurs*, the great semi-independent feudal overlords. As a class, they identified closely with the heroes of the *chansons de geste*, sometimes on a personal basis; many claimed to be able to trace their lineage back to the court of Charlemagne. Their ancestors were often martial heroes in their own right. Charles de Montmorency, a Marshal of France and one of King Philippe's closest confidantes, had ancestors who had distinguished themselves in the crusades and fought in the Norman conquests of England and Ireland. Another seigneur close to the king, Edouard de Beaujeu, also came from a family of crusaders; his great-uncle, Guillaume de Beaujeu, had been Grand Master of the Knights Templar and had been killed at the siege of Acre in 1291 (presumably no one in the family mentioned that, prior to the siege, the Grand Master had been suspected of treasonable correspondence with the enemy). Jean de Châlon, Comte d'Auxerre, was one of those who claimed descent from Charlemagne's paladins; another ancestor, Otton, was a brother of Hugh Capet, the founder of the previous dynasty.[26]

One of the greatest families of France was that of Châtillon. They traced their ancestors back to Charlemagne, and had a history of crusading; one of the family, Raynault de Châtillon, Lord of Kerak and Oultrejourdain, had been executed – some said by Saladin personally – after the battle of Hattin. The current head of the family was Louis de Châtillon, Comte de Blois et Dunois, who had inherited the title following the death of his father, Guy, in 1342. His mother was Marguerite de Valois, the sister of King Philippe; his sister Marie was married to Raoul, Duc de Lorraine, one of the powerful semi-independent nobles on the eastern borders of France; his brother Charles had married Jeanne de Penthièvre, the heiress of Brit-tany, and claimed the title Comte de Bretagne; and Louis himself had married Jeanne, Comtesse de Soissons, only child and heir of John of Hainault, Lord of Beaumont and one of the most powerful men in the Low Countries. A cadet member of the family, Guy de Châtillon, held the title Comte de St-Pol. Louis de Châtillon's connections thus included not only the crown of France but many powerful figures on the periphery of the country. Quite probably, he was wealthier and more powerful than the king himself.

The Briennes were another ancient family with a history of crusading. One branch of the family had established themselves as Dukes of Athens following the Frankish conquest of Greece in the thirteenth century; another member of the family had married Yolande, daughter of the Holy Roman Emperor Frederick II and thus also claimed the title of King of Jerusalem. Their descendants had been dispossessed, but Gauthier de Brienne, now serving with the French army in Gascony, still titled himself Duke of Athens. The senior branch of the family was represented by Raoul de Brienne, Comte d'Eu and Constable of France. His father had been a close friend and supporter of King Philippe, and had been appointed Constable in 1332; he had also participated in Jean of Bohemia's Italian expedition in the 1330s (see Chapter 3) and had close links with the rulers of Savoy. He had led French armies in the initial invasion of English Gascony upon the outbreak of war, but in 1344 he had been killed in an accident during a tournament held to celebrate the marriage of King Philippe's younger son. His death robbed Philippe of an important supporter. His son, the new Comte d'Eu, was only in his mid-twenties and had relatively little experience of warfare, certainly not enough for the duties now thrust upon him.

Of the individuals in this group we know only a little; as a class, according to contemporaries, they were characterised by pride and ambition. The author of the *Grandes Chroniques* rails bitterly at their hauteur and arrogance, and maintains that France's military disasters of the Hundred Years War were a punishment by God visited upon them. Another chronicler, Jean le Bel, maintained repeatedly that 'pride and envy' had led to French defeats. On the battlefield, we see time and time again how a powerful belief in their own primacy and superiority led the French nobles to commit incredible folly. At the battle of Courtrai in 1302, believing they were facing only a rabble of townsmen that were no match for their fighting powers, they launched into a foolhardy charge, and in the process heedlessly rode down some of their own foot soldiers. The charge ended in disaster and death; but no lessons were learned from it, and the incredible self-belief was not dented.

Below the *grands seigneurs* was another class of lesser nobles and knights based in the various provinces of France. These were largely separate from the great families; there was little marriage between them, and the provincial nobles seldom entered the national stage. There were exceptions; the Norman baron Robert Bertrand, Seigneur de Bricquebec, had a distinguished career in French royal service, first as ambassador to Bohemia in

1321 and then as Marshal of France in 1325. He had led French forces in the St-Sardos war of 1323–5, stood behind King Philippe at Amiens in 1329 when Edward of England did homage for Gascony, and in the present war had fought at Auray and Hennebont during the Breton campaign. He was now an elderly man, but his son Robert, Vicomte de Longeville, was preparing to follow in his footsteps. Other Norman nobles such as Jean, Comte d'Harcourt, and Jean de Melun, Comte de Tancarville, had rendered service to King Philippe and been rewarded as a result. But most were like the extended families of Bacon and Groussy, local lords conducting local affairs, making local marriages and building up local power bases. Their interests seldom if ever extended outside their own province.

The same was also largely true of the minor nobles and knights of Picardy. Along the valley of the Somme, and in southern Picardy, local seigneurs such as Jean de Picquigny, Jean de Hangest, Mathieu de Cayeu and Alerin de Brimeu had, until the war broke out, little interest in affairs outside their own area. Again, they married locally and, when called upon for military service, fought locally as well. The war would change this to some extent, with Picquigny and Hangest going on to become captains of mercenaries, although Picquigny's interests still remained concentrated in Picardy. There were a few more exotic individuals. The Tyrel family, Seigneurs de Poix, claimed ancestry back to Charlemagne's day when they were said to have held the title Prince de Poix. That title, if it had ever existed, had fallen into obscurity and the Tyrels were now just another rustic Picard knightly family. The Croï family, including Guillaume, Seigneur de Croï-sur-Somme and Jean, Seigneur d'Airaines, were descended by five generations from Andrew III, King of Hungary, and through him from St Stephen of Hungary himself. Guillaume de Croï's father Pierre had been more usually known as Pierre d'Hongrie. As might be expected, this family was more adventurous; Guillaume de Croï had served in Gascony during the St-Sardos war, and while there had married Jeanne de Pons from Bergerac. But these families were exceptions; for the most part the Picard knights and lords, like the Normans, kept to themselves.

Below these were the esquires and serjeants. Their careers are shadowy, and it is rare to find an individual about whom we can learn much; only if they later rise to prominence is anything more than their mere names recorded. A list of forty-two of King Philippe's serjeants-at-arms, members of the king's household who served in a variety of functions and rode with the king into battle, has survived from 1346. This group included another of the Hangest family, Jacquet, and a few other recognisable family names such as Jacquet d'Auxonne, Mahieu de Quiedeville, Gile de Douay, Lyon de Chambly and several members of the Lalemant family.[27] Pierre d'Auvilliers came from a small hamlet near Neuilly-sous-Clermont in the Oise, and in 1346 was one of the group of professional fighting men who had gathered around Jean de Luxembourg, King of Bohemia. In the 1350s he emerges as a commander of crossbowmen in the service of Jean de Hangest, and he went on to fight in Normandy, Guernsey, Spain and La Rochelle, on one occasion serving with the exiled Welsh prince Owen Glendwr. Auvilliers became wealthy enough to buy land and found a minor dynasty. Of his comrades in Bohemian service, men like Colin Petit de Maubuisson and Lambequin de Pé, we know very little, and the same is true of the vast majority of this class.

* * *

Looking at the English nobles and knights, one quickly gets the impression that they were both more cosmopolitan and less stratified than their French counterparts. This may be due to the fact that they came from a smaller country with a smaller population, but whatever the reason, the great noble houses such as the Fitzalans and the Lancasters seemed to rub shoulders much more comfortably with the minor members of the aristocracy. Further, the English barons and knights were more likely to marry outside their own region and to have lands and interests in diverse parts of the country. This is particularly true when we look at the membership of retinues. It was beginning to be the custom for noblemen and well-to-do knights (and others: see Chapter 3) to retain the services of other men-at-arms, usually but not exclusively for military service. It might be expected that these would be very regional in focus – that the Earl of Suffolk would recruit most of his retinue in Suffolk, and so on – but this is rarely the case. As it happens, a high proportion of the Earl of Suffolk's retinue in 1346 *did* come from East Anglia (or at least had surnames denoting places in East Anglia). In the Earl of Huntingdon's retinue, on the other hand, the largest geographical grouping of names comes from Kent. In the retinues of the Earls of Northampton, Arundel and Warwick, no geographical pattern is apparent, and men come from all over the country.[28]

Nor are family connections always evident; men of different families could and did serve in different retinues. For example, John Botetourt served in the retinue of the Earl of Huntingdon, while Robert Botetourt was in the retinue of the Earl of Oxford. Walter Paveley was in the retinue of Bartholomew Burghersh, while his brother John was in that of the Earl of Arundel. John Montacute was to be found in the retinue of the Prince of Wales rather than that of his nephew the Earl of Salisbury, and so on. The retinue system was, like English noble society itself, fluid; men could, and did, change retinues. When the Earl of Huntingdon was forced to return to England due to illness, his retainers John Botetourt and Henry Braillesford accompanied him to England, but William Setvantz transferred to the king's retinue. When at the end of the summer the Bishop of Durham returned to England to help confront the Scots, several of his retainers transferred to other lords. This seems to have been considered perfectly normal.

Thanks to England's superb administrative records, it is possible to know a fair amount about the men who made up the English army. We have been able to identify nearly three thousand individuals – about one member in five of the army – who can with a fair degree of certainty be said to have fought in France in the summer of 1346, from earls and barons to archers and clerks. It is about the former, of course, that we know most, and a few pen portraits will help give an idea of the individuals themselves and the nature of their society.

William Bohun, Earl of Northampton and Constable of England, was born probably in 1312, which would have made him thirty-four years old in 1346 (coincidentally, the same age as the king). His family had been established in Herefordshire since the twelfth century at least, but it was William's father Humphrey who first rose to national prominence during Edward I's wars in Scotland. Edward I recognised Humphrey Bohun's talents and promoted him quickly, appointing him Earl of Hereford and Essex and Constable of England and later marrying him to his younger daughter Elizabeth, Countess of Ormond.

The elder Bohun was present at Bannockburn, where he was unable to prevent the disaster and was taken prisoner by the Scots. Later he had joined Lancaster's revolt against Edward II and was killed at the battle of Boroughbridge in 1322. The titles and the post of Constable then passed first to his eldest son John, who died in 1336, and then to his second son

Humphrey. William Bohun and his twin brother Edward (who drowned on campaign in Scotland in 1334) were both close to the young King Edward III, and William was one of the king's companions in Nottingham on the night of the *coup d'état* against Roger Mortimer. As a reward for this and other services, he was made Earl of Northampton in 1337, with a grant of lands worth £1,000 a year. In 1338, ill health forced Humphrey Bohun to relinquish the post of Constable, and this passed naturally to his brother.

The Constable was in effect the king's chief military deputy, and on campaign was responsible for the conduct of the whole army. It was customary for deputy constables to be appointed as staff officers to do much of the routine work, and in 1346 Northampton's deputy constable was the energetic Adam Swynbourne;[29] but responsibility for tactics and planning rested still with the Constable. It is hard to imagine a better man for the post than Northampton. Already an experienced soldier, he had been present at Halidon Hill and had seen the new English tactical system in action. In 1339–40 he was in the Low Countries, where he played a leading role in the naval victory at Sluys and at the siege of Tournai. In 1342 he led a small army to Brittany where he had a string of successes, relieving the siege of Brest and defeating the French field at Morlaix.

By 1346 Northampton was probably the most experienced and proficient military commander in England. Everything about the events of that year speaks well of him: the meticulous organisation of the army, the methodical nature of its movements, the flexibility and determination with which it fought. When crises came, as they often did, Northampton was always near to hand. At Caen he overrode his king's orders and won a quick victory; at Poissy his personal courage and quick thinking probably prevented disaster; at the Blanchetaque and at Crécy his interventions in the battle were timely. Among all the English soldiers in the summer of 1346, Northampton stands out as one of the most capable and talented.

He was ably complemented by Thomas Beauchamp, Earl of Warwick and marshal of the army. In theory the marshal functioned as a deputy to the Constable with particular responsibility for the mounted portion of the army, but in practice Warwick and his fellow marshal, Godefroi d'Harcourt, were much more flexible and could be found doing everything from commanding reconnaissance parties to leading attacks on fortified strongholds. They too had a deputy, the under-marshal or 'lieutenant marshal' Thomas Ughtred, a very experienced soldier and veteran of the Scottish wars, who looked after much of the administrative and other detail.[30] Another deputy, Robert Houel, served as a marshal of the camp during the period before the embarkation of the army that summer. But Warwick, like Northampton, stands out for his energy and personal courage. Born in 1314, he had inherited the earldom from his father when he was less than a year old. In 1325, aged eleven, he married Catherine Mortimer, daughter of the Earl of March, but despite the latter's treason and disgrace, they remained married and produced ten children. In 1343, following vigorous actions at Nantes and Vannes, Warwick was appointed Marshal of England for life. He was also sheriff of Warwickshire and Leicestershire and Keeper of Southampton, and had also served as a diplomat in Scotland and France. In 1346 Warwick was thirty-two, and a veteran of a dozen campaigns in Scotland, France and Brittany.

The third important commander in 1346 was Richard Fitzalan, Earl of Arundel, who bore the nickname 'Copped-Hat'. His father, Edmund, had been a loyal supporter of Edward II, and in 1326 was arrested and beheaded without trial by supporters of the queen and Mortimer. Richard himself, then thirteen, was not allowed to inherit his father's title. Upon taking power, Edward III quickly corrected this and Richard Fitzalan was confirmed as Earl of Arundel in 1331. He quickly became a valuable member of Edward's circle, serving as justiciar of Wales, sheriff of Shropshire and admiral of the fleet west of the Thames, though he had relinquished the latter post to William Clinton by 1346. Like Warwick, he had been married while still a child, in this case to Isabel Despenser, but in the 1340s he began a liaison with Eleanor of Lancaster, sister of the Earl of Derby. Despite the fact that both were married, they seem to have lived together openly, and Eleanor accompanied her lover and her brother on embassies to Avignon and Castile. In 1344, Eleanor's husband having conveniently died, Arundel was able to get his own marriage annulled by papal decree – incidentally making bastards of his children by Isabel – and he and Eleanor finally married in 1345. She gave birth to their first child in 1346. Ruthless and extremely rich, Arundel was now thirty-three, with a long experience of military command and administration that made him a valuable member of Edward's circle.

Robert Ufford, Earl of Suffolk was one of the older commanders. Now forty-eight, he came from a relatively minor family with lands in Suffolk and Oxfordshire, but had become attached to the king at an early stage in his career. He too was present at the arrest of Mortimer, and joined the king's inner circle after the latter's assumption of power. He had married Margaret Norwich, the daughter of a neighbour, in 1324; however, unlike Arundel, he did not feel the need to put her away and acquire a grander wife upon his rise to prominence. He was one of the seven men given earldoms by Edward in 1337. He served on diplomatic missions in France and Scotland, and as well as holding military commands on land he was also serving as admiral of the fleet north of the Thames; in 1346, however, he handed over responsibility for his portion of the fleet to William Clinton.

Clinton was also one of the 'class of '37', having been made Earl of Huntingdon. He too came from a modest background, and his early links seem to have been with Queen Philippa rather than the king, but he was also present at the arrest of Mortimer, personally killing two of the latter's retinue who tried to resist. Thereafter he served as justice for Chester and for Kent, constable of Dover Castle, Warden of the Cinque Ports and admiral of the fleet west of the Thames. In 1346 he was about forty-two years old, and beginning to suffer from ill health. His marriage in 1328 to Juliane, widow of Thomas Blount, had produced no children.

Among the knights and bannerets (senior knights who were entitled to fly their own banners, which knights bachelor were not allowed to do), perhaps the most important was Bartholomew Burghersh. Now in his fifties, both Burghersh and his brother Henry, Bishop of Lincoln, had a long history of service to the crown. He had joined Lancaster's revolt against Edward II and had been captured and imprisoned. In the early years of Edward III's reign he was fairly quiet, but by the 1340s was engaged in diplomatic work, and he had recently been appointed as tutor to the Prince of Wales, with the task of teaching the young man the arts of war and governance. Burghersh's son Bartholomew, often known as 'le fitz' to distinguish him from his father, was about the same age as the Prince and would accompany his father on campaign. Another important figure was Reginald Cobham of Sterborough, Surrey. A little younger than Burghersh, he had served with the latter on some of the same embassies, notably to Rome in 1343.

Older than the others was John Darcy, by now in his sixties or even early seventies, who had been steward of the household and was now chamberlain to the king. His son, John Darcy 'le fitz', would accompany his father in 1346 with a retinue of eight knights, twenty esquires and twenty-four archers; while his father's career was almost over, that of Darcy le fitz seemed to be headed for greater things. The Darcys are good examples of men who turned administrative jobs in royal service into the material for founding dynasties. On the other side of the coin was Hugh Despenser, whose father and grandfather had both been highly visible favourites of Edward II, and as a consequence had been executed by Mortimer and Isabella soon after the king's overthrow. Despenser himself was now known as a reliable and effective soldier, but it would be surprising if something of his family's reputation did not still hang over him.

There were many other bannerets, usually attached to the retinues of one or another of the great lords. The bannerets John Neville of Essex and Fulk Fitzwaryne served with Northampton, while Robert Scales and Aylmar de St Amand served with Warwick and John Lestraunge of Whitchurch, Gerard Delisle and Thomas West were in Arundel's retinue. The Lincolnshire banneret Robert Colville of Bytham served with Suffolk, William Fitzwayne served under his fellow banneret Reginald Cobham, and Ralph Daubeny and Thomas Astley were in the retinue of the Bishop of Durham.

The ordinary men-at-arms included some colourful characters. James Audley, serving in the retinue of the Earl of Arundel, was about twenty-eight years old and a minor member of the Audley family which also included Hugh, Earl of Gloucester. His father was a knight, James Audley of Stratton Audley, Essex; his mother was one of the more remarkable women of the day. Eve Clavering had already been married and widowed twice, once to Audley's cousin Thomas. Around 1314, James Audley senior and Eve began living together, and continued to do so until his death in 1334; but, probably because they could not afford the necessary dispensation, they never married. Technically their two sons, James and Peter, were illegitimate, a fact that does not seem to have hindered them socially in any way. In 1346, James Audley was in the early stages of his glorious career; as too was John Chandos, knighted for valour on the battlefield at Cadzand eight years previously and now serving in the king's retinue. Audley and Chandos were both young men on the make, who hoped to find in military service a route to honour and riches. These men found them; others, like Edward atte Wode, did not.

A more prosaic character, though with an equally eventful life, was the Devonshire knight John Sully of Iddesleigh, also in the retinue of the Earl of Arundel. His exact age is not certain, but he was probably in his fifties or sixties, and he was a veteran of Halidon Hill, the siege of Berwick and the Flemish campaigns of 1339–40. He went on, astonishingly, to be present at the battles of Winchelsea (1349), Poitiers (1356) and Najera (1367) before finally retiring around 1370. His esquire, Richard Baker, who was in his service in 1346, retired with him and continued to look after the old man, who in 1385 was still lucid enough to give evidence to a commission of heralds; he claimed then to be 105 years old. In 1361, in recognition for his unparalleled service, Sully received a unique grant: once a year, in any royal forest or park, he might have freely one shot with his bow, one course with his hounds and one chase with his dog, who was called Bercelette.[31]

Other figures of note included the Lincolnshire knight Hugh Cressy and Hugh Wrottesley, ancestor of a later historian of the campaign, both in the Prince of Wales's retinue; mention should also be made of the Prince's standard-bearer, Richard FitzSimon. Guy Bryan from County Pembroke was another rising member of the king's inner circle. The cousins Ralph Basset of Cheadle and Ralph Basset of Sapcote were to be found in the retinue of the Earl of Warwick, while a third Ralph Basset, of Drayton, was in the service of Northampton. Oliver Bohun was also in Northampton's retinue, but two other members of the Bohun family, John and Edmund, served in Arundel's extensive retinue, which also included Henry Percy, Emery Rokesley, Hamon Lestraunge, Robert Hotot, Adam Shareshulle, John Trussel, Walter de la Garderobe (whose name suggests he came from humbler origins), Hubert St-Quinton and John Tudor of Kyrkeby Hornblowers. Robert Brent served with James Audley. Henry Colville and Robert Erpingham served with Suffolk, as did the latter's brother-in-law Roger Norwich; another of the family, Thomas Norwich, served with the Prince of Wales.

At the bottom end of the social scale among the English men-at-arms came men like the Yorkshireman John Rither, who had been at Sluys, and the Northumberland man William Hesilrigge, who had first seen action at Halidon Hill at the age of seventeen. Both were from humble backgrounds, and went on to distinguished careers as professional soldiers; never knighted, they were nonetheless respected by their peers. The supreme exemplar of this class is probably Nicholas Sabraham, then about twenty years old and preparing to go to war for the first time. The next forty years would see Sabraham practising his trade in Scotland, France, Spain, Prussia, Egypt, Turkey, Cyprus and Constantinople.[32]

The soldiers

It is an interesting commentary on the comparative survival of document-ary records in England and France that we know more about the king of England's servants in 1346 than we do about many French knights and nobles. Even so, details of the common soldiers of the English army are often vague. For example, we do not know whether the bowyer Robert Aubyn of London accompanied the army in his professional capacity or as an ordinary soldier; probably the former, but we cannot tell for certain. The same applies to the fletcher John Kyng and the cook John Saunford of Ipswich.

A few archers are known to us by name. They include Henry Torpoleye and Richard Whet in the retinue of the Earl of Warwick, and the Notting-hamshire man Richard Glaston in the king's retinue. Others for whom no retinue is given include William Quatfield from Shropshire, John Tony from London, William Dun of Ocle, Ralph son of Thomas Longdon, Henry Sturthrip and Adam Warewyk. Six men – William Gravenore, Richard Gravenore, Henry Gold, Richard Smyth, William Hockumbe and John Tybynton – are named in a document of the following year as having been in Huntingdon's retinue at Caen in 1346.[33] A dozen and a half hobelars, or light cavalrymen, are also known by name; they include John Branescome, William Brompton, Henry Godeslawe, John Slope, John Smythewyke, William Tidenhangre and John Tidenhangre, all from St Albans, Hugh Bromham and Richard Rameshulle from Watford, and the Warwickshire man Thomas de Stonleye.

Often we only know of these men from passing references in admin-istrative documents, which refer to pardons or other legal documents, or to their deaths. Very occasionally they speak to us directly. Many years after the battle the Cheshire foot soldier Thomas Crue, who had fallen on hard times, petitioned the Prince of Wales for aid. He reminded the Prince of how he and his brother, who is not named, had come aboard the Prince's ship, the *Thomas*, off the Isle of Wight to offer their services, and of how later his brother had been wounded and Crue had helped him off

the battlefield and taken him to hospital, and in so doing had missed
the rewards the Prince handed out to his followers when the fighting was
over.[34]

Others

There were also plenty of non-combatants, although it is not always possible to draw a clear distinction: Thomas Hatfield, Bishop of Durham, was
both a clergyman and a military commander. Many other clergy accompanied the army, and most of the major retinues had at least one chaplain:
John Anotson was in the service of the Earl of Northampton, John Loundres
was in the retinue of Warwick, John Place was in the service of the banneret
John Strivelyn. Robert Morley's retinue included two chaplains, William
Coke of Ockley and William Fyncham of Lavenham. The Earl of Suffolk's
retinue also had two chaplains, William Fuller of Dunwich and William
Rokaill, the latter described as 'chaplain of the retinue'. These were not
always the peaceable men of God one might expect; in October 1346,
William Fuller had to be pardoned for killing a man named Gilbert
Chouket.[35] There were also a number of parsons, men like Thomas
Beaumond, Martin Godsib and John Serle, who presumably ministered to
the spiritual needs of the ordinary soldiery.

Unsurprisingly, we know most about the royal household, beginning
with the steward, Sir Richard Talbot, and the keeper of the wardrobe,
Sir Walter Wetewang. In the kitchen the list starts with the yeoman of the
kitchen, Giles Coloyne, and includes the sauce maker, John Clerebaud, the
valet of the scullery, Thomas Poleyne, and the men of the Office of
the Poultry, John Kyngeston and another simply known as Hussee. The
surgeon who accompanied the king on campaign was Master Roger de
Heyton; Edward's valets included John Clavesowe, John Thornton, Geoffrey
Thoresby and Roger Sturdy. The household staff included a blacksmith,
Andrew le Fevre, and a team of carpenters including William Hurley the
chief carpenter and Richard St Albans.

Other important members of the household were the serjeants-at-
arms, hard-working men who served as bodyguards in battle and general
factotums at other times. In the months before the campaign began we
find men such as Henry Bath, Richard Cortenhale, John Coventre, Robert
Flambard, Robert Seint Oweyn and William Weston delivering orders and

messages (although a separate body of men, the king's messengers, also existed for this purpose), enforcing royal commands, organising the collection of shipping and escorting convoys of goods. They seem to have been paid at the standard rate for a mounted serjeant, a shilling a day, but were rewarded in other ways; for example, John Mounceaux was granted a pension of a shilling a day for life, and Adam Walton and William atte Wode received grants of land and houses.[36] After the 1346 campaign another serjeant-at-arms, John la Warde, was knighted, receiving also a grant of money to uphold his new status. Other large retinues had serjeants-at-arms too, such as Roland Daveys who served the Prince of Wales.

Even in the field, records had to be kept and letters written, and large retinues also included clerks. Gilbert Kertmell was employed by the Earl of Warwick, William Middleton and Nicholas Wynnesbury by the Earl of Arundel, and William Northwelle and Roger de la Hulle by the Prince of Wales. The king's staff included a number of clerks of the royal household such as William Hungate, Burgundus de Lia, Adam Neubold, Richard Eccleshale and William Campanea, who kept the king's personal seal. More senior members of the clerical staff included Philip Weston, Richard Wynkeley, Adam Offord and Michael Northburgh; Offord and Northburgh later received grants of 100 marks (about £66) a year for their services in 1346,[37] and Northburgh went on to become Bishop of London in 1354. The household staff also included the Chancellor of St Paul's cathedral, Thomas Bradwardine. Probably the most intellectual man in either army, Bradwardine had studied and taught at Merton College, Oxford in the early 1330s, where he was a prominent member of the group of philosopher-mathematicians known as the Oxford Calculators. His treatise *On the Ratio of Velocities in Motions* was enormously influential in the mathematics of the day, and he produced several other important works on geometry and theology. Plucked from Oxford by Richard Bury, Hatfield's predecessor as Bishop of Durham, Bradwardine then embarked on a career in public service, and was appointed a chaplain to the king and became an important member of the royal household. It was a long way from writing commentaries on Aristotle and Peter Lombard to preparing an army to invade France, but medieval men were expected to be versatile.

Last but by no means least, the royal household included Rodolfo Bardi, senior member of the London branch of the Florentine banking house of Bardi. Since the king's grandfather's day, the Society of the Bardi had been among the most important financiers of the English crown. Although King Edward had knighted Rodolfo Bardi, relations between the king and his bankers remained tense following the English financial crisis of 1339–40. Now, Rodolfo Bardi was preparing to accompany the army on campaign, presumably to keep an eye on his investment. In 1346, Edward III was taking his bank manager to war.

These, then, were some of the men who were preparing to fight each other in 1346. Before describing the events that followed, we need to look at how they were armed and equipped, and at the methods and systems by which they did battle. Both these issues would be of critical importance in the summer to come, and it is necessary that we see clearly how the two armies were armed and how they fought.

Weapons and armour: men-at-arms

Armour

Personal armour in the mid-fourteenth century was undergoing a transition, from the old style of head-to-foot chainmail covering with more solid protection for vulnerable areas such as the head and perhaps the chest, to full plate armour, the 'harness blanc' of the fifteenth century.[38] Chainmail, composed of many hundreds of interlocking iron rings, had been the standard protection for the mounted horseman and some foot soldiers for several centuries; the Normans who conquered England, Italy, Sicily and Palestine in the eleventh century had worn chainmail and open-faced iron caps. In the twelfth century the cap was gradually replaced by a heavy iron helm, the heaume or 'pot helm', which completely protected the head barring a narrow slit for vision and holes for breathing; and in the thirteenth century iron breastplates began to appear, sometimes worn beneath the mail tunic.

Chainmail was fairly effective against personal weapons such as swords; a hard blow could split the iron rings apart, but they would still absorb much of the force of the blow. It was also effective protection against arrows from lightweight bows or shot from long range. However, bows with heavy draw weights such as Genoese crossbows and English longbows could penetrate chainmail with ease.[39] The increasing use of archery on the battlefields of Western Europe was important in stimulating the development of solid metal body armour, although other factors played a role as well; the thirteenth century saw advances in mining and metal-working technology, and general economic growth and rising prosperity meant that more people could probably afford to buy armour.[40]

By the mid-fourteenth century, a well-equipped knight would wear first a padded or quilted tunic and leggings, the original purpose of which was to protect his own skin from abrasion by the chainmail, and to prevent the mail rings from being driven into the flesh by a hard blow. Over this would come the chainmail, and then fastened on top of these would come various protective pieces of armour. Chest- and backplates, collectively known as a cuirass, were widely used, as were cuisses, or thigh pieces, and vambraces, or forearm guards. Epaules or shoulder pieces would protect against a downward strike with a sword or axe, and guards for the upper arms and shins might also be worn. Most important of all was the head protection. The heavy helms had now largely been phased out; a few poorer knights might still wear these as hand-me-downs from their fathers and grandfathers, but most now wore the lighter bascinet, which had begun to come into fashion early in the century. The common style of the day was known as the dog-faced bascinet, which had a round head and a long pointed visor, shaped to deflect arrows away from the face and eyes. The visor could be raised when there was no immediate threat, allowing the wearer to see and breathe more easily, and then brought down into position just before going into battle. Even so, the bascinet could be uncomfortable to wear, and on hot summer days men would often take them off and ride or march bareheaded until they came into contact with the enemy.[41]

Armour was made of wrought iron, steel being far too scarce and expensive, and its strength depended on the quality of the iron being used. Armour thicknesses were pretty well standard across Europe. A helm or bascinet might be 3–4 millimetres thick, and chestplates and backplates were usually 2–3 millimetres; arm and leg pieces might be only 1 millimetre in thickness.[42] However, there were considerable variations in the iron used. In England, iron from the Weald of Kent and Sussex was soft and more likely to break under a heavy blow; iron from the Forest of Dean was of better quality, but was correspondingly more expensive. French knights had access to good iron from several sources, notably the region around Pont Audemer in Normandy, and armour made at the nearby arsenal of the Clos des Gallées at Rouen was of fine quality. The best iron, however, came from Spain and Sweden, and armour fashioned from Spanish iron was expensive and sought after.[43]

One final item of protective equipment needs to be noted; the shield. The Normans had used long, kite-shaped shields which protected much of the body of a mounted knight, but since the twelfth century shields had been slowly declining in size. The shield of the mid-fourteenth century was probably no more than three feet from top to bottom, with flat upper rim and pointed at the bottom. Shields were made of wooden planks, usually oak, and sometimes stiffened with a metal rim or braces. They were useful for deflecting glancing blows, but tended to split when hit by hard blows from a sword, and were easily penetrated by arrows or crossbow bolts. The face of the shield was painted with the owner's heraldic device, which was usually repeated on the surcoat, a light cloth tunic worn over the top of his armour. The shield would continue to decline in importance, virtually disappearing in the fifteenth century, but for the moment it remained an indispensable item of armour.

The above might be regarded as the standard armour of a well-equipped man-at-arms, but there were considerable variations depending on what the individual could afford. Poorer men might not wear the leg and arm guards, simply making do with a mail coat, breastplate and bascinet. The lowest rank of man-at-arms, the mounted serjeant, might not have plate armour at all, but might wear a mail coat or a quilted gambeson, a kind of tunic padded and stuffed with wool, animal hair, rags or other material which would hopefully absorb the force of a blow; or perhaps the two together, a gambeson worn over the top of a mail coat (a trick which had been picked up by the crusaders in Palestine, and which offered reasonable protection against the light bows of the Saracen mounted archers). Light cavalry such as English hobelars and German panzerati probably also made do with a simple gambeson, or even a tunic of stiffened leather. There was no standard 'suit of armour'; some generous lords might give items of armour to their followers, and some wealthy towns would outfit the men-at-arms they raised, but for the most part men wore what they themselves could afford.

A fully-armoured man-at-arms of the mid-fourteenth century carried about 80 to 100 lbs of armour and other equipment, including his sword, dagger and shield. This is considerably less than the full kit and weapons of a modern British paratrooper, for example, and is more evenly distributed about the body, but is still a considerable weight. To ride and move and fight in this ensemble for long periods required very high levels of physical fitness. It is small wonder that, in times of peace, knights continued to practise for war in tournaments; the need to maintain fitness would have been even greater than the need for glory and money.

Surcoats and heraldry

Medieval armies, especially those with large contingents of men-at-arms, were colourful spectacles, with many banners and standards and bright heraldic devices.[44] Most prominent, of course, were the banners of the kings and senior nobles. As noted in Chapter 1, since 1340 Edward had been displaying a banner with the colours of England, three gold leopards on red, quartered with those of France, gold lilies on blue. His son, the Prince of Wales, flew the Welsh colours, a red dragon on a field of green.[45] On the other side, Philippe of France rode under the famous Oriflamme, a semi-sacred banner said to date back to the time of Charlemagne, which normally rested in the great cathedral of St-Denis near Paris when the king was not on campaign. In 1346 it would be carried by Miles de Noyers, son of a former Marshal of France and a well-known knight in his own right.

The nobles too flew their own banners, as did the knights banneret, each with their own armorial devices. Knights bachelor were not allowed to fly banners, but they wore their arms painted onto the faces of their shields and stitched onto their surcoats, the open-sided tunics that they wore over the top of their armour. Esquires of good families could likewise wear their coats of arms. There was, indeed, still some haziness as to who exactly was entitled to bear arms. Like so much else in warfare, the mid-fourteenth century was a time of transition in heraldry. Heralds, the officers of the crown and senior nobles who served as emissaries and spokesmen, were slowly transforming themselves into professional custodians of knowledge about coats of arms. English royal heralds Andrew Norroy and Andrew of Clarenceux would later play a role in this process, becoming 'kings at arms' who laid down rules and guidelines as to who could bear arms and what arms they could bear.[46] But this development was still in its infancy in 1346, and the atmosphere was still fairly *laissez-faire*.[47] Devices, too, were simple; geometric devices such as chevrons, bends, crosses of various forms including saltires, and animals such as lions, leopards, eagles and martlets. Bright colours predominated, with blues, reds, white and yellow most common (for the more wealthy, white and yellow could become red and gold), and black, green and other colours also occasionally visible. Occasionally two or more knights bore the same or very similar colours, which could lead to confusion on the field; possibly as a result of this, in 1346 the English heralds reported as killed several French and allied nobles who are known to have survived.[48]

A few examples will suffice. On the English side, Richard Fitzalan, Earl of Arundel, displayed a yellow lion rampant on a red field, and Robert Ufford, Earl of Suffolk, wore a yellow cross on black. Among the barons and knights, Richard Stafford's device was a red chevron on gold, Bartholomew Burghersh's was a red lion on yellow, James Audley had a stylised yellow knot on red, John Darcy had three red quintrefoils on a white field, Hugh Despenser a black bend on white, Reginald Cobham had a distinctive badge consisting of a black and white ermine patterned lion and several small crosses on a red field; John Sully also had an ermine field with four blue horizontal bars. On the French side, King Philippe's brother Charles, Comte d'Alençon wore a yellow eagle on a blue field; the same device was displayed on his banner, carried by another famous knight, Jacques d'Estracelles. The Comte de Blois wore a blue and silver countervair on red, and his brother-in-law Raoul, Duc de Lorraine wore a red bend decorated with three martlets on a yellow field. The Constable of France, the Comte d'Eu, wore a gold lion on a blue field; the Burgundian knight who commanded the defences of Picardy and upper Normandy, Godemar de Fay, wore a rather unusual device of a gold stag on a blue field. There were thousands of other similar devices on both sides, and the arrayed armies would have presented a magnificent sight, glittering armour and weapons alternating with the brilliant colours of surcoats, shields and banners; that is, until they closed for battle, and the brilliance became obscured by mud and blood.

Hand-held weapons

The first striking weapon of the man-at-arms was the lance.[49] War lances were smaller and lighter than those used for jousting at tournaments. Although no lances from the mid-fourteenth century survive, manuscript illustrations suggest that the war lance was usually eight to ten feet long, with a shaft of ash or similar wood and a sharp-pointed steel head. This was a powerful striking weapon, particularly when grasped by a man riding a horse at full gallop, for even if the lance did not penetrate armour or shield, the kinetic energy delivered by the blow could knock an opponent off his feet or out of his saddle. However, the lance did not usually survive long in combat, either shattering on impact or becoming transfixed in the body of an enemy and having to be discarded. The real work of the man-at-arms in battle was done with the sword.

Although maces, hammers, axes and other more exotic weapons were favoured by a few, the great majority of men-at-arms used the sword as their primary weapon. Indeed, it was more than just a weapon; in popular culture of the day the sword was emblematic of chivalry and knighthood. Its shape, with the long pommel and straight crossguards reminiscent of a cross, also had symbolic religious overtones. In the great *chansons de geste* of medieval Europe, the *Song of Roland*, the *Nibelungenlied*, the Arthurian tales of Chrétien de Troyes and others, men swore solemn and binding oaths on their swords. Epic heroes like Roland and Siegfried and Arthur gave their swords names. In the real world this practice was sometimes imitated, or pious inscriptions might be inlaid on the blade or hilts. Fine blademakers such as those of Toledo, Solingen or Passau would also stamp blades with their own marks, and over time these took on associations similar to a modern trademark or brand marque, with particular blademakers achieving cult status.

Swords developed histories of their own. R. Ewart Oakeshott, one of the leading historians of the medieval sword, points out that, unlike armour and shields which wore out or became damaged easily, tempered steel sword blades could have very long lives.[50] A single blade might be handed down through a family for several generations, complete with oral accounts of how grandfather had wielded it at Falkirk or al-Mansourah. Or a sword might be taken from a captured or dead opponent, which is how some Mamlûk emirs could be found wielding French swords, or a Spanish nobleman might wear a blade originally fashioned in Moorish Granada. Good swords were expensive and highly prized, and the man who acquired one not only had a formidable weapon, but increased his own status and self-esteem.

The mid-fourteenth century was also seeing a change in sword design (although, as Oakeshott reminds us, older thirteenth-century swords were still being used well into the century). The primary change, probably sparked by the increasing use of plate armour, was a change from cutting to thrusting weapons. Older blades tended to be broad and tapered only gradually to a point, or might even have a rounded end with no sharp point at all; they were primarily intended for slashing or cutting at an opponent. Newer swords had a more pronounced taper and a much sharper point; they could still be used for cutting, but were designed primarily for stabbing into gaps in an opponent's armour. There were considerable variations in sword design. Blades might range from 30 to 40 inches in length and $2\frac{1}{4}$ to $3\frac{1}{4}$ inches wide at the base. Ordinarily the sword was used in one hand only, but hilts were usually long enough to allow a two-handed grip (proper two-handed swords were relatively rare). Crossguards were straight and usually unornamented. Pommels went through fashions; in the mid-fourteenth century the wheel- or disc-shaped pommel was most popular but other designs existed.

A number of popular misconceptions exist about medieval swords, one of which is that they were heavy and clumsy weapons. They were not; the average weight of those swords that have survived is between two and three pounds, and they are usually beautifully balanced. Oakeshott, indeed, goes so far as to liken them to works of art.[51]

Horses

The other great emblem of the medieval man-at-arms was the horse. A horse was probably the single most expensive item of equipment he would own. Trained warhorses were very expensive indeed; in 1342, the warhorse taken by Sir Walter Manny to Brittany was valued at £100, and similar valuations can be found throughout the period.[52] The historian Andrew Ayton has calculated that the mean value of all warhorses belonging to knights on that same expedition was £29, while the mean value of horses belonging to esquires was £12. Very similar values would have applied in 1346. Something of the value of the French warhorses can also be gleaned from the claims of those who lost them in battle; in 1346, the esquire Millet le Beuf lost a horse valued at 40 livres.[53]

There was clearly a social pecking order, with the horses of bannerets being on average worth more than the horses of bachelor knights, and those of knights worth more than those of esquires. However, individual economic circumstances meant that there was wide variation, and the horse of an esquire from a wealthy family might well be more expensive than the horse of a poor knight with a single manor. But whatever their station, the horse of a man-at-arms was a major investment. In the mid-fourteenth century it was common for the crown to pay a man-at-arms the value of his horse if it was killed on active service, a practice known as *restauro equorum*. Without this, it is hard to see how knights could have been persuaded to expose their valuable beasts to the rigours of campaigning, with its risks of death by disease, accident and lack of fodder as well as in battle.

The medieval passion for classification extended to horses as well. The heaviest and most expensive warhorses were called destriers or 'great horses'. Although larger than normal horses, they were probably not outstandingly large by today's standards; Ann Hyland, a former horse trainer, using measurements taken from fifteenth-century horse armour in the Royal Armouries, believes the average to be about 15 to 16 hands.[54] Lighter than the destrier but still comparable to today's hunters was the courser, some-times simply known in records as *equus*, and lighter still was the rouncy, which by the mid-fourteenth century was fading out of fashion as a war-horse and being used mostly for riding purposes. The palfrey was used for riding while on the march and was not normally taken into battle; there-after the scale descends to common hacks, ponies and carthorses. The best warhorses and palfreys were carefully bred at studs owned by the crown or the great nobles; ordinary mounted serjeants and hobelars got along on whatever horses they could find.[55] Individuals may have had preferences for colours, and on one occasion we read of King Edward surveying the Eng-lish army mounted on a white palfrey, but an account of horses being purchased in Northamptonshire for the royal stable in 1346 includes blacks, bays, greys, roans and piebalds.[56]

By the mid-fourteenth century, the twilight of the medieval warhorse was fast approaching. Already, English tactical doctrine called for men-at-arms to dismount and fight on foot; after the events described in this book, other armies would begin to copy them. Horses would still play an import-ant role in war, for scouting, raiding, transporting supplies and equipment and carrying men to the field of battle, but great combats between armies of mounted men-at-arms were becoming a thing of the past.

Weapons and armour: foot soldiers

Both French and English armies of the period raised large numbers of foot soldiers. These are known by a variety of names in French, English and Latin, and were often armed and armoured in an equally haphazard fashion. The ordinary provincial or town levy soldier in the French army was probably armoured with a quilted gambeson, if he was lucky, and possibly a metal or toughened leather skullcap. His weapon might be a short sword or long dagger, a hand axe, a clubbing weapon of some sort, or a short spear, a cut-down version of the mounted man's lance with a wooden shaft five or six feet in length and a steel head. Other armies had more exotic weapons, such as the Swiss halberd or the Flemish *goedendaag*, a long-handled wooden mallet with its head weighted with lead, but the ordinary French foot soldiers made do with whatever weapons were available.

The English armies of the day included some ordinary foot soldiers raised through the commissions of array, armed and equipped much as above, but they could also call upon a highly effective body of spearmen raised in North Wales. During the conquest of Wales in the 1280s and 1290s, these had proved to be formidable fighters, and when well led and on favourable ground could hold their own against mounted men-at-arms. Whether these men had armour is not known, although they probably had some form of protection similar to the gambeson. All were armed with spears and usually carried a back-up weapon such as a dagger or an axe.

The most important foot soldiers of either side, however, were the troops armed with missile weapons, crossbows in the French army and longbows in the English. Both types played important roles in the tactical doctrine of each army, and both were to figure prominently in the events of 1346. It is therefore worth discussing each in more detail.

Crossbowmen

Since the late thirteenth century, French armies had included increasing numbers of men armed with crossbows. Sometimes these were native Frenchmen, but more often they were hired mercenaries. They are usually referred to as 'Genoese' (and for convenience we have adopted this usage in this book), but in fact they probably came from all over north Italy, if not further afield. In the early years of the Hundred Years War the French crown used two contractors, the exiled Genoese nobleman Ottone Doria and the newly established lord of Monaco, Carlo Grimaldi. Both were freelances who offered men and ships for hire to anyone who could pay; King Robert of Naples and King Jaume of Majorca were among Grimaldi's other clients.[57]

Whatever their origin, the crossbowmen serving in the French army were fairly uniformly equipped. They even on occasion wore uniform white tunics, though it is not certain that they did so in 1346. They wore some body armour, apparently steel caps and quilted gambesons, but their main protection was the pavise, a large and heavy wooden shield which was meant to be set up on the ground and braced on a wooden strut. This was to protect the archer while he reloaded; standard practice was to load while kneeling behind the pavise, step out from behind it to shoot, then move back into shelter to load again. This was difficult to do, however, in a fluid battle where bodies of men were advancing and retreating rapidly.

The crossbows used by the Genoese in the mid-fourteenth century looked very much like the modern hunting crossbow, with a wooden stock and a horizontal steel bow, known as a 'prod'.[58] The prod was attached to the stock by sinews which had first been soaked in water; these shrank when dry, making the binding almost unbreakable. The bowstrings were also made of sinew, one of the strongest materials available. The steel prods were far too heavy to allow the bowstring to be drawn back by hand, so a separate tool, a hand-crank device called a 'cranequin', was employed to pull the string back. The bow was then cocked, and a bolt was fitted to the string, resting in a channel on to the upper surface of the stock. The crossbowman sighted on his target much as a modern rifleman would do by looking down the stock and the bolt channel, and pulled a trigger which released the bowstring and sped the bolt to its target. The bolts themselves were made of iron with steel tips, and came in different types. Bolts with bodkin points, very sharply pointed, were for use against men wearing chainmail; those with heavier square heads, later called 'quarrells', were used to penetrate plate armour.[59]

This was a weapon of considerable power. A bow's strength is indicated by its draw weight, which is calculated by holding the bow vertically and attaching weights to the string; the amount of weight which will draw the bow fully back is its draw weight. The Genoese crossbow of the fourteenth century probably had a draw weight of from 140 to 160 pounds, and some may have been heavier still. The powerful steel prod launched bolts towards their target at velocities of around 240 feet per second, or about 165 miles per hour.[60] This meant that at close range the heavy bolt had terrific kinetic energy, and could punch through the plate armour of the day without difficulty. However, that same weight meant that velocity, and thence kinetic energy, fell off rapidly over distance. At 100 yards the cross-bow was still capable of significant armour penetration, but at 200 lacked real punch except against unarmoured targets. An effective range was prob-ably between 250 and 300 yards.[61]

The greatest weakness of the crossbow was its loading time. One nineteenth-century authority reckoned that to wind back a crossbow cord six inches, the archer's hand had to travel about 180 feet as it turned the cranequin, with consequent loss of time and energy.[62] It takes a very skilled archer to shoot four bolts a minute, and three was probably the average under good conditions. That apart, the crossbow was a powerful and lethal weapon which could potentially give an army command of the battlefield. By 1346, the French crown was employing many thousands of mercenary crossbowmen both to garrison fortresses and with its field armies.

The English also used crossbows in warfare, but at sea rather than on land. In 1346 we find crossbows being supplied to the crews of ships assigned to transport the army to France, and in some cases every crewman would have been armed with a crossbow.[63] These were lighter weapons than those described above, with prods of yew wood rather than steel, but they would still have been adequate for use against lightly armoured enemy seamen. How many of these bows were supplied is not known, but they may have numbered several thousand. Among the foot soldiers on land, however, the longbow was now the dominant missile weapon.

Longbowmen

So enshrined has the longbow become in English folklore that it comes as something of a surprise to learn that archery is not native to Britain; the early Celts relied on slings and javelins for missile weapons. The Angles and Saxons used bows, but only in a limited way. Although archery was critical to the Norman victory at Hastings, the Norman and early Plantagenet kings never developed native military archery in any systematic way, preferring to rely on hired foreign crossbowmen. By the twelfth century, archery had taken hold in parts of south Wales, notably in Gwent; the chronicler Gerald of Wales wrote with awe of the skill of the Welsh archers and the power of their bows. Small contingents of Welsh archers often served with English armies, notably in the conquest of Ireland and with Simon de Montfort during the revolt of 1265–7.

It was during the final English conquest of Wales that recognition of the power of the longbow began to dawn. Many South Welsh archers served in the English armies against their neighbours in the north, and Edward I quickly recognised their worth. Large contingents of archers accompanied his forces in the invasions of Scotland, and played a crucial role at the battle of Falkirk in 1298. His successor Edward II seems not to have understood how to use archers, and it was left to Edward I's grandson, Edward III, to bring English military archery to its full development.

The English – and Welsh – longbowmen who formed an increasingly large part of English armies of the Hundred Years War were probably the most lightly equipped troops on either side.[64] Their standard garb was soft leather boots, tunics and hose of dull green or russet brown, and heavy leather belts from which were suspended quivers for their arrows (the quiver slung over the shoulder is a later innovation) and usually a simple hand weapon such as a short sword or a dagger. In terms of armour, a tough leather cap, sometimes stiffened with internal metal bands, was commonly worn; we have no record of other armour, but many may have provided themselves with some sort of home-made body protection such as a padded gambeson or leather tunic. At the belt, a small pouch held the tools of the trade, such as a spare bowstring, fine thread for repairing damaged fletchings, a leather finger guard to protect the fingers of the right hand from the bowstring, and another leather guard, known as a bracer, which covered the inside of the left forearm, the arm that held the bow. Finally there was the bow itself, which was usually carried unstrung to reduce the tension on the wood. This, plus a haversack for food and other necessaries, was the sole equipment of the longbowman.

There has been much myth-making about the longbow over the centuries. It is difficult to see why, when the facts are impressive enough. The longbow is a very simple weapon, made through a craft process, and every specimen will be slightly different, which makes creating general data a tricky process. However, a few medieval specimens have survived, and examination of these plus experiments in the nineteenth and twentieth centuries enable some conclusions to be drawn.

Medieval longbows were cut from a single piece of wood. The best wood was generally believed to be yew, but British yew trees were rarely tall enough or straight enough for longbow staves.[65] Elm was the most common wood, but ash and hazel were sometimes used. The average war bow was between 6 feet and 6 feet 4 inches in length, though longer specimens were known; ideally, a bow should be about four inches taller than the archer (the reader is reminded that the average male height in the fourteenth century was probably about the same as today). The bow stave was thickest at its midpoint, being anything up to three or four inches in circumference depending on the strength of the bow, tapering to perhaps an inch and a half at top and bottom. Notches, or nocks, for the string were cut into the bow near the tips, though fancy versions might have nocks made of horn. The strings were usually made of flax or hemp, and according to some accounts were impregnated with beeswax to ward off damp.[66]

The draw weights of medieval longbows are a matter for some debate. Most archers today shoot longbows of 60–70 pounds draw weight, but all the evidence suggests that medieval bows were very much heavier. Specimens recovered from the *Mary Rose*, dating from the early sixteenth century, have draw weights of as much as 180 pounds, and would have required men of considerable musculature to shoot them. Regular practice enables archers to shoot heavier bows, so it is by no means impossible that the brawny farmhands and herdsmen of the fourteenth century shot heavier bows than their flabby descendants do today. It is likely that the average draw weight of a war bow in the mid-fourteenth century was around 100 pounds, and might well have been higher.[67] Draw weight is important because heavier bows not only shoot arrows faster, imparting greater kinetic energy to the target, but they also shoot on a flatter trajectory, making them more accurate.

Arrows ranged in length from 27 inches to 36 inches; shorter, lighter arrows would fly further, but longer heavier ones had greater penetration. The nock was a simple notch cut in the base of the arrow to receive the bowstring. Arrows were fletched with three feathers, the wing feathers of geese being preferred. Fine thread was used to lash them in place, and then some form of adhesive such as pitch was applied to the lashings and dried. There were various types of arrowheads: the broadhead was roughly triangular with two backswept points, while the bodkin was a simple steel head like a chisel but coming to an acute point at the tip. Broadheads were used for hunting, and in war for shooting at unarmoured targets such as horses; long bodkin points were used for shooting at men with chainmail, while a straight metal point known as a pile was used against men in plate armour. As the war progressed more specialised forms of arrowhead developed, but in 1346 the broadhead, bodkin and pile were the types commonly found in most men's quivers.[68]

When shooting, the archer stands at a right angle to the target, with one foot planted a little forward towards the target. Holding the bow in his left hand, he nocks an arrow with his right hand,[69] and then draws arrow and bowstring back in a single fluid motion while at the same time raising the bow towards the target. The string is drawn back until the nock of the arrow is about level with the archer's ear; the bow is now fully drawn. Sighting is done briefly; few men are strong enough to hold a heavy bow fully drawn for long. Then the string is released, smoothly; plucking at the string causes it to reverberate from side to side and can result in painful blows on the outstretched forearm holding the bow (it is to protect against such an eventuality that the bracer is worn). The energy which transferred itself from the archer to the bow during the drawing process is now released through the string, propelling the arrow.

Many tests on longbow velocity, range and penetration have been carried out, some with greater scientific rigour than others. There are difficulties in doing comparative analysis, as the strength of the archer, the draw weight of the bow and the weight of the arrow are all important variables. As far as range goes, nineteenth-century experiments with bows of around 65 pounds draw weight and short, lightweight arrows found that it was perfectly possible to shoot arrows in excess of 300 yards.[70] It is likely that 300 yards was about the maximum range of a medieval war bow, but at that range the arrows would have had little penetration.

Velocity declines the further the arrow travels from the bow. Gareth Rees, a physicist with the Scott Polar Research Institute at Cambridge, has calculated that an arrow shot from a heavy longbow has a starting velocity of around 60 metres per second (around 195 feet per second, or 133 miles per hour), but at 240 metres distance, velocity has fallen to about

45 metres per second (146 feet per second, or just under 100 miles per hour).[71] This is probably very similar to the velocity of the medieval war bow. In terms of kinetic energy, the American writer Edward Ashby has calculated that a heavy arrow of 1,286 grains weight (just under three ounces) travelling at the comparatively modest speed of 154 feet per second will strike its target with 0.88 pound-seconds of momentum. This is almost exactly equivalent to a bullet from a .357 Magnum revolver. In other words, getting hit by a longbow arrow at close range is roughly the same as being shot with a powerful handgun.[72]

From this, it follows that at close range a longbow arrow will penetrate most forms of armour if it strikes squarely on, or nearly so. One experimenter, using plates attached to straw dummies, found that at twenty yards a longbow arrow would pierce two millimetres of iron and penetrate six inches into the dummy, more than enough to find a vital organ in a human. However, if the arrow strikes metal plate armour at an acute angle, it will probably be deflected and glance off (later in the war armourers began developing plates with more curved and deflective surfaces, but in 1346 most plate armour was worn flat to the wearer's body). Chainmail is penetrated easily, even at ranges of 100 yards or more, and quilted armour such as gambesons offers no protection except at extreme range when kinetic energy is low. Layering armour will help, and an arrow that penetrates a breastplate might do so with insufficient energy to pierce the mail coat underneath; but at very short range, even this is doubtful. In conclusion, bascinets and breastplates were probably able to protect the wearer from serious injury except at very close range, but Gareth Rees believes the light one-millimetre leg and arm plates would have been penetrated easily at longer ranges.[73] One of the authors of the present work, who shoots a light bow with a draw weight of 54 pounds, once inadvertently hit a water trough while conducting range trials and found that the arrow's pile-type point had penetrated two millimetres of galvanised metal at 180 yards.

Added to this must be the longbow's rate of fire, which astonished even contemporaries. The Florentine chronicler Villani thought that the English longbowman could outshoot the crossbowman at a rate of six to one. This is an exaggeration, but at a demonstration witnessed by the authors at Restormel Castle, Cornwall in 1988, a longbowman mangaged seventeen aimed shots in a minute, against a crossbowman's four. Both archers were experienced professionals, but even a longbowman of modest skill can manage twelve to fifteen shots a minute, especially if he is shooting at a large target such as an advancing body of cavalry. Fast, accurate and powerful, the English longbow was one of the most effective killing instruments to emerge during the whole of the Middle Ages.

Firearms

Gunpowder weapons were still very much in their infancy at the outbreak of the Hundred Years War. France was slightly more advanced than England in this respect, and a variety of small cannon could be found in French service, commissioned either by the crown or by some of the wealthier communes. Cannon mounted on the walls of Cambrai had fired on the English army in 1339, and ship-mounted weapons called *pots de fer*, which apparently fired large iron lances or spears, were used on at least one occasion during the French raids on the south coast of England. These spear-firing cannon do not appear to have caught on, and most French artillery of the period fired small stone or iron cannon balls and were employed in defensive positions. The Flemings also had some firearms of their own called 'ribaudequins' (literally, 'little rascals') which consisted of a collection of small-bore weapons grouped together and mounted on a cart or wagon; the barrels could be fired individually or all at once, rather similar to nineteenth-century prototypes of the machine-gun such as the *mitrailleuse*.

In England, there are records of purchases for the ingredients for gunpowder as early as 1333, suggesting that cannon might have been employed at the siege of Berwick that year; however, as the historian T.F. Tout pointed out, there is no documentary evidence for the existence of cannon at this time, and the accounts of chroniclers and contemporaries are not conclusive.[74] It was long believed that cannon were in use on English warships from 1338, until Tout discovered that the records on which this was based had been incorrectly dated. It is not until 1345 that we find hard evidence for firearms in the royal armouries at the Tower of London. From the records of the armourer, Robert Mildenhall, and one of his subordinates, the clerk Thomas Rolleston, it is possible to see that the English were clearly experimenting with several different types of firearms. These included small weapons firing lead pellets, which were ordered for the abortive Flanders expedition of 1345; ribaudequins of the Flemish type, which were ordered in the autumn of that year; and larger bombards, what we would think of today as cannon. Archaeological evidence suggests that the bombards were of slightly different sizes; balls of 82 mm, or about 3.2 inches, and 92 mm, or about 3.6 inches, have been found and traced to cannon used by the English army.[75] All three types were constructed in much the same way, as simple wrought-iron tubes which were loaded with gunpowder and either stone or cast-iron shot. Work orders still survive; the ironwork was done by Walter le Fevre, the blacksmith at the Tower, and one of the royal carpenters, Richard St Albans, built the wooden carriages on which the guns rested.[76]

Large quantities of gunpowder were also ordered. Medieval gunpowder (like all gunpowder down to the nineteenth century) was made of a mixture of charcoal, sulphur and saltpetre; recipes again vary, showing that much experimentation was going on. The gunpowder of the time burned comparatively slowly, meaning that greater quantities were needed in order to achieve the required force. Charcoal was cheap and plentiful, but both sulphur and saltpetre were expensive, and Rolleston's accounts of the spring of 1346 show him buying large quantities of both.[77] Whatever the king's plans might be for the forthcoming campaign, it was certain that he intended to take gunpowder weapons with his army.[78]

Tactical doctrines

As noted, the use of these missile weapons played a key role in the tactical doctrines of both French and English. The words 'tactical doctrine' should be seen in context. Neither side had a set of written instructions for commanders (although the Scottish king Robert Bruce had written a short set of strategic and tactical precepts earlier in the century), but there were common tactical methods and formations which were transmitted orally and were employed over and over again. We shall close this chapter with a brief look at how both armies fought.

French tactics were still essentially those of the Normans, though with some added refinements. The Normans had relied on shock; their armoured men-at-arms fought together in close order, and relied on the speed and impetus of their charge to break up enemy formations which could then be destroyed piecemeal or driven from the field. Fighting in this way, relatively small numbers of Norman men-at-arms had defeated much larger enemy forces in southern Italy, Sicily, Greece and Palestine. They had not been uniformly successful, and at Hastings in 1066 the Anglo-Saxon shield wall had initially repelled the charges of the men-at-arms; it was only when William of Normandy brought up archers to disrupt the enemy that his horsemen were able to break through. The Normans were also capable of considerable tactical flexibility; for example, at Dorylaeum in 1097, Bohemond had dismounted his men-at-arms and ordered them to stand on the defensive against the Seljuq horse archers.[79] Over time, however, this initial flexibility disappeared, and by the fourteenth century a certain rigidity had crept into French military thinking.

The main purpose of the man-at-arms was to charge the enemy en masse and rely on impetus to break through the enemy ranks. This was true whether attacking men on foot or other men-at-arms. Over time, fed in part by the *chansons de geste* and other legends of chivalry and valour, the charge of the mounted man-at-arms began to be seen as the *only* truly honourable way of fighting. Foot soldiers were seen as ignoble and therefore unimportant; on several occasions, notably at Courtrai in 1302, the French men-at-arms simply rode over their own foot soldiers when these got in the way. Like their descendants who commanded the cavalry regiments of Napoleon, they lived for the moment of the charge; *toujours l'audace* would have been a good motto for them. An unfortunate consequence was that the French man-at-arms began to believe in his own superiority. In his own eyes, at least, he was the finest fighting man in the world. The attack of the French men-at-arms even had its own name, *furor franciscus*, the French fury, implying unstoppable violent power.

Although often successful, this was also an all-or-nothing method of fighting. If the men-at-arms could break up the enemy formation, then the day was usually theirs and the enemy would flee the field. If they failed, however, the consequences could be dire; the charging formation would itself be disrupted and vulnerable to counter-attack. This had happened in 1302 at Courtrai, when the rebel Flemish army, composed mostly of foot soldiers, had taken up positions on a hill fronted by marshy ground and invited the French to charge them. The French duly obliged, but their impetus was slowed by the marsh and the hill, and as they struggled to regain momentum the Flemings, showing remarkable discipline, counter-charged and broke up the French formation. The French suffered very heavy losses and were driven from the field.

Courtrai showed the limitations of the French tactical method. With hindsight, military historians have called this battle a turning point; taken in conjunction with Bannockburn (1314) and Morgarten (1315), where the Scots and the Swiss respectively defeated mounted men-at-arms while fighting on foot, Courtrai is supposed to have been the beginning of the end for the mounted knight. Perhaps it was, but the French fighting man of the day was not prepared to believe it. After the fashion of defeated armies since the beginning of time, the French constructed elaborate excuses for their defeat, including a charge that their allies had betrayed them, and then went out into the field and reversed the decision of Courtrai, inflicting bloody defeats on the Flemings at Mons in 1304 and again at Cassel in 1328. Honour and pride were now restored.

Courtrai does seem, however, to have taught some lessons. The French had attempted to use crossbowmen at the start of the action to break up the Flemish formation, and had initially been successful, forcing the Flemings to retreat out of range. This promising start was spoiled when the French commander, the Comte d'Artois, then ordered a premature attack by his men-at-arms, with the consequences noted above. But the ability of crossbowmen to break up strong enemy forces was duly noted, and especially once Philippe of Valois came to the throne in 1328, crossbowmen were employed in ever-increasing numbers. By mid-century they were an important part of French tactical thinking.

The French tactical system, then, was to first deploy a large body of crossbowmen to shoot at the enemy from long range, to cause casualties but even more importantly to disrupt the enemy and perhaps force them into withdrawing. When this had been achieved, the men-at-arms would attack. These were typically drawn up in three *batailles* or divisions behind the crossbowmen, and would attack one after another, the second division being sent in if the first failed to break through, and so on. A succession of hammer blows from the men-at-arms would complete the work begun by the crossbowmen. Philippe VI, perhaps again thinking of Courtrai, also refused to give battle unless he felt sure that his forces were strong enough to gain an overwhelming victory. At La Flamengerie in 1340 and again in Brittany in 1342, Edward III openly invited Philippe to attack, but on both occasions the king refused, not trusting in his own superiority. This, needless to say, irked some of his noblemen who still believed that the *furor franciscus* would carry all before it.

English tactical doctrines were very different. Unlike the French, their primary enemies in recent years had been the Welsh and the Scots. The English conquest of north Wales in the 1280s and 1290s had met with dogged resistance, and the Welsh spearmen had proved to be tough opponents. Ironically, it was the employment of archers from south Wales that had helped give the English the victory; twice, at Orewell Bridge in 1282 and Conway in 1295, archers had been used to break up formations of enemy spearmen who were then finished off by the English men-at-arms.[80] The English duly learned their lesson, and in Scotland they employed archers in large numbers, notably at Falkirk in 1298. Here, the Scots commander William Wallace had drawn up his spearmen in three dense formations called schiltrons, and these initially repulsed the attacks of the English men-at-arms. The archers were then brought up and shot repeatedly into these tight formations, inflicting heavy casualties and finally disrupting the formations so that the English mounted men could charge home.[81] The importance of the tactical combination of archery and men-at-arms was well learned.

But the English also took another important lesson from the Scots wars, one that was reinforced after the disaster of Bannockburn. Here Robert the Bruce's army had fought largely on foot, and Bruce himself had famously concluded that 'on fut suld be all Scottis weire'.[82] The English were beginning to agree with him, particularly where defensive battles were concerned. A generation later, it was just such a defensive battle that laid the foundations for the English tactical system. The invasion of Scotland by Edward Balliol and the so-called 'disinherited' in 1332 was met by a sizeable Scottish army under the Regent of Scotland, the Earl of Mar, at Dupplin Moor near Dunfermline. Seeing himself greatly outnumbered, Balliol dismounted his men-at-arms and placed them in a tight body, then divided his archers into two groups and placed them on the flanks of this body. When Mar advanced, his men also on foot, the flanks of his army recoiled from the arrows of the archers and moved in towards the centre. The whole Scots army thus became compressed as it pushed forward against the English line, so densely packed that some men were suffocated or trampled in the press. The issue hung in the balance for a time, for the greater numbers of the Scots threatened to simply roll over the top of the English; one of the English knights, Ralph Stafford, shouted to the others to turn their shoulders to the enemy and push rather than trying to cut at them with swords, and at the front the battle began to resemble a rugby scrum. At the flanks, however, the archers were still shooting steadily, doing great execution at close range. Eventually the Scots broke and fled; the piles of bodies in some places stood as high as the length of a spear.[83]

Dupplin had shown what archers and dismounted men-at-arms could do when working in combination. The following year came the chance to repeat the experiment on a larger scale, when a Scots army moved to relieve the siege of Berwick and the English royal army moved out to meet it, taking up positions on Halidon Hill. Two of the leaders of the disinherited, Edward Balliol and Gilbert d'Umfraville, were in the English army, and their hand is visible in the formation adopted by the English. With more men than at Dupplin, the English deployed in three divisions, each with dismounted men-at-arms and spearmen in the centre and archers on the wings. The Scots advanced, and were killed in great numbers as they came up the slope of the hill. When they finally broke, Edward ordered his men-at-arms to mount and ride in pursuit. Seven earls, a multitude of knights and bannerets and thousands of common soldiers were killed; English losses were negligible.[84]

This formation had shown it could work against armies composed of foot soldiers. Would it work against the French men-at-arms who attacked on horseback? A worry must have surely been that the charging French horsemen would move at such speed that the English archers could not shoot them down in time. However, there were remedies; taking positions on hills or other difficult terrain could slow the French advance, and artificial obstacles could also be created which would slow and disrupt the enemy advance. A common practice of the day was to dig shallow pits in the ground over which the horsemen would have to advance (the hedges of wooden stakes such as were deployed at Agincourt were a later innovation). At Morlaix in 1342, despite nearly running out of arrows, Northampton showed that the combination of archers and dismounted men-at-arms could hold off the vaunted French men-at-arms.[85] The formation used at Dupplin Moor, Halidon Hill and Morlaix became the orthodox English tactical formation for the rest of the century and beyond.

Thus, while the French tactical system was primarily offensive, the English system was primarily defensive. There were of course many exceptions to this, and engagements such as attacking or defending a town or castle called for quite different approaches. But in set-piece battles in the open field, the French generally preferred to attack and the English generally preferred to stand and wait for them. Morlaix had indicated that the French tactical system was flawed, but two points need to be noted. First, the French commander Charles de Blois did not have any archers of his own; and second, Charles himself was a military incompetent who lost virtually every major battle at which he commanded.[86] The real trial of strength between the two systems had not yet occurred.

Notes

1 W.M. Ormrod, *The Reign of Edward III: Crown and Political Society in England, 1327–1377*, London, 1990, p. 44; see pp. 43–5 for a more detailed assessment of Edward's character.

2 Ibid., p. 43.

3 Ibid.

4 James Bothwell, 'Edward III, the English Peerage and the 1337 Earls: Estate Redistribution in Fourteenth-Century England', in J. Bothwell (ed.), *The Age of Edward III*, York, 2001, pp. 13–34.

5 Ormrod, *The Reign of Edward III*, p. 44.

6 For a detailed examination of events leading up to the fall of Edward II, see N. Fryde, *The Tyranny and Fall of Edward II, 1321–1326*, Cambridge, 1979.

7 Ormrod, *The Reign of Edward III*, p. 44.

8 Ibid., p. 45.

9 PRO E101/399/1 m. 17; see also Chapter 3.

10 A.K. McHardy, 'Some Reflections on Edward III's Use of Propaganda', in J. Bothwell (ed.), *The Age of Edward III*, York, 2001, pp. 171–92.

11 Ormrod, *The Reign of Edward III*, p. 45.

12 P. Boitani and A. Torti, eds, *Literature in Fourteenth-Century England*, Cambridge, 1983.

13 For example, Raymond Cazelles, *La Société politique et la crise de royauté sous Philippe de Valois*, Paris, 1958.

14 Philippe Contamine, 'The Norman "Nation" and the French "Nation" in the Fourteenth and Fifteenth Centuries', in David Bates and Anne Curry (eds), *England and Normandy in the Middle Ages*, London, 1994, pp. 215–34. For a more general overview of France at this time see the same author's *Guerre, état et société à la fin du moyen âge*, Paris, 1972.

15 A point made in more detail by Christopher Allmand, *The Hundred Years War: England and France at War, c.1300–c.1450*, Cambridge, 1988.

16 *Les Grandes Chroniques de France*, ed. Jules Viard, Paris, 1937, vol. 9, pp. 269–70.

17 See Chapter 9.

18 Maurice Keen, *Chivalry*, New Haven, 1984, p. 41.
19 'Chivalry was nurtured in France, but took its shape in a European context': Keen, *Chivalry*, p. 42.
20 Though not always; see Peter Noble, 'The Perversion of an Ideal', in Christopher Harper-Bill and Ruth Harvey (eds), *Medieval Knighthood*, vol. 4, Woodbridge, 1992, pp. 177–86.
21 Charny, *Livre de Chevalerie*, printed in Kervyn de Lettenhove (ed.), *Oeuvres de Froissart*, vol. 1, Brussels, 1873, pp. 463–533; see also Keen, *Chivalry*, pp. 12–15.
22 E.L.G. Stones, 'The Folvilles of Ashby-Folville, Leicestershire, and their Associates in Crime, 1326–1347', *Transactions of the Royal Historical Society*, vol. 7, 1957, pp. 117–36.
23 N. Fryde, 'A Medieval Robber Baron: Sir John Molyns of Stoke Poges, Buckinghamshire', in R. Hunnisett and J.B. Post (eds), *Medieval Legal Records Edited in Memory of C.A.F. Meekings*, London, 1978, pp. 197–221.
24 *CPR 1345–48*, pp. 310–11, 313, 319–20.
25 Terry Jones, *Chaucer's Knight: The Portrait of a Medieval Mercenary*, London, 1980.
26 Much of what follows is taken from La Chavanne-Desbois, *Dictionaire de la noblesse*, Paris, 1866. This is the most reliable of French genealogical sources (though that is not saying much) and we have supplemented it where possible with other sources including secondary literature and local histories. The footnotes to Jules Viard's 'Le Campagne de juillet–août et la bataille de Crécy', *Le Moyen Age*, 1926 (January–April), pp. 1–85, are valuable and reliable for factual data.
27 le Clerc, 'Philippe VI à labataille de Crécy, *Bibliotheque d'ecote de Chartes*, vol. 50, 1889, p. 296.
28 Information in this section is drawn from a variety of sources including the *Calendar of Patent Rolls* for 1343–45, 1345–48 and 1348–50; the *Calendar of Close Rolls*, *Calendar of Inquisitiones Post Mortem*, *The Complete Peerage*, the Kitchen Account (PRO E101/390/11) and G. Wrottesley, *Crécy and Calais*, London, 1897.
29 His energy can be inferred from the frequency with which he shows up in the records.
30 For more on Ughtred see Andrew Ayton, 'Sir Thomas Ughtred and the Edwardian Military Revolution', in J. Bothwell (ed.), *The Age of Edward III*, York, 2001, pp. 107–32.
31 N.H. Nicholas, *The Controversy Between Sir Richard Scrope and Sir Robert Grosvenor in the Court of Chivalry, AD MCCCLXXXV–MCCCXC*, London, 1832.
32 Ibid. The king's serjeants-at-arms will be included below.
33 PRO SC1/39/190.
34 *Register of Edward the Black Prince*, 4 vols, London, 1930–3, p. 413.
35 *CPR 1345–48*, p. 475.

36 *CPR 1345–48*, pp. 303, 271, 503.

37 *CPR 1345–48*, pp. 80, 91, 293.

38 A good introduction to the evolution of medieval armour is to be found in Michael Prestwich, *Armies and Warfare in the Middle Ages: The English Experience*, New Haven, 1996, pp. 18–26. More detailed works include C. Boutell, *Arms and Armour in Antiquity and the Middle Ages*, London, 1907, and C. Blair, *European Armour*, London, 1958.

39 See the discussion on archery, below.

40 On mining and metal-working see Jean Gimpel, *The Medieval Machine: The Industrial Revolution of the Middle Ages*, London, 1976; L.F. Salzmann, *English Industries of the Middle Ages*, Oxford, 1923; H. Cleere, D. Crossley and B.C. Worssam, *The Iron Industry of the Weald*, Cardiff, 1985; D.W. Crossley (ed.), *Medieval Industry*, London, 1983.

41 As, for example, Jacques d'Estracelles in Chapter 10.

42 See for example P. Jones, 'The Target', appendix in Robert Hardy, *Longbow*, Cambridge, 1976, pp. 204–8.

43 Gimpel, *The Medieval Machine*; Salzmann, *English Industries*; Cleere, Crossley and Worssam, *Iron Industry*.

44 F.E. Hulme, *History, Principles and Practice of Heraldry*, London, 1892; N. Denholm Young, *History and Heraldry*, Oxford, 1965; M. Keen, *Chivalry*, New Haven, 1984, chapter 7.

45 Noted by the contemporary chronicler Geoffrey le Baker, p. 783, who apparently misses the Welsh connection and embarks on a complex symbolic explanation of the dragon.

46 A.C. Fox-Davies, *A Complete Guide to Heraldry*, New York, 1978, pp. 29–36.

47 See the discussion in N.H. Nicholas, *The Controversy Between Sir Richard Scrope and Sir Robert Grosvenor*.

48 See Chapters 10 and 11.

49 For a concise survey of medieval swords, see Prestwich, *Armies and Warfare*, pp. 27–30. The outstanding work in the field is still R. Ewart Oakeshott, *The Sword in the Age of Chivalry*, London, 1961.

50 Oakeshott, *The Sword*, pp. 13–14.

51 Ibid., p. 12.

52 Andrew Ayton, *Knights and Warhorses: Military Service and the English Aristocracy under Edward III*, Woodbridge, 1994, p. 226. For more details on horses in medieval warfare, see this work and also Ann Hyland, *The Horse in the Middle Ages*, Stroud, 1999; and R. Ewart Oakeshott, *The Knight and his Horse*, London, 1962.

53 Contamine, *Guerre, état et société*, p. 105.

54 Hyland, p. 105.

55 This classification is hugely simplified, and many other types of horses can be found in records of the day.

56 PRO E101/103/8.

57 See Chapter 3.
58 Early writers doubted whether steel prods were in use by the fourteenth century, but more recent work concludes that they were: see Frank Bilson, *Crossbows*, Newton Abbot, 1974.
59 Ralph Payne-Gallwey, *The Book of the Crossbow*, London, 1995; see also Bilson.
60 Modern crossbows have much higher velocities: see Bilson, p. 48.
61 Although Robert Hardy thinks that the effective range of the crossbow of the 1340s was probably not more than 200 yards; a century later, advances in the technology had greatly increased the range. Hardy, p. 75.
62 C.J. Longman and H. Walrond, *Archery*, London, 1884, p. 115.
63 PRO E101/25/12 m. 1–3.
64 We have used the simple term 'English' throughout this book rather than the more cumbersome 'English and Welsh', on the grounds that the army was raised and commanded by the king of England. Similarly, the polyglot French army is referred to throughout as 'French'.
65 The crossbow prods of yew wood, noted in the previous section, required much shorter lengths of wood.
66 There were of course variations in all of the above, usually as a result of bowyers making do with what materials were at hand. Expert archers would of course have their own particular favourites as well. For more details on bow construction, see Edmund Burke, *The History of Archery*, London, 1958; Longman and Walrond, *Archery*, especially chapter 7; Hardy, *Longbow*; Tom Foy, *A Guide to Archery*, London, 1980.
67 See Hardy, *Longbow*, pp. 53–4, who estimates that the mid-fourteenth-century longbow probably ranged from 80 to 160 lbs draw weight; the average, though, was probably closer to the bottom of the range.
68 See Hardy, *Longbow*, pp. 54–5, who says the large hunting broadheads were no longer used in war, but smaller broadheads were used for soft targets.
69 Reverse this, obviously, if the archer shoots left-handed.
70 Longman and Walrond, p. 450.
71 Gareth Rees, 'The Physics of Medieval Archery', *Physics Review*, January 1995; see also the excellent technical appendices in Hardy, *Longbow*.
72 Edward Ashby, 'Arrow Lethality: Part IV, The Physics of Arrow Penetration', www.tradgang.com/ashby/arrow%20lethality%20204.htm (19 July 2004).
73 Rees; this is supported by Hardy, *Longbow*, p. 54.
74 T.F. Tout, 'Firearms in England in the Fourteenth Century', in *The Collected Papers of Thomas Frederick Tout*, Manchester, 1934, vol. 2, p. 237; Clifford J. Rogers, *War Cruel and Sharp: English Strategy under Edward III 1327–1360*, Woodbridge, 2000, pp. 64–5. Rogers adds that there are even hints that cannon may have been used by the English in an earlier attack on Berwick in 1327.
75 A.H. Burne, *The Crécy War: A Military History of the Hundred Years War from 1337 to the Peace of Bretigny, 1360*, London, 1965; repr. London, 1999, pp. 197–8.

76 Tout, 'Firearms in England', pp. 238–9.
77 Ibid., also *CCR 1343–46*, p. 340.
78 For a full discussion of the evidence for cannon in the English army in 1346, see Tout, 'Firearms in England', pp. 239–40 and the extensive discussion in Burne, pp. 192–202.
79 Steven Runciman, *The First Crusade*, Cambridge, 1980, p. 127.
80 Sir Charles Oman, *History of the Art of War in the Middle Ages*, London, 1924, vol. 2, pp. 69–70.
81 Ibid., pp. 78–81; Michael Prestwich, *Edward I*, Yale, 1988, pp. 480–3.
82 Quoted in Oman, vol. 2, p. 99.
83 Rogers, *War Cruel and Sharp*, pp. 42–6; Oman, vol. 2, pp. 103–5. Dupplin Moor is generally regarded as the genesis of the English tactical system, but T.F. Tout has argued that the true origin of this system lies in the formation adopted by Sir Andrew Harcla at the Battle of Boroughbridge in 1322; see his 'The Tactics of the Battles of Boroughbridge and Morlaix', *English Historical Review*, vol. 19, 1904, pp. 711–15.
84 Rogers, *War Cruel and Sharp*, pp. 69–74; Oman, vol. 2, pp. 106–7.
85 'The Tactics of the Battles of Boroughbridge and Morlaix'; Burne, pp. 68–86.
86 Morlaix, Josselin, St-Pol-de-Leon and La Roche-Derrien, all in the space of just five years; in the last three cases he was beaten by the same English commander, Thomas Dagworth.

Chapter 3

Preparations

Philippe VI said expressly that for the defence of the kingdom and the seacoast, he had ordained the raising of a good and great army.

Jules Viard

England's strategy

The campaigning season of 1345 had begun badly for the English, with the death of van Artevelde and the loss of yet another opportunity in Flanders; it had ended well, with the brilliant victories at Bergerac and Auberoche changing the course of the war in the south. As the year drew to its close, Edward and his councillors faced three immediate tasks: first, to exploit the opportunities Lancaster had created in the south; second, to re-start the war in Brittany and maintain the pressure on Charles of Blois; and third, to maintain the Flemish alliance and if possible to promote an offensive in the north. Anxious to maintain momentum, Edward sent out orders on 1 January to begin assembling ships at Portsmouth as soon as possible.

Meanwhile, the English king and his councillors had been discussing how to deal with the new opportunities presented to them. Prominent at court from late in 1345 was the Norman exile Godefroi d'Harcourt, who had crossed over to England from the Low Countries at the end of the summer and was quickly drawn into the king's inner circle. This latter event was particularly significant, for it was almost certainly on Harcourt's advice that Edward made his final decision. The choice was a bold one. Rather than, as in past years, reinforcing their troops in one of the three existing theatres of war, the English would open up a completely new front by landing in Normandy.

There has been much debate over Edward's strategic intentions for the 1346 campaign. The orthodox opinion in the nineteenth century was that Edward intended to go to Gascony to reinforce Lancaster, and only landed in Normandy when his ships were blown off course by unfavourable winds.[1] This has now been discredited, but some modern historians still believe that Edward changed his mind about Gascony at the last minute, late in June, and only then decided to land in Normandy.[2] That Edward had made the decision to attack Normandy much earlier is supported by, among other things, the fact that French spies in London knew such an attack was being planned as early as 18 March.[3] Even when it is accepted that Normandy was the chosen destination, historians are unsure as to his actual purpose in landing there. Jonathan Sumption believes that he intended, on Harcourt's advice, to conquer Normandy outright; Clifford Rogers argues that Edward's intention was to launch a raid or *chevauchée* into France and compel Philippe to fight a pitched battle, which would hopefully prove decisive; Alfred Burne believed that Edward intended to coordinate the activities of his forces in Gascony, Brittany, Normandy and Flanders to put maximum pressure on the French, but that the final purpose was to effect a juncture between the armies in Normandy and Flanders and confront the French from a position of strength.[4] All of these are useful theories, and all probably have a strong element of truth about them, although it must be stressed that minutes of the English royal council, if taken, do not survive, and any estimation of Edward's strategic intent must be a matter of informed speculation. To a limited extent, we can try to deduce Edward's motives from what he actually achieved; but this is risky, for it assumes that his strategic intent remained unchanged throughout the summer. Just because the campaign ended with the siege of Calais in September does not mean that Calais was the ultimate objective back in the spring.[5]

Plans for an invasion of Normandy had been discussed in England since the beginning of the war,[6] but the arrival of Harcourt made such an invasion seem a much more realistic possibility. Exactly when Harcourt and his followers arrived from Brabant is not clear, but certainly some of the exiles were in England by the end of the summer (the Groussy brothers were among those who took part in the attack on Castle Cornet).[7] The final decision to attack Normandy was probably made not long after; as early as 1 October 1345, the king ordered the armourer at the Tower of London, Robert Mildenhall, to build cannon to accompany 'the king's passage into Normandy'.[8] Harcourt's role was important, for not only did he have local knowledge of the countryside and suitable places for a landing, but he also had strong connections among the Norman nobility. It is possible that Harcourt suggested that Edward would find widespread support for his cause there (it is even possible that Harcourt himself believed this). Added to this, Normandy had been a thorn in the side of England for the last decade, and Norman ships had raided English shipping and coastal towns on many occasions, causing widespread destruction and loss of life and revenue from coastal areas.[9]

Thus, Edward and his commanders may have reasoned, a landing in Normandy would have one of two results. Either the Normans would rise up in support against the Valois usurper, in which case Edward could occupy and garrison the duchy with local loyalists (the Sumption hypothesis); or, if they did not, he could give the duchy a thorough drubbing, destroy as much of its shipping and port facilities as possible and hopefully defeat any French field armies he encountered (the Rogers hypothesis), and then move off north-east to link up with his Flemish allies and seek a confrontation with his adversary King Philippe (the Burne hypothesis). This is, in fact, more or less what he did: attempts (not very successfully: see Chapter 4) were made to protect private property and win over the Normans upon arrival, but when these failed, Edward proceeded to destroy Norman shipping and devastate the coastline of western Normandy. And letters sent from St-Vaast soon after landing and again from Caen two weeks later show that he intended from very early in the campaign to join forces with the Flemings before the end of the summer.[10]

Just as Philippe had spies in London, so Edward had them in Paris, and he was aware that the French were concentrating powerful forces in the south, intent on rolling back Lancaster's gains of the previous autumn. He also judged, correctly, that Lancaster was capable of standing on the defensive with the forces he had in hand. The campaign plan for 1346 was, we conclude, as follows. Lancaster would defend key fortified points against the French field army now assembling, and give as little ground as possible. Small reinforcements would be sent to Dagworth in Brittany, who would undertake a limited offensive so as to occupy Charles of Blois and prevent him from marching eastwards into Normandy and menacing Edward's right flank. Another small force would be sent to Flanders under the command of Hugh Hastings. Despite the death of van Artevelde, the leaders of the rebellious Three Towns alliance of Ghent, Bruges and Flanders remained committed to the English cause, and Hastings's task was to persuade them to raise an army and advance south into Artois and Picardy. Meanwhile, Edward would land with a sizeable army in western Normandy. This force, after doing what it could to either raise revolt or cause destruction in Normandy, would advance north to link hands with Hastings. The combined force would then be able if it wished to seek a confrontation with Philippe and the French royal army. A landing place in Normandy was chosen: the bay of St-Vaast on the north-eastern side of the Cotentin peninsula, a few miles south of the port of Barfleur. Sheltered from bad weather and largely free of rocks and reefs, it was an ideal place for a medieval army to disembark. It was also quite near Godefroi d'Harcourt's former home at St-Sauveur-le-Vicomte.

This was a complex plan, which could – and did – go wrong at several points. Fortunately, Edward and his commanders possessed the mental flexibility to change their plans to suit changing events. Edward's changes of plan were often cited by earlier generations of military historians, notably Sir Charles Oman, as evidence that Edward was a bad strategist, or even had no strategy at all.[11] In fact, these qualities of flexibility and adaptability suggest that Edward was actually quite a *good* strategist, one who could change his plans while still keeping his ultimate goal in sight, and who would probably have agreed with Field-Marshal von Moltke's dictum that no plan survives contact with the enemy. This kind of strategic thinking was to prove an important asset in 1346. While Lancaster and Dagworth fufilled their parts of the plan admirably, events in the other two theatres of war did not turn out as planned.

Edward funded the Crécy campaign using a mixture of taxation and loans, on top of the benefits of purveyance. In 1344, Parliament had granted him a tax subsidy of a fifteenth and a tenth of movable goods of the laity for two years. This latter subsidy was hedged about with conditions, primarily that it was for the use of the king in wartime, and not for general expenses. The financial and political crisis of 1340–1 had left Parliament somewhat cynical about Edward's warlike activities.[12] The 1344 subsidies were intended to bring in about £38,000 for each year, and they yielded over 95 per cent of that assessment.[13] A clerical subsidy was also levied, although it brought in a slightly smaller amount of money. The king also had the benefit of an ongoing tax of 40 shillings per sack on wool exports,[14] and also allowed a syndicate to farm the customs revenues; a group of merchants advanced the crown £50,000, which they were to recover from customs dues. Between 1343 and 1345 this syndicate was headed by William de la Pole, although Thomas Melchbourn appears as its official head on all documents. This company was unable to carry on past August 1345, and the farm of the customs was handed over to John Wesenham. Edward also borrowed from Italian bankers such as the Bardi, promising to pay them back out of subsidy revenues. It is clear that he also intended to raise money through an old-fashioned feudal levy which arose from the knighting of his eldest son, for although this event did not take place until the army's arrival in France, the administrative wheels were in motion whilst the campaign was still under way.

The French response

Edward tried to keep his plans secret, but failed. It was impossible to disguise the fact that large-scale military preparations were under way, but throughout the winter and spring Edward maintained that his next destination was Gascony. However, the English court leaked like a sieve and, as noted, French spies in Paris quickly brought word that in the summer the English would attack Normandy. By this time, however, Philippe had already committed much of his strength to the south. By mid-March an army of around 20,000 men, led by Philippe's eldest son Jean, Duc de Normandie, was assembling in the valley of the Garonne, and in early April 1346 this army laid siege to the strategically important fortress of Aiguillon at the confluence of the Garonne and the Lot. The garrison of Aiguillon was well prepared for a siege, and was ably supported by Lancaster, who raided forward from his base at La Réole and managed on at least one occasion to run supplies into the besieged town. Not only did they manage to tie down virtually the whole French strength in the south, but Aiguillon was still holding out in July when the English invasion of northern France began.[15]

But while part of Philippe's strength was committed in the south, he still had the manpower of much of northern France, including Normandy, Picardy, Champagne and the Île-de-France, to draw upon. Upon receiving intelligence of Edward's plans, Philippe took steps to put the north into a state of defence. The Constable of France, the Comte d'Eu, was placed in overall command, and two experienced captains were appointed to organise the coastal defences of Normandy. The Burgundian Godemar de Fay was put in charge of the coast of Upper Normandy, north of the Seine, while Robert Bertrand, Seigneur de Bricquebec and Marshal of France, was given Lower Normandy, south and west of the Seine.[16] Judging that his old enemy Harcourt would probably lead the English to the Cotentin, Bertrand, assisted by his brother Guillaume, Bishop of Bayeux, concentrated his resources to the west.

But of resources the French commanders had few. The Constable, who moved to Harfleur at the beginning of the summer, had only a few thousand men under his command, mostly raised from Normandy itself; Godefroi d'Harcourt's brother Jean, Comte d'Harcourt, and Jean de Melun, Comte de Tancarville, were the only senior nobles to raise men on his behalf. Bertrand and Fay were given some penny packets of Genoese crossbowmen from Doria's contingent and told to raise the troops they needed through local musters. The French fleet was also scattered into small forces and based in various harbours along the Normandy and Channel coasts; a mistake, since it meant that the fleet was never strong enough at any given point to ward off a full-scale invasion. Bertrand, whose instincts were clearly working well, deployed a sizeable force of crossbowmen to St-Vaast, but unfortunately he lacked the money to pay them; early in July these mutinied and withdrew to Caen.

French royal finances had now reached a crisis of their own, and money was in short supply. While the English king had sources of national taxation to raise money for military activity, the French crown was in the less enviable position of having to negotiate with regions and with individual towns.[17] In 1345 Philippe had been granted funds by Paris and some other cities to pay for 'a certain number of men-at-arms' until September of that year. Paris, for example, offered to fund 500 men-at-arms at 6 *sol* per day, and three Normandy towns offered a total of 8,523 *livres* for a period ending 30 April 1346. Tax collection was not controlled centrally, however, and local nobility sometimes took as much as half the revenue in return for organising its collection. Knowing that he was likely to face war on at least two fronts, the French king called for a military muster for the defence of the realm in August 1345, but he did not call a general assembly of nobles until very late in 1345 for the southern regions, and not until January 1346 for the northern regions. In February 1346 nobles and town representatives from places such as Arras, Lille and Amiens headed for Paris for the Estates General. They aired their grievances to Philippe and he responded by agreeing to a number of reforms, including a declaration that the *gabelle* (salt tax) and the sales tax would not remain as permanent national levies. The local representatives returned to the communities without agreeing to any specific financial help for the crown, but over the next few months local assemblies were held which did agree to grant support for men-at-arms; unfortunately these were still ongoing when the English invaded Normandy in July 1346. These assemblies calculated their assistance on the basis of how many hearths (or households) could support a single man-at-arms, with the city of Sens judging that 200 hearths would supply a single man-at-arms. Philippe did not rely solely on the grants of local assemblies; the *gabelle* and the sales tax both added useful revenue. Philippe also floated loans from individuals and from the Italian banks, as did his English adversary.

In summary, the attempt to defend the entire north-western coast of France was Philippe's first mistake of the summer. He had too little money, and too few men and ships spread too thinly. And having arranged his coastal defences he then hesitated, unsure of where the first threat would come from, Flanders or directly from the sea. He did not yet call up troops from the northern counties, judging that his frontier defences would be sufficient to contain the enemy until these could be summoned. Importantly, Philippe was also waiting for very sizeable contingents of troops from his foreign allies to arrive before making his next move. He had called upon these allies late in the previous year, for purposes which are not entirely clear (he may have been planning offensive action of his own in the north, until news of the projected English invasion forced him onto the back foot). Thousands of troops from many countries were on their way to France already, and these would play an important role in the months to come. The nature and role of the French allies in the 1346 campaign are often overlooked, and it is worth considering them in more detail.

The French allies

Five important bodies of allied troops had been summoned to join the French army late in 1345. These came from, first, the Genoese military contractors, Carlo Grimaldi and Ottone Doria; second, the rump of the Kingdom of Majorca, now consisting only of the city of Montpellier and its adjacent territories; third, the County of Savoy; fourth, King Jean of Bohemia and his son Charles; and fifth, from various counties of the Low Countries, notably Flanders, Hainault, Namur and Salm.

Grimaldi and Doria

As noted in the previous chapter, during Philippe VI's reign there was an increasing reliance on foreign mercenary crossbowmen. These are nearly always referred to as 'Genoese', but they were not provided by the Republic of Genoa; French relations with Genoa at this point were not particularly good.[18] Those Genoese who did serve with the French army were mostly exiles from the city, and many of the crossbowmen came from elsewhere in Italy.

The two key figures were, as noted, Ottone Doria and Carlo Grimaldi. Doria was a member of an old Genoese noble family and a member of the Ghibelline political faction, while the Grimaldis were *arriviste* and strongly Guelph in their leanings. Grimaldi's father Rainier had commanded warships in French service for many years, but Grimaldi himself in the 1320s had taken service under the pro-Guelph King Robert of Naples. In 1331, with the king's support, he had established himself on the rock of Monaco, to which his family had a decidedly shaky claim (it having been seized from its rightful owners by a previous Grimaldi, Francesco 'the Spiteful', in 1297). A revolt in 1335 overthrew the Guelphs and brought the Ghibelline faction to power, but Grimaldi was able to hang on to Monaco thanks to the fact that he now controlled a sizeable mercenary army and fleet of galleys.

In 1338, both Grimaldi and Doria, the latter still living in Genoa, were contracted to supply warships, marines and crossbowmen for French service. This was tricky, for as their commanders were on opposite sides of the political fence, the two contingents could not serve together. Arrangements had to be made to ensure that the ships sailed by separate courses to the English Channel, and, once there, Grimaldi's ships were based at Calais while Doria's sailed from Harfleur, so as to avoid contact with each other.[19]

This ridiculous state of affairs ended the following year when a popular revolution established Simone Boccanegra in power in Genoa, temporarily eclipsing both of the older political factions.[20] Doria went into exile, ultimately seeking refuge in France.[21] Here he continued to recruit men and ships for the French crown, though on a reduced scale. Meanwhile, he and Grimaldi, united by their hatred of the popular government in Genoa, worked out a *modus operandi* and together served France well. Their ships were particularly valuable after 1340, when France lost a number of warships at the battle of Sluys, and their crossbowmen were an important part of the French armies on land.

Late in 1345, both men were contracted to provide sizeable contingents for French service. Doria's contingent was the smaller of the two, probably about 3,000 men in all, and a few ships; having lost his power base, he was now little more than a recruiter of mercenaries. Grimaldi, however, had gone from strength to strength. Profits from the early French contracts had enabled him to buy up several neighbouring territories including Roquebrune, Menton and Ventimiglia, laying the foundations for the modern principality of Monaco. His contract, which he signed on 27 December, was to supply thirty-three ships and 7,000 crossbowmen; these were to be available on the Channel coast by mid-April. Between them, the two contingents totalled somewhere between 8,000 and 10,000 men (it is not clear whether Grimaldi supplied the full number of troops for which he was contracted).[22]

Doria's men arrived early in the season. This was fortunate, for the French were aware of the increasing threat of invasion in the north, and the crossbowmen were a valuable addition to their defences. Doria's men were used to garrison key points along the coast, including Caen and Harfleur and, as noted, St-Vaast. Grimaldi, however, delayed his departure, probably in part because of uncertainty about the intentions of Genoa, which was trying to bring Monaco back under its control; he was aware that a Genoese fleet was fitting out under the admiral Simone Vignoso, and needed to make Monaco secure in his absence.[23] Then he was contracted by King Jaume III of Majorca (of whom more below) and offered a contract to raid the king's former dominions in the Balearic Islands. The first of July found Grimaldi's galleys loitering off the mouth of the Tagus, still seven hundred miles from their destination. So dilatory was he that one later French historian accused him of accepting bribes from the English to delay his passage; another believed that Grimaldi, who was only contracted to serve until the end of October, was trying to do as little fighting as possible and still get paid.[24] Whatever the cause, Grimaldi's personal participation in the campaign was half-hearted, and it is significant that his contract was not renewed the following year.

Majorca

The kingdom of Majorca was one of those odd ephemeral states that medieval politics occasionally created; and this one indeed was already sliding toward eclipse. When King Jaume I of Aragon died in 1276, the kingdom was divided. Aragon and Valencia went to his elder son, while the Balearic Islands and other territories on the mainland, including Roussillon and Montpellier, went to his younger son, who became known as Jaume II, King of Majorca.[25] Jaume II was succeeded by his elder son Sanç, who died childless in 1324. Jaume's younger son Ferran had married Isabel, daughter of the Count of Andria, and through her had claimed the titles Prince of Achaia and Count of Clarencia (the Latin version of the Greek town of Glarentza), but had been killed in battle in 1316 while trying to enforce his claim.[26] Upon the death of Sanç, the throne then passed to Ferran's infant son Jaume III.

Jaume inherited his father's restless streak, and much of his life was full of grandiose plans; at one point he contemplated seizing the Canary Islands, at another he planned an invasion of North Africa. In the early 1340s he revived his claim to the titles of Achaia and Clarencia, and it looked at first as if the Greek and Frankish nobles might be prepared to accept him. However, Jaume had also quarrelled with his cousin, the unpleasant King Pere IV of Aragon. At stake was the issue of whether Majorca was a client state of Aragon or independent in its own right; Pere argued the former, while Jaume insisted on his independence. In 1343, Pere invaded Majorca with a large army. Jaume was quickly defeated and took refuge on the mainland. In the following year Aragonese troops entered Roussillon and seized its capital, Perpignan. Jaume was now confined to the city of Montpellier and its surrounding districts, and appealed to Philippe VI of France for assistance. Philippe provided financial aid which allowed Jaume to continue to survive at Montpellier and slowly begin building up a small army. It was probably through French agents that Jaume also came into contact with Carlo Grimaldi at Monaco. The two began to plan a campaign to recover Majorca, and the early months of 1346 saw Pere of Aragon hurriedly strengthening the defences of Roussillon and the Aragonese coast in anticipation of a joint Monaco–Majorcan attack.[27] However, the plans went into abeyance when, late in 1345, Jaume was requested to provide troops for French service in the following year.

It is not clear how many troops Jaume actually provided, but the number is likely to be small, perhaps five hundred or so; probably fewer than Philippe expected or hoped for. Although he had more men at his disposal (his army that fought at Lluchmayor four years later during the attempted reconquest of the Balearics numbered about 4,000), it is unlikely that he would have left Montpellier unguarded. It is also not clear how he joined the French army, whether he marched overland or travelled by sea in Grimaldi's galleys, but the latter seems more likely in that Grimaldi obligingly stopped off to raid the Balearics on his way to the English Channel.[28] Of all the French allies, the Majorcan contingent was the smallest and made the least contribution.

One final footnote to the Majorcan participation in the campaign of 1346 merits mention. Jaume III still claimed the County of Clarencia in Greece, but he had a rival: Philippa of Hainault, Queen of England, who claimed to have inherited Clarencia from her aunt Matilda (who was also the aunt of Jaume's mother, Isabel of Andria). Philippa later went so far as to ask that her third son, Lionel of Antwerp, be given the title Duke of Clarence, probably more in hope than in expectation that he would ever take possession of the lands that went with the title.[29] The title itself would continue in the royal family for many generations.

Savoy

Savoy, by contrast, was a well-organised and well-governed state that was beginning to rise to prominence in European affairs. The original county of Savoy was a mountainous state based around the town of Chambéry, but in the thirteenth century it expanded westwards into the Rhône valley to encompass the prosperous counties of Bugey and Bresse, and eastward over the Alps. The Counts of Savoy were long-standing allies of France, although by the 1340s that alliance was coming under strain; the increasing French interest in Dauphiné (see Chapter 1) was threatening to change the balance of power in the region, and in June 1345 Savoy went so far as to send an embassy to England to propose an alliance.[30] This seems to have been bluff, and all parties knew it; Edward received the ambassadors courteously but made no commitments. When in December 1345 Philippe wrote to the regents of Savoy to request a contingent of troops for the following spring, the regents responded positively.

Count Aymon of Savoy had died in 1343, and his twelve-year-old son Amadeus VI was still a minor. Savoy was ruled by two regents appointed by Aymon shortly before his death, the Counts Amadeus of Geneva and Louis of Vaud (the county of Vaud lay to the north of Lake Geneva, with its capital at Lausanne). The regents divided their responsibilities, with Amadeus of Geneva looking after the internal affairs of the county and Louis of Vaud responsible for foreign and military matters. Now in his late fifties, Louis was one of Europe's most experienced soldiers and diplomats. He had represented Savoy at the coronation of Edward II in Westminster Abbey. He had fought for the Emperor Henry of Luxembourg during the latter's Italian expedition of 1310–13, and had been appointed a Senator of Rome. He had become friendly with Henry's son Jean, King of Bohemia and had supported Jean's Italian venture in the 1330s, until his own son-in-law Azzo Visconti, Lord of Milan, decided to oppose Jean; Louis then retreated to neutrality on the far side of the Alps. He had commanded troops for the Counts of Savoy on several occasions, and in 1340 had deputised for Count Aymon and led a Savoyard contingent to join the French army in Flanders.[31]

It was natural, therefore, that the Count of Vaud should lead the Savoyard contingent this time as well. Savoy agreed to provide a thousand men-at-arms plus foot soldiers; the total contingent was about three thousand men. This was a small force by Savoyard standards; ten years later Amadeus VI would lead twice that many men to join the French army at Poitiers, and later in the 1350s Savoy was fielding armies of twelve thousand men or more. But the needs of local defence, plus perhaps a continuing discontent over Dauphiné, meant that the Savoyards provided only a modest force. They also left late; they were expected in Paris in July, but it would be well into August before they finally appeared.[32]

Bohemia and the Empire

Apart from the rival kings themselves, perhaps the best-known and most respected figure on either side was Jean, Count of Luxembourg and King of Bohemia. This fascinating man has often been written off as simply a military adventurer or mercenary. Adventurer he undoubtedly was, but he was also a highly cultured man, a complex and driven figure who seemed to inspire respect, if not necessarily regard, wherever he went. Born in Luxembourg on 10 August 1296, Jean was the eldest son of Henry of Luxembourg, who became Holy Roman Emperor as Henry VII, and his wife Marguerite of Brabant, a niece of King Philippe III of France. Like his father, Jean was educated in France and retained strong ties with that country throughout his career.

In 1310, at the age of fourteen, Jean married Eliška, last heir of the Přemsylid ruling dynasty in the kingdom of Bohemia. In the thirteenth century Bohemia had risen to become a substantial power in eastern Europe, and King Přemsyl Ottakar II had aspired to the imperial throne; but after his death in battle in 1278, Bohemia collapsed into chaos. Its various satellite states asserted their independence, and the remaining members of the Přemsylid dynasty either died of natural causes or assassinated each other in rapid succession. Although they later became estranged, the young king and queen initially worked well together to bring order to the state and its administration, and in the early years of his reign, Jean did much to restore Bohemian pride and security.

The Bohemians reacted to Jean in one of two ways; either they thought he was a foreign interloper whose adventurous nature would drag Bohemia down to ruin, or they regarded him as a champion of Bohemian greatness who would restore the kingdom to the glorious days of Přemsyl Ottakar II. Curiously, the former group coalesced around Jean's eldest son Václav (Wenceslas), who, having a Czech mother, was regarded as being one of them. After Queen Eliška's death, Václav became an increasingly important figure, and in 1337 at the age of twenty-one he took over the formal rule of the state in his father's name. Like his father, he was educated in France; one of his tutors, Pierre de Rosières, went on to become Pope Clement VI, and Václav took the French name Charles, by which name he is better known to history. While Jean extended Bohemian territory through conquest and embarked on his own imperial ambitions, Václav/Charles governed the state well; he went on in later years to become one of Bohemia's most beloved kings who made his capital, Prague, into the cultural and political centre of eastern Europe.

Jean's military achievements are described in detail elsewhere.[33] He conquered the iron-rich county of Silesia and added it to the Bohemian crown, and won further territory in successful wars with King Casimir III of Poland. He was an active ally of the Teutonic Knights, and served on several crusades against the pagan Lithuanians. In the early 1330s he attempted to carve out another base for himself in northern Italy around the cities of Bergamo and Brescia, but this project failed in the face of opposition from the powerful city of Milan. By now Jean was aware that he himself would never become emperor, but, undaunted, he set about campaigning for the election of his elder son. In the early 1340s the reigning emperor, Ludwig of Bavaria, was in conflict not only with the papacy but increasingly with his own nobles, and Jean, with the aid of France and Charles's old tutor Pope Clement VI, was manoeuvring Charles into position to replace him.

Meanwhile, Jean led a contingent of Bohemian and Luxembourg troops to support the French army in Flanders in 1340. His links with France were stronger than ever now that his daughter Bona of Luxembourg had married the heir to the French throne, Jean, Duc de Normandie. He was on crusade again in Prussia in 1344; he suppressed a rebellion in Silesia, and menaced Poland once again. This activity is particularly remarkable because Jean was now wholly blind. Some time around 1340 an accident (the exact nature of which is unknown) left him blind in one eye, and gradually the sight of the other eye weakened and failed as well. On the surface, he seemed as indomitable as ever. He fought, he attended tournaments, he laid the first stone of the new cathedral of St Vitus in Prague, he corresponded with his old friend the poet and musician Guillaume Machaut, he patronised painters and illustrators of books even though he could no longer see their work. Underneath it all, however, his power was beginning to fade. Most critically, rifts were opening between him and Charles. The latter resented his father's intrusions into Bohemian affairs, and increasingly wished to be free of Jean's domineering influence. Within Bohemia, factions were building in support of both men; the conflict between their camps was not yet open, but could not be long delayed.

Yet in March 1346, all appeared to be harmony, and the king and his son rode out together from Prague at the head of a glittering array of men-at-arms to attend the Imperial Diet at Trier. Here, in April 1346, ambassadors from Pope Clement VI declared Emperor Ludwig of Bavaria deposed. A series of tortuous negotiations ensued while the last of Ludwig's supporters were won over, but finally on 11 July the electors of the Empire met at Rense and elected the pope's former pupil Charles as King of the Romans.[34] All that remained was for him to be formally crowned as Holy Roman Emperor. However, this would have to be delayed. While Jean and Charles were still in Prague, messengers had arrived from Paris asking for assistance in the war against England. The two kings now rode on to Luxembourg and thence to Liège, where the Bishop of Liège and Count of Salm were facing a revolt by the commune of the city. The Bohemians crushed the revolt, but hardly had they done so when more messengers arrived from Paris, requesting assistance, this time urgently. With the Count of Salm and his men in company, the Bohemians began marching south.

How many men did Jean and Charles between them bring to the French army? No figures survive, but the answer must surely be several thousand. These were two of the most important political figures in Europe, and for both personal prestige and personal security, they are unlikely to have ridden from Prague with much fewer than a thousand men, including the Count of Rožmberk and other Bohemian nobles. Knowing that they were needed in France, they probably recruited more men in Jean's own lands in Luxembourg, and certainly did so among Charles's new subjects elsewhere in the Empire; six German counts, including the Count of Saarbrucken, are said to have served with the new King of the Romans.[35] It seems highly likely that Jean and Charles between them brought three thousand men to join the French army, including men-at-arms, panzerati light cavalry and foot soldiers; and the total may be higher. Whatever the true figure, none was more important than King Jean himself, who would show before the summer was out that, blind or not, he was still one of the finest soldiers in Europe.

The Low Countries

Finally, there were contingents from the Low Countries, notably Flanders, Hainault, Namur and Salm. The Count of Flanders, Louis de Nevers, was himself a French vassal and already had a substantial force in the field ready to fight the rebels of Bruges, Ghent and Ypres. Hainault had once been a staunch ally of England, but Count William of Hainault, King Edward's brother-in-law, had been killed trying to suppress a rebellion in Zeeland in January 1346. As he had no heirs, the power vacuum was temporarily filled by John of Hainault, Lord of Beaumont, an old friend and companion-in-arms of the English king. He now indicated to France that he was willing to consider a change of allegiance, and after a series of negotations conducted by one of Philippe's officers, Godemar de Fay, and two senior nobles, the Comte de Blois (who was also Hainault's son-in-law) and the Duc de Lorraine, Hainault agreed to change sides in exchange for a substantial pension.[36] He brought with him not only his own powerful retinue but a strong following among the other nobles of Hainault, who despised the English for encouraging the Flemish towns to revolt and feared their example would be followed in their own lands. Hainault did more than just serve King Philippe; he became a close advisor and confidant, and through the summer of 1346 was seldom far from the king's side. This was a stunning act of treachery, fully comparable to Godefroi d'Harcourt's defection to the English; a fact not always appreciated by the French historians who condemn Harcourt for betraying his country.

The motives of the other two counts, Guillaume of Namur and Simon of Salm, for joining France are not clear. Both had extensive lands in the Meuse valley around the cities of Namur and Liège, and both may likewise have feared the spread of rebellion from Flanders; both also had ties of blood and culture with France, and Salm was also to some extent a client of both Luxembourg and the Duc de Lorraine. Their contingents, including foot soldiers, were probably modest. All in all, taking into account the troops under Louis de Nevers facing the rebel cities of Flanders, these four contingents probably mustered about five thousand men.

The English preparations

Preparations for the 1346 campaign got under way in October 1345. Anxious to launch his campaign early, Edward initially hoped to embark for France early in March of the following year, and throughout the winter a steady stream of orders and instructions issued from the court. The army that would invade Normandy in 1346 would, it was initially hoped, consist of around 20,000 men. The final figure was rather fewer, but it was still the largest army England had raised since the start of the war.

In the 1340s, the English crown used two methods to raise armies. The first was the raising of what are generally known as arrayed troops, summoned for service by the issuing of commissions of array. Three or four commissioners were appointed for each county and shire, and in 1345 these commissioners included men like William Lucy in Warwickshire, John Coggeshale in Essex, Andrew Peverel in Surrey and Simon Basset in Gloucestershire. These were experienced administrators, most of them knights, and many would serve themselves in the forthcoming campaign.[37] The commissioners in turn required local administrative units such as hundreds to supply some portion of the total required; the communities were also required to meet the costs of clothing and arming the men being raised. Individual towns were also expected to provide troops. Each county and town had a fixed quota of men it was expected to supply, ranging from 280 for Kent to a mere 40 for Rutland. The counties and shires largely supplied archers on foot, while the towns supplied a mix of mounted archers, lightly armoured horsemen known as hobelars, or ordinary foot soldiers.[38] The principality of Wales was expected to supply around 7,000 men, a mix of archers and spearmen. Altogether, the commissions of array were expected to supply around 13,000 men.

In reality, the historian Andrew Ayton believes the total was probably closer to 9,000. Some counties provided only half or two-thirds of their quota; the town of Norwich negotiated a reduction in its quota from 120 to 60 men, and the commissioners of array for Norfolk only raised 129 of the 200 men they had been asked to supply.[39] Scores of exemptions from service were applied for and received, often in exchange for payment; for example, on 10 March, one Otto de Halsale paid £4 for an exemption, having previously been ordered to serve in exchange for a pardon for various felonies.[40] Even the king's own daughters, Isabella and Joan of the Tower, asked for exemption for three men, presumably of their own households, who had given them 'service'.[41] In other cases, people simply failed to show up when ordered to do so. Also, at least some of the men raised would have proved unfit for service and been rejected by the commissioners. The troops raised by the commissions of array were not always of the highest quality; as the historian Michael Prestwich says, 'what commissions of array produced was quantity, not quality'.[42] In one instance, in Warwickshire, the commissioners met with open resistance and one commissioner, John Lodebrok, was assaulted and unable to carry out his duties.[43]

The other method of raising troops, which was becoming increasingly common on both sides of the English Channel, was through contracts known as indentures. Under this system, nobles, bannerets and other prominent individuals raised troops themselves, which they then hired to the crown on a contract basis. It is estimated that between 4,000 and 5,000 men were raised in this way, including men-at-arms and archers. The total size of the army that had been raised by the spring of 1346 through both methods, array and indenture, has been debated, but was likely somewhere between 14,000 and 15,000 fighting men, plus some non-combatants who would have taken the total over 15,000. The former figure included perhaps 2,500 men-at-arms, between 8,000 and 9,000 foot soldiers of whom perhaps 6,000 were archers, and around 4,000 other mounted troops, a mix of hobelars and mounted archers.[44] Unlike the French army, which was a polyglot mix from many parts of Europe, virtually all this force was recruited within the British Isles. A few German knights, probably legacies of Edward's failed alliances of the late 1330s, did come to serve with the king, but seem to have played little part in the fighting. A knight from Hainault, Oliver de Ghistels, played a more active role, and there may have been a few others of his fellow countrymen in the army, and at least one Florentine accompanied the royal household (see above). Beyond these, however, the army was composed entirely of Edward's own subjects.

Pay was at standard rates, which had remained largely unchanged since the reign of the king's grandfather; as Prestwich points out, 'the king was in a monopoly position, able to dictate wage rates with little reference to market forces'.[45] Rates of pay depended on man's rank and armament, as follows:

Banneret	4 shillings per day
Knight bachelor	2 shillings per day
Mounted serjeant	1 shilling per day
Hobelar	6 pence per day
Mounted archer	6 pence per day
Foot archer	3 pence per day
Foot spearman	2 pence per day[46]

Mariners, or ordinary seamen, were also paid 3 pence per day while in the king's service. Neither they nor the foot soldiers were particularly well paid. In 1346, for example, the king was employing harness makers at 4 pence per day, and other craftsmen earned similar or higher wages.[47] At the outbreak of the war Edward had briefly experimented with offering double rates of pay to men serving overseas, but the financial crisis that quickly engulfed him meant that pay had to be returned to the standard rates.[48] Plunder, rather than pay, was doubtless the chief motivating force of the great majority of ordinary soldiers.

While the commissioners of array were struggling to find suitable men and the great nobles and bannerets were recruiting their retinues, royal officials were busily collecting weapons, equipment, supplies and ships. As noted in the previous chapter, men were expected to come ready equipped with weapons, including bows, but spares were provided in case of damage or loss. The most important items to be collected were arrows, of which the army would need a great number if a pitched battle was to be fought. The sheriff of each county was instructed to supply a fixed number of bowstaves and arrows, the latter usually in sheaves of twenty-four. Robert Hardy has calculated the total number of arrows ordered in 1346 at 133,200: a low figure, but Hardy reminds us that very large orders had also been placed in previous years, around half a million in 1342 and 1343 together and a further 300,000 in 1341, and many of these would still have remained in stock.[49]

A quantity of crossbows were also ordered for maritime service. On 25 November two men were appointed to fell trees on the royal manors of Eltham, Kent and Easthampstead, Berkshire and use the wood to make crossbows.[50] Forty crossbows at 12 pence each were provided for the crew of the ship *La Magdeleyne* of Lynn, effectively one for each member of the crew; 30 sheaves of crossbow bolts were also provided, at 18 pence per sheaf. Another ship, the cog *La Seinte Mary*, also from Lynn, received 30 crossbows and 32 sheaves of bolts, this time at 16 pence per sheaf.[51] Some additional armour was also provided for the crews of these ships, who, unlike the soldiers raised for the army, were apparently not expected to provide their own weapons and armour.

As noted in Chapter 2, Edward had determined early in the campaign to take firearms with him on the coming campaign, and was ordering ingredients for gunpowder in large quantities. The London merchant William

Stanes provided 2,021 lbs of saltpetre, at a price of £151 11s. 6d., and 466 lbs of sulphur for £15 10s. 8d. Stone and iron cannon balls were also provided, probably made by the royal armourers. In the end Edward seems to have decided to take only the larger bombards and leave behind the ribaudequins and other smaller pieces; the difficulties of transporting not only the weapons themselves but the required supplies of gunpowder may have been a deciding factor.[52] Walter le Fevre, the smith who had done the ironwork for the cannon, had died in November 1345, and his son Andrew (who had probably worked with him) was ordered to accompany the army to France, leaving his mother Katharine to carry on work at the Tower's forge. She, like her son, was paid 8d. per day for her services.[53]

As well as men, many thousands of horses were required for the campaign, ranging from the great warhorses of the nobles and knights to carthorses for the baggage train. Unfortunately the horse accounts for 1346 have not survived as well as for other years, but we know a little about some of the king's own horses. The documents are often surprisingly detailed. In one instance, a document noting the movement of twenty horses from Northampton to Portchester, the embarkation point, describes the appearance of each; there are a piebald with three white feet, another with four white feet, and five black horses including one with a star. Each had his own groom, who was paid 2d. per day with a 2d. bonus at Pentecost.[54] A black mare called Juele is also mentioned in another document, and the Prince of Wales had a grey horse called Liard. Carthorses were also purchased for the wagons to carry the king's baggage, and again a surprising amount of detail is given; in one undated document we read of a white horse and a bay horse, each costing 46s. 8d., two roans at 38s. and 39s. and three other horses all with values of from 32s. to 33s.[55]

Fodder was also collected. Warhorses in particular could not be fed on grass alone, and required a heartier diet. On one occasion, William de Ferour, the custodian of the king's warhorses, collected 122½ quarters (980 bushels) of beans and peas, which he delivered to the receiver of victuals for the horses.[56] Altogether, 5,200 bushels of corn, peas and beans were collected as fodder for the horses of the royal household, filling several large ships and twelve small ones.[57] This gives us an idea not only of the large quantities of fodder which were shipped, but also of the organisation that looked after these valuable animals. Fodder was shipped for carthorses as well; another document mentions oats for seven carthorses at a cost of 2*s*. 6*d*. per day.[58] The other great households, that of the Prince of Wales and the earls and barons, would probably have ordered similar, if smaller, quantities of fodder. Large quantities of horseshoes and nails were also needed; shoes for the twenty horses mentioned above cost 20*s*. Saddles and spurs were also ordered. These were expensive items, with even an ordinary saddle for a hobelar costing 10*s*. and those ordered for the king's riding horse costing 20*s*.[59] Along with these went all the equipment needed to keep horses healthy, including medicines, strigils, combs and hoof picks.

A mass of other equipment was also being collected. An important requirement was for material for building or repairing bridges; an expedition to Brittany in 1343 had taken timber for three complete bridges and 120 hurdles, the whole carried in twenty-two carts.[60] Similar or even larger quantities were shipped in 1346. In March of that year, the sheriff of Hampshire had been ordered to deliver 1,000 hurdles, twenty bridges (possibly loading ramps) and 'other necessities' for the equipment of the king's house.[61] Nails, hinges, brackets and tools for carpenters, smiths and farriers were also supplied, and the smiths and farriers also required portable forges, charcoal to heat them, and iron for use in making and mending horseshoes and tools. Hurdles for fencing were constructed, and thousands of bundles of faggots, which could have the dual purposes of being used to fill in ditches and serving as firewood, were collected. £16 worth of hemp was purchased from the London merchant Nicholas Chaucer, who also supplied the royal household with sealing wax; another merchant supplied 320 lbs of 'Bridport cord' at 2*d*. per pound.[62]

For the bulk of the army, accommodation on the march would be whatever billets or shelter they could find, or else they slept in the open wrapped in whatever cloaks or blankets they carried. The knights and nobles would also expect to be able to commandeer housing at some points, but for times when this was not possible they brought tents and furnishings. These ranged from what were probably fairly ordinary tents for the poorer knights bachelor to large and well-furnished pavilions for the king, the Prince of Wales and the great nobles. Some of these were doubtless made new, but there are also references to pavilions being mended, suggesting that they had been brought out from storage.[63] An undated document from around this time records payment for hundreds of pennons and banners: 340 small pennons or 'penecells' of one ell length, 1,000 penecells of three and a half ells length, longer streamers of four and five ells, 104 standards, a number of 'vexels' or banners and so on. Many of these bore the device of St George along with the royal arms.[64] It is highly probable that some of these, or similar pennons and banners, were taken on campaign. Medieval warfare was a showy business, with plenty of pomp and display, and especially on occasions such as the reception of embassies, the triumphal entry into captured towns and so on, kings were judged in part on the quality of spectacle they could produce.

Stocks of food and other supplies were also beginning to arrive. Throughout the winter, royal purveyors had been active throughout the country, in what one modern-day historian has called the largest purveyancing operation undertaken in England so far.[65] Purveyors, who could force compulsory sales of food and other goods at fixed prices, were among the most hated of royal officials, and they often met with non-cooperation or even active resistance.[66] On 15 February, purveyors had been assaulted at Wells in Somerset, and there was a suspicion of a plot to kill royal officials.[67] A large number of people, including one knight, were arrested and indicted. In general, though, the collection of food stocks passed off peacefully. Indeed, the purveyors were so thorough that in the end they collected more food than was needed or could be shipped, and later in the summer we find royal officials hastily selling off hundreds of bushels of grain, casks of flour and carcasses of meat that had been spoiled.[68]

The most common foodstuffs collected were corn of various kinds, peas and beans. The ordinary peasant diet of the mid-fourteenth century was pottage, either peas, beans or oats cooked in water along with whatever came to hand, including onions, garlic, whatever wild herbs that could be gathered, and perhaps bacon or salt fish or other meat if available. Thousands of bushels of peas and beans were shipped, serving equally well as fodder for horses and food for men; light and easy to carry and requiring only a simple pot and an open fire, they were a good source of nutrients. Oats, barley and wheat were also shipped, and also flour in casks; if the commoners got by with pottage, the better-off would still have demanded their bread. Meat, both preserved and fresh, was also provided; salted and spiced beef and mutton formed a minor but consistent part of the diet of the royal household over the course of the summer, but many live cattle and sheep were also collected. Meat, especially in the summer, would only keep for so long, and it thus may have been easier to herd beasts along and slaughter them as needed, at least for short periods of time. It is also probable that some dairy animals accompanied the baggage train, as milk, butter and cheese often appear on the tables of the royal household throughout the campaign. Where they appear they are valued, indicating that they were not simply pillaged. Hurdles for fencing and material for building stock houses were also shipped. The royal household included several herdsmen, and also keepers for the large quantities of chickens, hens, capons, geese and even more exotic birds such as swans that were kept alive until needed. Fish were a different matter; most of the cod and salmon collected were either salted or dried (stockfish), but fresh eels could be kept alive in barrels of water. Apart from these and whatever could be caught along the way (a fisherman also appears in the accounts), the king and his nobles would have to do without fresh fish, and items such as shrimps, oysters, roach, gurnard and even porpoise which sometimes graced the royal table would have to be left behind. Finally, the royal and well-to-do households brought along luxuries such as pickled vegetables, vinegar, mustard and verjuice for making sauces, as well as a variety of herbs.[69] Bundles of firewood and bushels of coal for cooking were also collected for use during the opening days of the campaign.

As well as food, large quantities of wine were also procured and shipped from all over the kingdom. Two ships laden with ninety tuns of wine came from London; two more came from Bristol, *La Gracedieu* and *Le Focra* in charge of the royal butlers John Wayte and Alan Norman, with 232 tuns. William Eastry brought seventy-four tuns of wine from Sandwich to Portsmouth in *La George de Stonore*, and Hugh Kechel brought a further ninety-seven tuns in *Le Botolf de Grimsby* down from Boston.[70] It is possible that some of these were specialist wine-carrying ships normally employed in shipping wine from Bordeaux. On arrival, the wine would have been decanted from the large tuns into smaller casks more easily transportable on land. Some was also sent directly to the royal household at Southwick for immediate consumption. It is interesting to note that an allowance was made for losses in transit; of the ninety tuns shipped from London, four and a half tuns were lost to leakage and evaporation (it is not clear whether these were the real cause of loss, or the terms were a euphemism for pilfering).

Last but by no means least among the stores being prepared for France were the king's own private effects. Even more than most monarchs of his age, Edward was fond of luxury and display, and seldom stinted himself when it came to personal comfort. In the months before the campaign began, the offices of the household – the Wardrobe, the Great Hall, the Chamber – were keeping the merchants of London and elsewhere busy. An incomplete fragment of one account lists some of the clothing and personal effects being bought for the king: twenty pairs of boots at 4s. the pair, ninety-six pairs of shoes at 6d. the pair, covers or cases for clothing, two portable folding thrones at 12s. each, a privy seat covered with cloth at a cost of 14s. 6d., six beaver caps at 5s. each, six felt caps at 2s. each, an ivory-framed mirror and two ivory combs, each item costing 10s. John Morreys of London provided a pair of scissors, a further pair of small barber's scissors and a case for both, as well as two other 'cutters', one hundred chamberpots at 2d. each, two iron-bound cases for chamberpots and three pounds of down for pillows. Nicholas Chaucer provided thirty-two pounds of cotton, then an imported luxury item. John de Colon provided pigments for paint, including azure, white lead, red lead and vermilion, candle wax and 600 small straw rings, purpose unknown. Purchases of cloth, silver leaf and gold plate are recorded.[71] Another document records payment for a velvet scabbard and gold decoration for the use of the king. While by no means all these items were taken on campaign, it is likely that many were. The King's Hall was also busily buying various bits of furniture, and the accounts list not only the items but also the cost of their carriage to Portchester. As late as 26 June the King's Hall was buying two tables for the household. The King's Hall and the Chamber also purchased many smaller items such as hooks, nails, locks, iron mallets and spits.

Every order made, every shipment received, every payment handed over to merchants and craftsmen left its own parchment trail as the clerks of the royal household meticulously recorded transactions and expenses for everything from gunpowder and crossbow bolts to chamberpots and shoes. Although not all these records have survived, enough remains for us to appreciate the scale of the bureaucratic machine that organised it. By the standards of the day, the army that Edward took to France was very well prepared and well organised, and these 'staff officers' of the household are among the unsung heroes of the summer that was to come. Many of these men themselves were also preparing to accompany the king. Although by the mid-fourteenth century a permanent administrative apparatus was in place in London, the king still travelled with an extensive administrative staff.

Two of his senior officials, Richard Talbot, the steward of the household, and Walter Wetewang, keeper of the wardrobe, would accompany the king to France, as would a batch of other clerks and officials including Michael Northburgh, Richard Wynkeley and Thomas Bradwardine; the correspondence of the last three forms one of our most important sources for the events of that summer. Tables, chairs and extensive stores of parchment, ink and sealing wax were prepared for transport so that the clerks could continue the work of government even in the field.[72]

*　*　*

As the spring of 1346 began to arrive, the process of moving men, horses and supplies to the embarkation point began. Portsmouth harbour had been chosen for this purpose, as it was large enough to accommodate a number of ships in sheltered conditions, and building works were undertaken at Portchester castle by the constable, John Haket, including the construction of a new chamber and repairs to the hall, chambers and kitchen.[73] Portchester, an ancient coastal fort with a medieval keep inside Roman ramparts, was to be Edward's headquarters during the embarkation. The king himself was still in the London area, with the main household quartered at Stratford-atte-Bow, while Edward seems to have divided his time between Westminster and Mortlake. On 10 April the household moved by river to Kingston, and thence to Guildford on the following day; twenty tuns of wine were also sent by river to Guildford.[74] There the king joined them, and the household passed Easter at Guildford. On 16 April, Easter Sunday, there was an enormous feast at which were consumed the carcasses of 24 cattle, 9 sheep, 77 deer and 26 pigs, along with 10 swans, 4 bustards, 4 herons, 50 geese, nearly 500 chickens of various kinds, 342 doves, 12 rabbits, 37 whole cheeses, 4,600 eggs and 300 loaves of bread; 53 bushels of coal, 900 quarters of faggots and 403 bushels of smaller firewood were required to cook it all. The total cost of food was £58 12s. 1½d. On 25 April, his digestion having presumably recovered, the king seems to have returned briefly with part of the household to Westminster, while the remainder moved on in slow stages, leaving Guildford on the 27th and travelling via Farnham and Alton to Southwick, just north of Portchester, on the 29th.

The rest of the army was already beginning to arrive, either taking up billets in Portsmouth and Southsea or camping in the fields nearby. On

5 May, Robert Houel, deputising for the Earl of Warwick, was appointed by the king to organise the assembly of the army.[75] Houel also served on a commission of oyer and terminer appointed two days later, along with the steward of the royal household, Richard Talbot, and the officials John Leukenore, Thomas Aspale and John Roche, to examine felonies and trespasses committed by troops on the march in Hampshire, Wiltshire, Somerset, Dorset, Surrey, Sussex, Oxford and Berkshire on their way to Portsmouth.[76] Whether this commission was set up in order to deal with criminal acts already committed by the troops against the local populace along their line of march, or in anticipation that such crimes would be committed, is not clear.

Some of the mariners of the fleet were also proving a problem. There were a number of fights on land between sailors and locals or members of the army. Two men, Philip Kent, a citizen of London, and John Burnewell of Sparkewell, Devon, had their ears cut off during these brawls. This was particularly unpleasant, as the cutting off of ears was a common judicial punishment for sedition and other crimes, and a man with no ears would commonly be presumed to be a criminal. The hapless Kent and Burnewell had to apply for royal 'notifications to avert suspicion', documents which would show that their mutilation was not due to any offence committed.[77] Worse, at least one ship, the *Escumer* commanded by Simon de Rathby, had been indulging in acts of piracy, raiding wine ships coming into Southampton.[78]

These were exceptions, however, and by and large the assembly of the fleet passed off without incident. The chief problem had been poor spring weather. Initially the king had asked for the fleet to be assembled by February, but this proved to be impossible. The end of March was then set, but storms in the Channel kept ships in their harbours and made sailing impossible. Finally the assembly was ordered for 30 April, the earliest practicable date. The other problem was the shortage of suitable ships. The crown owned a handful of ships, such as the cogs *George* and *Thomas*, purpose-built warships of somewhere between 100 and 150 tons displacement with permanent fighting towers or 'castles' at the bow and stern to give protection to archers and men-at-arms. Crews for these ships were correspondingly large: the *George* had a crew of two masters, two constables, a clerk, four carpenters, 130 seamen and 26 pages.[79] Both the *George* and the *Thomas* underwent repairs prior to the campaign.[80]

The vast majority of the fleet, however, were commandeered or 'arrested' ships from ports around the kingdom. These ranged from big cogs of 70–80 tons to smaller 'ships' of various types, ranging down to 10 or 20 tons. Some of the larger of these might have had permanent fighting castles, and others had temporary castles added, but the smaller vessels almost certainly had neither the space nor the buoyancy to support such structures and were used to transport stores only. An undated list of ships from the reign of Edward III gives an idea of the numbers of ships in each port and the total number of ships at the disposal of the king. For example, Margate was said to have fifteen ships and 160 mariners, and the total available to the southern fleet was 493 ships and 9,630 seamen.[81]

Assembling the fleet was an expensive business. The owners of La Magdeleyne of Lynn, mentioned above, submitted a bill to the crown for refurbishing the ship, including repairs to sails (46s.), two heavy cables weighing 100 stone (£4 3s. 3d.), 100 hand ropes (£3 6s. 8d.), a thirteen-foot-long anchor (45s.), provision of a small boat (£4 5s.) and repairs to hatches as well as compensation for lost income during the time of the arrest and wages for the crews. The same owners submitted a similar bill for their ship La Seynte Marie; the total came to nearly £240. Admittedly the owners, Thomas and Peter Melchbourn, were sub-admirals of the fleet north of the Thames, and Thomas Melchbourn was also heavily involved in the procurement of royal finances, so they were probably able to claim for rather more expenses than the ordinary shipowner; but even so the costs were high.

The heaviest item of expenditure would have been wages for the seamen themselves. La Magdeleyne was crewed by a master, a constable, 38 mariners and four pages, and La Seynte Marie by a master, a constable, 36 mariners and three pages. These were fairly large ships, probably 50 tons or so, and smaller ships had correspondingly smaller crews. But the total number of ships finally gathered was between 700 and 800, and thousands of seamen were required to man them. It seems to have been the practice to pay these men – or at least, to pay the shipowners and masters – in advance, and sizeable sums were doled out by one of the royal clerks, John Watenhoule: £300 on 10 April, another £300 on 2 June, and £420 and £641, both on 8 June.[82] Other royal officials were travelling throughout the spring trying to assemble the necessary ships, and as late as April Alan Killum was sent to Sandwich and the royal serjeants-at-arms Robert

St Oweyn and Henry Bath went to Bristol in an urgent attempt to make up the numbers. Ships also came from the pro-English ports of Brittany, and in July Watenhoule paid out another £196 to their crews.[83]

Ultimately, however, they were successful, and the fleet filled not only Portsmouth harbour but spread down the Solent towards the open sea, a vast and motley armada ranging from the royal ships of war down to ungainly merchant ships, coasters and probably even a few fishing vessels; the whole reminiscent more of Dunkirk than of D-Day. In ordinary times the English fleet was organised into two divisions: Robert Ufford, Earl of Suffolk, commanded the fleet north of the Thames, while William Clinton, Earl of Huntingdon, commanded the fleet south and west of the Thames. Possibly because it was in his bailiwick, Huntingdon was now given command of the entire fleet and Suffolk prepared to join the land forces. Some of Suffolk's officers seem to have transferred to Huntingdon; William Redenhale, lieutenant of the fleet under Suffolk, was still serving in that capacity in July under Huntingdon.

While many goods came by sea, much was also transported by land. Hundreds of wagons and carts were required, and while some of these were probably purchased, others were built using wood from trees felled in the royal forests. Some came provided with covers in order to protect perishable goods such as food, and also gunpowder. These wagons were expensive to build. One such, built from materials provided by Robert atte Spyne, cost 61s. 11d. for the wheels alone, including iron rims for the wheels and the pay of the wheelwright. The harness for the draught horses cost a further 3s., and 26d. was spent on cords or ropes, presumably to secure the cargo. Many carts and wagons would also be required on the other side of the Channel, and so were built so that they could be easily dismantled and stowed on board ship.

*　*　*

By mid-May the great concentration was well under way. The king, leaving a few of his officers in London, rejoined the household at Southwick on 2 May, and on 5 May moved on to Portchester. The bulk of the household did not follow until a week later, suggesting that perhaps the refurbishment of the castle had not been carried out as quickly as planned. A major feast was held at Pentecost, the last before embarkation; this was another gargantuan meal at which were consumed ten and three-quarter carcasses of beef, eleven carcasses of salt mutton and forty-nine of fresh mutton, twenty sides of bacon, eight pigs, twenty piglets, thirty-three deer, seven swans, seven herons, four spoonbills, thirty geese, seven capons, 202 hens plus three hens 'in pastry walls', ten pullets, 110 chickens and 2,200 eggs.

The clerks of the household were busier than ever, issuing letters of protection – effectively, passports – for men going overseas in the royal service, and letters of exoneration from other services for men who had come to serve with the army. Men also made sure that their own lands and property would be looked after in their absence, and there survive a large number of letters nominating attorneys to safeguard the property of men going overseas. On 10 June there appears a long list of quittances for not going abroad, as more men decided to pay cash rather than experience the dubious delights of invading Normandy.[84]

Throughout all this, the minor affairs of governance had to continue. Several Spanish ships coming from Bayonne with cargoes of wine were arrested off Guernsey on suspicion of trading with France, and brought into English ports; the merchants argued false arrest, claiming they were on their way to Flanders. Edward rejected the argument, but returned ships and crews to Castile as a gesture of good will, after first confiscating the wine.[85] And almost while he was preparing to board ship and sail for France, the king had to deal with one of his most cantankerous and difficult subjects, the former outlaw John Molyns of Stoke Poges, and issue orders to his officers not to molest Molyns's swans or take them for the king's use.[86]

By the end of June, however, all was at last ready. The gathered supplies were sent aboard ship; the payment of cellarage for the wine for the royal household ends on 24 June, suggesting it may have been put aboard ship on that date. The other parts of the royal household also began loading under the direction of Richard Talbot, steward of the household. Giles Coloyne, yeoman of the kitchen, had responsibility for ensuring that the kitchen equipment, personnel and foodstuffs, including the live animals, were safely transported. Thomas Poleyne, valet of the scullery, had been stocking up on equipment such as spits, sconces, hurdles, pots and drinking vessels – 600 of the latter were bought on 17 June alone – and these were loaded along with the rest of the gear.[87] It is interesting to read that the twelve small ships carrying fodder for the king's warhorses each flew a small pennon with the device of the king's receiver so that they could be identified, and it is tempting to believe that other similar devices were used to identify particular storeships.[88]

Loading of the horses must have taken some time, and cannot have been an enjoyable prospect. It is not so much water that horses dislike as confined spaces, and many would have needed to be coaxed or dragged up the loading ramps into the waists of the transport ships. Small ponies and carthorses could probably be managed more easily, but dealing with the powerful and bad-tempered – and extremely valuable – warhorses would have required persistence and ingenuity. Compared to that, the embarkation of the men was probably a fairly easy process. Spirits in the army seem to have been high; those who did not want to go had by now purchased their quittances and gone home. Few knew officially where they were going (although rumours were doubtless circulating), but for most this probably did not matter. Some were looking forward to a chance of action, especially those from the south coast who had scores to settle with the French; and nearly all were dreaming of riches, the common soldiers looking forward to opportunities for loot, the knights and esquires hoping to capture a wealthy nobleman whose ransom would set them up for life.

By 27 June most of the army was embarked. The king handed over the reigns of government to the regent who would govern the realm in his absence, his young son Lionel of Antwerp. Lionel was only seven, but this was considered old enough to manage the ceremonial aspects of government, while the real work was done by a council consisting of John Stratford the Archbishop of Canterbury, the Bishop of Winchester, Thomas Berkeley, William Shareshull, Robert Sadyngton and the clerk Peter Gildesburgh. The king himself went on board his flagship, the *George*, and the Prince of Wales and his household went aboard the cog *Thomas*. The king moved down the Solent and anchored off Yarmouth while he waited for the rest of the fleet.[89] But there were more delays; the huge fleet, confined in the waters of the Solent, took longer than expected to organise. On 1 July the king landed again on the Isle of Wight, presumably so as to wait in greater comfort. The Kitchen Account for 27 June has a separate list of food for the king and the household on board the *George*; it states that they were at sea on the 28th, 29th and 30th before arriving at Freshwater on the Isle of Wight on the 1st July. While at sea they continued to eat a variety of food including fish, beef, mutton, bacon and venison. The saucery appears to have been baking bread while at sea, and continued to do so until the army disembarked in Normandy, at which point presumably the usual household bakery was up and running again.

Slowly, order began to emerge, and by 5 July much of the fleet had concentrated off Yarmouth and around the Needles. Then the weather changed, with the wind blowing steadily out of the south-west. The clumsy roundships could not sail close to the wind, and most could not even get out of the Solent, let alone steer a course for Normandy. Most were driven back up the straits towards Portsmouth.[90] The king remained at his shore station at Carisbrooke, very probably wondering if the weather was going to balk him yet again and all this preparation and effort and time and money would go to waste. On 6 July he was even forced to send back to Portchester for more wine as supplies were running low.[91] The king's kitchen and other household departments remained at Freshwater, providing some food for the king and other members of the household; costs for boats and boatmen for carriage remain high throughout this period. Even at this late date, the scullery continued to buy large amounts of firewood as well as, on 9 July, eight hurdles, four pestles, twenty vessels, ten bowls, two sconces and a ladle.

But on the 11th of July the wind changed again. Quickly the king re-embarked and the vast fleet began streaming out of the Solent and into the open sea, following the *George* and the other leaders on their way south. By nightfall they formed a long column stretching across the Channel, hundreds of ships running south before the wind. Most of the army were still in ignorance of their destination, although rumours were probably circulating; it was not until they were at sea that the ship's captains were told that they were not going to Gascony at all, but were instead bound for Normandy. 'Our lord helped the king of England', says the *Acta Bellicosa*, the anonymous campaign diary kept by an official of the household, 'and the winds and tides were favourable.'[92] They were indeed, and as dawn broke on 12 July, the *George* and her consorts were sailing off the east coast of the Cotentin peninsula, the little port of St-Vaast and its harbour lying before them. The invasion of Normandy was about to begin.

Notes

1 An enigmatic statement by Bartholomew Burghersh in a letter written shortly after the landing provides the only direct evidence for this: 'he [the king]

decided to land wherever God should give him grace to do so' (quoted in Richard Barber (ed.), *The Life and Campaigns of the Black Prince*, Woodbridge, 1986, p. 14). Burghersh was a senior figure and tutor to the Prince of Wales, so this cannot be dismissed as simple ignorance; Burghersh must have had some other purpose in mind that we cannot fathom. But the idea that a complex and expensive army which had taken months to raise and equip should simply be left to drift before the wind is unlikely in the extreme.

2 Sumption, pp. 497–8; which seems slightly at odds with Sumption's view that Edward intended to occupy and annex Normandy.

3 Richard Barber, *Edward, Prince of Wales and Aquitaine: A Biography of the Black Prince*, London, 1978, p. 48.

4 Sumption, pp. 497–8; Rogers, *War Cruel and Sharp*, pp. 233–7; Alfred H. Burne, *The Crécy War: A Military History of the Hundred Years War from 1337 to the Peace of Bretigny, 1360*, London, 1955, pp. 136–9.

5 The chronicler Jean Froissart suggests exactly this when he puts a speech into the mouth of Godefroi d'Harcourt after the battle at Caen, in which Godefroi urges King Edward to concentrate on his goal of taking Calais; this is almost certainly an invention of the author; *Oeuvres de Froissart*, ed. Kervyn de Lettenhove, Brussels, 1868, vol. 4, pp. 412–13.

6 Sumption, p. 497.

7 H. Marett Godfray, *Documents relatif aux attaques sur les Îles de la Manche, 1338–45*, Jersey, 1891.

8 From the privy wardrobe account, cited by T.F. Tout in 'Firearms in England in the Fourteenth Century', *The Collected Papers of Thomas Frederick Tout*, Manchester, 1934, vol. 2, p. 238. Even if the final decision to attack Normandy had not been made by this time, this reference clearly shows that Normandy was playing a leading role in the king's military thinking in late 1345.

9 See Livingstone, map 7.6, for the extent of the damage caused up to 1340.

10 The fact that Edward was contemplating a longer occupation of Normandy is also suggested, if only tangentially, by his order for cannon to be taken with the army; until 1346, cannon had rarely if ever been used by a land army except during sieges. The need to reduce fortified places hints at an intention to occupy rather than to raid; cannon and gunpowder were cumbersome objects to include in the baggage train of an army that merely intends a raid or *chevauchée*.

11 Oman, vol. 2, p. 126.

12 See Fryde, 'Edward III's War Finance 1337–41', and Livingstone, chapter 2.

13 W.M. Ormrod, 'The Crown and the English Economy, 1290–1348', in B.M.S. Campbell (ed.), *Before the Black Death*, Manchester, 1991, table 5.1.

14 *Rotuli Parliamentorum*, II, p. 161, no. 18.

15 For a full description of the siege of Aiguillon and its outcome, see Sumption, pp. 485–8 and 519–20.

16 J. Viard, 'La campagne de juillet – aout 1346', *Le Moyen Age*, vol. 27, pp. 5–6.

17 The material in this section is derived from J.B. Henneman's comprehensive study of Valois finances, *Royal Taxation in the Fourteenth Century: The Development of War Financing, 1322–56*, Princeton, 1971, particularly pp. 180–201.

18 France supported the Angevin king Robert of Naples, whose Guelph allies had been expelled from Genoa in the early 1330s. For the sake of convenience we have continued to refer to these allies as 'Genoese' despite their having no formal connections with the city of Genoa.

19 Françoise de Bernardy, *Princes of Monaco*, London, 1961, p. 17.

20 For the power struggles within Genoa at this point, and for a valuable general history of the city, see S.R. Epstein, *Genoa and the Genoese*, Chapel Hill, 1996.

21 M. Émile Vincens, *Histoire de la République de Gènes*, Paris, 1842, vol. 1, p. 474.

22 Vincens, vol. 1, p. 476, believed the total was 15,000, but this is an exaggeration.

23 Vignoso did raid Monaco in April, after Grimaldi had sailed, but was repulsed by the strong defences; Epstein, pp. 209–10.

24 C.G.B. de la Roncière, *Histoire de la marine française*, Paris, 1879; Bernardy, p. 18. Jonathan Sumption more charitably suggests they were delayed by bad weather: Sumption, pp. 494–5.

25 Called thus to distinguish him from his father, although technically he was Jaume I of Aragon, and some historians refer to him as such. See David Abulafia, *A Mediterranean Emporium: The Catalan Kingdom of Majorca*, Cambridge, 1994; J.L. Shneidman, *The Rise of the Aragonese–Catalan Empire, 1200–1350*, New York, 1970; C.R. Markham, *The Story of Majorca and Minorca*, London, 1908.

26 William Miller, *The Latins in the Levant: A History of Frankish Greece (1204–1566)*, New York, 1908.

27 J. Zurita, *Anales de la Corona de Aragon*, Zaragoza, 1973, vol. 4, pp. 14–16.

28 This is speculative of course, but it does seem reasonable that Jaume would accompany Grimaldi if the latter was raiding his former kingdom. Jaume and the Majorcans do not appear in the French army until the assembly at St-Denis in mid-August, meaning they could have either come overland or marched from Rouen when Grimaldi arrived there earlier in the month. But if Jaume was marching overland from Montpellier, would it not have made more sense for him to join the French army in the south?

29 Or so says C.R. Markham, *The Story of Majorca and Minorca*, London, 1908. The more common view is that the title Duke of Clarence derives from the manor of Clare in Suffolk, which Lionel held; the extension from Clare to Clarence was to avoid confusion with the Irish earldom of Clare. There is no reason why both cannot be true; Philippa, notoriously quick to claim her rights where money was concerned and every bit as symbol-conscious as her husband, may well have seen this as a happy coincidence, and intended the creation of the title of Duke of Clarence as laying down a marker in case it should ever become possible to enforce her claims in Greece.

30 Eugene L. Cox, *The Green Count of Savoy*, Princeton, 1967, p. 58. See also C. Dufayard, *Histoire de Savoie*, Paris, 1922; M. José, *La Maison de Savoie*, Paris, 1956; A. Perrin, *Histoire de Savoie des origines à 1860*, Chambéry, 1900.

31 Cox, p. 37.

32 The date of their departure from Chambéry is not recorded, but given that the Regents had agreed to provide troops late in the previous year and yet the Savoyards had still not arrived in Paris by mid-July, a degree of foot-dragging would seem to be indicated.

33 Notably in Raymond Cazelles, *Jean l'Aveugle*, Paris, 1947, and Lenka Bobková, 'The Royal Crown of Bohemia: A Central European Empire of the House of Luxembourg', in *The Czech State from the Hussite Wars to NATO Membership*, Prague, 2002, pp. 51–63.

34 Ibid., p. 282.

35 Reports and casualty lists from later in the campaign mention that a number of German nobles were present: see Chapter 10. Cazelles, *Jean L'Aveugle*, p. 283, says that Jean and Charles arrived in Paris with 500 knights, but this is likely to be the Bohemians only, not taking into account the Luxembourgeois and Germans; nor does it include other mounted men or foot soldiers.

36 H.S. Lucas, *The Low Countries and the Hundred Years War, 1326–1347*, Ann Arbor, 1929.

37 These were among the commissioners of array for October 1344; *CPR 1343–45*, pp. 414–16. There appear to be no enrolled commissions of array for 1345, but it is possible that the late 1344 commissions were simply 'rolled over' and applied to the next year's campaign.

38 These are generalisations, and it should be noted too that the 'mounted archers' were intended to fight on foot; their ponies were merely a form of transport. How many mounted archers served on the 1346 campaign is not known, but the number is likely to have been fairly small.

39 Andrew Ayton, 'The English Army and the Normandy Campaign of 1346', in David Bates and Anne Curry (eds), *England and Normandy in the Middle Ages*, London, 1994, pp. 262–3.

40 *CPR 1345–48*, p. 86.

41 PRO SC1/40/5.

42 Michael Prestwich, *Armies and Warfare in the Middle Ages: The English Experience*, New Haven, 1996, p. 124; see pp. 123–5 for a discussion of how the commissions worked.

43 *CPR 1345–48*, pp. 112–13.

44 See the discussion in Ayton, 'The English Army and the Normandy Campaign', especially p. 268. Burne, p. 138, similarly puts the total at about 15,000. Barber, *Edward, Prince of Wales*, p. 48, prefers a lower figure of 10,000 and Sumption, p. 497, says between 7,000 and 10,000, but Ayton's careful analysis is preferred. Unfortunately a muster roll for 1346 has not survived.

45 Prestwich, *Armies and Warfare*, p. 84.
46 Ibid.
47 PRO E101/25/13.
48 Prestwich, *Armies and Warfare*, p. 84.
49 Hardy, *Longbow*, p. 60.
50 *CPR 1345–48*, p. 9.
51 PRO E101/25/12 m. 1–3.
52 See Tout, 'Firearms in England', pp. 239–40.
53 *CPR 1343–45*, p. 572; *CPR 1345–48*, p. 131.
54 PRO E101/103/8.
55 PRO E101/25/13. These animals and their costs appear as part of a note about the cost of making and repairing carts.
56 PRO E101/103/13.
57 PRO E101/25/11.
58 PRO E101/25/13.
59 PRO E101/391/1.
60 PRO E101/612/39.
61 *CCR 1346–49*, p. 32.
62 PRO E101/391/7 m. 2.
63 PRO E101/35/16.
64 PRO E101/399/1 m. 17.
65 Sumption, p. 491.
66 'The 1341 Royal Inquest in Lincolnshire', ed. B.W. McLane, *Lincoln Record Society*, vol. 78, 1988.
67 *CPR 1345–48*, p. 106.
68 PRO E101/25/11.
69 All of the above information about the food of the royal household at this time is drawn from the Kitchen Account, PRO E101/390/11.
70 PRO E101/79/14.
71 PRO E101/391/7.
72 It is clear that at least some accounting procedures were being carried out on campaign. The Kitchen Account, for example, while summary in its enrolled state, is clearly drawn from daily accounts recording food consumed, and these accounts must have been prepared en route.
73 *CCR 1346–49*, p. 31, which records payment for the work on 6 June.
74 Dates of movements of the household and the king are taken from the Kitchen Account, PRO E101/390/11.
75 *CPR 1345–48*, p. 79.
76 *CPR 1345–48*, p. 113.
77 *CPR 1345–48*, pp. 146, 154.
78 *CPR 1345–48*, pp. 109–10.
79 Prestwich, *Armies and Warfare*, p. 266.

80 PRO E101/257 for the *George*, PRO E101/25/13 for the *Thomas*.
81 This list appears at the end of copies of lists of retinues for the 1346 campaign which exist in several copies in British Library manuscripts: BL Harley 246, fos 15v ff.; BL Stowe 574, fos 434 ff.; BL Add. MS 38823, fos 654 ff.
82 PRO E101/326/8.
83 PRO E101/326/8.
84 *CPR 1345–48*, p. 122.
85 *CPR 1345–48*, p. 135. The case was enrolled on the day of Edward's departure, but was heard in the days and weeks prior to this.
86 *CPR 1345–48*, p. 154.
87 Kitchen Account, PRO E101/390/11.
88 PRO E101/25/11.
89 *Acta Bellicosa* in Barber, *Life and Campaigns*, p. 27.
90 *Acta Bellicosa*, ibid., seems to suggest that the entire fleet returned to Portsmouth, but other contemporary sources place the king on the Isle of Wight throughout this period until the 11th. The kitchen, or most of it, stayed at Freshwater, but the king moved to Carisbrooke Castle.
91 PRO E101/79/14. The wine was brought to Carisbrooke through the port of Yarmouth.
92 *Acta Bellicosa*, in Barber, p. 27.

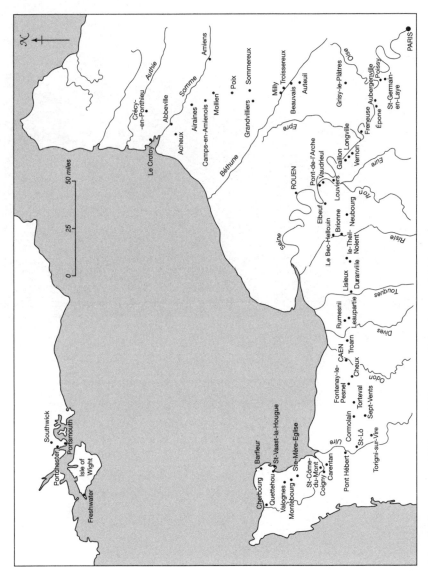

Map 1 The route of Edward III's army, July–August 1346.

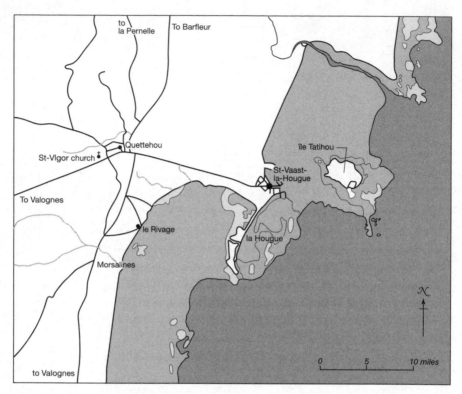

Map 2 St-Vaast-la-Hougue and environs.

Chapter 4

St-Vaast to Carentan

At dawn on the twelfth the inhabitants woke to bitter and disturbing news.

Acta Bellicosa[1]

Wednesday 12 July

At first light on 12 July, the people of the town of St-Vaast and the nearby village of Quettehou looked out to the east to see the sea crowded with ships. The leading vessels were already nearing the port itself, while the dawn light showed hundreds more coming down from the north, in a broad column stretching as far as the horizon. The meaning of this sight was at once apparent; the English invasion, so long rumoured, had at last begun. Most did not wait to see more. By the time the English troops began to come ashore, the Norman peasants and fishermen and their families had already abandoned their homes and were rushing inland towards safety. 'When they saw the terrible sight of the ships', records the author of the *Acta Bellicosa*, 'they fled from the enemy king as quickly as they could to caves and woods, leaving all their possessions.'[2]

The bay of St-Vaast is enclosed on the north and west by the mainland of the Cotentin peninsula, and on the east by the island of La Hougue, now connected to the mainland by a causeway (see Map 2). St-Vaast town sits at the easternmost point of the mainland, north of La Hougue, surrounded itself on the north and west by flat marshes that, in the fourteenth century, were probably partially inundated at high tide. To the north of

St-Vaast the coast is either flat marshland or dangerous rocks, with no further possible landing places apart from the tiny port of Barfleur to the north. To the south there are more marshes, which then give way to the long open beaches leading down to Quinéville and beyond, beaches that six centuries later would see the approach of another, very different invasion force, the American 4th Infantry Division landing on Utah Beach.

Behind the coast itself the ground rises steeply in an escarpment some 150 feet in height. The village of Quettehou, with its church of St-Vigor, sits on the edge of this, looking down over the bay and the marshes around St-Vaast.[3] Further north and higher still is the ancient chapel of La Pernelle, its tower clearly visible from the sea; this formed an important navigation marker for the ships coming down from the north. Behind Quettehou and La Pernelle lies a rolling tableland which was, and still largely is, covered in dense woodland.

The bay of St-Vaast is shallow, and in modern times is empty at low tide, with a long expanse of sandy mud stretching from St-Vaast town around to the seaside villas of Le Rivage below the village of Morsalines in an arc of about a mile and a half. There are a few rock formations, known today as the Rochers Arnaud and the Rochers la Pie, but these would have posed little difficulty to experienced seamen. The bay was likely to have been somewhat deeper and more free of silt in the fourteenth century, but in any case the shallow-draft, round-hulled ships of the English fleet could have easily grounded on the mud and been floated off again at high tide. However, only a limited number of ships could fit into the bay at any one time, and many vessels would have had to heave to and wait in the open sea for their turn to land.

In any amphibious landing, one of the keys to success is to get a strong force ashore as quickly as possible to hold the beachhead. This the English proceeded to do. By mid-morning at latest, the first ships were entering the bay. One of their first sights was the squadron of ships that King Philippe had sent to bolster the defences of the Cotentin. The invaders counted fourteen French ships drawn up on the beach, eight of which were clearly intended for use as warships as they had been fitted out with fighting castles at bow and stern.[4] This force, which might have been adequate against a mere raiding force, was hopelessly inadequate against a full-scale invasion, and as soon as their crews learned the magnitude of the threat they faced, they abandoned their ships and fled inland. The English ships eased themselves onto the beach below Quettehou not far from the abandoned warships, and the first troops landed unopposed, four hundred dismounted men-at-arms and eleven hundred archers under the command of the Earl of Warwick and Godefroi d'Harcourt.[5] These quickly established a beachhead, and by late morning the whole of the shore from St-Vaast to Morsalines was lined with ships disembarking their cargoes of men, horses and stores. The fourteen abandoned ships were quickly burned by the landing party, the first of many fires that would soon fill the sky over the Cotentin with smoke and ash.

At midday the king himself landed near Quettehou. The chronicler Jean Froissart, ever one for a colourful story, records that when the king first stepped ashore he overbalanced and fell forward, hitting his head hard enough to start a nosebleed. The same source tells us that the superstitious knights of his household urged him to immediately return to his ship and not attempt to land that day, as the omens were clearly unfavourable. The king, however, rose to the occasion. On the contrary, he said, this was a good sign, as it showed the land was ready to receive him and he was its natural ruler; as a sign of this, the land had taken his blood to itself. Now, he continued, in the name of God and St George, let us go and seek our enemies. It is a good story, and it is quite possible that the monarch did indeed have trouble with his balance after a long period at sea in a relatively small ship, and did fall as described. The notion that the hard-headed veterans in his household would be alarmed at this is, however, unlikely in the extreme. The little speech by Edward, if delivered, might easily have been a joke.[6]

After landing, the king met with his senior commanders including Warwick, Harcourt and Northampton. These joined the royal household, and so too did the Prince of Wales and his own household and associates including the young Earl of Salisbury. Heavily armed and bright with banners and surcoats bearing heraldic devices, the party climbed the hill to Quettehou, most if not all of its members on foot.[7] From the heights they could see all of the bay of St-Vaast before them, and the sea beyond full of ships. If they had been expecting a clear view to the west, however, they were disappointed, for the rolling plateau and woodlands beyond barred their line of sight. Instead, the party entered the church of St-Vigor and, as recounted in the opening chapter of this book, the Prince of Wales and a number of other young nobles including the Earl of Salisbury and Roger

Mortimer were knighted. Godefroi d'Harcourt then did homage to Edward as king of France, and the royal standard with the leopards of England quartered with the lilies of France was unfurled. These acts, symbolic and full of meaning, not only marked the 'official' commencement of the campaign, but restated and reiterated Edward's purpose in making war in front of his most important commanders. In effect, he was reminding them of why they were here.

The ceremonies concluded, Edward then returned to the more practical business of the day: finding out where the enemy was. To do this, he needed to see the lie of the land. With his household knights and senior commanders, he proceeded to the tower and chapel at La Pernelle, two miles north of Quettehou. At around three hundred feet, La Pernelle is one of the highest points on the escarpment and offers a splendid view out over the whole of the north-east Cotentin, from St-Vaast to Barfleur and its rocky point, then along the north coast and into the distance towards Cherbourg to the west. Its strategic importance has long been apparent; there has been a lookout tower there since Viking times, if not before, and in 1944 it was the site of a German radar station and battery of long-range artillery, which harassed the Americans on Utah Beach for nearly three weeks until finally put out of action.

The visit to La Pernelle offered Edward some useful information. The little harbour of Barfleur, four miles to the north-east, was clearly visible, and keen eyes in the royal party would have been able to make out the masts of ships moored or beached in the port. The view to the west remained obstructed by high ground and woodlands, but Edward could by now be confident that no sizeable force opposed him. But the view from La Pernelle also showed something else, rather less to his liking: columns of smoke rising at various points along the coast. Already the more adventurous among the English foot soldiers were working their way across the marshes towards the hamlets of Réville and Jonville, plundering and burning. Only a few hours after the king had proclaimed his sovereignty, he was watching the property of his new subjects being pillaged and destroyed.

And as the looters moved inland, the first clashes of arms began. Robert Bertrand of Bricquebec, Marshal of France, had read the English intentions well. Whether informed by spies or by an understanding of the tactics his old enemy Godefroi d'Harcourt was likely to use, he had forecast that the English would land in the northern Cotentin, and had picked St-Vaast as a likely landing place. He had despatched a troop of several hundred Genoese crossbowmen to St-Vaast earlier in the summer, but lacked the funds to pay them, and on 9 July, three days before the landing, these had deserted their post.[8] Had they remained to oppose the landing, the English might have found the task rather more difficult. Bertrand had also called a muster of local levies at St-Sauveur-le-Vicomte several days previously,[9] and now had a force of perhaps three hundred men-at-arms and foot soldiers at his disposal; and, as luck would have it, he had called a similar muster for the St-Vaast district for 12 July. Riding towards St-Vaast on the morning of the 12th, Bertrand encountered the refugees fleeing inland from the coastal districts and thus learned that he had been pre-empted. Gathering his small company, he made straight for the bay, where he found the English already ashore in force.

Bertrand was a skilled and able commander, but his men were now heavily outnumbered. An outright attack on the English beachhead would have been suicidal, and he contented himself with observing and waiting for a chance to harass the enemy.[10] The bulk of his men remained concealed in the woodland behind Quettehou while little parties of French troops ambushed the English at various points, initially creating some alarm. Thomas Bradwardine, the Chancellor of St Paul's, was under the impression that the English were confronted with a force far larger than themselves.[11] Casualties are not mentioned, but are likely to have been light: this was a series of sudden quick raids rather than a full-scale battle. But there was nearly one high-profile casualty. Returning from La Pernelle to the beachhead, the Earl of Warwick, accompanied by a single esquire, became separated from the rest of the royal party and was ambushed by a group of a dozen Frenchmen. Although mounted on a 'poor horse', Warwick and his esquire managed to fight their way free.[12] Had this talented commander been killed or captured at this early stage, the English army would have suffered a major blow.

But the French were not pressing their attacks home with vigour, and before long, dismayed at the size of the army that was coming ashore, Bertrand's force began to disintegrate. One by one his men-at-arms withdrew, riding back to their own homes to either evacuate them or put them into a state of defence.[13] 'They fled in haste,' says the *Acta Bellicosa*, 'leaving the way into Normandy clear for the king and the English army.' By the end of the day fewer than thirty men of Bertrand's own household remained with him; the rest of his force had evaporated.[14] Few options remained to the marshal, and he resolved to abandon the northern Cotentin and retreat to the strategic river crossing point of Carentan, meanwhile sending couriers to Caen to alert the defences of the rest of Normandy. This was a hard decision, for Bertrand would have known full well that his own home at Bricquebec would then be defenceless before the enemy, and the vengeance he had visited on Godefroi d'Harcourt's lands three years earlier would shortly be paid back in full.

Meanwhile, the attacks beaten off and the beachhead secure, the king and his household made for St-Vaast, where they found quarters for themselves in the deserted town.[15] The beach and bay remained a hive of activity. The long summer days meant that unloading could carry on far into the evening, and men, horses and stores continued to come ashore through a thin haze of smoke from the afternoon's burnings. The Prince of Wales and his household also established themselves in the town, at a separate location. The royal kitchens were ashore and established (at least in part) and the king and his household were able to sit down and eat their first full meal in France. Wednesday was a fast day on which no meat was to be eaten (although, unlike Fridays, poultry was allowed: the Wednesday pro-hibition applied to red meat only), and the primary items on the menu were cod, salmon and eel. According to the Kitchen Account, the house-hold dined on ninety-three cod, possibly fresh (given that they were valued at a total of 54s. in the Account), sixteen 'salt salmon' (valued at 26s. 1d, more than a shilling and a half apiece), along with twenty-four stockfish, and eleven conger eels and four lampreys. The latter were accounted a delicacy in the Middle Ages, and the account values them at 4s. apiece, equivalent to over three weeks' wages for an archer.[16] A few geese and hens were also eaten, but most of the poultry was still on board ship. The fish was eaten with sauces of garlic and mustard: a good solid meal by the standards of the time, but by no means a feast. Despite the arson going on around them, the kitchen staff avoided plundering for firewood and unloaded three quarters (twenty-four bushels) of coal from their ships in order to cook the meal.

As night finally fell, the English – or at least, those who had debarked – could rest reasonably content. They had managed to land sufficient men and stores to maintain the beachhead, and had seen off all opposition to date. If the population had chosen to flee rather than to welcome their rightful king with open arms, well, that was a small matter that could be put right later. The real test would come when the army moved inland and approached the first towns, Valognes and Montebourg. Meanwhile, there remained the tasks of landing the rest of the army and cleaning up the remaining local opposition.

Thursday 13 July

The day following the landing, however, brought a new and more urgent problem. The general indiscipline of medieval armies, especially their foot soldiers, was exacerbated by the disorder that inevitably accompanies amphibious landings, and a good many of the men were roaming at will over the beachhead area. And as the successful looters returned to camp and displayed their booty, more men were tempted to go out and try their luck. Those men still on ships could only watch in frustration as their more fortunate comrades foraged through the surrounding area and then through St-Vaast itself, looking for valuables.

The temptation to loot is easy to understand. Archers were paid 3*d.* a day, and were by no means the worst off; grooms, servants and camp followers were paid substantially less. Even a small find of silver coins or spoons represented a substantial sum to these men, and there was always the hope of a larger find, gold or jewels or valuable spices. The lure of plunder exercised a strong fascination on the mind of the medieval foot soldier,[17] in much the same way that the hope of acquiring huge ransoms from captives fascinated his knightly comrades-in-arms.

Less easy to understand to the modern mind, perhaps, is the arson that accompanied the looting. Fire does of course provoke an atavistic response in many people, even today (witness the continued popularity of Bonfire Night), and modern warfare sees its fair share of arson especially where paramilitary troops are involved; but indiscriminate burning of civilian property was a particular feature of medieval warfare. Often this was carried out as an act of policy, but there is plenty of evidence to suggest that even when kings and commanders desired that civilian property be left in peace, their orders were not obeyed. As well as causing terrible hardship for the hapless population, this could also create real political problems, particularly when commanders desired the support of the local inhabitants. People whose homes have been burned and livelihoods destroyed by marauding soldiers are seldom likely to look kindly on their conquerors.

And it was just this position that Edward now faced. In Brittany, he had largely been able to restrain his troops; but in Brittany he had nearly always campaigned with local allied troops, the presence of which would have been a considerable deterrent to looters in his own ranks. A sizeable allied Norman contingent might well have been able to guard Norman property. But there was no such contingent, only Godefroi d'Harcourt and his few followers, and so the looting and the burning began almost as soon as the English army was ashore. And on 13 July, having exhausted the potential of the nearby countryside, the looters began working their way through St-Vaast itself, and then set the little town ablaze.

Possibly provoked by this act, the king now issued his famous proclamation of protection:

> *However, the English king, feeling for the sufferings of the poor people of the country, issued an edict throughout the army, that no town or manor was to be burnt, no church or holy place sacked, and no old people, children or women in his kingdom of France were to be harmed or molested; nor were they to threaten people, or do any kind of wrong, on pain of life or limb. He also ordered that if anyone caught someone in the act of doing these or other criminal acts and brought him to the king, he should have a reward of forty shillings.*[18]

This was, of course, only a partial protection. Houses, towns, manors and holy places were to be spared, but there was no mention of villages and isolated farms (though the final catch-all clause, 'or do any kind of wrong', could be used at need to cover these). There are several possible reasons for this. First, and most cynically, the proclamation itself may have been a propaganda stunt: Edward was either indifferent to the sufferings of the Norman people, or actively encouraged the destruction in order to damage the economy of the country. Issuing this proclamation provided him with cover should his enemies accuse him of atrocities. Alternatively, the *realpolitik* of the time was that Edward could afford to ignore the harm done to the Norman peasantry, but needed to keep the towns, monasteries and gentry on side, and this could best be done by preserving their property.

Both are possible explanations, and certainly at later – and earlier – points in his career, Edward did sanction large-scale destruction of property in order to damage the enemy's economy and ability to make war. His son, the Prince of Wales, would become even more proficient at this, his career culminating in the infamous sack of Limoges in which churches and hospitals were pillaged and burned and several hundred people were killed.[19] But because he did so on other occasions does not necessarily mean that was his intent in July 1346. Regardless of whether he planned to conquer Normandy outright, establish a base for further actions or simply punish the Norman pirates for their attacks on English shipping, in this first phase of the campaign he seems genuinely to have desired the support of the populace, and hoped to win over at least some of the locals to his cause as he had done successfully in Brittany. There is much evidence to suggest that Edward hoped for support from the local population, not just from the former followers of Harcourt and the executed Olivier de Clisson but from others who, as in Brittany, might seek personal advantage by deserting France and joining his cause. As well as the proclamation, shortly after landing Edward also sent out emissaries to local leaders and communities asking them for their allegiance, stating explicitly that he had 'come into this land not to lay waste to it, but to take possession of it'.[20]

The partial nature of the proclamation can be explained another way: Edward knew that a blanket protection for every house in the land was simply not enforceable, and sought to protect those properties and lives that he could. As a later historian of the campaign, Lieutenant-Colonel Alfred Burne, has pointed out, low-level pillaging 'came under the category of "living off the country" and was usual procedure for an invading army at the time, and indeed for centuries later'.[21] In addition, as Burne also points out, at least some of the invading English army came from towns and villages along the south coast of England, and would have scores of their own to settle.[22] It was all very well the king asking that the Normans be treated with kindness; but to the men of Southampton and Portsmouth and Folkestone and other places up and down the coast, whose own homes had been reduced to ashes not so many years before, this was the time for revenge. And these, of course, would have carried their fellows along with them.

The proclamation, then, might well have been *realpolitik*, with respect not so much to the property of his new subjects, but to his ability to command and discipline his own army. We are used to thinking of medieval monarchs as having the power of life and death over their subjects. But even where this might be true in theory, in practice the monarch's powers were hedged about by severe restrictions. Even if Edward personally managed to capture an arsonist red-handed, unless the man belonged to his own retinue, it was the arsonist's own overlord or captain who had the power to discipline him, not the king. To enforce such an edict, therefore, required first the cooperation of the nobles and knights; and if even a few of these chose to turn a blind eye, then problems would start to mount.

Also, even if his officers enthusiastically supported the proclamation – and there is no evidence that they all did: Godefroi d'Harcourt appears to have been understandably enthusiastic about pillaging and burning the property of his enemies – the problems of command and control in a medieval army meant that it was in practice difficult, if not impossible, to apprehend malefactors. And Edward had also to contend with the nature of his army. He knew as well as anyone that the archers and foot soldiers, on whom his tactical system depended, were ill paid and motivated largely by hopes of plunder. A blanket ban on looting might well have resulted in a disastrous fall in morale, even large-scale desertions as the men saw their hopes of riches dashed. An old military adage suggests that an officer should never give an order unless he knows it will obeyed; and the balance of probabilities is that at St-Vaast, Edward sought a pragmatic solution. If so, it was a vain hope. The appetites of his army for looting and pillage, once aroused, could not be easily checked.

One more observation may be offered on this subject. It is easy to assume – and was assumed by contemporary observers and chroniclers, French and even English – that the entire army was involved in this destruction. That may not have been the case. Strict captains may have kept their men in line, and many of the men themselves may well have had a sufficiently moral outlook to disapprove of at least some of what was going on around them. Modern experience shows that in civil society, the majority of serious crimes are committed by a tiny minority of people. A small number of determined soldiers could wreak a large amount of havoc in a short space of time, if they put their minds to it. It is dangerous to assume that every soldier in the English army was completely out of the control of his officers; if this were true, this army could not have functioned as an efficient fighting force.

Whatever the case, and whatever the purpose behind Edward's proclamation, the fires continued to burn. The troops, says the *Acta Bellicosa*, 'boldly and cheerfully set fire to the countryside around, until the sky itself glowed with a fiery colour'.[23] With the town of St-Vaast beginning to burn around them, the households of the king and the Prince of Wales moved further inland. The king rode to the village of Morsalines on the left flank of the landing, overlooking salt marshes and dunes to the south and overlooked in turn by the steep slope leading up to the Bois de Rabey to the west. This was a somewhat exposed location, close to the English front lines, but by now Edward was surely confident that the opposition of the day before had evaporated. There was a deserted manor house near the village, which he occupied and made his headquarters for the next several days.[24]

Meanwhile, back in the bay, the disembarkation went on, now under a growing pall of smoke. Steadily, the roundships sailed into the bay, grounded on the mud and began unloading their cargoes of men, beasts and stores. The scenes on the beach can only be imagined. Even in modern times, with better communications and organised systems of beachmasters, the beachhead of an amphibious landing can best be described as organised chaos. In 1346, the beach at St-Vaast would have been full of captains looking for their companies, companies looking for their captains (and at least some of the men quietly slipping away and moving inland to see if the earlier pillagers had left anything worth taking), heaps of stores, dismantled wagons waiting to be assembled, and animals being rounded up and herded away to their rightful destinations. A particular feature of this beachhead would have been the thousands of horses, who had been cooped up on board ship for two weeks and were now finally being released. Horses, after being transported by sea for long periods, normally celebrate their freedom by stampeding, and rounding them up and getting them to their owners must have been a monumental task.[25]

But horses were not the only animals coming ashore. Strange though it might seem, the king's household, at least, brought its own fresh meat, and in warm summer weather, much of that meat had to be kept on the hoof.[26] Several dozen head of cattle, sheep and pigs were among the more unwilling members of the army disembarking at St-Vaast, along with their own herdsmen, three men who were each paid 4*d.* a day for their services. This was a substantial wage, more than that of the archers.[27] Large amounts of poultry – including not only hens, chickens, capons and geese, but also swans, doves, herons, spoonbills, woodcock, plovers and partridges – were brought ashore in crates, all destined for the high tables of the great households.

Nightfall saw large numbers of men and stores ashore, though many ships were still waiting their turn to enter the bay. In their new quarters at Morsalines, the royal household sat down to a rather more substantial meal than the night before; the Kitchen Account reports that the household consumed three and one-quarter carcasses of fresh beef, one of salt beef and one of spiced beef, as well as three carcasses of mutton, one of salt mutton and one of spiced mutton, two dozen chickens and hens, four geese, a heron and a spoonbill, as well as 200 eggs, 200 onions, ten gallons of milk, garlic, parsley, mustard, pickles and two bushels of salt.[28] A deer was also butchered and cooked, presumably shot by an enterprising archer in the nearby forest. What the household ate, both the provisions themselves and their quantity, gives some interesting clues as to the condition of the army as a whole. While the king and his companions of course ate much better than did the common soldiers, their food supplies too were subject to fluctuation and interruption. At the moment the household was dining well despite being in the field. As the campaign progressed, the situation deteriorated.

* * *

A hundred miles to the south-east, Robert Bertrand's messengers had reached Caen by the middle of the day.[29] They had already passed through Bayeux and raised the alarm there. More messengers went speeding east to Rouen and Harfleur, where the Constable of France was mustering more troops, and then on to Paris to alert the king. The game was now afoot, and the French counter-measures were being set in motion. The marshal's brother Guillaume Bertrand, Bishop of Bayeux, hastened to Caen to put the city into a state of defence. Further west at Carentan, the marshal himself was waiting to delay the English advance until the garrison of Caen could be reinforced.

Friday 14 July

By the morning of the 14th the English army ashore was sufficiently strong to begin expanding from the beachhead. The first target was Barfleur, a few miles to the north. While the disembarkation in the bay continued, a squadron of ships full of armed men moved north along the coast to seal off the entrance to the harbour, while a detachment of men-at-arms and archers approached the town from the landward side. The expedition was commanded by the Earl of Warwick and Ralph Stafford, and numbered several hundred men in all.[30]

Barfleur was a small port, but by all accounts a wealthy one. Michael Northburgh compares it in size to Sandwich, though its harbour was considerably smaller. Like other ports in the Cotentin it had been prepared for defence, with a garrison and a small squadron of ships; the harbour had also been partially protected with stakes driven into the harbour bottom, intended to rip the bottoms out of ships attempting to approach.[31] The defenders, however, would have spent the last two days looking out at a sea covered in English ships and becoming more and more apprehensive about their own fate. Upon the approach of the English force, both sailors and garrison abandoned the town and its inhabitants to their fate.

While the sailors landed and burned the ships in the harbour, including eleven warships with fighting castles fore and aft and three other vessels, Warwick and Stafford and their men descended on the town.[32] The defenceless inhabitants surrendered at once, and the English troops occupied the town. The pillaging that followed seems to have been thorough and systematic, and the inhabitants were robbed of gold, silver and other valuables. Froissart comments that the town was so wealthy that even ship's boys turned up their noses at valuable furs (though carrying heavy furs as booty in the heat of July may have been unattractive for several reasons).[33] Even allowing for later exaggeration, the town seems to have been remarkably wealthy, and it is tempting to believe that at least some of the spoil taken from Barfleur had itself been looted from the coast of England. Whatever the truth, stories about the raid spread through the army, and the temptation to other looters increased.

As the pillage continued, the population of the town were rounded up and taken aboard ship. Froissart thought this was for defensive purposes, in case the townspeople should later arm themselves and attack the English.[34] The idea of a few hundred badly equipped civilians mounting an attack on the whole of the English army is unlikely in the extreme, and it is more likely that they were simply held for ransom. Edward's proclamation had ordered that people should not be harmed, but kidnapping had not been mentioned and the sailors presumably felt themselves to be justified. Again, it should be remembered that many of them, or their families, would have suffered similarly at the hands of French raiders in recent years, and this would have been all the justification they felt they needed. No more is heard of the people of Barfleur, and it can be assumed that at some later point, having negotiated their ransoms, they were set free. How they paid these ransoms is hard to imagine: not only had the town been looted, but, as the hapless Barfleurois sailed away in the hands of their captors, they looked back to see columns of smoke rising. The sailors had set the town on fire, and soon, like St-Vaast before it, Barfleur was a burning ruin.

Back at St-Vaast the disembarkation went on. A number of later historians have commented unfavourably on the length of time it took Edward's army to complete the disembarkation, one in particular describing the process as 'leisurely'.[35] Others have been more charitable, with Burne in particular believing the process could not have been accomplished much more quickly. It was important to make certain not only that all the troops, animals and supplies were ashore, but that all were properly organised. Not only horses but men had been cooped up on ship for a long time before the landing, and required rest and feeding. Five days to disembark and organise up to 15,000 men, several thousand horses and tons of stores is not a bad effort when only muscle power is available.

Certainly the army, or at least its commanders, did not intend to stint themselves when it came to food. Friday was the primary fast day, on which no meat should be eaten, only fish; but creative cooks could do a great deal with fish, even when the army was in the field. That night the royal kitchens served up thirty-eight cod, sixteen stockfish and eight salted salmon, and also consumed supplies of oat flour, milk, mustard, vinegar and peas. The *pièce de résistance* of this medieval fish supper, however, was eels: a hundred quarters of the small eels known as pimpernels and two hundred lampreys, all transported barrels from England, as well as seven larger 'shaft' eels.[36] These may well have been stewed, along with garlic, onions and parsley, a rich and succulent meal which would have been much to the taste of men who had been riding or walking all day in full armour. Judging by the quantities of food, the kitchens were feeding rather more people than usual, but there is no indication of whether any special occasion was being celebrated; perhaps the king was simply indulging in the knightly virtue of largesse by feeding large numbers. Sunday night fell, with the sky still full of smoke, glowing with the embers of burning farms and the ruins of Barfleur.

Saturday 15 July

Emboldened by the successes of the previous day, the naval squadron that had attacked Barfleur rounded the point at Gatteville and sailed west along the northern coast of the Cotentin towards Cherbourg. Much of this coast is either rocky or full of shoals, but there are several places where landings can be made, notably the beach west of the Pointe de Néville, and then further west in the Anse de la Mondrée. Landing parties from the ships penetrated inland for some distance, pillaging and burning everything they found, and the hamlets of Néville, Réville and Fermanville went up in smoke. Rounding Cap Lévi they continued to press west, destroying more ships as well as villages on shore; these ships may well have been in the Anse du Bric below Maupertuis-sur-Mer, which according to local tradition was formerly a base for raiders and privateers.

The fires around Maupertuis alerted the inhabitants of Cherbourg, seven miles away, that the enemy was approaching. The town was protected by a large and powerful castle, which had been strengthened as recently as 1314, and the town walls had recently been strengthened as well. Robert Bertrand, appreciating the strategic significance of Cherbourg, had installed a sizeable garrison, under a commander who was made of sterner stuff than his fellows at Barfleur and St-Vaast had been; when the English arrived, landing along the shore to the east of town not far from the modern ferry port, they found the defenders were ready and prepared.

The castle was clearly impregnable, and it commanded the harbour. The raiders sheered off and skirted the town to the south, crossing the river Divette and then turning right to move up towards the southern faubourgs. The Augustinian abbey of Notre-Dame de Voeu, founded by the English Queen Matilda in the twelfth century, was pillaged and burned, and the raiders penetrated some way into the faubourgs around the town before withdrawing. The fighting, if any, was desultory; there is no mention of casualties in any of the sources, nor is there any mention of vast quantities of loot, as at Barfleur.[37]

The Cherbourg raid marked the western limit of the fleet's activities; the fertile west coast of the Cotentin remained unravaged, at least for now. By the following day the squadron had been recalled to rejoin the main fleet. Back at the bay of St-Vaast, the disembarkation continued and smoke continued to rise from burning farms and hamlets, more distant now as the pillagers moved out further from the beachhead. That night was quiet at the royal table; Saturday was also a fast day, though again without the strong restrictions of Fridays, and the Kitchen Account records that forty-four cod, twelve stockfish, eight salted salmon and three lampreys were consumed, along with peas, flour and sauces.

Sunday 16 July

There was no major activity this day, and the bulk of the army concentrated on finishing the unloading of the ships. By now most, if not all, of the men and horses were ashore, but there was all the paraphernalia of a medieval army on the march to be prepared. Scores of wagons and carts, dismantled for storage on board ship, were now reassembled, and the thud of carpenters' hammers reverberated around the bay. Bags of peas and flour and onions and dried or salted meat were augmented by finer foods for the nobles: cages of poultry, barrels of eels, kegs of vinegar and verjuice, bags of garlic and parsley, tubs of salt, kegs of wine and all the equipment of kitchen and scullery, including pots and turnspits. The bombards were brought ashore, together with stone shot and bags of gun-powder carefully sealed against the damp. Spare weapons were off-loaded, swords and spears and bowstaves, and, importantly, thousands of sheaves of arrows. The farriers and armourers had their forges and tools; the clergy had their vestments and portable altars; the clerks had their stores of parchment and pens and ink for the issuing of proclamations and writs, keeping records of expenditure and writing letters.

All these and other stores had not only to be brought ashore but also organised and made ready for transport. This would most likely have been the job of the under-constable, Adam Swynbourne, and the under-marshal, Thomas Ughtred, the equivalent of staff officers in a modern army, and the efficiency with which they carried out their duties needs to be recognised. Even in the days of greatest pressure the English army remained well-organised and had access to its supplies, dwindling though these would later be. Much of that success was undoubtedly due to the careful preparation and organisation undertaken during those five days around St-Vaast.

Monday 17 July

The army and its horses and supplies were now ashore, and the process of organisation was nearly complete. Preparations were made to march in the morning. The initial goal was to be Valognes, a few miles inland, which lay astride the main road leading up the Cotentin. The next stage would be to move south to Carentan, from where the army could choose a variety of routes into Lower Normandy.

As was customary, the army was now divided into three divisions: the vanguard, commanded by the Prince of Wales, the centre, commanded by the king in person, and the rearguard, in the nominal command of the Bishop of Durham. All three divisions were probably of roughly equal strength, though the division of the king may have been slightly larger. The various nobles and knights and their followings were then assigned their divisions. We have already met some of these men in Chapter 2; others were destined to come to public attention as the campaign went on.

The choice of the Prince of Wales as commander of the vanguard was another step in his confirmation as a leader in his own right. In fact his command was still a nominal one; real authority was exercised by the Constable, Northampton, and the Marshal, Warwick. The prince's tutor, Bartholomew Burghersh, was also assigned to this division, as were a variety of experienced barons and knights including the under-marshal Thomas Ughtred, Reginald Cobham, Richard Stafford, John Mohun from Dunster in Somerset, Thomas Holland, William Kerdeston, Robert Bourchier and William St Amand. Here too were some of the prince's younger companions including Salisbury, Mortimer, Richard de la Bere and the younger Burghersh. The other marshal, Godefroi d'Harcourt, was initially assigned to the king's division, along with John de Vere, Earl of Oxford. Salisbury's uncle Edward Montacute, John Darcy and his son, and the bannerets Robert Ferrers, Michael Poynings and Maurice Berkeley were also there. The rearguard, nominally commanded by the Bishop of Durham, was actually in the hands of the Earl of Arundel, with the Earl of Suffolk as his able lieutenant. Hugh Despenser, Robert Morley, John Grey of Rotherfield,

Robert Colville, Gerard Delisle and John Lestraunge were among the other senior members of this division.[38]

It should be noted at once that this was an extremely flexible organisation. Men could and did move back and forth from one division to another as needed; later in the campaign, Hugh Despenser is to be found fighting with the vanguard. Northampton seems to have swiftly resumed his charge of the entire army, and Godefroi d'Harcourt went forward to assist Warwick with the vanguard. Sometimes the army marched all together, sometimes with one or more divisions taking separate routes. In fact, almost immediately it was arranged that a small flying column should be separated under the command of Warwick and Cobham to guard the left flank, and two days later another column under Harcourt moved out on the right flank, both rejoining the main army at Carentan. Throughout the campaign, organisationally as well as tactically, Edward's commanders showed themselves capable of great flexibility and adaptability in the face of circumstances.

With all ready, the household sat down to dine for the final time at Morsalines, with their beef and mutton supplemented by a pig and two deer and around 150 geese, chickens and doves, as well as 300 eggs, while the troops ate their pottage in the fields around. By now the area around St-Vaast and Quettehou would have been pretty well scoured clean, and the ordinary soldiers would have been eager to move on in search of better food and more plunder. So far, apart from the skirmishes on the first day and the resistance at Cherbourg, there had been no fighting. Confidence within the army was high, and there was an appetite for battle. It is probable that at some time during these last days at St-Vaast, word reached the army of another English victory. On 9 July, at St-Pol-de-Léon in western Brittany, the English commander Thomas Dagworth had once again confronted Charles de Blois. Dagworth, with only a few hundred men-at-arms and archers under his command, was heavily outnumbered, but in a bloody battle lasting most of a day, he defeated Blois for a second time and forced the latter to retreat. Strategically the battle changed little, but the news would have been a further boost to English morale.

Tuesday 18 July

On the morning of the 18th, the army moved out of its billets and tents along the Bay of St-Vaast. A strong flanking force under the Earl of

Warwick and Reginald Cobham moved off south from Morsalines, initially following the coast and then moving inland around the salt marshes towards Fontenay-sur-Mer, covering the town of Montebourg from the east. The rest of the army advanced along 'thickly wooded and very narrow roads' through the Bois de Rabey towards Valognes, just over nine miles away.[39] There are three reasonably direct routes from St-Vaast to Valognes. The most northerly route follows the high ground north-west from Quettehou via Teurthéville-Bocage, and comes down to Valognes from the north. The central route, and the most direct, goes straight through the wood along the line of what is now the D902, probably following a Roman road, entering Valognes from the north-east. The third, southerly route follows the coast through Morsalines as far as Aumeville-l'Estre, then turning west through Octeville-l'Avenel, St-Martin-d'Audouville and Huberville and approaching Valognes from the east. It is likely that the three divisions each followed one of these tracks, though we cannot say for sure which used which track. The narrowness of the road and density of the woodland meant that the army moved cautiously, with frequent pauses to scout ahead in case Bertrand's men had resumed their activity and laid more ambushes. But the day passed without incident, and in the afternoon the three columns debouched from the woods and moved down a slight incline in the ground to find Valognes lying defenceless before them.

There had been a settlement at Valognes since Roman times, if not before, and in 1346 the town was prosperous. Sitting astride the Cherbourg–Carentan road, it served as a market and entrepôt for the surrounding region, and also had some industries of its own including tanneries and a parchment works. A small river, the Merderet, provided the water these industries needed, and also powered several mills. The big church of St-Malo dominated the town, but there were several other churches as well as a large Franciscan friary. Most of these can still be seen today, although the church of St-Malo was badly damaged by Allied bombing in the Second World War. The town was unwalled, not garrisoned and completely defenceless apart from a small and rather ancient castle.[40]

Whatever their personal feelings for the invaders, the inhabitants of Valognes now had a simple choice: surrender, or see their town go up in flames as Barfleur and St-Vaast and the villages around had already done. It was not a choice that appears to have taken them long to make. The *Acta Bellicosa* recounts that 'the inhabitants of the town came out and threw themselves at the king's feet, asking him only to spare their lives; the king most mercifully admitted them to his peace, and ordered his earlier edict to be repeated, with the same penalties and rewards'.[41] This was a classic piece of medieval public theatre, with the people – probably, in fact, only the senior figures of the town – begging humbly for their lives to be spared and the king graciously granting them not only their lives but their valuables. The townspeople got to keep their houses and possessions, the king was made to look magnanimous, and all were satisfied; all, that is, but for the more voracious among the soldiers, who looked with covetous eyes on the fine houses and churches of the town and wondered how much loot they contained. The king recognised this, and firmly repeated the proclamation he had issued at St-Vaast, forbidding the pillaging of towns and harming of their inhabitants.

The English then took over the town, with the men-at-arms being billeted in houses. The better houses went to the men of highest rank; the king himself took over a house belonging to the Duke of Normandy, the son of his adversary, and the Prince of Wales requisitioned a house belonging to the Bishop of Coutances, in whose diocese Valognes lay.[42] The foot soldiers were most likely camped in the surrounding fields. Some stocks of foodstuffs were commandeered; it is possible that the royal household, at least, was also buying some goods from the local populace, but this is not certain.[43]

The first day of the march had thus far been a successful one for Edward. He had achieved his first objective, cutting the road from Cherbourg to Carentan, and was now in a position to strike south himself towards the latter town. There had been no sign of enemy forces, and the difficult traverse of the Bois de Rabey had been accomplished without incident. A fine town had fallen into his hands intact, and its inhabitants acknowledged him (under some duress, admittedly) as their monarch. Sufficient supplies of food and water were also on hand. All seemed to be going as planned – until columns of smoke began to rise to the south-east.

Balked of their spoils at Valognes, the disgruntled foot soldiers began to spread out across the countryside around the town, pillaging isolated farms and hamlets. Four miles south-east of Valognes along the road to Carentan, they found the town of Montebourg. Smaller than Valognes, it nonetheless had an abbey and a fine church of St-Jacques, and a number of houses strung out along the road. It too was unwalled and defenceless, and here there was no king or marshals to stay the hands of the soldiers. There is no mention of the inhabitants of Montebourg, and it is possible that they fled across the fields rather than trying to resist. The town itself was then taken, robbed and burned. By the time the soldiers trailed back over the fields to Valognes, Montebourg was in ruins.[44]

Evening drew down on Valognes, the sky dark with smoke, and the army settled down to its evening meal, pease pottage and bread for the common soldiers with perhaps a bit of poultry or pork for those who had been successful at foraging. The royal kitchens served up mutton, pork, fresh and spiced beef and a variety of poultry including a heron and spoon-bill; large quantities of eggs, milk and flour were used, indicating perhaps the making of meat pies on a large scale. One deer was also consumed, for which the princely sum of 8d. was paid. The kitchen's supplies of coal had run out, and 12d. was paid for two cartloads of wood with a further 8d. for the carriage of water from Le Merderet.

Despite the destruction of Montebourg, this had still been a good day for the English king. As night fell, his scouts would have reported that apart from a few isolated garrisons, notably at Cherbourg and Bricquebec, there was no longer any resistance in the north of the Cotentin. The way to the south lay open. The next destination was Carentan.

* * *

On that same day, messengers arrived in Paris and King Philippe learned that the long-expected invasion had now arrived. He probably received messages at the same time from Harfleur, where the Comte d'Eu, the Constable of France, had gone to oversee the defences and raise new forces. Eu now left the Burgundian knight Godemar de Fay in charge of the coastal defences in the north and sent Jean, Comte d'Harcourt to defend Rouen, the capital of Normandy, with a strong force that included Harcourt's own son and the younger Robert Bertrand, Vicomte de Longeville and son of the marshal. Eu had then mustered all the remaining men that could be spared, probably about 3,000 in all, including Jean de Melun, Comte de Tancarville, and a number of Norman and Picard knights and barons including Alerin de Brimeu, Philippe de Pons, Friquet de Fricamps, Macio Choffin and Jean de Grimbault, and was now taking them by sea the short distance from Harfleur to Ouistreham and then up the river Orne to Caen.

Although the correspondence has not survived, we can assume that Eu concurred with the marshal's view that the defence of Lower Normandy should be concentrated on Caen, the main city of the region and a certain goal of the English army. The city itself was poorly defended, but Caen's castle was very strong. If the English could be stopped or delayed there, this would give the king time to muster more forces and move west to confront the enemy. It was a sound plan; there was nothing wrong with the young Constable's strategic sense. It was his tactics, as we shall see later, that let him down.

Philippe, not for the first time in the campaign, hesitated, remaining at his hunting lodge in the Bois de Vincennes for several days after receiving the news.[45] He was aware, thanks to his spies in London, that Hugh Hastings was on his way to Flanders and might land at any moment, at which point France might well be invaded from two directions, west and north. Most of the French troops that had been raised for that season had been sent south with Duc Jean to Aiguillon; more troops were being raised but had not yet assembled, and there was still a severe shortage of money. The foreign contingents were on the way but had not yet arrived: the Bohemians were on their way from Liège, where they had been delayed suppressing a local revolt, the Savoyards were reportedly on the march but had started late, and there was as yet no sign of Carlo Grimaldi from Monaco, who should have been at Harfleur by now to join his forces with those of Ottone Doria. So Philippe waited for reinforcements, and for further intelligence of his enemy. This particular delay, as it happens, was not fatal, but it shows the cast of mind of a man whose first instincts were usually cautious ones.

Wednesday 19 July

Having rested and eaten well during the night, the English army made an early start. It was still mid-July and dawn came early, and the troops were able to breakfast and begin their march in full daylight. Another flanking force was despatched, this one of 500 men-at-arms and 2,000 hobelars and archers under the command of Godefroi d'Harcourt. This force moved south from Valognes with the purpose of protecting the right flank of the army, but Harcourt had his own agenda as well. Ten miles south-west of Valognes lay St-Sauveur-le-Vicomte, his former home, and it was here that

Harcourt first marched. His motives may have been varied; a sentimental desire to see his home may have been one of them, although sentiment is not a word easy to associate with this lame and embittered Norman. More prosaically, he may have wished to try to recruit former tenants to join Edward's cause; if even a few Norman knights could be seen to be rallying to the latter, the propaganda value would have been considerable.

What Harcourt was expecting to find at St-Sauveur cannot be known, but what he found was the ruins of his castle, taken and dismantled by Bertrand three years earlier. The expected support did not materialise; most of the men-at-arms of the district had already been summoned by Bertrand a week earlier, and any who remained were clearly unwilling to commit themselves. The only Normans who remained loyal to Harcourt were those fellow exiles like the brothers Nicholas and Guillaume de Groussy who had accompanied him from England.

And their number was shortly to be reduced by one. Some time that day Guillaume de Vacognes, a former esquire of the executed Olivier de Clisson, was sent to the manor of St-Clément-sur-Gué with letters from King Edward, calling on the inhabitants to acknowledge him as their rightful overlord and to rise up against King Philippe. The locals responded by killing him out of hand. Vacognes thus has the dubious honour of being the first identifiable member of the English army to die during the course of the campaign. His death and the disappointment at St-Sauveur seem to have effectively ended Edward's attempt to spark an anti-French revolt in Normandy, though he of course continued to claim sovereignty over it.[46]

Leaving his shattered home behind him, Harcourt turned east, back towards the main body. By afternoon his flanking force was passing through Picauville, where it turned south, following a road across the marshes of the river Douve just above its confluence with the Merderet, and then climbing back up the hill to Coigny, having marched for about eighteen miles. Harcourt was now in position to block any attempt to relieve Carentan from the west, or to join the attack on the town itself if need be.

* * *

In the east, Warwick and Cobham were also on the move. The place of their halt the previous night is not known,[47] but can be assumed to be east or south-east of Montebourg, around Fontenay or St-Marcouf. The following day they resumed their march down the coastal road, inland of the salt marshes and dunes that would later form part of Utah Beach, through Ravenoville and Varreville. Out to sea, paralleling the marching column, the ships of Huntingdon's fleet could be seen making their own slow way south-east, a hundred sail or more with their own orders regarding the coastline of Normandy.[48]

By afternoon Warwick and Cobham had reached the high ground around St-Marie-du-Mont, overlooking the sandbars of the mouth of the Douve. Their further way south-east was blocked by the estuary, and they now turned south-west to rendezvous with the main body. They had encountered no opposition.

* * *

The first sight to confront the king's division when it moved out that morning was the still smouldering ruins of Montebourg lying along the road. From the tower of the looted church of St-Jacques, a fine view could be had down the length of the Roman road for many miles to the south. The road was clear and empty. Despite the possibility of ambush from the hedgerows of the *bocage* along the sides of the road, Edward pushed his army forward at full speed, moving swiftly down the road towards Carentan twelve miles away.

Six miles south-east of Montebourg the road ran through the little town of Ste-Mère Église, a market town built around a central square and church on which building work had been proceeding in a desultory fashion for some time. It too was defenceless, and had probably already been abandoned. English sources do not mention it, but local histories confirm that Ste-Mère Église was burned and destroyed that morning; indeed, it may be coincidence, but building work on the church is known to have stopped in the mid-fourteenth century and did not resume for another fifty years.[49]

And still no opposition had been met. Late afternoon brought the king's division to St-Côme-du-Mont, a handsome village with a fine manor house and a small but rich and highly decorated church sitting on the high ground overlooking the marshes between itself and Carentan. Here Warwick's force rejoined the main body, but at the same time the scouts brought back bad news. The bridges between St-Côme-du-Mont and Carentan had been broken, and the road was now impassable. Carentan itself was garrisoned by a force of unknown size. Any chance of seizing the town quickly had been lost.

Carentan sits at the confluence of three rivers: the Taute flowing up from the south to the east of the town, and the Sèves from the west and the Douve from the north-west, both passing north of the town. The combined stream then empties itself into the sea three or four miles to the north-east. A fourth river, the Vire, also flows into the sea a couple of miles to the east. The area around these rivers is a large salt marsh, the Marais du Cotentin. This has now been largely drained and the rivers canalised, but in the fourteenth century the marshes were still largely inundated at high tide, and even at low tide were impassable to horses and wagons. This was a wild area, inhabited by only a few hunters and fishermen, gatherers of reeds and wild plants and cutters of peat, whose produce, sold in the markets of Carentan, provided them with a bare living. There were danger-ous bogs, and an even more dangerous tidal bore, the *mascaret*, which sometimes washed across the entire area when strong incoming tides pushed back the river water.[50]

From the English position at St-Côme-du-Mont, the ground slopes away steeply to the northern arm of the marsh. The only route to Carentan was by a raised causeway, again almost certainly of Roman construction originally, high enough to remain dry at high tide, and with several bridges across the rivers. There are four significant river channels at this point: the Jourdan, a tributary channel of the Douve, then the Douve proper, then another tributary known as the Groult, and finally, a little closer to Carentan, the Madeleine, a separate small stream that drained the marshes immedi-ately around the town. The Douve is the most formidable obstacle, being some 40–50 feet wide today; the river has been channelled to some extent, and was probably wider in the fourteenth century. The other three streams are small and were probably fordable, but the deeper Douve could only be crossed by bridge.[51]

On the far side of the marshes lay Carentan itself, the largest and most important town the army had so far reached. Michael Northburgh described Carentan as being as large as Leicester, meaning it was a provincial centre of some importance. Then, as now, Carentan was a prosperous town deriving its income from agriculture and its position at an important cross-roads. Its wealth was reflected in the big church of Notre-Dame and many fine buildings, such as the row of arcaded shops still visible in the centre of the town.[52] Its strategic importance was considerable: not only did it command the only crossing place of the Marais, but from Carentan roads also ran south, west and – importantly – east towards Caen.

It was at Carentan that Robert Bertrand chose to reorganise his defence, and, like the German commander of Carentan in 1944, he broke the bridges along the causeway in order to delay the enemy advance. He also put the castle and town of Carentan into a state of defence. Carentan had strong walls, and these at some points rose almost from the edge of the marshes, using the latter as a kind of natural moat; there was also a sizeable castle in the centre of the town. But Bertrand did not intend to make a determined stand at Carentan. Still with far too few men under his command to risk an engagement, his aim instead was to buy time, to delay the English advance long enough to allow a sufficient force to be assembled at Caen to defend the city, and perhaps even launch a counter-attack. Accordingly he adopted a Fabian strategy, always withdrawing his main force before the English could catch up with him, luring the enemy in pursuit and yet at the same time holding up their advance as long as possible. He had no realistic hope that Carentan would hold out for long, but a delay of two or three days would be invaluable.

Such was not to be. The English army had come well prepared, and as the main army settled down to make camp – and pillage and burn St-Côme-du-Mont – and prepare a meagre dinner, even the royal household dining on cod, cheese and pease porridge with onions,[53] the royal carpenters were at work. Some bridging equipment had been brought with the army, while other timber may have been taken from felled trees or from local houses. Late in the day a strong force of men-at-arms and archers, commanded by the reliable Reginald Cobham and Bartholomew Burghersh and including also Hugh Despenser, John Stirling and the young Roger Mortimer, moved down the causeway to the banks of the Douve. Under their guard the carpenters worked throughout the night, dragging their timbers down the hill and out across the causeway to the broken bridge and then, working by torchlight, hauling the beams into place, making them fast and then laying down lighter planks to create a roadway.

What is most impressive about this episode is the speed and efficiency with which the operation was carried out. Admittedly, this was helped by the fact that Robert Bertrand was so short of men that he could not spare any to go forward and harass the bridging operation; even a handful of crossbowmen hidden in the marsh could have hampered the bridge repairs considerably. In sharp contrast, a few German machine-gunners were able to hold up American combat engineers repairing the same bridges for nearly three days in 1944. Even so, to find sufficient timber to repair a 30–40 foot bridge, carry it or haul it nearly a mile and then effect the repair by night, all in about twelve hours, is a feat worthy of some admiration. This was by no means the last time that the royal carpenters would earn their wages on this campaign.

Thursday 20 July

During the night the garrison and townspeople of Carentan had watched the burning of St-Côme-du-Mont, and also of Coigny and other points to the west, and knew they were about to be assailed on two sides.[54] The presence of the force at Coigny was an especially bitter blow, for it was from the west and south-west that Carentan was most vulnerable; only from these directions could an army deploy and advance over dry ground. The sight of torches reflected in the waters of the marshes around the Douve bridge only a mile from the walls told Bertrand that the game was now up, at least as far as Carentan was concerned. The early morning sun showed him that the bridge was not only fully repaired, but that Edward's army was advancing in a long glittering column across the causeway towards the town, while soon after Harcourt's force came marching up from the west.

Harcourt's men had the longer march, a little over eight miles, but apart from crossing the Sèves at Baupte they had good roads, while it would have taken time for the main body to cross the two-mile causeway, which, the *Acta Bellicosa* informs us, was extremely narrow.[55] By late morning at latest, however, the English were beginning to deploy in force against the town, and Bertrand realised he could do no more. Rather than simply retreating east to Caen, however, he chose instead to fall back still further south, towards St-Lô. If he could persuade the enemy to follow him, rather than advance east along the coast directly towards Bayeux and Caen, then there was a chance he could buy still more time for his brother the bishop and the other commanders gathering their troops in the east. One wonders if this tough old soldier occasionally spared a thought for his eldest son, the Vicomte de Longeville, then serving in the Norman contingent which had been gathering at Harfleur under the Comte d'Eu.

Accordingly, he detailed a small garrison to remain in the town and hold out as long as possible. Then, accompanied by the main body of his force – strengthened by further recruiting, but still only a few hundred men at most – Bertrand rode out of Carentan to the south-east, following the causeway across the marshes of the Vire and then up over the high ground to St-Lô seventeen miles away, pausing to break the bridge at Pont-Hébert to delay the enemy still further, and arriving at St-Lô by nightfall. As Bertrand abandoned the town, the small garrison he had left behind sealed themselves inside the castle, while the burgesses of the town took another look at the advancing English and opened their gates. The English were admitted to the town without a fight, and the leading companies rode into the centre of the town towards the castle.

What happened next has outraged generations of French historians. It appears that the garrison of the castle, far from putting up resistance as ordered, surrendered almost immediately, and it was said that the garrison commanders, Raoul de Verdun and Nicholas de Groussy, sold the castle to the English in exchange for money. This story is repeated in several chronicles of the day, and by many historians since. That the garrison of Carentan may have surrendered in dubious circumstances is highly possible, but Verdun and Groussy were not its commanders. Verdun, Groussy and the latter's brother Guillaume had been in English service as early as 1345, and Groussy was present at the attack on Castle Cornet that year. In 1345, too, their lands had been confiscated by Philippe VI, who gave them to the daughter of Robert Bertrand. Now they were part of the small band of Norman exiles who accompanied Godefroi d'Harcourt with the English army.[56] That they were traitors to their country is undoubted, but of this particular offence they must be exonerated.

At all events, Carentan fell without a blow being struck, and the wealthy town and its large stores of food and wine were delivered into the hands of the English.[57] But the advantage so easily won was quickly destroyed by the indiscipline of the troops. Looting began almost at once – Northburgh maintains that the first troops into the town immediately began to pillage – and then the inevitable fires broke out. By nightfall, the greater part of the town had been burned, and much of the valuable stores of food went up in smoke along with the houses. Other food stocks were pillaged by the soldiers.[58]

Edward's anger is easy to imagine. Fresh food stocks, especially meat, were already running out, and the army would become increasingly reliant on what food it could buy or commandeer as time went on. He issued yet another proclamation, ordering 'in the king's name that no one should waste more food than he needed', on pain of life and limb.[59] On balance, this proclamation was no more effective than the preceding ones. Meanwhile, more smoke was rising to the east as Huntingdon's ships descended on the coast east of the mouth of the Douve and the landing parties began going ashore.

In an atmosphere thick with smoke, the army made camp in and around Carentan. As mentioned, fresh meat supplies were running low, but the royal household was still able to dine on fresh beef, pork and mutton, a dozen geese and a dozen hens, and 100 eggs. The loss of the stored foodstuffs was unfortunate but not serious, for there was a great deal of rich countryside ahead of the army. Lessons had been learned, however, and from then on the royal foragers were very active in securing food stocks wherever the army went. The Kitchen Account records regular payments to foragers, huntsmen, fishermen and others who went out every day to forage for foodstuffs for the king's household, and doubtless other large households were doing the same.

Notes

1 *Acta Bellicosa*, p. 27.
2 Ibid.
3 The nave of the church looked substantially the same then as it does now; the tower is a fifteenth-century addition.
4 Letter of Michael Northburgh, 27 July, quoted in Robert de Avesbury, *De Gestis Mirabilis Regis Edwardi Tertii*, ed. E.M. Thompson, London, 1889, p. 358. The *Acta Bellicosa* mentions fourteen ships but does not distinguish between those which were fitted out for war and those which were not.
5 Froissart, vol. 4, p. 390. All references to Froissart are (unless otherwise indicated) to J. Froissart, *Oeuvres de Froissart*, ed. Kervynde de Lettenhove, vols 4 and 5.
6 What is more, Froissart is the only source to recount this; even Jean le Bel, never one to miss a potentially embarrassing story about Edward, does not mention this incident. However, a nearly identical story is told of William the Conqueror upon landing at Hastings!

7 A reasonable assumption; even if all their horses had been unloaded, which is unlikely, they would have been virtually unmanageable after the long confinement aboard ship (see below).

8 *Acta Bellicosa*, p. 28.

9 Ibid. Froissart, vol. 4, p. 378. Froissart states that Bertrand had 2,000 '*combattants*' at his disposal at St-Saveur-le-Vicomte. Clifford Rogers believes Bertrand may have had as many as 1,000 men at his disposal, but if so, he does not seem to have concentrated his whole force at St-Vaast; Rogers, *War Cruel and Sharp*, p. 219.

10 Sumption, p. 501, maintains that Bertrand made a brief attack on the beach, and Rogers, *War Cruel and Sharp*, p. 219, presents, largely from French sources, a picture of a spectacular pitched battle on the beach between Bertrand's French troops and an English company under Warwick. English sources, including eyewitness accounts, suggest that the fighting was much more scattered and sporadic, and did not begin until elements of the army had begun to move off the beach.

11 Bradwardine, letter of 17 July: 'On a number of occasions our handful of men defeated large numbers of the enemy, killing many, capturing more', quoted in Adam Murimuth, *Continuatio Chronicarum*, ed. E.M. Thompson, London, 1889, p. 358. Admittedly this letter, like many other similar letters, was written for propaganda purposes and Bradwardine may have been exaggerating the real situation.

12 *Acta Bellicosa*, p. 28. The 'poor horse' was probably badly out of condition after spending two weeks in the cramped hold of a ship, and would not yet have been fit for combat.

13 'The men at arms of the region have withdrawn into the castles and fortified towns', letter of Bartholomew Burghersh, 17 July, in Barber, *Life and Campaigns*, p. 14.

14 *Acta Bellicosa*, p. 28; Rogers, *War Cruel and Sharp*, p. 241; the figure of 30 men is provided by Sumption, p. 501, but is not sourced.

15 Barber, *Edward, Prince of Wales*, p. 49, says that the king spent the night of the landing at a small village two miles inland, but most sources including the Kitchen Account suggest that he did not move from St-Vaast until the following day. This seems sensible: Quettehou and Morsalines, the only villages that qualify, would still have been on the front line at this point whereas St-Vaast was protected and secure.

16 Fish sizes were larger in the Middle Ages than today. The stockfish were dried cod or any other white fish. As well as the eleven conger eels the Kitchen Account lists a further 'half a peck' of conger eel.

17 And of course, not only the medieval soldier. In the nineteenth century, even disciplined professional armies like that of Britain were capable of acts of wanton looting and destruction, perhaps most infamously at the Summer Palace near Beijing in 1860. And even today, militia armies in many parts of the world supplement their often uncertain pay through looting.

18 *Acta Bellicosa*, pp. 28–9.

19 Barber, *Edward, Prince of Wales*, pp. 224–5. Barber refutes the commonly held view, probably derived from Froissart, that the entire population of the town was slaughtered *en masse*.

20 *Registres du Trésor des Chartes*, ed. J. Viard and A. Vallée, Paris, 1979–84, no. 6544 OR 5676; quoted also in Rogers, p. 240.

21 Burne, p. 142. Burne, a professional soldier, explicitly rejects the idea that Edward ordered or sanctioned widespread destruction, insisting that there was no military advantage to be gained from such acts.

22 Ibid., p. 143.

23 *Acta Bellicosa*, p. 28.

24 Le Baker, p. 80. Sumption, p. 501, describes Edward as taking up his quarters in an inn, but Morsalines seems rather small to have had an inn, and the manor house would have made a more fitting location. The editors of le Bel's Chronicle assert that Edward spent the night 'near Barfleur', le Bel, p. 72.

25 The late Lieutenant-Colonel Lawrence Biddle, formerly an officer in a British yeomanry regiment, recalled taking a draft of 200 horses from Britain to Palestine by sea, again a voyage of about two weeks. Upon being disembarked near Haifa, the horses 'went wild', and it took most of the rest of the day to round them up again. This apparently was quite common in such circumstances (personal communication with the authors).

26 The Kitchen Account records that the households of the king and prince were still eating fresh meat brought ashore at St-Vaast by the time the army reached Carentan on the 19th, a week after landing. Some of this may have been bought locally, but, given the flight of many of the peasantry, this cannot have met the whole needs of the household. After Carentan, the Account increasingly no longer gives values for fresh meat, but instead records it as 'depreda' (stolen). See also the discussion in Chapter 3.

27 Kitchen Account, PRO E101/390/11.

28 This is a considerable amount of salt, and it is possible that some of the meat, not consumed, was then preserved for later use.

29 At latest, assuming they did not ride by night, and also that they were able to change horses at points such as Carentan and Bayeux.

30 Le Bel, pp. 71–2, Barber, *Edward, Prince of Wales*, p. 49, mention only an attack by sea. Froissart, p. 127 says that the town was attacked by both sea and land; this is most likely, given the narrowness of the harbour entrance and the fact that it was well protected.

31 No similar measures seem to have been taken at St-Vaast; the shallowness of the water and the muddy bottom may have precluded this.

32 Northburgh; *Acta Bellicosa* mentions seven 'curiously fitted-out warships', p. 29.

33 Froissart, pp. 388–90, 393.

34 Froissart, p. 388. *Acta Bellicosa* says simply that the raiding force 'returned unharmed with a number of prisoners, both citizens and peasants', p. 28.

35 Rogers, *War Cruel and Sharp*, p. 219.
36 A quarter was the equivalent of eight bushels.
37 Some of the above is conjecture. Detail is lacking on the Cherbourg raid; there is no unanimity as to the date it occurred. On one reading, Michael Northburgh states that the fleet did not begin its movement until after the army set out for Valognes on the 18th, and this interpretation is followed by Sumption, p. 502. But the Barfleur attacks show that the fleet was already in action, and the plunder taken at Barfleur undoubtedly concentrated the minds of its officers and men; our assumption is that, having attacked Barfleur, the squadron simply carried on to the west, raiding and burning after the manner described, until it reached Cherbourg. Northburgh's statement that the fleet began its attacks after the king left La Hogue could also be interpreted as meaning after he moved inland from St-Vaast, i.e. to Morsalines on the 13th. Jean le Bel explicitly links the attack on Cherbourg with that on Barfleur, as do several modern sources (Rogers, *War Cruel and Sharp*, p. 242; André Plaisse, 'Cherbourg durant la guerre de Cent Ans', in *La Normandie dans la guerre de Cent Ans, 1346–1450*, Caen, 1999). Both Northburgh and le Bel claim the entire town was burned although the castle held out, but this seems doubtful: the castle itself would have protected at least some of the town. The landing site and direction taken by the English raiders are based on the geography of the Cherbourg area, complicated by the considerable expansion of the port and consequent building work over the last several centuries.
38 We have followed the list given in *Acta Bellicosa*, p. 29, with some amendments. That source lists Huntingdon with the rearguard, when in fact he commanded the fleet. Reginald Cobham is given with the king's division, but if he served there at all, it was not for long, for he very quickly appears in the vanguard. A few others, noted in other sources as being in specific divisions, have been added.
39 *Acta Bellicosa*, p. 29.
40 Local sources.
41 *Acta Bellicosa*, pp. 29–30.
42 Ibid. It is possible that the 'house of the Duke of Normandy' was the castle, which had an eleventh-century keep and some later buildings, but this is by no means certain; the ducal lodging might equally have been a townhouse.
43 The evidence comes from the Kitchen Account, which occasionally lists purchases of items such as milk, and also of kitchen equipment including pots and turnspits, throughout the campaign. These items might simply have been stolen, but the account is fairly faithful at separating those goods which were *depreda* from those which were paid and accounted for. Kitchen equipment might have been bought from other households, and milk cows might have accompanied the army, but this seems nearly as unlikely as the idea of royal kitchen servants buying milk from people whose homes had just been burned down.

44 *Acta Bellicosa* says that the army left Montebourg to one side when it marched south the following morning, but by then the destruction had already been accomplished. The burning of Montebourg is sometimes dated to the following day, when the main body of the army passed through the area, but the circumstances are suspicious: why did not the inhabitants simply surrender as those of Valognes had done? Logic suggests that Montebourg was in fact burned before the main body arrived, and this in turn suggests that the destruction happened either early on the 19th or, more likely, during the pillaging of the country around Valognes on the afternoon of the 18th.

45 Jules Viard, 'Itineraire de Philippe VI de Valois', p. 100.

46 The death of Vacognes is recounted in RTC 6544, 5676. Rogers believes that he was one of a number of envoys sent out for this purpose, but no further attempts at propaganda of this type seem to have been made.

47 Froissart asserts that each night the flanking forces rejoined the main body, but this was not always the case. In this particular instance it would have made no sense for Warwick to march down the coast, then inland to join the king at Valognes, then back to the coast again for the following day's march.

48 The whole of the fleet that had sailed from the Solent did not remain at St-Vaast. Many of the smaller ships returned to England, probably immediately after discharging their passengers and cargo. Huntingdon retained only the larger ships, especially those fitted out for war. How many there were is hard to ascertain; the *Acta Bellicosa*, p. 34, later speaks of 'more than a hundred' ships, and this is probably right.

49 Of course, other factors such as the Black Death a few years later may also have been responsible for this.

50 The Marais du Cotentin remains an important nature and wildlife preserve, and readers wishing to know more about this unique area, its ecology and its human inhabitants are encouraged to stop at the excellent visitor centre on the banks of the Douve just north of Carentan. The rivers, especially the tributary channels, may have changed course to some extent over the centuries.

51 *Acta Bellicosa*, p. 30, confirms that only one bridge needed to be replaced, as the water in this channel was too deep to ford; this was almost certainly the Douve, which is a larger river with a much larger drainage basin than the Madeleine.

52 The old Norman church of Notre-Dame was completely ruined during the Hundred Years War, and was rebuilt in 'Gothic' style after the French reconquest of Normandy in the 1440s. The church was badly damaged again by bombing in the Second World War. The old arcaded houses can still be seen on the Place de la Republique.

53 Quite possibly the baggage train and livestock had not yet caught up with the main body, meaning dinner had to be prepared out of whatever was to hand.

54 There is no record of Coigny being burned but, especially given Godefroi d'Harcourt's record on this campaign, it would be astonishing if it was not.

55 *Acta Bellicosa*, p. 30.

56 The supposed selling of Carentan by Verdun and Groussy is noted in several chronicles: *Chronique de Richard Lescot*, Paris, 1896, p. 71; *Grandes Chroniques*, ed. J. Viard, Paris, 1887, vol. 9, p. 271; *Chronique Normande*, ed. A. and E. Molinier, Paris, 1882, p. 75, which mistakes Nicholas de Groussy for his brother Guillaume. However, their presence and that of Verdun at Castle Cornet is definitely identified in Godfray, *Documents relatif aux attaques sur les Îles de la Manche, 1338–45*. Froissart, in one of his more imaginative moments, says that the garrison of Carentan resisted for two days and only surrendered when they could fight no longer, but all other evidence points against this.

57 According to Michael Northburgh, although it is not known what these food stocks were; at this time of the year, just before the harvest, food stocks would normally have been low.

58 This again is on the testimony of Northburgh, and it is possible that his account of the destruction is exaggerated, though French historians also refer to the destruction of most if not all of the town. *Acta Bellicosa* says merely that much of the food was 'consumed' by the soldiers.

59 *Acta Bellicosa*, p. 30.

Chapter 5

Carentan to Caen

When the English came before Caen, they assailed the town . . . and shot arrows from their bows as dense as hail.

Grandes Chroniques[1]

Friday 21 July

The tenth day of the campaign dawned. Edward now had, thanks to the townspeople and garrison of Carentan, firm intelligence of his enemy, and was aware that Robert Bertrand had withdrawn south to St-Lô, and also had an idea of the strength of his force. A choice now confronted the English commanders: whether to move due east towards Bayeux and Caen, or follow Bertrand to St-Lô.

The latter choice was tempting, for a variety of reasons. St-Lô, like Carentan, was strategically important, commanding a main road crossing the Vire from Caen to the important western towns of Coutances and Mont St-Michel. Seizing the town would increase Edwards's own options and give him control over a further large area of western Normandy. The personal enmity between the French marshal and Godefroi d'Harcourt may also have been a factor; laying hands in person on the despoiler of St-Sauveur would undoubtedly have given the latter a great deal of satisfaction. Finally, if Edward could force Bertrand to give battle, at odds decidedly favourable to himself, he could score a propaganda victory and give his knights the chance to take some valuable ransoms.

And so the decision was made, and unwittingly the English followed exactly the course Bertrand had hoped they would choose. Had they advanced due east to Caen, they could have reached the town in three days, possibly before Eu's force from Harfleur could arrive and with the only garrison being the small force under the Bishop of Bayeux. Edward then decided to install a garrison in Carentan itself, protecting the vital crossing point and guarding his rear areas. The garrison was to be a mix of English troops and Norman exiles, and two of Harcourt's followers, Raoul de Verdun and Nicholas de Groussy, were appointed as captains; presumably they were also expected to continue to raise Norman support for the English cause in the region.[2] It was an appointment that would later cost both Groussy and Verdun their lives.

From Carentan the army first marched east, crossing the causeway and bridges over the Taute. Bertrand's troops had left these intact, presumably not having time to destroy them thanks to the proximity of the English army. Climbing up onto low rolling ground two miles east of the town, they came to the point where the road divides, one branch running east to Isigny and Bayeux, and ultimately Caen, the other turning south to St-Lô. They followed the latter, moving in a single column down the road over the marshes west of the Vire and crossing several more bridges; these too had been left intact. This was nonetheless a slow progression for the main body, for it would have taken many hours for the entire army to ride or march down this single narrow route.[3]

Ten miles south-east of Carentan the ground began to rise, and now the army could make better speed. However, there was more bad news: the bridge over the Vire at Pont-Hébert, four miles short of St-Lô, had been broken. The Vire at this point runs between steep banks a hundred feet or more in height, and is deep and swift-flowing. Today the road descends steeply from the high ground straight to the river, crossing by a modern bridge (with older foundations); the original road may have descended a few hundred yards to the south of the modern route, following a less steep gradient, but probably crossed at the same point. The crossing is a potential chokepoint, and even today Pont-Hébert is one of the few crossings of the Vire between St-Lô, where the town and castle effectively bar the passage, and the marshes nearer the river's mouth. Once again Robert Bertrand had done his work well, holding up the enemy advance at a critical point.

But once again, too, Bertrand himself had underestimated the energy and organisation of his enemy. As the vanguard division under the Prince of Wales reached the heights above Pont-Hébert in the late afternoon, the carpenters were once again sent for. There was no evidence of the enemy, although the Prince and his commanders clearly were concerned about the possibility of an ambush on the far side. Despite having marched thirteen miles already,[4] the men set to work. By nightfall the bridge was repaired and ready for use, but the crossing was delayed until morning when the army could advance in force. Dinner at the king's household was a meagre affair of cod, stockfish and salt salmon with pickles and eggs; presumably all of the wagons carrying the bulk of the food had not yet arrived, and there had been no time to forage. The number of men being fed also appears to have been lower than usual.

* * *

On that same Friday, the English commander Hugh Hastings landed in Flanders. He had with him a handful of men-at-arms, including John Molyneux, John Montgomery and John Maltravers, and about six hundred archers. This little force moved swiftly on to Ypres, arriving a few days later, and joining the Flemish forces already assembled under their nominal leader, Henry of Flanders. Hastings, bent on carrying out his orders, urged the Flemings to advance into Artois and Picardy to link up with Edward's army, which would be coming up from the south later in the summer. Reluctantly, the Flemings agreed. Their hearts were not really in this venture, but their economic interests depended largely on continuing supplies of English wool to feed the looms and spindles of their cities, and so they prepared to march. Hastings's arrival in Flanders was reported to Paris almost immediately by French spies, who had been expecting him.

Saturday 22 July

In the morning the English vanguard swiftly crossed the bridge and followed the road up through a gap in the bluffs along the river, reaching the high ground a mile or so east of Pont-Hébert and now within easy striking distance of St-Lô. Here they halted and drew up in battle order, preparing to resist any attack by the enemy that might materialise, and providing cover while the rest of the army crossed the river.[5] This was very cautious behaviour, but river crossings were a time when the army was at its most vulnerable; given the terrain, even a small enemy force might have caused considerable damage if it had got through to the bridge. But Edward and his commanders need not have worried. Unbeknownst to them, Robert Bertrand's force had left St-Lô, but instead of advancing to attack, it was already withdrawing east towards Caen.

The vanguard was followed by the king's own division, and then the long column of wagons, which crossed the bridge in single file and then laboured up the long slope beyond, where the steep gradient slowed the more heavily laden vehicles to a crawl. Arundel, Durham and the rearguard patiently shepherded them across. The vanguard, seeing the king's division coming up in support, paused for a little ceremony while the young Prince of Wales knighted another of his companions, Henry Burghersh.[6] This concluded, the vanguard began to advance on the town.

St-Lô was larger than Carentan, and more prosperous. Michael Northburgh describes it as being the size of Lincoln, meaning it was equivalent to one of the larger provincial towns in England. It occupied a strong natural position surrounded by steep bluffs on three sides and overlooking the Vire to the west. The imposing castle sits at the western end of the town, commanding the river crossing; the rest of the town stretches away to the east, around the imposing church of Notre-Dame. It had first been fortified in the eighth century, allegedly at the instigation of Charlemagne to protect against Viking invasion, and had since become a wealthy trading centre. One chronicler, Jean Froissart, estimated that there were between 160 and 180 'people engaged in commerce' (i.e. burgesses), putting the total population at about 8,000, and other contemporary sources mention its markets and trade, particularly in cloth. Two faubourgs had grown up outside the walls, one around the abbey of St-Croix to the east, and one in the Dollée and Torteron valleys under the shadow of the north walls.[7]

Impregnable on three sides, St-Lô was vulnerable to the east, especially if – as seems likely – the fortifications had been neglected and were in a state of poor repair.[8] The faubourgs were not walled at all and were extremely vulnerable. This probably explains Bertrand's decision not to try to defend the town. It probably also explains the decisions of the citizens themselves to abandon the place. The approach of the English seems to have inspired something close to panic, and most of the population fled at the approach of the English army, without even taking their valuables. A few brave, or foolish, souls remained behind, probably to protect their property.

The richness of St-Lô is one point on which all contemporaries, English and French, are agreed. No one could imagine, says Froissart, the riches the English found, especially the numbers of bales of cloth. Had any buyers been available, he adds, they might have been able to buy a great deal of cloth at a very cheap rate. Michael Northburgh says that 'at least a thousand barrels of wine' were found, along with many other goods, and the author of the *Acta Bellicosa* says that 'there was plenty of food of all kinds'. The town was thoroughly pillaged, and, according to the chronicler Jean le Bel, those inhabitants who had remained behind were roughly handled when they tried to defend their property; some were killed out of hand, and several women were raped. It should be added that le Bel's statement is not supported by other evidence.[9]

Edward himself had refused to enter the town, assuming – rightly – that his troops would burn the town down around his ears and that he himself would be in some danger. While his own foragers made the stocks of food secure and his men loaded themselves with plunder, a curious and slightly touching ceremony was taking place. Suspended over the gateway into the town were three grisly relics, the skulls of Guillaume Bacon, Jean de la Roche-Tesson and Richard de Percy, the three friends of Godefroi d'Harcourt who had espoused his cause in the revolt of 1343. They had been arrested and taken to Paris, tried and beheaded, and their heads returned to Normandy and hung over the gate at St-Lô as a warning to other rebels. Now the skulls were taken down and given a solemn burial. This might be seen as a piece of English propaganda, but no English participant in the campaign mentions it, not even Edward himself. It is more likely that this was a private matter, arranged perhaps by Harcourt as a tribute to his friends.[10] If so, it cannot have improved his mood; as the campaign went on, the lame Norman seemed to be growing more and more bitter and destructive.

Still camped outside the walls at St-Lô, the royal household ate another fairly simple meal of cod, stockfish and salt salmon. Poultry was permitted on a Saturday, but none appears in the accounts, either because the wagons were still coming up from Pont-Hébert or because local stocks had been foraged. Again, the number of people being fed seems to have been less than usual, and only one cartload of firewood was needed instead of the usual two. Many of the household may have been involved in other affairs; some, indeed, may well have been taking part in the plundering. It seems highly unlikely that the rest of the army observed the dietary requirements of the day, gorging themselves instead on looted food and wine. Although the king's foragers probably managed to save some of the thousand barrels of wine for themselves, there were probably quite a few sore heads in the English army on Sunday morning.

* * *

That night, Robert Bertrand and his men halted at Cormolain, fourteen miles to the east. They had been joined by the Constable, the Comte d'Eu, who had ridden forward from Caen with a small escort to see the situation for himself, and possibly also to order Bertrand back to Caen.[11] The old marshal had done all that he could. Nine days had elapsed since his message had arrived at Caen, time surely for the defence to have been organised and reinforcements to have arrived from Rouen and Harfleur. Now he was needed in Caen to help defend the city from the attack that must surely come. He had been unable to stop the advancing English, or to save the rich towns of the Cotentin, but he had delayed the invaders for a day at Carentan and another at Pont-Hébert, and had successfully deflected Edward from the direct route to Caen. He had acted with great resolution and skill, and if a few more of King Philippe's commanders had behaved equally well, the story of 1346 might have been rather different.[12]

Philippe himself was finally on the move. Leaving the Bois de Vincennes, he returned to Paris, where it may be presumed he spent the night.[13] On the following day he went to St-Denis, just north of the city, where in a solemn ceremony he received the Oriflamme, the semi-sacred standard of France which legend said had been given by angels to the emperor Charlemagne. The real banner was far too precious to take on campaign, so what Philippe received and gave into the care of his standard-bearer, Miles de Noyers, was one of several replicas.[14] This piece of symbolism announced publicly that the king himself was now taking the field against his enemies. Orders were sent out to raise troops in Normandy and Picardy, mustering at Rouen and Amiens respectively. Philippe also wrote to his ally King David of Scotland, suggesting that with so many English troops in France, the English border might have been stripped of many of its garrisons; now might be the time for a Scots invasion of England.[15] The Scots, however, knew differently; earlier in the summer they had raided into the northern counties of England, and had received a warm reception from the defenders under the command of Henry, Lord Percy and Sir Ralph Neville. At the end of July, so far from following Philippe's wishes, they agreed a three-month truce with England.

Philippe's plan was to move down the Seine and take charge of the forces gathering at Rouen, from where he could turn either west or north to deal with whichever threat seemed most significant. But, again, he seems to have hesitated. By the 25th he had progressed no further than St-Germain-en-Laye, only a few miles west of Paris (see Map 4), and by the end of the month was halted at Vernon on the south bank of the Seine.[16] We may assume that he was trying to raise troops, and money, as he went along, but this is still a curiously slow progress for a man whose kingdom was now threatened with invasion from two sides.

Sunday 23 July

Initially, at least, Edward and his commanders were deceived into thinking that Bertrand had continued his retreat to the south. They had received word of the arrival of the Constable of France and Tancarville at Caen, but do not appear to have been unduly disturbed, and continued to see Bertrand as their primary target. Accordingly, at dawn on Sunday the trumpets blew and the army, hangovers and all, prepared to march south to Torigni-sur-Vire. An advance party of men-at-arms and hobelars under the experienced commander Thomas Holland set out for Torigni, eight miles from St-Lô. Following the track of what is now the N174, Holland and his men crossed a rolling plain occasionally cut across with watercourses running down to the deep valley of the Vire to the west, and later in the morning came out on the high ground overlooking Torigni from the north. The little town, dominated by its large Cistercian abbey, was undefended and there was no sign of the enemy.

Torigni had been designated as the halting place for that night, and Holland's men occupied the town and began reserving houses as quarters for the commanders and senior nobles. They were midway through this work when news came from the north. The enemy had been located, and was retreating not south but east, towards Caen. Holland was ordered to rejoin the main army. Setting fire to Torigni, his men then withdrew to the north-east, some of his horsemen slipping away to indulge in further pillaging and arson and straggling in to join the main army somewhat later than Holland. Detached scouting expeditions like this were good opportunities for men in search of plunder, as they could work over ground that had been untouched by their fellows and get first pick of any loot that was available.

The intelligence of Bertrand and d'Eu's retreat to the east must have reached Edward early in the day, before the main army began to march. He now ordered a change of direction, and the army turned east. There are several roads leading east out of St-Lô: one runs north-easterly towards Cérisy-la-Fôret and Bayeux, while another divides soon after leaving St-Lô, with one road leading to Cormolain and another following a more southerly route through St Jean-des-Baisants and Vidouville towards Caumont. It was in this direction that Bertrand and d'Eu had withdrawn, and the English accordingly set off in pursuit.

There followed another long march, of twelve miles at least, and longer for Holland's contingent. Edward clearly wanted to catch up with the enemy force retreating from St-Lô, and it is possible that once again he was overestimating the size of the enemy force. Certainly Bertrand's little contingent was easily able to outdistance the English, and by the time the leading English troops reached Cormolain, Bertrand was riding into Caen. There he was reunited with his brother Guillaume, the Bishop of Bayeux, and, with the Constable and the other senior commanders, set about preparing the defence of the city.

There is, unusually, some confusion as to where the English actually halted for the night. The primary journal of the campaign, the *Acta Bellicosa*, puts the English night halt at Cormolain, indicating the northerly route, while the accounts of the royal kitchen, which scrupulously record the name of each place where it halted for the night, give a name which Alfred Burne translates as Sept-Vents, a mile south-west of Caumont.[17] There are several arguments to be advanced in favour of the northerly route. First, it is a much more level road, proceeding for most of the first ten miles across a flat plain, then descending to the crossing of the Drôme, a shallow, muddy stream which could probably have been forded without much difficulty, and then up a long gentle hill to Cormolain half a mile away. The southern route is much more hilly and would have offered more difficult passage for the wagons. Second, the Drôme offers a source of water for men and horses, while Sept-Vents is on high ground and water, though present, is less plentiful. Finally, the English believed that Bertrand had taken the northern route, and, indeed, knew that he had spent the previous night at Cormolain, a day ahead of them.

It is possible, of course, that the army was divided and different divisions followed both roads, and it is this explanation that Alfred Burne prefers.[18] That still makes Sept-Vents an unlikely night halt, as the divisions of the army would have been separated by about four miles over uneven ground. This is a much larger separation than was employed at any other time, and would have made it difficult for either division to come to the other's aid in the event of an attack; and even though an attack was considered very unlikely, caution and common sense both dictated that the rules of war be followed. An alternative explanation is that Sept-Vents is really Haut-Vents, about a mile east of Cormolain, but this cannot be verified.[19]

The past three days had seen the army cover more than thirty miles and take and loot a sizeable town. Some of that loot was now being consumed, and of the food eaten by the royal household that night, six head of cattle and two deer are listed as *depreda*, meaning plundered or stolen. However, six sheep, which were also slaughtered and eaten, have recorded values and thus were not plundered, as was a quarter of coal used to supplement firewood. The rest of the meal consisted of a variety of poultry, including geese, chickens, partridges, plovers, a heron and a spoonbill, all presumably taken from the poultry cages still travelling with the army, and 400 eggs are also listed. Fatigue was now beginning to set in; the horses, which had been cooped up at sea for two weeks and then ridden almost continuously for six days, must have been suffering particularly.

Monday 24 July

Accordingly, the march on Monday was a short one, only about five miles. Having failed in his immediate objective of catching Bertrand and the Constable and their force, Edward now resolved to advance on Caen slowly and deliberately, making sure of his quarry. He now ordered that Cormolain, described as a small town but probably no more than a large village, should be 'set alight, so that their enemies would know their intentions', as the author of the *Acta Bellicosa* put it.[20] Although this was apparently in violation of his own edict, Edward now had sound military reasons for this act. The smoke of burning towns and villages in the west would cause people living further east to abandon their homes and make for the nearest shelter, which was Caen. The presence of panic-stricken refugees – and the sight of smoke on the western horizon, for Cormolain was less than twenty-five miles from Caen – would be bound to prey on the nerves of the defenders, who themselves may not have known the strength of Edward's force.

Not all the locals had fled, however. One group of archers had taken shelter for the night in a building near Cormolain, and early in the morning they were discovered by some locals, who blocked up the entrances to the building and set fire to it. All the English troops inside were suffocated and died.[21] Acts of resistance like this are seldom mentioned in the sources, and were probably few, but it is certain that the population of Normandy, far from welcoming the English and seeing them as liberators, were beginning to develop an active hatred of them.

East from Cormolain, following roughly the modern D31, the road runs over mostly level ground, along a wide ridge with ground sloping away to both north and south and offering good visibility. After about four miles the road then descends to cross another small river, the Aure, at Pont Mulot and then climbs up onto the higher ground to the east to the village of Torteval. This offered a good place to make camp, with easy access to water from the Aure, and the main body and the baggage stopped here. The vanguard division under the Prince of Wales pushed a little further on to the next village, St-Germain d'Ectot, a little over a mile to the southeast and on high ground that slopes away sharply to the east and south; the position commands an excellent view over the surrounding countryside. There was water here too, a small stream and ponds on the western slope of the hill. This set the pattern of many future night halts; the main body encamped in one location, close to water and other necessary resources, the vanguard a little distance away, screening the main force but close enough to be quickly reinforced if attacked.

The shortness of this march has puzzled some modern historians, who wonder at Edward's apparent slowness.[22] There are several possible explanations. Fatigue, alluded to above, is one of them; Edward could expect a hard fight when he reached Caen, and both men and horses needed to be in condition. Lack of intelligence about the enemy was another issue; it could be assumed that the enemy would choose to defend Caen, but that did not preclude possible ambushes at points such as river crossings in the meantime, and Edward could not know the slenderness of the forces at Eu's disposal, or the dissension among the commanders that was already beginning to emerge. Lieutenant-Colonel Burne also suggests that Edward was waiting for the fleet, which was slowly progressing along the coast to the north. The assault on Caen was to be a combined one, from both land and sea, and Edward needed to know his ships were in position in the estuary of the Orne before launching his attack from the landward side.

The fleet was making slow progress, but not because of enemy opposition. Rather, and again at Edward's deliberate orders, Huntingdon and his squadrons were devastating the coast, burning harbours and ships and sending parties ashore to spread havoc as much as two or three miles inland.[23] Along the short stretch of coastline between the mouth of the Douve at Carentan and the little port of Ouistreham at the mouth of the Orne, Huntingdon's men destroyed sixty-one French and allied warships, thirty-two fishing vessels and twenty-one smaller vessels of around 30 tons displacement.[24] The little ports of the region, such as Arromanches, Courseulles and Ouistreham itself, were all burned and pillaged. Once again, this was a deliberate act of war. Many times in the past, these same Norman ports had sent out ships to attack the south coast of England. Now, Edward's intent was clearly to break the power of the Norman raiders and ensure that future attacks were curtailed.

The destruction of the ships was even more important than the destruction of houses. Many of the houses of the region west of Caen were made of cob; fire would destroy their roofs and contents, but the houses themselves could be fairly quickly rendered habitable again (in summer, with the harvest coming, there would have been no shortage of straw for re-thatching). But ships were costly and took time to build. Whatever one may think today of the actions of Huntingdon's men, they bought at least a few years peace for the coastal towns of Kent and Sussex and Hampshire.

But Caen remained the primary objective, and it was towards Caen that Edward was now concentrating his forces. The coast was about twenty miles north of Torteval, and scouts riding north from the main army could track the fleet's progress by the smoke of burning; and it is probable that the scouts made contact with Huntingdon's landing parties, thus enabling some coordination of the movements of the army and the fleet. So Edward slowed his advance, waiting until Huntingdon was ready to advance into the Orne. The bulk of the household dined that night on salt cod – fifty-two were consumed – stockfish and salt salmon. However, there were fresh fish to be had as well, probably from the nearby Aure, and the royal fishermen were paid 14*d.* for catching and carrying four pike, two carp and three tench. These, we can safely assume, were eaten by the king himself and his closest associates. The fish themselves were almost certainly larger than modern specimens, and would have made a welcome change from the usual diet.

Tuesday 25 July

On Tuesday the main body covered a little over eight miles, moving down the road to Caen and still following a wide ridge with good visibility to north and south. Once again the army moved deliberately and with caution, the Prince of Wales's division a little in front, and once again they burned each village and town through which they passed. Every day, says Michael Northburgh, raiding parties rode out from the main body, burning and destroying across a front of several miles.[25] Very deliberately, Edward was turning the screw on the defenders of Caen, and now he decided to give it one more twist. An emissary was sent to Caen, summoning the defenders to surrender.

For this role, Edward chose one of his own staff, the Augustinian canon Geoffrey of Maldon. Using clerics as emissaries between armies in wartime was not uncommon, in the days before heralds routinely took over this role, and it was to be hoped that Brother Geoffrey's habit and tonsure would prevent the enemy from maltreating him. Bearing Edward's summons, the emissary set off for Caen ten miles away, while the main body of the army crossed the river Seulles near Tilly and made camp around Fontenay-le-Pesnil. This was a sizeable village with a small Cistercian abbey and a large church dedicated to St Martin, which provided accommodation, and a number of large ponds which provided water for men and animals (these ponds are still a feature of the village).

The Prince of Wales's division had already crossed and moved up onto the high ground at Cheux, about two miles further on. Here they enjoyed a commanding position, looking out over the plain towards Caen eight miles away, and could both screen the army from potential attack and prevent enemy reconnaissance parties from estimating the size of the total force; not that the enemy were, by this time, in any fit state to attempt either. The Prince's men took over the church of St-Vigor and the big tithe barns owned by the abbey of St-Wandrille in Caen. These buildings, or rather their reconstructions, can still be seen; little else of medieval Cheux exists, the village having been almost completely levelled in July 1944 when the 2nd Glasgow Highlanders took the town from the 12th SS Panzer Division. The royal foragers had been active during the day, and the household, anticipating battle on the morrow, sat down to a full meal of plundered beef, mutton and venison; the Kitchen Account records the consumption of nine carcasses of beef, two deer and eighteen mutton, of which all but five of the sheep had been stolen. Fourteen geese, seventy-five chickens of various descriptions, 400 eggs and twenty-four gallons of milk were also included. Out in the fields around Fontenay and Cheux the foot soldiers, themselves undoubtedly well fed on plundered meat along with their bread and pease porridge and onions, cleaned their swords and knives and checked the fletchings on their arrows, everyone aware that the morning would bring battle.

Meanwhile, Geoffrey of Maldon had reached Caen. Upon arrival he was taken to the castle and appeared before the commanders, where he delivered his ultimatum. If Caen surrendered, the population would not be molested: all could keep their goods, and no one would be harmed. Resist, and the city would be sacked, according to the customs of war. Such ultimata were again perfectly common practice for the time, and it was not unknown for cities to negotiate a surrender with opposing armies on terms which spared the lives and property of the inhabitants. But there could be no question of surrender at Caen. The military commanders had resolved to fight, and in this they were supported by the redoubtable Bishop of Bayeux. The latter, incensed enough by the devastation of his diocese and the presence of his old enemy Godefroi d'Harcourt in the English ranks, now flew into a rage. Seizing the letter from Brother Geoffrey, he tore it into pieces, and then, showing no respect for his fellow clergyman, ordered the unfortunate monk to be thrown into the castle's prison.

This was a clear violation of the customs of war; unarmed emissaries were supposed to be respected, particularly if they were clergy, and by rights Geoffrey of Maldon should have been allowed to return to the English army. If anyone disputed the bishop's action, however, there is no record of it. The other commanders had problems of their own. The Constable, Bertrand and Tancarville were resolved to fight, but the burgesses of Caen, watching the sun go down through a haze of smoke and then seeing the western sky glowing with reflected flames at night, were not so sanguine. They were particularly perturbed when Eu made it known that he did not plan to defend the city itself, but rather to withdraw the whole of his force into the castle and conduct the defence from there. This was tantamount to sacrificing the city, which was not only home to thousands of people but also the place of refuge of hundreds of others who had fled from the villages and farms to the west. The young Constable, facing the first real test of his military career and aware by now that he was badly outnumbered, was begged to defend the town.

Caen, the second city of Normandy, was large and prosperous but virtually indefensible. Its population was estimated by King Edward himself at 30,000, and although this is probably an exaggeration, Michael Northburgh's view that Caen was larger than any English city apart from London is likely to have been correct.[26] It lies at the confluence of two rivers, the Orne and the Odon, a few miles from the sea, which can be reached easily down the broad estuary of the Orne. The Odon itself is divided into several channels, the Grande Odon, the Petite Odon and the Noë, which finally merge just before the confluence with the Orne (see Map 3). The area is low-lying and marshy, and in ordinary times, just as at Carentan, these marshes formed part of the natural defences of the city. But it had been a dry summer, and the river levels were probably low, with the marshes themselves drier than usual.

The old town, the Bourg-le-Roi, lay to the west of the castle, a massive fortification which had been greatly expanded by William the Conqueror and kept in good repair since. The castle had its own wells, and its storehouses could hold enough food to enable a garrison to withstand a lengthy siege. The castle lies a few hundred yards to the north of the Grande Odon, overlooking the big church of St-Pierre and, just beyond it, the main bridge crossing the Odon onto the Isle St-Jean. The Odon has been drained and paved over, but its course can still be followed west from the modern boat basin along the boulevard des Allies and then the boulevard Marshal Leclerc.

To the west of the castle and north of the Grande Odon lay the old town's great markets, the Halle du Blé, the Halle aux Draps, the Halle aux

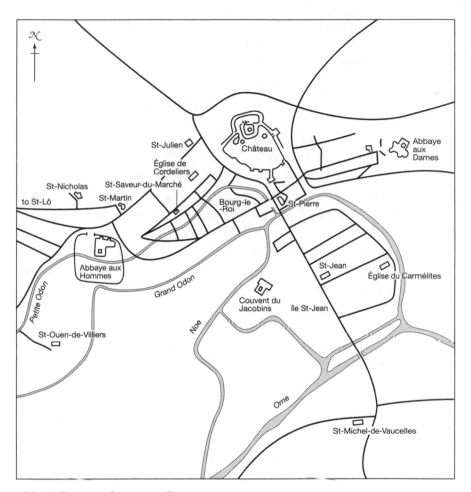

Map 3 Fourteenth-century Caen.

Laines and the Halle de Tanneurs. There were a number of fishponds and wells just under the western walls of the castle, along the line of the present rue de Gèole; these provided amenities for the city, and helped to drain the low-lying ground on which it was built. Further west the old buildings crowded tightly around churches such as Notre-Dame de Froiderie, still to be found on the modern Place Bouchard, and St-Sauveur-du-Marché a little to the west. Along the banks of the Grande Odon were concentrated many of the town's industries, including tanneries, fulling mills and butchers, the latter in the district of La Boucherie between Notre-Dame de Froiderie and the river. A smaller stream, the Petite Odon, flowed through the middle of the old town, joining the main channel just above St-Pierre. The Bourg-le-Roi had in the past been fortified, but its walls were now in bad repair, being in some places no more than a wooden palisade behind a moat. Such stone fortifications as existed were mostly on the south and east. These had not been well maintained and could not be held for long against a determined assault.[27]

When the city grew, it expanded to the south across the Odon. The Isle St-Jean was surrounded on three sides by channels of the Grande Odon and the Noë, and on the south side by the broad stream of the Orne, and was protected still further on the west by the marshes known as La Prairie. Here, away from the crowding and smells of the old town, the wealthy of Caen had chosen to make their homes. It was bisected from north to south by the rue de St-Jean, running from the bridge and gate of St-Pierre in the north down to the bridge over the Orne in the south, the Pont Millet. From here, roads ran away to the south towards Falaise and east to Lisieux and Rouen. St-Jean too was poorly fortified with wooden palisades, the inhabitants trusting to the rivers and marshes to protect them from attack.[28]

The St-Jean district could be reached from the Bourg-le-Roi in one of two ways. The main approach was across the bridge of St-Pierre, which spanned the Odon just west of the church of that name and led on to the district's main street, the rue de St-Jean. The bridge supported several houses along its span, and was fortified with two stone towers at the southern end. This was the only major fortification in the St-Jean district, and was potentially a strong defensive position. The second entrance was from the district of La Boucherie to the west, from whence a small gate gave access to the river. Either a ford or, more likely, a small bridge gave access to the marshes of La Prairie. A few hundred yards away across the marshes there was another bridge or ford over the Noë, and a 'back door' entrance into St-Jean not far from the church and convent of the Jacobins.

The third section of the city was the suburb of Bourg-l'Abbé, which had grown up outside the western walls. Its centrepiece was, and is, the great abbey of St-Etienne, also commonly known as the Abbaye aux Hommes, founded by William the Conqueror as an act of penance for his marriage to Queen Matilda within the grounds of consanguinuity; the Conqueror himself still lies buried before the high altar of the abbey church. Around St-Etienne there had grown up a sizeable community, including a separate church, St-Nicholas, and several streets of houses including the rue de Bretagne and the rue Neuve Bourg l'Abbé. Another notable feature near the abbey was the palace of the Logis du Roi, built in the first quarter of the fourteenth century.[29] Here, as in St-Jean, the density of building was lower, and the houses were built on burgage plots, that is, with long narrow strips of land running to the rear of each property. This was a well-established suburb with its own fountains and wells, bisected by the main road that runs west to St-Lô and ultimately to Brittany.

Although St-Etienne had originally been founded at some distance from the castle and the heart of the old town, with time the two districts, Bourg-l'Abbé and the Bourg-le-Roi, had grown almost together, with only a small amount of open ground between them. Unlike the Bourg-le-Roi, however, the Bourg-l'Abbé had never been fortified. There may have been some fortifications around the abbey of St-Etienne itself, but if so nothing is known of these.[30] Modern scholars of medieval Caen have commented that so little faith was placed in the fortifications around the abbey that it was evacuated before the arrival of the English king.[31]

A final feature of the city was the abbey of La Trinité, or the Abbaye aux Dames, on the high ground to the east of the castle and overlooking the city. This had been founded by Queen Matilda as her part of the penance, and she too lay buried before its high altar. It was a large and wealthy establishment, with about 120 nuns.[32] The abbey lay among gardens and orchards, although a small unwalled faubourg with a parish church had grown up on the hillside leading from the abbey down to the castle. Although it gave a commanding view over the castle and the city, La Trinité was unfortified and indefensible.

It was this large, complex and poorly fortified city that Raoul de Brienne, Comte d'Eu, had chosen to defend. In truth he had few options; Caen was the second city of Normandy, and sooner or later some attempt had to be made to stop the marauding English. And in the powerful castle he had a strong asset. Its storerooms were now well-stocked thanks to the efforts of Bishop Guillaume, and its deep fosses – probably partly flooded – and strong walls and defensive towers were impregnable against anything but heavy siege engines. Eu himself reckoned the castle could hold out for at least forty days, more than enough time for a relief force to arrive from the east.

With the men he had brought from Harfleur, Robert Bertrand's little band and the crossbowmen and others gathered by the Bishop, Eu had about 4,000 men under his command.[33] This was too few to attempt anything like a comprehensive defence of the entire city. The logical move was to withdraw the whole force into the castle and allow Edward to occupy the city. This would be pillaged and probably burnt – especially since the choleric bishop had torn up the summons of surrender – which would be hard on the townspeople but would preserve Eu's force intact. The English king would then have two choices. He could besiege the castle, which would take time, or he could simply bypass the place and move on, in which case Eu would then be able to move freely in the English rear areas, reconquering territory the English had already passed through and mopping up any garrisons that might have been left behind. Eu was prepared to gamble that Edward would not take this risk, and would try to attack or besiege the castle. Preparations were put in hand: the two abbeys were abandoned, their monks and nuns evacuated, and so were the two northern districts of the city, Bourg-l'Abbé and Bourg-le-Roi.

At this point came the fatal error. The inhabitants of Isle St-Jean, among the wealthiest of the city, were unwilling to see their homes burned and their valuables pillaged. They begged Eu to mount a defence of the island. Protected as it was by rivers and marshes, the district was only really vulnerable to attack from the north, across the Odon, and the main bridge of St-Pierre was well protected and fortified. Probably against his better judgement, Eu allowed himself to be persuaded and, over the objections of the Bertrand brothers, ordered the bulk of his force out of the castle and into positions on St-Jean. He himself, with Tancarville and the other senior nobles, Friquet de Fricamps, Jean de Coubray, Philippe de Pons and Alerin de Brimeux, took up positions on the Isle St-Jean at the southern end of the bridge with a strong force of men-at-arms and foot soldiers. The stone towers were garrisoned and the bridge itself was blocked with a heavy barricade. Thirty boats were brought up the Odon and moored or anchored in the stream to the east of the bridge, where the river was somewhat wider; these were filled with Genoese crossbowmen, who would cover the bridge and the north bank around the church of St-Pierre. The castle remained garrisoned by two hundred men-at-arms and a further hundred crossbowmen, under the command of the Bertrand brothers. These two redoubtable figures, having had their advice rejected, seem to have decided to have nothing to do with the foolish attempt to defend St-Jean.

For folly it undoubtedly was. Eu should have closed his ears to the pleas of the burgesses, and listened to the marshal and the bishop. His force, outnumbered nearly four to one, could not hope to hold the ramshackle defences of St-Jean against a determined assault. The water levels in the marshes and rivers, on which the inhabitants placed such faith, were low, for it had been a dry summer.[34] Even worse, low tide the following day would come in the middle of the morning, very near the time the English would attack. Even the deepest channels of the Odon could be easily forded by the lightly armed foot soldiers which constituted the bulk of the English army.

And, piling error on error, Eu seems to have made no attempt to defend the 'side entrance' to the Isle St-Jean from La Boucherie. Indeed, he may not even have been aware of it. He had marched the bulk of his small army out of an impregnable position and into one which was highly vulnerable, facing an overwhelmingly superior force. It was a decision that would cost France very dearly, and would ultimately cost the Constable his life.

Wednesday 26 July

The morning of the 26th in Caen was tense, and a curious little act on the part of King Philippe of France may have made things even worse. One of the last messengers to arrive in Caen before the battle brought letters from King Philippe, appointing Jean de Melun, Comte de Tancarville, a marshal of France. The purpose of this appointment is difficult to determine; already present with this force were the Constable of France and a veteran marshal, Robert Bertrand. Appointing yet another senior commander in a force of 4,000 makes little sense; unless Philippe had doubts about those commanders already present. Was Robert Bertrand's failure to stop the English in the Cotentin being held against him, and Tancarville's appointment thus an effective demotion of the former? If so, it might help to explain his actions over the days to come. Or was Philippe already having suspicions of his Constable? The elder Raoul de Brienne had been a loyal officer, but the son was an unknown quantity. The young Comte d'Eu had as yet given no overt sign of disloyalty, but Philippe, who was prepared to see treason at every corner in any case, may well have wanted one of his most trusted officials (Tancarville was also a royal chamberlain) on hand to keep watch over him. This cannot have done much to ease the mind of the Constable as he prepared to fight the most important battle of his military career.

At dawn on the 26th, says the author of the *Acta Bellicosa*, the trumpets sounded and the English army began to advance rapidly.[35] No breakfast was eaten; that could wait until they reached Caen. The failure of Geoffrey of Maldon to return from his mission was confirmation that Caen was intending to resist. The plan of battle had been worked out the previous evening, and now in the early morning the three divisions of the army began to move. Up on the high ground at Cheux, the men of the Prince of Wales's division set fire to the village; the defenders of Caen could clearly see the flames eight miles away. Then more fires were seen, closer now, as the oncoming English deliberately fired every building they passed. The signal was clear; if Caen intended to resist, then the English were equally resolved to attack.

The Prince's division led the way, angling gradually across the main line of march and sweeping across the open plain which is now occupied by Caen airport and the industrial districts of Carpiquet, then past the Premonstratensian abbey of Ardennes, which they also burned, before moving down on the city from the north. Their march covered ten or eleven miles and they moved quickly; the day was still young when the Prince and Warwick and their men moved down towards the northern outskirts of Bourg-le-Roi. Some elements moved up onto the high ground to the east and seized the abandoned abbey of La Trinité. The commanders had also embarked on a deception to confuse the enemy as to their real numbers. Behind the vanguard came all the non-combatants of the army, wagon drivers and carters and grooms, marching together; these halted some way behind the vanguard, presumably giving the impression that they were a further division of troops massing for an assault. The author of *Acta Bellicosa* describes the army approaching in full panoply of war, helmets gleaming, lances raised and banners unfurled, moving deliberately and in full view of the defenders.

Meanwhile, the king's division had moved straight in from the west along the road from St-Lô. They found the Bourg-l'Abbé deserted and moved swiftly into the faubourg, occupying the abbey of St-Etienne and no doubt remarking, as Michael Northburgh did, on the tomb of William the Conqueror. The king himself took over the Logis du Roi as his head-quarters, and ordered a halt until the exact disposition of the enemy could be determined. The rearguard division under Hatfield and Arundel was moving up on the town further south, towards La Prairie.[36]

The army halted, and breakfast was ordered and cooking fires lit. It became apparent that the Bourg-le-Roi was deserted as well, and at around the hour of terce, about eight in the morning, the leading elements of the Prince of Wales's division entered the town from the north and began seizing supplies of food and drink.[37] They found the castle apparently strongly held, and the rich market halls still full of great stocks of goods. The more venturesome spirits in the vanguard began to wander still further in search of loot. The big church of St-Pierre must have acted like a magnet for them, despite the fact that its entrance was within crossbow range of the gatehouse of the castle. But on reaching St-Pierre, they also discovered that the bridge beyond it was heavily guarded, with a strong force holding the houses and towers and boats full of Genoese crossbowmen moored in the river. It was quite possibly the sniping of these latter at the pillagers that drew the English into combat. The sounds of fighting began to reverberate around the old town, and more English troops hurried to the scene.

This was expressly contrary to the king's wishes. As at St-Lô and on the march east, he did not intend to take risks. His men had already marched several miles without food, and they needed to be rested and fresh before commencing their assault; they also needed to know more about the enemy dispositions. His commanders were aware of this, and at the first sounds of fighting the Earl of Warwick, with a small party of men-at-arms, hurried forward towards the bridge.[38] But when he arrived at the bridge, Warwick found that his lightly armoured troops, fighting like tigers against the French men-at-arms, were not only holding their own but gaining the upper hand. Quickly appreciating the situation, Warwick disregarded his orders and led his little force straight into the attack.

The fighting that raged around the bridge was confused and bloody, and lasted for several hours. Initially Warwick could make little headway along the bridge itself. The houses on the bridge were set on fire, probably by the English seeking to use the smoke as cover, but the barricade and towers at the south end were resolutely defended by Eu and Tancarville, and despite fierce fighting at close quarters Warwick could not dislodge the defenders. Further east, English and Welsh archers dodged around the buttresses of St-Pierre and shot into the Genoese in their boats at close range; the latter replied with volleys of crossbow bolts. But the high rate of fire of the longbow quickly made itself felt, and though the archers were few in numbers, their arrows, as the *Grandes Chroniques* described it, fell thick as hail. Someone seems to have had the bright idea of using fire arrows, for at least two of the boats were set on fire. As the numbers of the crossbowmen diminished, Welsh foot soldiers began wading out into the river. This showed almost suicidal courage, for as they approached the boats the crossbowmen could scarcely miss, but the Welsh came on, covered by their own archers, and then began stabbing the men in the boats with their spears. The crews of several boats were slaughtered and the boats themselves captured, and the victorious Welsh began landing on the south bank of the Odon. The remaining Genoese either abandoned their boats or rowed them down the river and fled.[39]

Meanwhile, word of the battle at the bridge had reached the king in Bourg-l'Abbé. He immediately ordered his Constable, Northampton, to go forward and halt the fighting. Collecting a small troop of men-at-arms, including the royal steward, Richard Talbot, Northampton hurried towards the bridge on foot. By the time he arrived, more men-at-arms from the Prince of Wales's division had also arrived, including the veteran Thomas Holland and a knight of the Prince's own household, Thomas Daniel. These had in all probability been summoned by Warwick, urgently needing reinforcements. Warwick and Northampton quickly conferred, and Northampton endorsed the marshal's decision. The attack on the bridge was resumed, the English archers moving through the smoke and shooting clouds of arrows at any French face that showed itself, the men-at-arms rushing forward to engage the defenders of the barricade with spear and sword.

Even now the defence held out, and might have done so for some hours yet. There is little doubt that the French men-at-arms fought with great courage, even though their casualties, mostly from English arrows, were very heavy.[40] But now came the fatal moment. Other English soldiers, again mostly from the Prince's division, had found the postern gate at La Boucherie. Crossing the Grande Odon, they made their way across the marshes and, crossing the Noë, forced their way through the gate into St-Jean. Here they almost immediately encountered resistance, not from the French men-at-arms, but from the townspeople. These, seeing their defences beginning to crumble and knowing what their own fate was liable to be, took up arms and rushed into the attack. Women as well as men took part in the fighting; the *Grandes Chroniques* speaks of women helping to tear doors and window shutters from their hinges to use as shields in the fighting, and also carrying wine to the men to help them recover their strength.[41] Desperate though the resistance was, the burgesses of Caen armed with swords and wooden shutters were no match in terms of either weapons or skill for the English and Welsh archers and spearmen. Once again the fighting was very bloody, but the end was a foregone conclusion. Forcing their way through the defences, the English turned east towards the embattled bridge.

Now the resistance began to crumble. As Northampton and Warwick resumed their assault on the front of the French position, the troops that had crossed from La Boucherie attacked from the rear. Some of the French broke and ran; others, seeing the situation hopeless, began to surrender. Others fought to the end. The final resistance came in one of the towers at the south end of the bridge, where, choking on smoke and under a deluge of grey-feathered arrows, Eu and Tancarville were still holding out with about two dozen men-at-arms and some foot soldiers. The end was clearly at hand, and little could now be gained by continuing the resistance. Considering that he had done all that was consistent with honour, Eu began looking for an opportunity to surrender.

He found one in the guise of the one-eyed knight Thomas Holland. The two men knew each other; they had even campaigned together, crusading against the Lithuanians a few years previously, and had come to know and respect each other even though their countries were at war. They had met again at Algeçiras, on another crusade against the Moors. In these desperate circumstances, Holland could be regarded as a friend, some-one who would see Eu and his companions safe rather than slaughtered out of hand by the archers. Like most noblemen of his time, Eu regarded being killed by a commoner as a far worse fate than being killed by one of his own class.

A parley was called, and Eu agreed to surrender. Holland made sure to claim the Constable as his own prize, aware that a very considerable ransom could be extracted from him; old comrades they may have been, but Holland was a man on the make, with an expensive court case to fight, and he needed the money. Tancarville was taken into the custody of Thomas Daniel, the Prince of Wales's man. The remainder surrendered to other English knights: Jean de Coubray surrendered to William Kildesby, and Macio Choffin, Friquet de Fricamps and Jean de Grimbault were also taken.[42]

The surrender, however, did not mean that the fighting was over. Else-where in St-Jean, battles still raged, as the citizens, bolstered perhaps by a few men-at-arms and crossbowmen who had not yet fled, fought doggedly on in defence of their homes. The English foot soldiers, who having bro-ken the defences at the bridge were now inclined to run riot, encountered repeated dogged resistance from townspeople hurling stone benches, baulks of wood and other heavy objects from the upper floors. The English retaliated by slaughtering those who resisted, and men and women both perished in the fighting. Other English troops reached the Pont Millet over the Orne, at the south end of the Isle St-Jean, and launched a pursuit of the French troops who were fleeing across the fields, killing a number of them. Further destruction was caused by the arrival of Huntingdon's ships, which had been delayed by the low tide but now came sailing up the river and landed their own forces to join in the mopping up.

By nightfall the fighting was over. The streets of St-Jean and the banks of the Odon were littered with dead. English casualties had been relatively light; among the men-at-arms, one esquire had been mortally wounded in the fighting around the bridge, and died two days later. The ordinary soldiers, including the archers, had suffered more heavily in the fighting along the river and in the streets of St-Jean. Two of Warwick's archers, Richard Whet and Henry Torpoleye, were among the dead. The total of English dead and injured may have been around 500. The French had suffered far more heavily. The author of the *Acta Bellicosa* puts the French dead at 2,500 in the town, not counting those who were killed later in the pursuit across country; this figure may also not include the Genoese who died in the vicious fighting on the river, some of whose bodies would not have been recovered.[43] The *Chronique Normande* puts the figure a little lower, at 2,000,[44] but Bartholomew Burghersh estimates the total of dead and captured together at around 5,000.[45] The dead included two noblemen, Alerin de Brimeux and Philippe de Pons. The bodies, says Michael Northburgh, lay in the streets and houses and gardens where they fell, and had been stripped of armour and clothing by looters so that it was impossible to tell the knights and squires from the townspeople.[46] As well as Eu, Tancarville and the other names mentioned above, a further 250 men-at-arms had surrendered and a number of important burgesses had also been captured.[47] What remained of the 4,000 men that Eu had mustered that morning were now fleeing to the east, wrecked as a fighting force.

One small contingent still held out. In the castle of Caen, Robert Bertrand and his brother the Bishop of Bayeux had watched as the English, fighting without apparent plan or direction, had overwhelmed Eu's men through force of numbers and courage bordering on recklessness, as evidenced particularly in the fighting along the river. The unarmoured and lightly armed English foot soldiers had shown themselves willing to take on heavily armoured French men-at-arms, trusting in their own courage and the power of the longbows to carry the day. They had watched the tragedy unfold, and had made no move to intervene. This has scandalised some chroniclers and later historians, French and English alike, who felt that the Bertrands abandoned Eu and his men to their fate. But the 300 men of the garrison would have made little difference to the result of the battle, except to risk the castle being captured as well. Their feelings that morning and afternoon can be imagined; but they had kept the vital castle safe, and although their force was terribly reduced, they still had the capacity to be a thorn in Edward's side.

Dusk fell in Caen, lit by the flames of the houses still burning on the bridge; these continued to burn thoughout the night.[48] The king's household settled down in the Logis du Roi and nearby buildings around St-Etienne, and the prince's household likewise settled in buildings around La Trinité, most of the rest of the army probably finding billets in the houses between. A watch was kept on the castle in case the garrison should attempt a sortie, and the victorious army went to its dinner. Wednesday being a fast day, the two households dined on cod, salt salmon, stockfish and eels, with eggs and cheese. A gallon of pickles, rather more than usual, accompanied the dishes; an unusually large quantity of garlic was also consumed, about four times more than usual. Order was gradually restored, and the king was forced to repeat his proclamation forbidding violence to women, children and the religious, and also prohibiting the pillage of churches and other religious establishments, on pain of life or limb.[49] Notably, however, the houses of the burgesses and the markets of the town were not protected. Caen had resisted when it had been ordered to surrender, and so Caen would pay the price. French historians sometimes repeat the legend recounted by Froissart, that when the king learned the scale of his own losses and that the burgesses of the town had been actively involved in fighting, he had threatened to put the entire population to the sword, but was dissuaded from this by Godefroi d'Harcourt.[50] This seems very unlikely – the reverse situation, with Harcourt wishing to destroy the city and the king forbidding it, seems more plausible – but there is little doubt that the king intended that the city should be thoroughly pillaged of all its valuable goods. This would, he hoped, serve several objects: it would enrich the army and the king himself, it would provide an outlet for the energies of his men, and it would teach the citizens not to resist him in future.

The first phase of the campaign was now over, and so far events had gone decisively Edward's way. All his immediate objectives had been achieved. Much of Lower Normandy had been overrun, and Caen, a major city, had been taken. The French army in the field had been destroyed and its commanders taken prisoner. Immense damage had been done to the ports of the region, and well over a hundred ships – ships which had been raiding English shipping and towns – had been destroyed. Casualties had so far been light. There had been disappointments, the chief of which was the failure of the Normans to rally to Edward's cause and recognise him as king. If his aim had been to conquer and annex Normandy, then he must have been beginning to realise the impossibility of this, at least with the forces currently at his disposal and without support from local lords. Another minor problem was the failure to take the castle at Caen, a failure which was to have ramifications. But on the whole, the king and his commanders could look back on the first two weeks of the campaign with real satisfaction. It would have been hard not to agree with Bartholomew Burghersh, who wrote to the Archbishop of Canterbury, John Stratford: 'so that praised be Our Lord! Our business hath gone hitherto as favourably as it could.'[51] The next two weeks, however, would be rather more difficult.

Notes

1 *Grandes Chroniques*, vol. 9, p. 273; translation in Rogers (ed.), *The Wars of Edward III*, p. 124.

2 Rogers, *War Cruel and Sharp*, p. 244, notes that the garrison were referred to as 'partisans anglais'.

3 *Acta Bellicosa*, p. 30, says that the army crossed four bridges and followed a narrow causeway over these marshes. There are patches of higher ground among the marshes and flanking parties could probably pass along these, but the main body, and the wagons, would have been confined to the main road.

4 A longer than usual march, says the *Acta Bellicosa*, p. 30.

5 Ibid.

6 *Acta Bellicosa*, pp. 30–1. The reason for his knighting is not given.

7 It was St-Lô's fate to be often in the path of invading armies. In 1944, 95 per cent of its houses were destroyed by Allied aerial bombardment during the Battle of Normandy.

8 Generations of neglect had taken their toll of the fortifications of many of the towns of lower Normandy, including Caen. Cherbourg, frequently the target of English raids, and Carentan seem to have been exceptions to this rule. St-Lô is often described as heavily fortified, and certainly it had been once, but local sources indicate that many of the key gates and towers were in poor condition in the mid-fourteenth century and were not strengthened until later in the war.

9 Northburgh states that the inhabitants had fled before the English approach, and that the town was empty when they arrived, and most accounts follow this (pp. 358 and 360). Le Bel's account, if true, is likely to be exaggerated; he also states that some burgesses of the town were taken to England for ransom, but there is no corroboration of this (vol. 2, pp. 83–4).

10 *Grandes Chroniques*, vol. 9, pp. 271–2.

11 Eu's presence at St-Lô was noted by *Acta Bellicosa*, p. 31. The small size of his force is inferred; there would have been time for a small mounted party to reach St-Lô from Caen, but not for a major contingent of foot soldiers. Viard, 'Le Campagne de juillet–août et la bataille de Crécy', *Le Moyen Age* (1926), pp. 16–17, is sceptical as to whether the Constable reached St-Lô at all.

12 Sumption's (p. 501) comment that Bertrand's retreat 'went badly from the beginning' is unfair. It is hard to see how he could have done more with the meagre forces under his command, and the two or three days time he had gained for the defenders of Caen might have made all the difference; that they did not, cannot be blamed on the marshal.

13 Viard, 'Itineraire'.

14 Philippe Contamine, *Guerre, état et société à la fin du Moyen Âge*, Paris, 1972, pp. 670–3.

15 Walter of Hemingburgh, *Chronicon*, ed. H.C. Hamilton, London, 1948–9, vol. 2, p. 422; noted by Sumption, pp. 503–4.

16 Viard, 'Itineraire'.

17 *Acta Bellicosa*, p. 31; Kitchen Account, PRO E101/390/11; Burne, p. 143.

18 Burne, p. 143.

19 Some French sources, notably Denifle, mistakenly assert that the English army travelled by way of Cérisy-la-Fôret: P. Henri Denifle, *La Guerre de Cent Ans et la désolation des églises, monastères et hôpitaux en France*, Paris, 1899, p. 37.

20 *Acta Bellicosa*, p. 31.

21 Ibid.

22 Burne, p. 143.

23 Northburgh, in Barber, *Life and Campaigns*, pp. 16–17.

24 Ibid., p. 17.

25 Northburgh says fifteen or twenty miles, which sounds unlikely unless he was also including the zone of devastation being caused by the fleet to the north.

26 Letters of Edward III in Barber, *Life and Campaigns*, p. 21; Northburgh, pp. 358 and 360–1.

27 The Tour le Roy on boulevard des Allies is a later building, but was probably built on the site of the original fortifications facing onto the Odon.

28 There is no archaeological evidence of fortifications until after 1346, but palisades are mentioned by some contemporary sources: Christophes Collet, Pascal Leroux and Jean-Yves Marin, *Caen, cité médiévale, bilan d'archeologie et d'histoire*, Caen, 1995. Much of the foregoing description of fourteenth-century Caen is taken from this work.

29 This was a large building, 47 metres long and 12 metres wide; Collet *et al.*, p. 161.

30 Ibid., p. 153.

31 Ibid., p. 72.

32 Froissart, pp. 407, 409 and 414.

33 Evidence on this point is confusing. King Edward later believed he had faced about 1,600 men-at-arms, but did not count the crossbowmen and other foot soldiers. Michael Northburgh thought there were rather fewer men-at-arms. Among modern historians, Barber, *Life and Campaigns*, p. 54 and Rogers, *War Cruel and Sharp*, p. 246 adopt the figure of 4,000, while Sumption, p. 507, as ever more cautious when it comes to numbers, suggests the garrison may have been as few as 1,500. This latter seems unlikely, given estimates of French casualties.

34 Sumption, p. 509; Viard, 'Le Campagne de juillet–août', p. 23.

35 *Acta Bellicosa*, p. 31. Dawn would have come early; first light would have been around 4 a.m. Greenwich Mean Time.

36 This division of the army into four units – the three fighting divisions and the 'mock' division of non-combatants – becomes somewhat garbled in the reporting. The *Grandes Chroniques* says that the town was assailed at four points, while the *Acta Bellicosa*, having given quite a clear picture of events, then

37 *Acta Bellicosa*, p. 32. Terce is mid-morning, midway between dawn and noon; Barber translates terce as about 8 a.m., which seems reasonable. Northburgh, p. 16, says the king only arrived at nones, or midday, but this may be a confusion; it is possible that the king did not enter the city proper, the Bourg-le-Roi, until midday, which would be consistent with the orders he had given.

38 This was a confused battle, and contemporary accounts reflect this. *Acta Bellicosa*, p. 32, says that Warwick deliberately set out to assault the bridge, but Warwick's comrade in arms Bartholomew Burghersh, in Avesbury, p. 17, says that Warwick went forward initially to stop the fighting.

39 *Acta Bellicosa*, p. 33.

40 Jean le Bel accuses the French men-at-arms of fleeing at the approach of the English, but other French sources, and all the English sources, testify to the doggedness of the resistance.

41 *Grandes Chroniques*, vol. 9, p. 273.

42 A comprehensive account of the surrender of Eu and Tancarville appears in Froissart, who says that Holland and his men entered the tower and received the surrender there; the *Grandes Chroniques* suggests that Eu and his men came out and surrendered in the open. Fricamps and Grimboux are mentioned in the *Chronique Normande*, vol. 9, p. 76. On 7 October 1349, Jean, Duke of Normandy, gave 29 livres tournois to Macio Choffin to help pay his ransom after having been captured at Caen: L. Delisle, *Actes Normandes de la chambre des comptes sous Philippe VI de Valois*, p. 419, no. 236. Jean de Coubray's capture by Kildesby is noted in *CPR 1345–48*, p. 362.

43 *Acta Bellicosa*, p. 33.

44 *Chronique Normande*, p. 76.

45 Burghersh, in Avesbury, p. 204. Viard, 'Le Campagne de juillet–août', reckons Burghersh's figure is close to the real one, and most modern French historians put the figures at 5,000 or even higher, including dead, wounded and captured and also including losses among the townspeople.

46 Northburgh, p. 16.

47 *Acta Bellicosa*, p. 33, says 95 captives, but Northburgh claims 100 knights and 120–40 esquires; King Edward later mentioned 140 knights and bannerets as well as many esquires and rich citizens.

48 *Acta Bellicosa*, p. 33.

49 The *Chronique Normande* (p. 76) claims that a number of men were killed and women raped after the fighting stopped; this is not unlikely, but again, as at St-Lô, the scale of the atrocities was almost certainly exaggerated by the French chroniclers.

50 Froissart, vol. 4, pp. 412–13.

51 Quoted in Murimuth, *Continuatio Chronicarium*, ed. E.M. Thompson, London 1889, p. 204.

Chapter 6

Caen to Elbeuf

Nothing more was done, except that the countryside was set on fire all round, so that at least the men were not idle for lack of work.

Acta Bellicosa[1]

Thursday 27 July

At daybreak on the 27th, the English troops guarding the castle spotted five men slipping out of one of its gates. What their purpose was is not known, but it is likely that they were messengers; the survivors of the disaster of the previous day would already be spreading word of the French defeat, but the marshal and the bishop would also have been concerned to let the authorities know that they were still alive and intended to carry on the resistance. Whatever their purpose, the five men were quickly trapped by the watchful English. Three were killed; the other two were captured and taken before King Edward. They were, however, not able to give much in the way of useful information. They confirmed the fate of Geoffrey of Maldon, still languishing in the castle's prison, and also that the bishop and his brother had no intention of surrendering. This cannot have come as any particular surprise to the English commanders.

In the city, the process of clearing up after the battle had begun. Burial of the dead, assuming even the lower casualty figures are correct, would have taken some time. Five hundred bodies were buried in the churchyard of St-Jean.[2] How the remainder were disposed of is not known; some may have been claimed by their families, some buried in parish churchyards, and others more simply in mass graves.

Then came the pillaging of the city itself. As noted, Caen was rich, rich enough for everyone in the army to have their share. The author of the *Acta Bellicosa* maintains that 'the English eagerly returned to the work of despoiling the town, only taking jewels, clothing or precious ornaments because of their abundance',[3] and Froissart maintained that even the common soldiers did not bother looting silver objects and coins, as there was enough gold for everyone.[4] This is almost certainly hyperbole, and Richard Wynkeley is more probably correct when he says bluntly that 'the town was taken and stripped to the bare walls'.[5] Although there was an immense amount of freelance looting, many of the larger houses and market halls were methodically stripped of their contents by servants of the king, the Prince of Wales and others of the great nobles. Most of the plunder was loaded on board Huntingdon's ships, a process which must have taken several days, and the *Acta Bellicosa* says that the quantity of goods taken from Caen and elsewhere was so great that there was not room for all of it aboard the ships.

This quantity of riches inevitably created temptations that not all could resist. Some ship's captains, their vessels loaded with loot, decamped from the fleet and sailed back to England without orders, and two days later the king ordered William de Redenhale, the lieutenant of the fleet north of the Thames, to chastise and punish insubordinate mariners.[6] Quarrels over plunder also led to fights among the pillagers, and may have been responsible for two deaths, that of Edwin Neuman at the hands of Henry le Smyth of Covehythe, Suffolk, and of William Randekyn of King's Lynn, killed by Hugh Pulter of the same town. All four men seem to have been seamen.[7] One William de Braye, however, was more adventurous: stealing a quantity of jewels, money and other valuables from the Prince of Wales and his household, he deserted the army and fled back to England. Here he seems to have remained on the run for several months, but was eventually caught, and on 20 March 1347 letters patent were issued ordering him to be brought to trial.[8]

Some, however, did not need to steal to get rich. Thomas Holland's capture of the Comte d'Eu changed the lives of both men forever, though the consequences were not immediately apparent. Eu was sent back to

England as a prisoner, and early in the following year King Edward purchased him from Holland for the very considerable sum of 80,000 florins. Holland had an expensive court case to fight in order to assert his marriage and his rights to Princess Joan of Kent (see Chapter 1), and he used the money to engage one of England's best lawyers, Master Robert Beverley, to plead his case before the pope. In 1349, despite the opposition of the king and Princess Joan's mother, the pope found in favour of Holland. His marriage to the princess was legally recognised, and in 1360 he himself was finally recognised as Earl of Kent through his wife. His sons became earls and dukes – and the stepchildren of the Prince of Wales, who married Joan after Holland's death.[9] But for the unfortunate Comte d'Eu, the ending was rather different. Quite unable to raise the huge sum demanded for his ransom, he eventually secured his freedom by swearing allegiance to Edward III. He may well have thought of this as a simple ruse to regain his liberty, but the new king of France, Jean II, thought otherwise. Upon his return to France, Eu was arrested and beheaded for treason. One new dynasty had been born; another had been extinguished.

It seems possible that at least some of the refugees from Caen fled north rather than south or east, for word of what had happened reached Bayeux, sixteen miles to the north-west. Late in the day on the 27th a delegation from Bayeux reached Caen, offering to surrender the town to Edward. He refused to see them; conditions were still somewhat chaotic in the aftermath of the battle, and Edward was probably being no more than honest when he said that he could not guarantee to protect Bayeux or its people.[10] However, arrangements were made to receive the surrender of the city at a later date when the situation had improved, and safe-conducts were issued to emissaries from Bayeux allowing them to return home.

The royal household's food consumption for this day is quite eclectic, and probably represents a gradual transition from using up some of the last supplies which had been brought from England to an increasing reliance on plundered food stocks. Beef, mutton, a moray eel, half a salt salmon, geese, chickens, four dozen doves and 300 eggs were consumed, with the usual pickles and sauces. From this point on the diet becomes increasingly monotonous, with plundered beef and mutton supplemented by dwindling stocks of salt fish on fast days. For the moment, however, the army was still well provisioned, and food was not yet an issue.

Friday 28 July

With Caen stripped bare, the army now proceeded to devastate the countryside around the city. The callous comment by the author of the *Acta Bellicosa*, quoted at the head of this chapter, suggests that even the army's commanders were no longer minding very much what their troops did. Indeed, the failure of the Normans to support Edward's cause may have led to tacit encouragement of such behaviour; one modern historian, Richard Barber, even suggests that Edward, having failed to persuade the Normans voluntarily, was now trying to terrorise them into surrendering.[11] Whatever the motives, however, the result was the same: the prosperous villages and market towns around Caen went up in smoke.

The mood of King Edward and his commanders was not improved by the discovery of a document, possibly in the Logis du Roi, recording an agreement reached between King Philippe of France and many of the leading nobles of Normandy in 1338.[12] On 21 March of that year, Philippe and the Normans, who included the Comte d'Eu, father of the present imprisoned Constable, the Comte d'Harcourt, Robert Bertrand of Bricquebec, and around forty of the leading barons of the duchy, had met at the Bois de Vincennes, near Paris, to lay down a blueprint for what was to be nothing less than a second Norman conquest of England. The invasion was to be led by Philippe's son, Jean, Duc de Normandie; the Norman barons were to contribute a force of 4,000 men-at-arms and 20,000 foot soldiers; King Philippe would provide a further 20,000 foot, including 5,000 crossbowmen. The expedition was to be financed from Normandy as well, and the terms of payment and length of the contract were spelled out along with the organisation of ships for transport. The agreement also specified that if it were not possible to attack England that year, 1338, then the services of the Normans could be called upon in future years, whenever the opportunity arose. Technically, therefore, the agreement was still in force and the threat of invasion remained.[13]

What was really inflammatory about the document was that it went on to spell out in detail how the conquered country was to be apportioned among the victors. Edward was to be deposed and his possessions awarded to the Duc de Normandie: 'all which the king of England hath shall be and remain unto the said my lord the duke, as king and lord, and with rights and honours as the King of England holdeth them'.[14] The Duc himself was to be crowned as King Jean of England. The English barons were also to be dispossessed and their property handed over to the nobles and towns of Normandy as a reward for their services. The property of the English church would not be confiscated, but the church would in effect be required to pay rent, £20,000 per annum, for its own property. Only lands belonging directly to the pope in England would be protected.

And, unlike the previous Norman Conquest, which had been an independent venture by Duke William, this one was to be controlled by the French crown, for the Duc de Normandie would also of course become king of France upon the death of his father. The agreement stated that 'the realm of England shall never be devised from the hands of my lord the duke and his heirs, the kings of France'.[15] England would no longer be independent, and a principal source of many of the conflicts from 1066, down to and including the present one, would be removed.

The contents of the document came as no surprise to one member of the English army. Godefroi d'Harcourt had been at the meeting at the Bois de Vincennes along with his brother, and had witnessed the document and agreed to take part in the invasion.[16] The terms of the document must have been known in England; certainly it was no secret in 1338 and the years following that the French were preparing to invade, and it was only with the defeat of the French fleet at Sluys in 1340 and the counter-invasion of Artois and Picardy that this threat had been reduced, at least temporarily. Nevertheless, reading its terms in full just yards from the tomb of William the Conqueror must have given Edward a great deal of satisfaction. Far from suffering his own country to be invaded, he had turned the tables with a vengeance. He ordered a copy of the letter to be sent to England and read out in public, as evidence of the perfidy and aggression of his adversary the king of France. This was duly done in the churchyard of St Paul's cathedral, London on the 12th of August by the Archbishop of Canterbury, John Stratford, with due pomp and ceremony, accompanied by a sermon and solemn procession; all present then offered up prayers for the success of the king's expedition on France.[17] A propaganda victory had been added to the king's military triumphs.

Friday being another fast day, the royal household dined on dried cod, salt salmon and stockfish, all of which had been soaked and then prepared with sauces of mustard, vinegar, verjuice, garlic and parsley. Two hundred pimpernels provided fresh fish, and 200 onions and a quantity of pease pottage were also consumed. The total kitchen expense for the day was £5 5s. 8¼d., including 4d. for the wages of the sergeant of the scullery, Thomas Redyng. The bill for the previous day had been just under £5, and by this stage of the campaign it was beginning to cost more to feed the household on fish days than on meat days, as supplies of captured livestock were being increasingly used while fish was still drawn from the household stores. It is notable too that the average daily kitchen bill is down to an average of around £5, from a high of £8–9 a day at St-Vaast.

Saturday 29 July

As previously arranged, a delegation from Bayeux now arrived to formally surrender the city. Travelling under passes of safe-conduct, fifteen of the leading burgesses of the city arrived and were presented before Edward, who promised to protect their lives and property.[18] On this occasion, at least, the king's guarantees seem to have been effective. There is no record of any molestation or damage in Bayeux, and the city seems to have survived the invasion without loss. It may simply be that the city was too far away from the main army for the pillagers to reach it.

The loading of the ships continued, and the bulk of the army rested. Prior to the battle the men had marched eighty-two miles in nine days, and, as the king himself pointed out, had not had a single day's rest. The next stage of the campaign was likely to be even more arduous, and Edward needed his men in fighting trim. That night saw another comparatively frugal meal of dried cod, stockfish, dried or salted salmon and pimpernels with the usual sauces of mustard, garlic and vinegar. There is not even any record of pottage, though possibly enough had been made the previous day to allow for leftovers. Whether the burgesses of Bayeux stayed to dine at the royal table is not known, but if so, like many Frenchmen since, they are unlikely to have been impressed by the standard of English food.

* * *

Philippe of France received the news of the fall of Caen while he was still at Vernon, about midway between Paris and Rouen. He had been moving slowly towards Rouen, apparently still uncertain as to what was happening in the field. Regular reports reached him of Flemish and English troops massing in Flanders, while the situation in Lower Normandy remained in the balance. The news of the disaster of Caen, however, changed things dramatically. For now the threat from the north would have to be ignored, and local nobles such as Louis of Nevers, the pro-French Count of Flanders, would have to contain the Anglo-Flemish army as best they could. Edward himself now commanded Philippe's full attention. On 29 July he issued a general summons to the nobles and communes of Normandy and the Île-de-France, ordering every available man to Rouen. He himself remained in Vernon the following day, then moved on to Rouen to join his army.[19]

Sunday 30 July

The army remained at Caen, but was beginning now to prepare to march onward. The next destination was Rouen, the capital of Normandy. Situated near the mouth of the Seine and even larger and richer than Caen, the city was a tempting target. As well as the wealth of the city itself, it was the site of the great French naval arsenal, the Clos des Gallées, the destruction of which would be another major blow to the French fleet. Importantly, too, the army needed to seize bridges over the Seine in order to continue its onward march, and the nearest of these were at Rouen. In the fourteenth century the tidal estuary of the Seine extended almost to the city, and was impassable on foot (even today, there are few crossings of the river west of Rouen). Finally, it seems likely that the English had already received intelligence of the new French army gathering at Rouen, and knew that King Philippe himself had arrived there.

The coast of Normandy east of Caen was largely sand dunes and salt marshes, with no harbours or ports of importance until the Seine itself, only a few insignificant fishing villages at the mouths of rivers such as the Dives and the Touques.[20] The most direct route from Caen to Rouen lay inland through Lisieux and Neubourg. This meant that the fleet could be sent back to England, at least temporarily. This move had several advantages. First, the prisoners taken at Caen and elsewhere, including Eu and Tancarville, required to be transported to England for safe-keeping. According to Bartholomew Burghersh, a decision had been taken that no ransoms would be arranged until the end of the summer when the campaign was over.[21] The plunder taken from Caen and St-Lô needed to be taken home and disposed of. As noted, large stocks of foodstuffs had been taken at both places, and some of the food was already beginning to spoil in the summer heat. Some of this surplus food was sold at Caen itself – very possibly back to the people it had been stolen from – while more was taken back to England and sold at Winchelsea. One account lists 644 quarters and 3 bushels of wheat, 443 quarters and 4 bushels of beans and peas, 992 quarters of oats, 142 tuns of flour, 70 carcasses of beef, 644 sides of bacon and 480 carcasses of mutton, all of which was 'spoiled' and therefore being sold.[22]

The army also had a number of sick and wounded, the latter from the fighting at Caen, who were no longer effective and needed to return home. Among the sick was the Earl of Huntingdon, William Clinton; the nature of his illness is not known and he had recovered his health by the end of summer, but the fact of his needing to return home at this point suggests the illness was serious.[23] Finally, Edward was already thinking forward to the next stage of the campaign, when he proposed to move north from Rouen across Picardy, ultimately linking up with Hugh Hastings and the Flemish army. Anticipating hard fighting in the weeks to come, he called for more reinforcements and supplies. As well as the infamous invasion plan and other letters from men like Northburgh and Wynkeley, which were meant to be read in public and inform the English people of the king's triumphs, Huntingdon also carried a number of orders to royal officials. A further 1,200 archers were to be raised; 2,450 bows and 6,300 sheaves of arrows were to be procured along with other supplies, and the whole was to be made ready to send to France. Anticipating that the greatest need would come in the north, Edward ordered the fleet to collect these reinforcements and supplies at the Sussex port of Winchelsea and to land them at Le Crotoy, a small port in Picardy near the mouth of the Somme, not far from Abbeville.[24]

Although the sources do not mention this, it is probable that not every ship returned to England. A small force may have remained at sea, raiding along the Channel coast; for example, the town website of Dives-sur-Mer claims that the town was burned in 1346, though it does not say exactly when.[25] Also, communications with Hastings in Flanders needed to be maintained, although the presence of the Genoese galleys at Harfleur would have made this hazardous. However, most of the hundred or so ships under Huntingdon's command returned to England, along with a sizeable number of his following including the bannerets John Botetourt and Henry Braillesford. Some others of his men-at-arms, however, transferred to other retinues.

Final preparations in place, the fleet and army both prepared to say farewell to Caen.[26] A small covering force was detailed to guard the castle, its members no doubt grumbling at having to remain behind in the city while their fellows went off to win plunder and glory in new fields. The detachment of this force and the Carentan garrison, plus battle casualties at Caen, those who were returning to England with Huntingdon, and general losses from sickness and desertion meant that the army was probably now a little over 13,000 strong. Making up for the frugality of recent days, the royal household dined in style. Several hunters and a forager had been employed to bring in food, and eight carcasses of beef and thirty-one of mutton, and also a foal, were consumed at the evening's banquet, along with thirty geese, four dozen hens and six dozen doves. The poultry may well have been made into pies, if the quantities of eggs, milk and flour used are anything to go by. This may have sounded like an excess, but the days ahead were likely to be difficult and the army would need all its strength. Napoleon's comment that an army marches on its stomach would have been heartily endorsed by Edward and his commanders.

Monday 31 July

On Monday morning the army resumed its march. Their road ran almost due east across a level plain to Troarn, eight miles away. Troarn was a small town overlooking the floodplain of the Dives, dominated by an imposing Benedictine abbey; the church of the latter, which has some fine decorated carving around the windows and door, still stands. The abbey had been fortified and could be defended, and at first the monks and inhabitants tried to resist the English approach. This resistance quickly collapsed, however, and the army occupied the town, the king doubtless commandeering the abbey buildings for himself. A halt was called for the day.[27] Once again the march was accompanied by the inevitable freelance pillaging and arson, and among other places the village of Argences, about four miles south of Troarn, was burned.[28]

Earlier in the campaign, Edward had made at least some efforts to prevent widespread destruction. Then, on the approach to Caen and in the immediate aftermath of the battle, he had deliberately burned large swathes of the country in order to put psychological pressure on his opponents. That motive was no longer present; the nearest enemy forces were sixty miles away. Once again, it is questionable as to how widespread the destruction really was during this stage of the campaign. Eyewitnesses such as Northburgh, Wynkeley and Burghersh, who give detailed accounts of the destruction elsewhere, make no reference to it at this point. Some other chronicles do mention pillage and arson in general terms, but the main source on this account is the anti-English chronicler Jean le Bel, who laments the destruction of many towns and villages. But le Bel at this point is talking in general terms, not specifically about the march from Caen to Rouen.[29] (Jean Froissart makes similar comments, but he drew on le Bel at this point, to the extent of copying some passages word for word, and is similarly not to be relied upon.) That there was destruction is undoubted, but le Bel's accusation that the two marshals, Godefroi d'Harcourt and the Earl of Warwick, rode out every day on the flanks of the army and burned and destroyed for many miles around is a gross exaggeration. The duties of the marshal were to order and maintain the army, and the job of getting 13,000 men and assorted animals and wagons down narrow Norman roads would not have left much time to indulge in systematic arson. Of course plundering happened – the king's own kitchen was paying foragers to look for foodstuffs, and much of the meat consumed by the royal household during this time is listed as *depreda* (plundered) – but the evidence for systematic widespread destruction *at this time* is too slim to bear much weight.

In particular, the problem that faced the commanders at Troarn was how to get across the Dives. Immediately to the east of Troarn the ground fell away into salt marshes a mile or more wide, with the river itself flowing in meandering channels through them. Even at low tide the marshes were impassable to horses and wheeled vehicles.[30] The nearest crossing point was at St-Pierre-du-Jonquet, a little over three miles to the south-east.[31] The halt at Troarn gave the commanders the opportunity to organise for the crossing, which was likely to be arduous and time-consuming. Dinner for the household was mostly roast meat: eight carcasses of beef and fourteen of mutton were consumed, with three dozen geese, and two dozen capons and hens, plus various sauces and two bushels of salt.

* * *

Exactly when is not recorded, but at some point not long after the English departure, Robert Bertrand and the garrison of the castle of Caen launched a sortie against the covering force the English had left behind. The latter, taken by surprise, were slaughtered to the last man. It was the first military defeat the English had suffered on the campaign, and showed that when properly led the French were redoubtable fighters; Bertrand's force cannot have outnumbered the English by much, if at all.

Leaving the city and castle secure, Bertrand turned west and began moving back towards the Cotentin in order to bring the area back under French control. He found no opposition apart from the little garrison at Carentan under the command of Raoul de Verdun and Nicholas de Groussy. These he compelled to surrender. What happened to the ordinary members of the garrison is not known, but it is unlikely to have been very pleasant. Verdun and Groussy were arrested as traitors and transported to Paris, where later in the year they were publicly beheaded. The last vestiges of English control in Normandy had been wiped out in a matter of days.

Tuesday 1 August

Unaware of what was happening behind it, the army began its crossing of the Dives on the morning of Lammas Day. The tide was out, and the vanguard division managed the crossing from St-Pierre-du-Jonquet to the east bank near the modern settlement of Le Ham fairly easily. The king's division followed, and the two divisions then moved off east, up a series of small roads towards the village of Rumesnil on the banks of the small river Doigt, where there was fresh water. The king's division halted here, having covered about ten miles, while the prince's men pushed on across the Doigt another mile to Leaupartie, a hamlet with an ancient chapel.[32]

Back at the Dives, the ponderous task of getting the baggage train across the river took most of the day. Unlike the Marais de Carentan, where the army had the benefit of the old Roman causeway, the crossing of the Dives was a poor-quality path through marshes and shallow, muddy streams.[33] Today the Dives itself has been diked and the marshes drained, but even so it is not hard to imagine the scene: wagons bogging down in the mud, teams and drivers straining to pull them free, and quite likely the men of the rearguard division being told to get off their horses and go forward to lend a hand, pushing the heavier wagons from behind while the

Plate 1 The Bay of St-Vaast at low tide.

Plate 2 The Bay of St-Vaast from Quettehou churchyard.

Plate 3 The church of St-Vigor, Quettehou. The Prince of Wales and others were knighted here on the day of the landing.

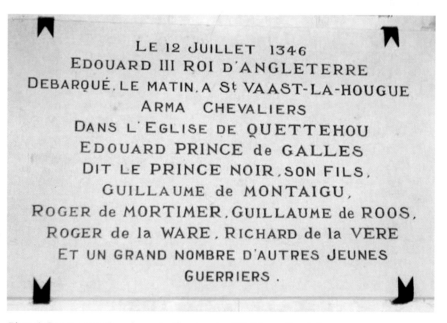

LE 12 JUILLET 1346
EDOUARD III ROI D'ANGLETERRE
DEBARQUÉ, LE MATIN, A St VAAST-LA-HOUGUE
ARMA CHEVALIERS
DANS L'EGLISE DE QUETTEHOU
EDOUARD PRINCE de GALLES
DIT LE PRINCE NOIR, SON FILS,
GUILLAUME de MONTAIGU,
ROGER de MORTIMER, GUILLAUME de ROOS,
ROGER de la WARE, RICHARD de la VERE
ET UN GRAND NOMBRE D'AUTRES JEUNES
GUERRIERS.

Plate 4 Commemorative plaque in the church of St-Vigor, Quettehou.

Plate 5 The tower and chapel of La Pernelle.

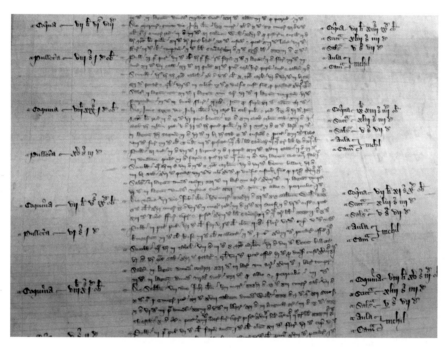

Plate 6 Page from the Kitchen Account, showing daily consumption and expenditure by the royal household during the campaign.

The National Archives, ref. E101/390/11 m.58.

Plate 7 St-Sauveur-le-Vicomte, home of the Norman baron Godefroi d'Harcourt. The keep was repaired and strengthened later in the fourteenth century.

Plate 8 Carentan, medieval arcades in the former marketplace.

Plate 9 A fourteenth-century army on the march, from *Chronique de Hainault*.
Courtesy of the Bibliothèque Royale de Belgique.

Plate 10 Cheux, the church of St-Vigor. The Prince of Wales's men camped here the night before the storming of Caen.

Plate 11 Medieval houses in Caen, from Robida's *Vielle France*.

Plate 12 Caen, the former site of the bridge of St-Pierre, looking towards St-Pierre church with the castle in the background. The cross street in the foreground follows the course of the Odon, now drained and paved over; the bridge was at the site of the present intersection.

Plate 13 Troarn, remains of the Benedictine abbey.

Plate 14 Tanneries at Lisieux from Robida, *Vielle France*.

Plate 15 Gaillon, view of the town and Seine valley from the site of the castle.

Plate 16 Vernon, remains of the medieval bridge from Robida, *Vielle France*. Parts of the bridge, including one of the old houses, are still standing.

Plate 17 La Roche Guyon, stormed by Sir Robert Ferrers on the night of 10 August.

Plate 18 Remnants of the bridge at Poissy, which the Earl of Northampton defended against the men of Amiens. The piers that still stand are probably from the late fifteenth century.

Plate 19 The church at Frocourt, south of Beauvais.

Plate 20 The former Knights Templar commandery at Sommereux.

Plate 21 The valley of the Somme at Longpré, looking north. In 1346 the valley was a tidal floodplain.

Plate 22 The bridge at Pont-Remy, where the King of Bohemia defeated Godefroi d'Harcourt. Both the current bridge and the church in the background are much later.

Plate 23 The Blanchetaque. The modern path follows the track of the ancient ford from Saigneville to the north bank.

Plate 24 The Blanchetaque from the north, looking across the Somme. On this hill Godemar de Fay waited for Hugh Despenser.

Plate 25 Crécy-en-Ponthieu, from the left flank of the Prince of Wales's position looking down the hill, with approximately the view that the English and Welsh archers had of the approaching French. The trees and buildings in the foreground were not present at the time; the line of trees beyond marks the line of the river Maye.

Plate 26 Crécy-en-Ponthieu, from the left flank of the Prince of Wales's division, looking back towards the king's division. The lookout tower is believed to stand on the site of the windmill which was the king's own post during the battle.

Plate 27 Crécy-en-Ponthieu, memorial to King Jean of Bohemia.

teams pulled from the front. Some of the thousands of faggots of wood the army had brought over from England in its baggage may well have been needed here to give the wheels purchases in the soft ground. By the time the last wagons crossed the river and began labouring up the slopes beyond in the wake of the king's division, the tide was coming in. Durham and Arundel and their men, cut off from the rest of the army, were forced to spend the night camped around St-Pierre-du-Jonquet.

Around Rumesnil and Leaupartie, the army made camp and celebrated the feast day. Lammas (technically the feast of St Peter ad Vincula), or 'Loaf Mass', was an important day in the medieval Christian calendar; traditionally, it was the day when bread was baked from flour ground from the first corn of the harvest and consecrated in churches. The household dined on the usual range of roast meats, including eight and half carcasses of fresh beef, fifteen carcasses of mutton, a pig and two young deer, plus assorted fowl including four geese and two dozen doves. Once again the beef and mutton were foraged from the local countryside, but the poultry still seems to have been from household stores. The most striking item in the accounts, however, is 1,000 eggs and twenty-four gallons of milk. We may assume that mass was also celebrated with more than usual splendour, with the Bishop of Durham officiating for the household and nobles and other clergy serving throughout the army.

Wednesday 2 August

On the third day since leaving Caen, the two leading divisions of the army pushed on through a series of little valleys in the Pays d'Auge, moving roughly east-south-east, and finally coming out on the higher plateau west of Lisieux. From there it was a fairly straightforward march on to Lisieux itself, which the vanguard reached after a march of about nine miles. Here they halted, waiting for the baggage and the rearguard to catch up. Durham and Arundel's men, having crossed the Dives in the morning, had a long and wearying march of nearly twenty miles, much of it uphill, and probably did not arrive until evening.

The apparently slow progress of the English army has puzzled some modern historians. Since leaving Caen the army had marched twenty-seven miles in three days, an average of nine miles per day.[34] In fact these figures are not much lower than the army's daily march for the whole of the campaign. The average for these three days will also have been dragged down by the slow crossing of the Dives, and by the fact that much of the subsequent march was up long hills; the gradients are relatively gentle, but would have slowed progress none the less.

Modern readers may be surprised at the slow progress of both armies more generally. It is perfectly possible for a person in good physical condition on good roads or paths to walk for eight or ten hours a day at an average rate of three miles an hour, thus covering from twenty-four to thirty miles a day.[35] It is quite another thing to expect this person to do this day in and day out without rest, carrying a load of equipment and weapons, and on a diet of bread, pease porridge, onions and whatever poultry or other meat they are able to scrounge from the countryside they pass through. Marching armies become tired, and tired armies do not fight well. Conserving the strength of their troops to ensure they are fit for battle has been a preoccupation of commanders since the beginning of time. To be sure, men can march longer distances and still fight, and later in the campaign they would be called upon to do exactly that, but generally commanders like to husband the strength of their troops unless there is no other option.

And what is true of men is also true of horses. Although horses move considerably faster than men on foot over short distances, they also become tired quickly if forced to move at speed, especially if carrying close to three hundred pounds of man, armour, weapons and harness on their backs. Many generals, including some great ones, have made the error of overestimating the endurance of their horses, and have paid the price. For example, in 1812, Napoleon's *Grande Armée* repeatedly overtaxed its horses during the first month of the invasion of Russia, and lost tens of thousands of horses as a result, badly hampering the effectiveness of the French cavalry and interrupting supply arrangements. Although – as we shall see later on this campaign – a mounted force can move faster than one largely on foot for short periods, over the long duration, average march distances are about the same.

An army also moves at the speed of its slowest unit. In medieval armies, this was nearly always the baggage train. On level roads, over open fields, wagons and carts should experience little difficulty in keeping up with marching troops. All this changes when steep hills must be climbed or descended. Heavily laden wagons – loaded, for example, with cannons and gunpowder, or portable forges and charcoal – slow to a crawl when going up hills, and on steep hills, such as that coming up from Pont-Hébert earlier in the campaign, it may well be necessary for the men from the units marching behind to put their shoulders against the backs of the wagons and push (remember that the hills of medieval roads would not have been graded as modern ones are, and may well have been much steeper than they are now). On downhill slopes there is the risk of gravity taking over completely, the wagon overrunning its team and crashing out of control; in these cases, men will be required to brace against the *front* of the wagon to slow its descent, an occupation not without its hazards. Soft ground also slows progress; we saw above how the crossing of the Dives delayed the rearguard of the army by nearly a day. Unglamorous and sometimes ignored by historians, the baggage train is nevertheless vitally important. Without it, the army lacks food, medical supplies, tents, spare weapons and armour and much of the equipment for maintaining them. Later in the summer the Genoese troops in the French army became separated from their baggage, with fatal consequences (see Chapter 10).

Lastly, even on good level roads, it is not always possible for an army to march at its optimum speed. A man may be capable of marching twenty-four miles in a day, but often his commanders will have cause for congratulation if he is able to march twelve or fifteen. In much the same way, an automobile capable of being driven at over a hundred miles an hour will, in heavy traffic, struggle to make an average of forty or fifty. Narrow roads, sometimes hemmed with ditches or hedgerows, mean that congestion becomes a major issue. At many points during the 1346 campaign the English commanders tried to avoid this by sending different divisions down different roads, using two or even three routes at once. Even so, congestion still occurs. Some men move faster, or slower, than others. Bottlenecks develop, such as at bridges or fords, meaning men tend to bunch up and come to a stop as they wait their turn to cross. When the time comes for rest halts the march commanders, the under-constable and under-marshal and their officers, must pass the word down the column; when it comes time to move on again, the word must again be passed. All of this takes time, and the average marching speed is pressed still further downward.

For all of these reasons – the slow progress of the wagons and the rearguard, the need to not overtax his men, the narrowness and condition of the roads – Edward halted his leading divisions at Lisieux and waited.

With hindsight he can be criticised for doing so; it was urgent that the crossings of the Seine be seized before the enemy could defend them, and he had already tarried some days at Caen. It is possible that after the victory at Caen he and his commanders had succumbed to overconfidence, and believed the force King Philippe had at Rouen was small enough to be easily challenged. But this would be in contrast to the prudence they showed through much of the campaign, and it seems rather more likely that they intended to proceed in the careful, methodical manner which had characterised their actions so far.

*   *   *

Lisieux was a sizeable city in the valley of the river Touques. From the west, the road from Caen ran down from the high ground into the faubourg west of the river. Crossing the bridge, the army entered the old town, with its long main street climbing, sometimes steeply, up to the east and running on towards Neubourg and Rouen. Lisieux, like so many of the provincial centres of Normandy, was a prosperous place, particularly noted for its tanneries along the river. Its main street was lined with fine houses, some of which escaped the devastation of the city by Allied bombers in 1944 and can still be seen on the higher slopes of the hill. The market square lies about halfway up the hill, and the cathedral and bishop's palace lie on the north side of this.

The town was not defensible – it may have been unwalled at this point – but the cathedral and its precincts did have a defensive wall. At the first sign of the English approach, the Bishop of Lisieux, Guillaume Guitard, opened the gates of the precinct and gave refuge to the entire population, most of whom took shelter inside the bishop's palace or the cathedral itself. Arms were served out, and when the English army crossed the bridge and approached the cathedral they found it defended, the bishop himself in a defiant mood.[36] Whether out of respect for the episcopal cloth or because they were too busy plundering the deserted town, the English troops left Bishop Guitard and his people alone.

The same could not be said of the next clergy they encountered. That evening a small party rode into Lisieux from the east, led by the red-robed figures of two cardinals. The princes of the church and their escort were greeted with delight by a party of Welsh foot soldiers, who held them up, stole their horses, and sent them discomfited and on foot into the city to meet the king.[37] Edward, for his part, cannot have greeted the new arrivals with any great enthusiasm. Of the two men, one, the Italian Annibale Ceccano, Cardinal-Archbishop of Naples, was of comparitively little importance. But the other, the Frenchman Étienne Aubert, was a man of considerable importance. Formerly Bishop of Clermont, he had since 1342 been Cardinal-Bishop of Ostia, and was close to both Pope Clement VI and King Philippe (in 1352 he would become pope in his turn, taking the name Innocent VI).[38] He could not be simply brushed aside, much as Edward must have longed to do so.

Ostensibly, the two cardinals had been sent by Pope Clement VI to make peace between the two warring kings. However, as was doubtless evident to every man present, they had in fact been sent at the direct behest of the king of France, and their mission was not to make peace – the impossibility of that at the present time must surely have been manifest – but to buy time. Philippe was still mustering men and waiting for reinforcements, and was watching with some anxiety events to the north in Flanders. Indeed, that very day, Hugh Hastings and Henry of Flanders marched out of Ypres on their way south, although the news did not reach Philippe for another two days. By forcing Edward to stop and go through the charade of discussing a peace proposal, the cardinals could buy Philippe a further day or two in which to reorganise his defences behind the Seine. Knowing all this, Edward attempted to put a good face on events. Courteously, he entertained the cardinals to dinner, salt cod and stockfish and peas augmented by a variety of poultry and another 800 eggs and fourteen gallons of milk, the latter for making sauces thickened with flour and ground almonds. This fine meal was probably eaten through gritted teeth on all sides.

Thursday 3 August

The English army remained halted all day at Lisieux, under the watchful eyes of Bishop Guitard and his little garrison, who were doubtless aware that they were unlikely to be massacred in the presence of the two cardinals. Edward and his commanders spent the day locked in conference with the cardinals, while his men continued the plunder of Lisieux.

The atmosphere of the meeting was polite, but far from cordial. Richard Wynkeley, writing a month or so later, maintained that the envoys were received courteously, out of respect for their position as princes of the church, and that Edward adopted a reasonable tone. In response to their homilies on the need for peace and concord among Christians – the need for unity against the Saracens and the recovery of the Holy Land was probably mentioned at this point, as it nearly always was on such occasions – Edward responded that he was, as a dutiful son of the church, always anxious to make peace and was ready to do so if a reasonable offer could be made. Indeed, he claimed (according to Wynkeley) that he himself had frequently offered to make peace and suggested terms for a lasting treaty, but these had always been rejected. He was still ready to come to terms, even though these terms might be to the detriment of his own cause, so great was his desire for peace.

The preliminaries over, the negotiators now stated their terms. The proposal from the cardinals confirmed the English view that this was no more than a delaying tactic. King Philippe's offer was merely that in exchange for peace, Edward should hold Gascony and Ponthieu on the same terms as his father had done, in other words, as a vassal of the French king. This was tantamount to saying that the last nine years of warfare had been for nothing, and Edward would gain no advantage whatsoever; Philippe would be able to resume hostilities, seize Ponthieu and invade Gascony again at whatever point he saw fit. The offer was rejected out of hand. Angrily, Edward responded that he would make a proper answer when he received a reasonable offer of terms.

The cardinals urged further discussions, but the king refused; he would waste no more time, and in the morning he would continue his march. He ordered that the twenty horses stolen by the Welsh should be restored, and gave the two cardinals written safe-conducts through his army.[39] Because magnanimity was a princely virtue, he ordered that they should be entertained at a banquet as lavish as an army on the march could muster. Meats included spiced and fresh beef, mutton, pork, venison and such exotic poultry as a swan, a spoonbill and a heron, plus geese, chickens and doves, and two whole cheeses. An unusual household expense is the payment to an unnamed individual to watch the cooking pots over the fires, presumably to keep hungry archers from stealing their contents while the cooks' backs were turned. This item appears fairly frequently from then on, suggesting that for the other ranks, food may have been starting to become a problem.

More than this comparatively lavish meal, however, Edward would not provide. He held the upper hand still in this campaign, and was determined to keep it. As the royal household feasted, the officers of the Constable and the marshal made ready to march early in the morning.

Friday 4 August

The pace of the campaign was beginning to quicken once more. Hugh Hastings and Henry of Flanders marched steadily south from Ypres. The French royal army was assembling along the Seine, and at long last Carlo Grimaldi's thirty-three galleys arrived from Monaco, bringing with them welcome reinforcements of crossbowmen and possibly also the small force of the King of Majorca (see Chapter 2). Grimaldi himself, to Philippe's apparent disappointment, stayed with his ships, but several thousands of his infantry were sent ashore. With these and troops collected in Normandy and the Île-de-France, Philippe was beginning to assemble a respectable army. The English royal army also resumed its advance. Early in the morning the English marched from Lisieux, setting fires in the town behind them. French historians generally assert that the entire town was burned, but it is possible that the residents, emerging from the cathedral after the last troops had gone, were able to save some of the buildings.

East of Lisieux the road climbs a long gentle slope onto the plateau once more, and then runs fairly straight and level across country to the east. Along this level route the army marched, making steady progress, with once again the pillagers fanning out on either side of the march, looting and burning.[40] After passing through the sizeable village of Thiberville, the vanguard pushed on to the hamlet of Le Teil Nollent, while the main body of the army halted around Duranville. They had covered between fourteen and fifteen miles.

At first sight Duranville and Le Teil look like a poor choice of camping spots. There is little water today, nor is there any sign that there ever was anything beyond a few wells and a tiny stream running to the west of Duranville. Horses as well as men needed water after such a long march in the summer heat, and this may have been an uncomfortable night (the household, who dined on salt fish, eels and cheese, may similarly have wished they had more water). The choice of halting points may have been determined by Godefroi d'Harcourt, who apparently knew the local landholder, Robin de Lombelon.[41] There is no suggestion that Lombelon was an active traitor, but he may have cooperated at least passively in order to protect his property.

The shortage of water would have had other, less pleasant consequences. We have frequently noted the food and fodder consumed by the army and its horses, but have not so far touched on the end result of this consumption. When the army was camped near running water, such as at Lisieux, the stream could serve as a sewer and much waste would simply be washed away (to the discomfort of those locals who used the stream, of course). There seems to have been no such stream at Le Teil, and it must be assumed that the thousands of men and horses left behind them – not to put too fine a point on it – large quantities of shit. Given that the indications are that the summer of 1346 was hot and dry, Le Teil would have been a place best avoided for a few days after the army's departure.

Saturday 5 August

The following day saw another early start, with the army moving east in long columns across the high plateau from Duranville towards the valley of the Risle. The rapidity of Edward's march is hard to explain, unless he was aware that Philippe had briefly, and rashly, advanced south of the Seine. Possibly the cardinals had let something slip in Lisieux; possibly rumours had reached the ears of Lombelon in Duranville. (Philippe had quickly come to his senses and retired behind the Seine, but Edward may not have realised this.) Scenting his adversary in the open, out from behind the protective barrier of the river and probably with only a small force, Edward pushed his men down the road as quickly as possible. Ten miles from Duranville, they began descending the road into the valley of the Risle, crossing by bridge at Brionne.

Here the army were passing through country that Godefroi d'Harcourt would once again have found familiar. The great seigneurie of Brionne was the property of his brother, the Comte d'Harcourt; the ancestral home, the village of Harcourt, lay a few miles to the south-east. Family feeling, however, no longer counted for much in this war. Brionne was burned, along with the abbey of Le Bec-Hellouin to the north,[42] and the English pressed on up out of the Risle valley, across the plateau through Harcourt, and so, after a march of nearly twenty miles, to the town of Neubourg.

Neubourg was eleven miles from Elbeuf, on the south bank of the Seine, and a little over twenty miles from Rouen. Despite his long march, Edward had failed to catch his adversary, and must now have realised that he was too late and the latter had withdrawn north of the river. Here he halted his tired army. The town, though fortified, was not defended and his men entered without opposition. The king himself took over the small castle in the centre of the town for his household. This place was steeped in the history of his own ancestors; Stephen had been proclaimed king of England here by the barons of Normandy following the death of Henry I, and in 1160 Henry II's son and heir, Henry the Young King, had been married to Marguerite of France at Neubourg castle.[43] Prior to the conquest of Normandy by Philippe Augustus, Neubourg had marked the boundary between France and Normandy. Beyond this point, the English would be advancing into France proper.

The seigneurs of Neubourg, the Meulans, were neighbours of the Comtes d'Harcourt and were related several times by marriage. The current seigneur, Amaury de Meulan, had himself married a Harcourt, and was a veteran soldier who had fought against the English in the campaigns of 1338 and 1340 and, like the Comte, was loyal to King Philippe. He himself was away in Rouen, serving with Harcourt.[44] There is no indication that the town was occupied when the English arrived, and it is likely that Meulan had evacuated the town. The English occupied and plundered the town, and the household ate a fairly simple meal of salt fish and eels with onions, sauces and pickles. The number of fish being consumed per day was now about a third less than at the start of the campaign.

Sunday 6 August

After marching nearly thirty-five miles in two days the army halted, the men and horses to rest and the commanders to take stock. The first step was to find out whether the bridges over the Seine at Rouen still stood, and to ascertain how strongly the city itself was garrisoned. Godefroi d'Harcourt was sent out with a strong force of mounted men towards Rouen itself, while the main body remained at Neubourg ready to either advance directly on Rouen or to make a dart at one of the nearer bridges at Elbeuf, eleven miles away, or Pont de l'Arche, seven miles further on. It is perhaps a little surprising that Edward did not simply move towards these bridges immediately, or at least reconnoitre them as well;[45] if they still stood, he would have the egress to the north bank of the Seine that he so badly needed, and could move his whole force towards Rouen from the landward side. Was he once again simply being methodical in his approach, not moving until he had firm intelligence of his enemy? In fact the issue made little difference to the outcome, as Philippe had already been in possession of the bridges for some time and had made his own preparations. But it is still a curious omission.

The Seine in its lower reaches describes a series of great U-bends across a broad valley. Rouen lies at the northernmost extent of one of the largest of these bends; the old city centre was on the north bank of the river, connected with the south bank by the Pont-Mathilde and another smaller bridge. There was a faubourg on the south bank, including the monastery of Notre-Dame-du-Pré, and there was a large leper sanctuary, founded by Henry II of England in the twelfth century, still further south in the parish of Petit-Quevilly, on the edge of a large woodland. Harcourt's men rode forward through the Forêt de Rouvray, along the neck of land within the loop of the river towards the distant city. Passing through woods, they fired all the houses they came to, once again it would seem with the intention of putting pressure on the defenders of the city.[46] According to a legend recounted by a later Rouennais writer, the notary Pierre Cochon, while passing near the leper sanctuary, Harcourt's men stopped a lone woman – presumably one of the lepers – and asked her for news. She confirmed that King Philippe was in the city, along with Harcourt's brother Comte Jean and the Comte de Dreux, and that the bridges had been broken down. The people were said to be in a state of fear, but the defenders were resolute.[47] Whether this story is true or not, it appears Harcourt was resolved to see for himself. Moving on towards Notre-Dame-du-Pré, still applying the torch as he went, he drew closer to the Pont-Mathilde. A second monastery was also burned, the monks fleeing before the approach of the English.

But the information Harcourt had received earlier was correct. The bridge was broken, and was also heavily defended at the southern end, where barricades had been erected and the defenders were waiting and ready. Harcourt probed, and there was a short skirmish, probably confined to a brief exchange of arrows and crossbow bolts. One chronicle reports that two men, Thomas Holland and Richard de la Marsh, rode up to the point where the bridge was broken shouting 'St George for King Edward!', but they must have been dodging crossbow bolts as they did so. Another of the party was the banneret John Daunay, a West Country man in his forties serving in the Prince of Wales's division; he was killed, as was another unnamed Englishman.[48] There was no point in the marshal's pressing the issue; even if he had managed to force the barricade, he would have achieved little. He had come close enough to Rouen to see the banners of King Philippe flying over the walls, the lilies of France and the Oriflamme, and he would also have seen the red and gold colours of his brother flying there as well.[49]

Harcourt's men returned to Neubourg late in the day, having covered more than forty miles. They had done a great deal of damage to the southern suburbs of Rouen, but they had also confirmed that the French held the city in force, and were likely to hold much of the north bank as well. An attack on Rouen, at least from the south, was impossible. As Alfred Burne suggests, Edward must have been prepared for such an eventuality. It was now urgent, however, that he find a crossing over the Seine; otherwise his carefully prepared strategy for the summer was in danger of collapse, and his army would be stranded deep inside enemy territory. That night his household dined well, the usual plundered beef and mutton augmented by a heron, two bitterns, four geese, almost six dozen chickens, 400 eggs and three cheeses, with almonds and parsley featuring heavily in the sauces. Even at this distance one can almost sense the king and his commanders bracing themselves for hard times ahead. Like all seasoned soldiers they believed in eating well when they could, as leaner times would surely come.

Monday 7 August

On Monday morning the entire army marched, well fed and (apart from those who had accompanied Harcourt) rested. Their destination was Elbeuf, the nearest crossing point over the river. The road from Neubourg runs north-east, gradually descending past the villages of Iville and Amfreville, descending into the valley of a little river, the Oison, climbing briefly past St-Pierre-des-Fleurs, and then descending sharply through a cleft in the steep bluffs, three hundred feet high, that overlook Elbeuf and the Seine.

Elbeuf sits on the south bank of the river, on the southern tip of another of the great U-bends. The town, another of the seigneuries of the Comte d'Harcourt, was a prosperous one. A single bridge spanned the river, extending from the town's high street to the village of St-Jean on the north bank. The river here is about a quarter of a mile across, swift-flowing and tidal, and the bridge would be required intact if the army was to cross.

But the bridge was not intact. The span had been broken, and on its north bank there was a strong defending force of Normans, who jeered and taunted the English as they approached. Some of them turned and exposed their buttocks to the English. One modern historian, Richard Barber, interprets this as being a reference by the Normans to a bit of then-current folklore to the effect that Englishmen had tails. Possibly; but this is also an ageless gesture of insult that has been used by peoples as diverse as the Vikings and the Maori, and its meaning may have been much simpler and more scatological.[50]

They soon had cause to regret their defiance. Several Welsh foot soldiers of the vanguard, perhaps the same daredevils who had waded into the Orne at Caen in the teeth of the Genoese crossbow bolts, had spotted some small boats apparently unguarded on the north bank, and these Welshmen now swam the perilous stream, stole the boats and brought them back over the river. A party of English troops, including some men-at-arms, then rowed across the river, landed on the north bank and attacked the defenders, killing a number of them apparently without loss to themselves.[51] This was a daring piece of enterprise, and had the English been able to reinforce this party they might have seized both ends of the bridge and made repairs. However, it seems the raiders then recrossed the river and rejoined the English army; the reasons for this are not known, but it can be conjectured that the Norman defenders were already being heavily reinforced by Harcourt's main force to the north. The only advantage gained had been the capture of the boats, which were taken along with the army and proved useful on several occasions in future.

Balked again, the English settled down near Elbeuf, and pillaged and burned the town. Once again, one of Jean d'Harcourt's fine properties was reduced to ashes by his brother's allies. But a pattern was also being set; the defenders of the north bank, despite taking losses, were standing firm and barring the English from crossing the river. Despite their courage and tenacity in combat, the English were not going to be able to force their way across the Seine this close to Rouen. Still, all was not yet lost. There were a number of other bridges along the river to the east, starting with Pont de l'Arche seven miles away. Tomorrow the English would try again.

Notes

1 *Acta Bellicosa*, p. 34.
2 Viard, 'Le Campagne de juillet–août', p. 27, no. 3.
3 *Acta Bellicosa*, p. 34.
4 Froissart, vol. 4, p. 413.
5 In Barber, *Life and Campaigns*, p. 18.
6 *CPR 1345–48*, p. 473. The admiral of the fleet north of the Thames was Robert Ufford, Earl of Suffolk, but as he was serving with the army in France at the time, the instruction instead was sent to his lieutenant.
7 In both cases the killers were pardoned, Smyth on the 28th and Pulter on the 29th; *CPR 1345–48*, p. 483.
8 *CPR 1345–48*, pp. 308–9.
9 Wentersdorf, 'The Clandestine Marriages of the Fair Maid of Kent'.
10 Northburgh, in Avesbury, p. 362. This letter has caused some confusion among later historians, who take Northburgh as evidence that Bayeux did not surrender; but Northburgh's letter was dated 27 July, two days before the city did surrender.
11 Barber, *Edward, Prince of Wales*, p. 55.
12 The discovery of the letter on this date is conjectural, and it could easily have happened a day either side; Viard, 'Le Campagne de juillet–août', p. 25, discusses it in the context of events on the 28th, but does not identify this date specifically. The circumstances of the finding of the document are not clear, but the Logis du Roi seems the most likely location given that the English did not have access to the castle.
13 A further clause specified that should France itself be invaded, the same force of 4,000 men-at-arms and 20,000 men could be summoned by the king, on similar terms. See Philippe Contamine, 'The Norman "Nation"', pp. 215–34.
14 Translation in Murimuth, p. 210.
15 Murimuth, p. 211.
16 On 4 April 1338, Harcourt was one of a number of Norman lords, including his brother, the Comte d'Eu and Robert Bertrand, who were witnesses to a separate document in which King Philippe promised to recognise Norman liberties in exchange for their services in the projected invasion; Contamine, 'The Norman "Nation"'.
17 Murimuth, p. 211; Avesbury, p. 363. It was almost certainly read out in other places as well; it was customary for such letters to be copied to each diocese and read out in public in other cities as well.

18 Wynkeley, in Barber, *Life and Campaigns*, p. 18; *Acta Bellicosa*, p. 34.

19 Viard, 'Itineraire'.

20 Most of this area remained lightly populated until the nineteenth century, when the beaches of Cabourg and Deauville were developed as holiday resorts.

21 Burghersh in Avesbury, p. 204.

22 PRO E101/25/11.

23 Murimuth, p. 205.

24 Sumption, pp. 510–11. Accounts survive concerning the raising and expenses of archers in several counties at this time, notably Essex and Hertfordshire: PRO E101/556/30.

25 www.dives-sur-mer.com (19 July 2004).

26 The departure of the fleet at the same time as the army is conjectural. The fleet was still at Caen as late as 29 July, and would be unlikely to leave any later than the army.

27 Viard, 'Le Campagne de juillet–août', p. 32. The *Eulogium* on the other hand says that Troarn was deserted when the English arrived.

28 Denifle, p. 38. Barber, *Edward, Prince of Wales*, p. 55, takes this to mean that part of the army halted for the night at Argences. See also Baker, p. 80.

29 Le Bel, pp. 84–5. Le Bel's geography is so muddled at this point that it is almost impossible to tell what he is talking about. Froissart repeats le Bel's comments almost word for word, and likely drew on him for a source at this point, as evidenced by similar geographical conclusions. Rogers, *War Cruel and Sharp*, p. 252, interprets le Bel to mean that the swathe of destruction was thirteen leagues (thirty-nine miles) broad. This seems an improbable figure; it would have included towns as far south as Livarot, for which there is no evidence. Denifle, usually eager to mention examples of English barbarity, rarely mentions places very far from the main line of march.

30 The N175, which today crosses the valley between Troarn and St-Samson, looks to be built on modern foundations. There may well have been footpaths across the marshes, passable at low tide, but, as at Carentan, the army needed firm roads for its horses and baggage.

31 Viard, 'Le Campagne de juillet–août' (p. 32), says St-Pierre-de-Jonquet was called St-Pierre-sur-Dives, but there may be some confusion; the modern town of St-Pierre-sur-Dives is some distance to the south.

32 The Kitchen Account mentions only Leaupartie; Rumesnil is mentioned by le Baker, p. 80.

33 Inferred, quite simply from the length of time it took the army to cross. So slow was the crossing that the rearguard division was cut off by the rising tide and had to spend the night on the west bank (see below). The scenes in the marsh are readily imaginable to any reader who has ever helped to push a bogged-down vehicle out of mud.

34 Sumption, p. 512, says the average was only five to six miles per day, but the map figures tally with those given by Burne, p. 148.

35 Indeed, it is possible to walk longer distances still. The father of one of the authors, who formerly worked for the US Forestry Service, recalls walking forty-four miles in the course of a fifteen-hour day. He was not, however, in fit condition to walk long distances again for several days. Much more famously, in 1809 the Light Division of the British army marched forty-four miles in twenty-two hours before the battle of Talvera, but suffered heavy casualties through sheer fatigue in the process.

36 This incident is not mentioned in the chronicles, but is attested to by local sources in Lisieux. It is entirely consistent with Guitard's later career, when he several times mediated with local warring factions in attempts to save the city, and escaped only just before its pillage by the Bastard of Savoy's free company in 1357.

37 *Eulogium Historiarum*, ed. F.S. Haydon, London 1863, p. 207. We have assumed that the cardinals arrived on the 2nd, the theft of the horses having most likely taken place during the plundering of the city, but arrival early on the 3rd is also possible. None of the contemporary French chronicles even mentions the arrival of the cardinals in Lisieux, testimony to the fact that the so-called 'peace mission' was not taken seriously by the French.

38 Aubert is sometimes referred to in sources by his former title, as Cardinal of Clermont. Some later historians also include an unnamed archbishop in the delegation, but Viard, 'Le Campagne de juillet–août', believes this is a misinterpretation stemming from the fact that the Cardinal of Naples was also an archbishop.

39 Wynkeley, p. 18; Letter of Edward to Sir Thomas Lucy, quoted in Barber, *Life and Campaigns*, p. 21; *Eulogium*, p. 208.

40 Viard, 'Le Campagne de juillet–août', pp. 36–7; also Nangis. The *Grandes Chroniques* and the chronicle of Richard Lescot both say that the English followed a slightly more northerly route, through 'Falaise' (presumably not the town of Falaise south of Caen, which lies in the opposite direction) and Le Bec-Hellouin, but there is no confirmation from the usually accurate English sources.

41 In the following year, Lombelin and other landholders from the area were ordered to raise troops by Harcourt; M. Charpillon, *Dictionnaire historique de toutes les communes du départment de l'Eure*, Les Andelys, 1868, vol. 2, p. 959. It is possible that Lombelin, or his servants, may have been able to help the English find water.

42 Denifle, p. 39.

43 Charpillon, vol. 3, p. 584.

44 Ibid. Meulan's presence with Harcourt is not specifically mentioned by Charpillon, but he is noted as having been present in all the major campaigns of the time. He survived the summer, and was active as late as 1356.

45 That he did not reconnoitre these bridges at the same time we can infer from the fact that when Edward did move on Elbeuf the following day, it was in hope that the bridge would still be standing.

46 The *Chronique de Pierre de Cochon* (p. 68) refers to the sack of Caen having already aroused great terror in the minds of the people of Rouen.

47 Ibid.

48 *Chronique Anonymous de Valenciennes,* reprinted in *Oeuvres de Froissart,* ed. Kervyn de Lettenhove, p. 493, notes the death of two Englishmen. The death of Daunay is noted in the *Calendar of Inquisitiones Post Mortem,* vol. 8, no. 648, which notes he had a daughter aged 18 or 19 and held lands in Somerset, Devon and Cornwall. There is some debate as to whether he died on 6 or 13 August, but the inquisition seems to prefer the former date.

49 *Chronique de Pierre de Cochon, Chronique des Quatres Premiers Valois,* also Viard, 'Le Campagne de juillet–août', pp. 38–9.

50 *Eulogium,* p. 208; 'A French peculiarity', the editor notes in the margin of the edition. Barber, *Edward, Prince of Wales,* p. 35.

51 *Eulogium,* ibid. The text says the Normans suffered 105 killed, which seems high for so small a raid, and the figures are almost certainly an exaggeration. There is no mention of English losses, but this means only that no one of prominence was killed; the deaths of common soldiers are rarely recorded.

Chapter 7

Elbeuf to Poissy

We found all the bridges broken or strengthened and defended, so that we were in no way able to cross to our enemy.

King Edward III[1]

Tuesday 8 August

In the morning the army marched east, leaving the embers of Elbeuf still smouldering behind them. The road took them along the south bank of the Seine, through Criquebeuf and past the abbey of Bomport, which had been founded by Richard I of England in the late twelfth century. From there they passed on to the small fortified town of Pont de l'Arche. This town too lay on the south bank of the river, with a large bridge over the broad, deep main channel. Pont de l'Arche was well fortified; it was also strongly defended by Jean du Boys, the vicomte of the town, with a small body of men. Du Boys (sometimes also referred to by the Norman version of his name, Du Bosq) was a royal official of some experience who was known and trusted by King Philippe, and he was supported by the captain of the castle, the knight Richard de Mesnil, one of the Mesnil family who owned St-Barbe-sur-Gaillon a few miles further up the river.

The vanguard approached the town with menace, but du Boys, Mesnil and their men held firm. They knew that reinforcements were coming from the main body of the French army along the north bank; indeed, they could probably see these approaching, for the French army was watching every English move and tracking it up the river. And the English army could likewise see the French, and realised that Pont de l'Arche, already well defended, would be impossible to take, at least without very serious losses. Some skirmishing seems to have taken place, again probably confined to exchanges of arrows and crossbow bolts, but there is no indication of losses on either side.[2] As Alfred Burne remarks, Edward's attempt to take the town was probably not very serious, as it was well known to be heavily fortified.[3] However, the attempt had to be made.

A curious incident also took place at Pont de l'Arche when the English received a messenger under flag of truce from King Philippe, challenging Edward to settle their differences by personal combat. This sort of rhetorical flourish was not uncommon in the Middle Ages, and back in 1340 Edward himself had challenged Philippe to personal combat. On that occasion Philippe had refused. This was not the done thing; a true knight should always answer an opponent's challenge, or so the code of chivalry said. There had been perfectly sound reasons for Philippe refusing; Edward was younger and more vigorous than he was, and was well known for his prowess in tournaments and would almost certainly emerge the victor. This, of course, would prove absolutely nothing in political terms. Doubtless his advisors had pointed to all this at the time, but Alfred Burne is probably right when he suggests that the incident still rankled with Philippe.[4] Now he could return the challenge at a time when Edward, finding himself in an increasingly difficult position, was equally likely to refuse. The English army needed its commander, and would hardly benefit if by some mischance he was killed or incapacitated in single combat.

And refuse Edward did, flinging back the retort that he would meet Philippe in battle at Paris. He almost certainly had no intention of going as far as Paris if he could avoid it; once he was across the river, he and his army would be away to the north. But there was no harm in letting his adversary think he was intent on raiding Paris, and sowing as much confusion as possible about his true intentions.

Drawing off from Pont de l'Arche, the vanguard turned south-east, following now the bank of the Eure, which flows up from the south and enters the Seine through several channels around the town, and skirting the northern edge of the large Fôret de Louviers. They pressed on to Notre-Dame-de-Vaudreuil,[5] the main crossing over the lower Eure. North and east of here the land became progressively more marshy, crossed by several channels of the Eure and the Seine. The main body apparently halted at Léry, a prosperous small town with an old church dedicated to St Ouen, three miles back along the road to the north-west. By coincidence, Jeanne de Bourgogne, wife of King Philippe, had property in the area, which the English doubtless took special pleasure in burning.[6] It is possible that the army was strung out to some extent along the road; the royal household seems to have gone on to Notre-Dame-de-Vaudreuil, as this is the location given in the Kitchen Account. Notre-Dame-de-Vaudreuil itself was a sizeable place. Today it is a handsome market town, its medieval houses covered with eighteenth-century fronts, but in the Middle Ages it was an important small town on the crossings of the several channels of the Eure, with a priory, a market and several mills. Generations of French kings had visited and stayed at the royal palace in the town; St Louis had been a frequent visitor.[7] The town had, with nice circularity, furnished a contingent of archers for the army of William the Conqueror that had defeated the English at Hastings. Settling here, the household dined on beef and mutton and poultry, augmented with a small amount of salt fish and some partridges and widgeon which had been shot by the huntsmen. Roasted or grilled meat and salt fish were now the staples of the diet, although the household retained enough stocks of flour, mustard, parsley and other ingredients for sauces.

The position around Notre-Dame-de-Vaudreuil and Léry had an advantage in that it was four or five miles from the north bank of the Seine, and although French troops watching from the high ground to the north-east around Amfreville and Senneville could see movement in the English positions, they were unable to make out details. The picture was further obscured by smoke from the many burnings. Richard Wynkeley wrote that the army was devastating everything for twenty miles around.[8] Edward was now again deliberately employing fire as a tactic; by destroying the countryside of the Île-de-France, he was striking a very deliberate blow at his adversary. This was the French king's heartland, where he and his family had many of their own lands, as did many of his closest supporters and officials. Being forced to watch from the far side of the river as their lands and property went up in smoke would, Edward and his commanders reasoned, be a bitter pill for the French king to swallow. Indeed, he might even forget himself so far as to cross the river and offer battle. Watching the French march along the north shore had given Edward a reasonable idea of his enemy's strength, now probably about the same as his own, and he was confident that at this point he could match the French in an open contest. Once again, he was putting psychological pressure on his adversary and hoping, as at Caen, to force him into making a mistake.

But Philippe was older, wiser and, above all, more cautious than his Constable had been, and however painful he may have found it to watch so many fine towns and villages burn on the south bank, he knew also that he had Edward trapped. All the French had to do was follow the English up the river, matching their speed and blocking or destroying the crossing points. Eventually, Edward would be forced up against the walls of Paris and there, deep in enemy territory without reinforcements or supplies, he could be hemmed in and destroyed. More French troops should have been gathering at St-Denis, north of Paris, and Philippe had also ordered the Duc de Normandie to raise the siege of Aiguillon and march his army north. Soon, he would have Edward heavily outnumbered.

So thorough were the French preparations at this point that it is tempting to believe that this was exactly the objective Philippe had in mind. All along the south bank of the Seine, from Rouen to Paris, French *bailis* and vicomtes had been working hard. Strong places such as Pont de l'Arche, Gaillon, Vernon and Mantes were garrisoned and made ready for defence. Smaller towns and villages were evacuated, so that when the English moved up the river they would find the countryside deserted. Homes and livestock could not be saved, but many lives would be spared and at least some valuable goods removed from the path of the marauders.

As long as Philippe held his nerve and concentrated on blocking or breaking down the bridges, Edward stood little chance of achieving his campaign objectives. And Edward knew it. In his own letter home after the end of the campaign, he reported being 'greatly annoyed' by the French tactics, and Richard Wynkeley expressed what was probably a common frustration throughout the army when he accused the French of being afraid to cross the river and fight.[9] The English army was causing considerable damage, but every mile they travelled east meant further diversion and delay. Edward needed to move north to the Somme, where reinforcements would shortly be arriving at Le Crotoy, and then press on through Picardy to make his rendezvous with Hastings and Henry of Flanders. Instead, the combination of the impassable river and the constant presence of the French army on the north bank was forcing him south-east. His options were limited; for the moment, all he could do was press on and hope that chance or a French mistake would present him with the opportunity he needed.

Wednesday 9 August

In the morning the English attempted to increase the pressure still further by burning Notre-Dame-de-Vaudreuil,[10] and also by sending a party south from the main line of march to Louviers, five miles up the Eure. This was a large and rich town, famous for its cloth manufacturing and markets, and with a fine church of Notre-Dame; there were said to be two thousand houses in the town.[11] But it was indefensible, apparently not even fortified. The inhabitants had been evacuated some time before, and the English found it empty. After pillaging such goods as had been left behind, the English raiders set the town ablaze. Both the main body, marching swiftly south-east from Notre-Dame-de-Vaudreuil towards Heudebouville, and the French on the far side of the river tracking their movements could see the rising cloud of smoke, soon joined by other smaller clouds as the devastation continued.

For the last few miles towards Heudebouville the road runs along the top of high wooded bluffs that fall sharply away to the river, which here is at the southernmost point of one of its bends. Now the army could clearly see, and be seen by, the French on the north bank. The main body of Philippe's army was probably some distance away, cutting across the bend from Vatteville towards La Roquette and Noyers, but scouts would have been sent down into the bend to watch the English in case they should double back towards Rouen. East of Heudebouville the river bends back to the north, towards Les Andelys and Château Gaillard, Richard I's great castle that still glowers out over the valley. There was no crossing point at Les Andelys and Château Gaillard was widely known to be impregnable, and so the English marched on south-east, cutting across the base of the next bend and making for Gaillon. They reached the town around midday.

The castle of Gaillon sits at the top of a steep escarpment, looking down into the town and then across the Seine towards Les Andelys six miles away.[12] Much of the layout of the old town survives, though with more modern buildings. At the castle, the motte still survives but the remainder of the medieval castle has long since gone, replaced by a large and splendid palace built for la Reine Margot, wife of Henry IV, in the late sixteenth century. Town and castle were then the property of the Archbishopric of Rouen. In previous centuries Gaillon had been regarded as an important strongpoint, and its castle had been besieged many times, including by Richard I in 1196. Now it was heavily garrisoned with a strong force of men-at-arms, and more troops were waiting in the town below. The day was wearing on; the English needed to get to Vernon as soon as possible to attempt a *coup de main* on the bridge. Once again, the Prince of Wales's division moved in to the attack.

Details of the fight that followed are sketchy; on the English side, we are told that both Thomas Holland and the steward of the royal household, Richard Talbot, were wounded in the assault, though not badly enough to keep them out of action for long.[13] It can be safely assumed that the English archers and spearmen also suffered casualties. For the rest we must use our imagination; English archers moving in towards the walls, clouds of arrows rising towards the battlements and embrasures to pin the defenders down, men-at-arms and spearmen moving in under cover of the arrows to batter down the gates, the defenders resisting with crossbow and spear and sword but being slowly driven from the gate and walls by superior English numbers and the deadly hail of longbow arrows. This was a bloody fight without quarter; when the resistance finally did break, the French defenders were methodically hunted down and slaughtered.

Now it was the turn of the town. Here the defenders, perhaps believing the castle to be impregnable, lost their nerve and withdrew through the east gate towards the road towards Vernon. They were at once intercepted by other elements from the Prince's division and, as at Caen, the retreat turned into a rout. An unknown number of the French men-at-arms were cut down as they fled. The town's civilian population had been evacuated earlier, and the victorious English looted it swiftly and burned it, along with the nearby village of Ste-Barbe, before resuming their march towards Vernon.[14]

From Gaillon the army pressed on east. Three miles further on a small tributary of the Seine, the St-Ouen, flows down through a steep wooded valley from the south, entering the river at Le Goulet. The manor of Le Goulet was the property of one of the Duc de Normandie's officials, the esquire of his kitchen.[15] This again was deserted, and was burned by the English, who now pushed on towards Vernon. Here the road closely follows the river and is overlooked by high wooded hills, now called the Bois de St-Just but then rather more extensive and known as the Forêt de Longueville. This had been the property of the Knights Templar until their suppression early in the century; it had then been seized by the French crown, and was now the property of Queen Jeanne de Bourgogne, King Philippe's wife.[16] So too were the villages of St-Pierre-de-Longueville,[17] St-Just and St-Marcel, all on the banks of the river just north-west of Vernon. The villages had been evacuated, their people taking shelter inside the walls of Vernon, and the advancing English burned them, advancing through the smoke clouds towards Vernon. Half a mile away on the north bank of the river the French army, remorsely dogging its foe, advanced also.

Vernon was one of the richest towns of the Île-de-France. It was a royal town and trading centre, and its fairs and markets had been important for over a century. During the thirteenth and fourteenth centuries Vernon was often given as a dowry to queens of France, and so the town was currently the property of Queen Jeanne. The town itself was on the south bank of the river, in the plain below the wooded bluffs of the Forêt de Bizy, and controlled access to the only bridge over the Seine between Pont de l'Arche and Mantes. The bridge itself was large, built on stone piers and covered with houses, with a mill on the fifth pier; parts of the bridge and houses can still be seen today.[18] To get to the bridge, however, the English army needed to take the town. This was well fortified with walls and fosses, which ironically had first been built by an English king, Henry I. Now Vernon was strongly defended, and had been reinforced by contingents from the French royal army on the north bank.

Once again, Edward and his commanders were stymied. Ranging futilely around the walls of the town, they set fire to the faubourgs south and east of the town, outside the walls. The Benedictine abbey of La Croix Saint-Leufroy and the priory of St-Louis-de-Vernon, both also outside the protection of the walls, likewise were burned.[19] But although they could raze the outlying districts right up to the edge of the fosse, so that the whole area was covered in ash and smoke, they could not tempt the French garrison into sallying out. An attack on Vernon, even if successful, was likely to be very costly in terms of lives. Even if the English could take the town, which was by no means certain, and gain the south end of the bridge, they would then have to fight their way across the bridge in the teeth of opposition from Philippe's main army, which now included thousands of crossbowmen, and which would have the advantage of a strong defensive position on the heights overlooking the bridge.

That night the army camped around Longueville, with the king probably taking up quarters at the little priory of St-Pierre-de-Longueville and dining on eels and crayfish taken from the river.[20] The English had marched eighteen miles and had one sharp fight, at Gaillon, and a great deal more futile manoeuvring around Vernon. Despite the victory at Gaillon, nothing had been achieved. Between Vernon and Paris there were three more bridges, at Mantes, Meulan and Poissy. Three more chances to cross the Seine, one of which would have to be seized. Things were not yet desperate; but they were becoming serious.

Thursday 10 August

The first stage of the march was spent skirting Vernon and its smouldering faubourgs. This was a delicate operation, for the steep hills and the Forêt de Bizy to the south meant that in order to pass Vernon, the army had to march close to the town itself. The plain was wide enough for the troops to pass by the walls outside of crossbow range, but the risk of a sudden sortie from the town against the open flank of the army had to be guarded against. A more enterprising commander than King Philippe might well have strongly reinforced the town in the night with just such a sortie in mind. A masking force moved towards the town itself in order to protect the English flank and watch the gates, and the remainder of the army marched carefully past. When all were clear the masking force itself pulled back and rejoined the main body, which then moved on up the Seine towards Mantes.

Halfway to Mantes, however, the army was interrupted by unwelcome visitors: the peacemakers were back. The Cardinals of Ostia and Naples reappeared before the English army, asking for audience with King Edward. Reluctantly, the army halted after a march of eleven miles while the emissaries were brought before the king at the village of Freneuse, on the flat plains overlooking the Seine. The Prince's division marched on across the neck of another bend in the river to Mousseaux, a small village on a high bank overlooking the river, some of whose houses were actually troglodyte caves. From here the vanguard could cover the strong castle of Rolleboise to the south-east, which was heavily garrisoned.

The king and the cardinals conferred, without much hope on either side. At Pont de l'Arche Philippe had offered to fight Edward hand-to-hand; was he now likely to be sincere about making peace? It was at once clear that he was not. The terms – Edward to hold Ponthieu and Gascony as fiefs of the French crown exactly as before the war – were identical to those offered at Lisieux. The negotiations were correspondingly short. The cardinals received what the author of the *Acta Bellicosa* terms 'a light-hearted answer', and were sent on their way, this time without even the offer of dinner.[21] The two cardinals returned to the French army by way of Mantes with news that Edward was resolved to fight, and then both took their leave and returned to Avignon, clearly feeling that no more could be done in the cause of peace. They had, however, slowed the English march on Mantes at a critical time.

The timing of the cardinals' meeting with the English cannot have been coincidence. Just at the point where they met, the Seine takes another of its great U-bends, this time to the north. The bend, from its base at Bonnieres and Rolleboise, to its tip at Moisson, is over five miles. Edward, in his march on Mantes, could cut across the base of this bend, while the French on the north bank were forced to go around it, meaning they had many more miles to march in order to reach Mantes. By halting Edward near the base of the bend, the cardinals had – even if unwittingly – given Philippe several additional hours to get his army around the north side of the bend and in position to cover Mantes.[22]

That evening the English commanders planned their riposte. Anger over the lost time, and more general frustration with their enemy's tactics and the need to relieve this frustration through action, may have been part of their motive. More clinically, they may have hoped that a sudden sally onto the north bank of the river, into the flank and rear areas of the French army's line of march, would cause confusion and might slow or even halt the French march towards Mantes while they turned to deal with this new threat.[23]

The plan was for a daring night attack on La Roche Guyon, on the north-west side of the bend. The small town of La Roche nestles under a steep bluff on the north shore of the river, while its powerful castle stands on the heights above, looking out over the valleys of both the Seine and its tributary, the Epte. It was known as one of the strongest fortifications in northern France. It had been fortified by Charles the Bald in 863 as a defence against the Vikings, but the latter had stormed it in 911 and it had thereafter become one of the pivotal defensive positions on the frontier between Normandy and France. It had returned to French hands in the late twelfth century. In the 1190s, in response to the building of Château Gaillard a few miles down river at Les Andelys, the town's lords, the

Seigneurs de la Roche, had fortified the town and greatly strengthened the castle. It consisted of two fortified courts or baileys, one near the bottom of the hill and the second further up the slope. At the highest point there was a very tall and strong round donjon. Like Château Gaillard, it was widely considered impregnable. According to local folklore, if La Roche Guyon should be taken, then the fleur-de-lys would wither; and this was perhaps yet another motive for the English, who resolved to seize the castle.

A force was assembled under the leadership of the banneret Robert Ferrers of Chartley, who served for most of the campaign in the king's division. Men were drawn from other divisions as well, however, including Edward atte Wode, who had been serving in the vanguard.[24] Atte Wode, from southern Staffordshire, had recently been knighted; he may even have been among those young men knighted at Quettehou in July by the Prince himself. He had left behind a wife in England, who unbeknownst to him had become pregnant shortly before the army left for France. He was typical of many of the men in the Prince's service, with little land and a need to make his name and fortune; he may well have volunteered for the attack.

At dusk the boats seized at Elbeuf were brought to the river bank below Freneuse, and Ferrers and his men climbed into them and began rowing upriver. Stealthily, under cover of darkness, they approached La Roche Guyon and landed on the shore below the town. The garrison were on the alert, and by the time Ferrers's men had stormed the town the French were standing to the defence of the lower bailey. Ferrers ordered several houses next to the castle to be set on fire to provide light, and then launched his assault. The defenders resisted strongly, hurling heavy stones from the battlements. One of these struck Edward atte Wode on the head and killed him outright. The rest of the English force, covered by arrows that swept the battlements, crashed into the lower bailey and, by sheer brute force of their assault, drove the enemy up the hill into the second bailey. Pressing home their attack before the defenders could reorganise, they carried this bailey as well. Suddenly the defenders were calling for quarter, and Ferrers, remembering the massacre at Gaillons, restrained his men and received the defenders' surrender.[25]

Those who surrendered included a number of knights and esquires. There was no way these could be transported back across the river, and in a chivalric gesture Ferrers accepted their word of honour that they would pay ransoms if released. Present also were a number of what the author of

Acta Bellicosa describes as 'noble ladies' who had taken shelter in the castle; these may well have been refugees from the south bank, either wives and daughters of local seigneurs or even nuns from the convents at Louviers and Vernon.[26] Ferrers assured these women they would not be harmed. It may have been their presence that decided him against attempting to damage or destroy the castle itself; or he may simply have decided that with powerful French forces in the vicinity, there was not time to hang around. Releasing his prisoners, Ferrers retreated swiftly to the waterfront, re-embarked and rowed back down the river.

It had been a daring raid, and testified to both the confidence and the fighting qualities of the English army. The author of the *Acta Bellicosa*, who does not normally waste words, gives considerable space to this incident, which suggests that Ferrers and his men were much admired by the rest of the army (although he himself does not seem to have received any special reward from the king, as might have been expected on such an occasion). Ferrers himself comes out of the affair particularly well; he had led his men boldly, seemingly undaunted by the reputation of the castle. In the moment of victory he had been magnanimous and had controlled his men. He had killed or captured more than forty of the enemy, and his losses, apart from the unfortunate Edward atte Wode, had been light.[27] But we should also spare a thought perhaps for atte Wode's unnamed widow waiting at home in Staffordshire, knowing by the time the news of his death reached her that autumn that she was also carrying his child. Many similar tragedies doubtless occurred during the summer of 1346; this one is unusual only in that we can still read about it today.[28]

* * *

In the north, Hugh Hastings and his Anglo-Flemish force had fought their way past several French attempts to block them from crossing the river Lys, and on the 10th of August they stormed the town of St-Venant, putting the garrison to the sword. Pressing forward into French territory, they now threatened the important town of Béthune. The town itself was well garrisoned, and a strong force of several thousand men under Louis of Nevers, Count of Flanders, was in the field. There was no immediate danger, but news of Hastings's progress over the next few days doubtless increased the pressure on the French king and his officers.

Friday 11 August

Despite the excitement of the night, the army was soon on the move in the morning, and conducted a difficult march of about thirteen miles. From Freneuse and Mousseaux, the Prince's division and the main body converged on Rolleboise, bypassing its strong castle,[29] and pressed on up the Seine towards Mantes. By midday they were approaching the town itself.

Mantes, like Vernon, is on the south shore of the river, built on a low hill overlooking a broad floodplain. Much of medieval Mantes has disappeared, and it is hard to reconstruct the English approach through the grim tower blocks that now dot the northern outskirts of Mantes-la-Jolie. But medieval Mantes was a large and prosperous town, walled and defended, with a bridge to the north shore. Despite its longer march the previous day, Philippe's army had gained the north end of the bridge and thrown a strong force into the town.[30] Mantes was now impregnable. The dash and courage that Ferrers's men had shown would be futile against walls lined with hundreds of crossbowmen. Once again Edward drew his men off, burning every building and hamlet they came to in an attempt to lure their enemy out to the attack, but to no avail. The swathe of destruction was now immense; the author of the *Acta Bellicosa* says that the country was burned in every direction on 11 August, and as the English army skirted Mantes, again throwing out a masking force to protect against sorties from the town, they were moving under a cloud of smoke.

With Mantes safely behind them the English pressed on east towards Meulan, site of one of the two remaining bridges. Here again the road followed closely the south bank of the river, and the English army could now see clearly the French tracking them on the north bank, the lilies of France and the red and gold banner of Harcourt flying over their ranks, the thousands of Genoese crossbowmen tramping steadily onwards.[31] By late afternoon the English were crossing the Mauldre, a small tributary stream running into the Seine from the south. It was too late now to attempt an attack on Meulan that day, and the main body halted at Epône on the west bank of the Mauldre while the vanguard pushed on across the river to Aubergenville.[32] Both towns sit on low hills on either side of the river, looking out over the floodplain to the north towards the Seine. Here the army made camp, watering horses in the Mauldre, and the royal fisherman and foragers went out to look for fresh fish to supplement the dwindling stocks of salt cod and stockfish. They were in luck, and the king's table were able to dine on a pike and also a carp that had been given as a gift (by whom, sadly, is not recorded, nor is the donor of four carp and bream eaten the following night) along with the usual salt fish and sauces based on mustard and vinegar.

In the evening a strong force of men-at-arms and archers under the command of the Earls of Northampton and Warwick, the two best commanders in the English army, set out to the east. Under cover of night this force drew close to Meulan and then made a separate camp. In the morning, the two earls would attack Meulan and, with luck, at last seize a crossing over the river.[33] Much depended on this venture; if it failed, there was only one more bridge before Paris, and only an incurable optimist would expect the bridge at Poissy not to be guarded as well. Edward and his commanders were too experienced in war to be prone to panic; but there can be little doubt that by now they were worried men.[34]

Saturday 12 August

Unlike Pont de l'Arche, Vernon and Mantes, Meulan was on the north shore of the Seine, with a single unwalled faubourg, Les Mureaux, on the south bank. Its bridge was large and well defended, with a strong tower at the southern end. Nothing remains of the medieval bridge, but it is possible that the tower referred to in the *Acta Bellicosa* was in fact a gate tower, through which the attackers would have had to pass to reach the bridge itself.

In the morning Northampton and Warwick marched towards the bridge and deployed their contingent for battle. As they approached the tower they saw that it was full of armed men, both men-at-arms and crossbowmen, and these in turn began to shout insults at the English. Perhaps provoked by these, perhaps simply desperate to get to the bridge, the English lost their discipline at this point and rushed towards the enemy position. They were at once met with a volley of crossbow bolts. The commanders managed to restrain their men but not until the English had come perilously close to the tower; close enough for the crossbow bolts to penetrate armour, and several English men-at-arms were wounded in this fashion.[35] The hobelar Thomas Stonleye, from William Careswelle's retinue, was killed outright,[36] and we can infer that there were other losses among the common soldiers as well. Order was restored, and the archers began shooting rapidly at the crossbowmen on the battlements, killing or injuring several of them. The English commanders saw that it might be possible to storm the tower under the cover of their own arrows, but they were now close enough to the bridge to see that even if they did so, nothing would be gained. The middle of the span had been destroyed, and there were more French troops waiting on the north shore to oppose any crossing.

Doubtless with heavy hearts, Northampton and Warwick pulled their men back, setting fire to the faubourg of Les Mureaux in order to vent their frustration.[37] Messengers were sent to the king at Epône to inform him of yet another failure. The king's response was to get his army moving again. Already at dawn he had sent out parties to burn and devastate the countryside, still hoping vainly to provoke the French into crossing to attack him; he did not yet know that the Meulan bridge had been broken. Red tongues of flame appeared at many points in the morning, and smoke and ash covered the valley.[38]

One bridge remained: that at Poissy. If this could not be taken, then the English were trapped on the south side of the river. Unable to move north to rendezvous with the Flemings, they would be forced to retreat, either west through lands they had already devastated, or south towards the Loire. Either way, they would be remorselessly pursued by Philippe's army, augmented by the additional forces he was gathering at St-Denis and by the Duc de Normandie's army coming up from the south. And already, as the king received Northampton's news, the day was well advanced. By the time the forces sent out to burn the countryside had been collected and Northampton's own men had returned and had their hurts tended to, there was no longer time to reach Poissy that day, at least not in any condition to fight a battle should one be necessary.

Edward at this point seems to have retained a remarkable calm. He resolved on a short march, turning away from the river and moving southeast up over rolling higher ground, much of it thickly forested, part of the great belt of royal and noble hunting preserves that stretched out from Paris. After just five miles the army halted and made camp, the main body settling in around Ecquevilly (sometimes also known as Fresnes). The Prince of Wales's division moved on a couple of miles to Bures, on the summit of the bluffs overlooking the Poissy bend of the Seine. Here the commanders looked out over the heartland of the Île-de-France. Poissy itself lay peacefully on the south bank of the river, perhaps six miles away. And on the eastern horizon, sharp eyes could see, or at least fancy they could see, the church spires of Paris itself, less than twenty miles distant.[39]

* * *

Although King Philippe had successfully contained the English army south of the river, he had also driven them perilously near to his own capital. The Seine west of Paris runs through another set of long bends: first running south-west; then turning just before St-Cloud and swinging north and north-east to St-Denis; then running south-west to Bougival and St-Germain-en-Laye; then a long sweep back to the north past Herlay and Conflans, with a sizeable tributary stream, the Oise, flowing in from the north; and then finally a much shorter sweep south to Poissy before turning back north-west to Meulan (see Map 4). By accident of geography, Edward was now somewhat nearer to Paris than Philippe. A march of less than twenty miles from Ecquevilly and Burcs would take Edward past St-Germain-en-Laye and St-Cloud to the southern faubourgs of Paris, whereas Philippe would have to march nearly twice as far from Meulan to reach Paris from the north.[40] Philippe needed urgently to put Paris into a state of defence, and so on Saturday, following the repulse of the English at Meulan, he gathered his men-at-arms and rode swiftly towards the city, leaving his foot soldiers to follow on.

A hard decision now had to be made. Poissy, the site of the last remaining bridge, was a royal town, much loved by generations of kings. An older royal palace had recently been supplemented by a fine new one. There was also a rich priory of Dominican nuns; Philippe's own sister, Isabelle de Valois, was the prioress there. But Poissy was not walled and could not be defended. With a heavy heart, Philippe ordered the vicomte of the town to break down the bridge and render it impassable and then evacuate the town and priory.[41] The bridge was broken down, some of its beams left lying in the river, and the nuns and townspeople left hurriedly for the safety of Paris. A contingent of men-at-arms coming south from Amiens to Paris was ordered to divert from its line of march to defend the crossing point on the north shore, rendering all secure.

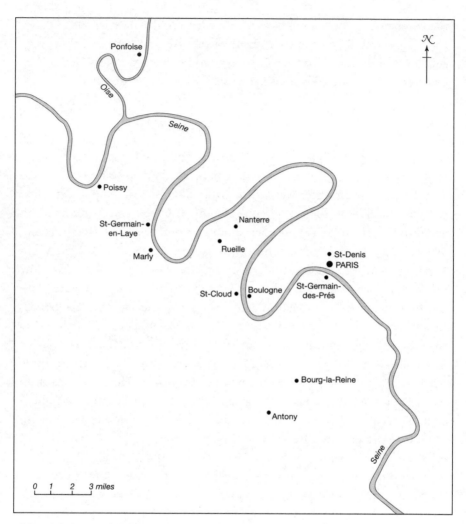

Map 4 Poissy and Paris.

Sunday 13 August

Sunday morning saw the English army moving early, coming down off the heights around Bures and entering Poissy, six miles away, by late morning. They found the rich and handsome town empty, and if the author of the *Acta Bellicosa* is to be believed, some of them indulged in a little sightseeing, admiring the beautiful priory church and its fine altar and wall paintings, and the equally fine royal palaces. Particularly impressive was the fact that no expense had been spared in their construction. At the priory, even the outbuildings were built of smoothly planed wood and ashlar blocks rather than the more common rough beams and rubble, and the author of the *Acta Bellicosa* was so moved that he described it as the finest priory in the world.[42]

More practically, the English also examined the bridge, which consisted of a series of stone piers on which was built a wooden roadway, this resting on heavy beams spanning the piers. As they must have expected, it had been broken; about sixty feet of the centre of the span had been cut down. However, all was not lost. At least one of the beams was still lying in the river, presumably wedged against one of the stone piers against the current of the river.[43] What is more, the north bank of the river was, for the moment at least, unguarded, meaning that repair work could be carried on without interruption. The north shore was flat and marshy in places, with a road running north-east along the river towards Chanteloup and eventually to Pontoise. The high ground of the escarpment could be seen in the distance to the north.

Orders were quickly given, and the army began to occupy the town. The royal household took over the new royal palace, next to the empty priory, while the Prince of Wales's household took over the old palace. Meanwhile, William Hurley and the royal carpenters unloaded their tools and materials and set to work on the bridge, no doubt assisted by a labour force drawn from the rest of the army and with the aid of the boats captured at Elbeuf. Other parties began looking for wood to use for further beams and supports, and for laying down a roadway. Slowly and painstakingly, the fallen beam was hoisted from the river and lowered into place on the piers and made fast. Of course the carpenters had already had some practice at this sort of work, at Carentan and Pont-Hébert, but this bridge was rather larger and probably also more badly damaged, and work proceeded slowly.

They were hard at work, with still only the single beam in place, when the alarm was raised. French horsemen could be seen to the north, coming down the riverside road from Chanteloup. There were several hundred of them, with foot soldiers and a small column of wagons.[44] This force had been raised in and around Amiens and sent south to join the army mustering at Paris; it was led by two minor Picard barons, the Sire d'Aufremont and the Sieur de Revel, along with other knights and men raised by the commune of Amiens.[45] This was the force which Philippe had ordered to guard the north bank to prevent the English from repairing the bridge. They had arrived just too late.

The Amienois, however, did their valiant best. They had crossbows and also several ballistas, large crossbows which fired heavy stone shot and were apparently mounted on the backs of carts. These were formidable weapons which had a longer range than the ordinary crossbow and would do considerable damage to even an armoured man.[46] They were normally used in siege operations, and it was unusual to see them in the field; it is probable that Aufremont and Revel intended to emplace these on the north bank to cover the bridge. Now, seeing the English already in possession and working on the bridge, they quickly formed up and moved into the attack, 'like a ravening wolf on the sheepfold', as the *Acta Bellicosa* says. The only Englishmen on the far side of the partly mended bridge were a few carpenters.

The senior English commander on the spot was the Constable, the Earl of Northampton. There was no time to gather the boats; the only way across the river was the single wooden beam, sixty feet long and a foot wide, with the murky waters of the Seine swirling twenty feet below.[47] For a fully armoured man-at-arms, encased in eighty or a hundred pounds of chainmail and metal plate, falling into the water would mean certain death by drowning. On the other hand, unless an armed force could cross the river and hold off the Amienois, the latter would occupy one end of the bridge and prevent the vital repairs from being completed. There was, in the end, no choice.

Fully armoured and sword in hand, Northampton walked across the foot-wide beam. Others followed him, dismounted men-at-arms moving in single file along the narrow walkway above the swirling waters of the river. Encumbered by weapons and armour, they must have moved slowly. Whether any fell to their deaths is not recorded; some may well have done so. But many others crossed, and by the time the French approached the bridge, twenty-five banners had been raised on the north bank and several hundred English troops were preparing to defend it. It was a slender force, but it proved to be enough. Aufremont and Revel attacked hard, knowing full well what the stakes were, but the English men-at-arms, their backs to the river, were equally desperate, and in the end their courage and skill, aided by the arrows of those archers who had either crossed the beam as well or were still standing on the far side of the bridge, carried the day. The French were driven back, then broke. The English pursued them, hacking and shooting down the fugitives. In their desperation to escape, some of the French foot soldiers unharnessed the carthorses and leaped onto the backs of these, sometimes with two or three on a single horse.[48] The carts, abandoned, were overrun by the English, and proved to contain foodstuffs as well as crossbow bolts and stone shot for the ballistas. The food was taken back to the army, and the carts and munitions were then burned. Once again the French had suffered heavy losses, while English casualties had been minimal.[49]

It was one of the most astonishing episodes of the campaign so far, and, like Ferrers's capture of La Roche Guyon, displayed to the full the fighting qualities of the English. Full credit here must go to Northampton, who led from the front, crossing the beam and leading the defence against the French. The crossing of the river was a remarkable act of courage in its own right, but it probably also saved the English army. If the Amienois had gained the north end of the bridge and prevented its repair, then Edward would have been trapped exactly as his adversary planned. Indeed, Philippe himself continued to believe that Edward *was* trapped, and behaved accordingly; and when, the following day, he was informed that the Amienois had been defeated and Edward was repairing the bridge at Poissy, his nobles refused at first to believe it.[50]

A combination of luck, mistakes by his enemy, and courage and quick thinking by his Constable had saved Edward from great peril. By nightfall, more beams had been put in place and planks laid down so that a horse and cart could be driven across the bridge, though more strengthening was required to make it safe for the whole army to pass and another day's work would be needed to ensure this.[51] Now, with his exit route to the north finally secure, Edward turned his attention once again on his adversary. Calculating as ever, he reckoned that a feint towards Paris might throw his enemy off balance and distract the French while the English made their own preparations to march north. A more cautious commander would have marched north towards Picardy at once; Edward instead made preparations to strike south and east towards the enemy capital. That night he and his household dined in his adversary's fine new palace off plundered beef and mutton along with geese, chickens, doves, partridge and widgeon, with four cheeses and the usual pickles and sauces.

His adversary, meanwhile, had reached Paris and ordered his army to begin congregating at St-Denis, to the north of the city. The first foreign contingent, that of the King of Bohemia with his son the newly elected King of the Romans, and other allies including the Count of Salm, had arrived, and more levies were coming in from the communes and countryside of the Île-de-France. Taking a strong force, Philippe marched through Paris and went to the abbey of St-Germain-des-Près on the left bank, standing by in case Edward should attempt a sudden assault on the city. Panic over the close approach of the English was already beginning to grip Paris.

Monday 14 August

On Monday the main body of the army rested at Poissy. The carpenters continued to work on the bridge, while for the army itself there was plenty of ongoing maintenance to be carried out; they had been marching without rest for a week, and some at least had been engaged in the fighting at Pont de l'Arche, Gaillon, La Roche Guyon, Meulan and Poissy itself. There were wounds to be tended, provisions to be foraged and stored, weapons and harnesses to be mended and repaired. The thud of carpenters' hammers from the bridge competed with the ring of farriers and armourers striking their anvils.

For the vanguard division, however, there was no respite. Early in the morning the Prince of Wales's men, with the two marshals leading the way, set off south-east through the Forêt de St-Germain. Three miles away the village of St-Germain-en-Laye nestled between the forest and the river, and here too was another royal palace. Village and palace were both put to the torch. Here it seems that the prince and much of the division halted, while Warwick, Harcourt and other commanders led smaller raiding parties forward to spread devastation towards Paris.

The French chronicles at this point are full of woe. They list the castles and palaces and fine places that were destroyed, and they were many. The royal castle of Montjoie, near Marly, was burned, and with it yet another royal palace, the Chastel le Roy, completed within the last two years and described as one of Philippe's favourites. Some parties went north, burning Nanterre and Reuil, though attempts to burn the ancient abbey at Reuil, which had been founded by Charles the Bald in the ninth century, apparently failed. The French chroniclers attributed this to the divine intervention of St-Denis, as Reuil was a daughter house of the cathedral of St-Denis, but why the headless saint should have intervened to spare this monastery when so many others went up in smoke is not clear.[52] Further south, a raiding column under the command of Godefroi d'Harcourt penetrated as far as St-Cloud, on the west bank of the last bend in the river before Paris and only about four miles from the city's western gate. The bridge linking St-Cloud to Boulogne had been broken down on King Philippe's orders; had it still stood, the raiders might well have penetrated all the way to the western edge of the city itself.[53]

As the flames and smoke grew nearer and nearer, alarm broke out in Paris. It had been centuries since an invading army had menaced the city, and its fortifications, constructed by Philippe Augustus a century and a half earlier, had not been maintained. The city itself had outgrown the walls, especially on the north and west where the faubourgs, known collectively as 'nouvelle Paris', were extensive and defenceless.[54] Now the people were terrified, 'and not without cause', noted the author of the *Grandes Chroniques*.[55] Paris had never been fond of Philippe de Valois, and now, as he rode back through the city from St-Germain-des-Près on his way north, he was besieged by anxious citizens who demanded to know where he was going. He responded that he was going to St-Denis, five miles north of the city, where his main army was now concentrated. The citizens demanded that he not leave them defenceless, to which he replied that it was he and his army that the English king sought to attack; by leaving the city, he would draw the English after him and Paris would be safe. Only the more simple-minded among his listeners could have been satisfied by this, but there was little they could do. The king rode away to St-Denis, and the people of Paris began making desperate preparations to defend themselves, the smoke and ash of Nanterre and St-Cloud drifting over the city.

The great basilica of St-Denis, burial place of French kings for centuries, looked out from a high hill over the Seine valley. On the plain nearby, the French army was gathering. To the Normans and Genoese whom Philippe had led up the river had now been added the strong forces levied in the Île-de-France and elsewhere. The king's brother, the Comte d'Alençon, and his nephew Louis de Châtillon, Comte de Blois, were there, along with the Comte de Sancerre and the Comte de Dammartin. Also recently arrived was a powerful force under King Jean of Bohemia, who had celebrated his fiftieth birthday four days before, his own Bohemians and Luxembourgeois accompanied by the troops of Simon, Count of Salm.[56] King Jaume of Majorca had arrived in the capital also, and the Savoyards under Louis of Vaud were said to be on their way. Philippe also believed that his son, the Duc de Normandie, was on his way north with his own powerful army; he could not have known that the latter was still dithering before Aiguillon, trying unsuccessfully to negotiate a truce with Henry of Lancaster.

Still smarting from his reception in the streets of Paris and stung by the damage being done to his country and his reputation, Philippe called a council of war, summoning the senior nobles already present at St-Denis. This was not a spectacular success. No course of action could be agreed on, and in the end the great army, now considerably larger than that of his opponent, sat at St-Denis and did nothing. News arrived from Poissy, allegedly from a common soldier who had been captured and then released, that the bridge had been seized by the English and was being repaired; this was met with frank disbelief. The author of the *Grandes Chroniques* says that the man was not believed because he was a commoner, and comments dolefully: 'Thus was proved the truth of the saying: "The poor man speaks and they mock him, saying, who is this? The rich man speaks, and all fall silent out of respect." '[57]

The only positive measure taken was the sending of a letter to Edward at Poissy, challenging him to, in effect, stand up and fight. After accusing Edward of being a false vassal and invading France and committing various offences against its people – and the latter at least was true enough – Philippe reminded the English king of his throwaway line at Pont de l'Arche, that he would fight him before the walls of Paris. Before the walls of Paris he now was, and the time had come to make good on his promise. Philippe offered four dates for the set-piece battle, the 17th, 19th, 20th or

22nd, and two possible venues, on the plain south of the city beyond Bourg St-Germain and near the village of Vaugirard, or to the north-west between Franconville and Pontoise. If Edward was as eager for battle as he had claimed he was at Pont de l'Arche, Philippe said, then he should take up this offer. He asked that the English king confirm his acceptance of the offer in writing, and added hopefully that in the meantime Edward's army should refrain from burning and pillaging.

The offer was sent to Poissy by means of another ecclesiastical messenger, the Archbishop of Besançon, riding under a flag of truce.[58] Edward received him late in the day, and must have been hard pressed not to laugh. In Philippe's letter could be detected the note of a man who thought he was in control of the situation; but Edward knew that, since the previous afternoon, this was no longer true. He could march away to the north any time he wanted. What was most important now was to distract Philippe away from the north, particularly from the Pontoise area, which was very close to his own projected line of march. Whether he responded in writing as requested is not known, but he reportedly told the archbishop that he was very pleased with Philippe's offer and was ready to fight his adversary at any time. He declined, however, the offer of a meeting on a set date and place, and said that if the French wished to find him, all they had to do was look for the smoke of burning towns.[59] He then trailed a heavy hint that after leaving Paris he planned to move south, ostensibly to link up with Lancaster.[60]

Quite what Edward said and quite what Philippe heard appear to be two different things. Edward seems to have been clear that he was refusing his adversary's offer, but Philippe seems to have been convinced that it had been accepted. Believing that he would meet his enemy on the 17th, not at Bourg St-Germain but further south near the village of Antony, he remained at St-Denis and prepared to celebrate the forthcoming feast of the Assumption of the Blessed Virgin Mary, while the smoke still rose from the west and the murmuring in Paris grew still louder. The word 'treason' began to appear, and finds its way into the texts of the chronicles as well. The chronicle of Jean le Bel, the *Chronique des Quatre Premiers Valois*, even the normally loyal *Grandes Chroniques* accused Philippe of vacillation and his senior nobles and councillors of outright betrayal of their country, claiming that the latter advised the king to do nothing while towns and abbeys and palaces burned and the English ravaged the heartland of France with impunity. Why, they demanded, did not the large and powerful French army move to Poissy and confront Edward? They could think of no reasons apart from the cowardice of the king and the treason of his advisors.[61]

But it appeared that Philippe was now preparing to fight. And in the evening the ravaging of the country to the west of Paris was also coming to a halt. Orders had gone out from the English headquarters at Poissy to the marauding units in the field, ordering that on the following day, the feast of the Assumption of the Blessed Virgin Mary, no raiding or burning was to be done on pain of life or limb. The author of the *Acta Bellicosa* says glibly that this was on account of the feast day itself; all warlike activity was to be suspended while the army made its devotions to the Mother of God.[62] In fact, as the author almost certainly knew, the raiding parties were being ordered to fall back in the morning on the vanguard's main position at St-Germain-en-Laye, and the vanguard itself was then to rejoin the main army at Poissy.

*   *   *

Hugh Hastings's expedition had become increasingly bogged down. It had taken him too long to force his way across the Lys, but he had finally done so and reached Béthune. When the Anglo-Flemish force arrived on the 14th, they found the town covered by a pall of smoke; the faubourgs had been burned and the town was apparently deserted. The unwary Flemish vanguard made straight for the town, and was promptly ambushed by the garrison under the command of Godefroi d'Ennequin, who had hidden in a nearby wood. The Flemings tumbled back in disorder, and Ennequin returned to the town, which was already in a state of defence. The following day a series of attempts to storm the walls were beaten back with heavy casualties, and the Flemings the settled down to besiege the town. The allies themselves were growing increasingly fractious; the leaders of the Three Towns were highly jealous of each other and disinclined to listen to Hastings, who urged them to bypass Béthune and continue south. He was unsuccessful, and the siege of Béthune began. This venture was never destined to have much success. Béthune was well provisioned and garrisoned and Ennequin had already shown himself to be a very able commander. A key element in Edward's strategy was beginning to unravel.

Tuesday 15 August

The feast day of the Assumption of the Blessed Virgin Mary dawned with the air around Paris heavy with smoke and ash. The day was one of the most important in the Christian calendar, and in both armies preparations were made for its celebration. The more immediate business of war, however, continued without pause. In the French camp at St-Denis, preparations were made for the forthcoming move south of the river to confront the enemy on the plain around Antony. Some units of foot soldiers may have begun moving off that morning, for it would take many hours for the army to negotiate the streets of Paris and the bridges over the Seine. With the King of Bohemia and other senior nobles, King Philippe attended mass in the cathedral of St-Denis, perhaps taking comfort and inspiration from the tombs of his illustrious predecessors. Afterwards the nobles feasted (French records are much less complete than English ones, so we do not know on what), and in the afternoon the main body of the army began marching south to keep their rendezvous.[63] However, a strong force, probably including the Bohemians, remained at St-Denis.[64]

At Poissy the English too were preparing to march, but in the opposite direction. Edward could not yet know if his bluff had succeeded, but his time in the Paris area was running out. In late morning he too celebrated mass, probably in the fine church of Princess Isabelle's priory. Afterwards, in a splendid piece of theatre, he dressed in a sleeveless red robe trimmed with ermine and gave a feast for his nobles.[65] Two herons and a swan formed the centrepieces of a meal which also saw the consumption of four geese, four dozen hens and chickens, four dozen doves, twenty-six carcasses of mutton and eight of beef, and two fresh carp. Two gallons of lard and a bushel of salt were used in the cooking, and the entire meal cost a little over £5, the cost being greatly reduced by the fact that the beef and mutton had been plundered from nearby.

Honour having been done to the Mother of God, the fine robes were packed away and the preparations for the march resumed. The main body of the army had had plenty of time to make do and mend while camped in and around Poissy, but the Prince of Wales's vanguard, which arrived back in the camp during the afternoon, required rest for men and horses. Ahead of them lay a week of hard marching. The first objective was to gain the river Somme, about ninety miles to the north. Reinforcements should be arriving soon at Le Crotoy at the mouth of the river, and on the far side Edward expected to make rendezvous with Hugh Hastings and Henry of Flanders; the size of the combined force would allow him to turn the tables on the enemy. But speed was of the essence; if the French should gain the Somme before him, then they could break down the bridges and bar his passage north exactly as they had done along the Seine. The next day would show whether Edward's bluff had worked, and whether he had gained a head start over his adversary.

The second phase of the campaign had largely gone Philippe's way, and had come very close to giving him victory. Later historians have charged him with being irresolute, but on the march down the Seine he seems full of resolve, willing to sacrifice fine towns and his own property to pen Edward south of the river and force him onto the barrier of Paris. His behaviour at the end smacks not of indecision but of overconfidence; believing he had Edward trapped, with the only choices for the latter being inglorious retreat or battle against a greatly superior force, he moved slowly and methodically, gathering his army and issuing a formal challenge that would, he hoped, force his enemy to commit himself. Only in the last few days did a combination of his own mistakes and the courage and quick thinking of the Earl of Northampton undo all his plans. Now it remained to be seen if he could retrieve the situation.

Notes

1 Letter of Edward III to Thomas Lucy, in Barber, *Life and Campaigns*, p. 21.
2 *Actes Normandes de la chambre des comptes sous Philippe VI de Valois*, ed. L. Delisle, Paris, 1871, p. 347, no. 195. In December, when settling back wages owed to du Boys, Philippe acknowledged that he had encountered many difficulties and sorrows in recent months. Sumption, p. 513, and Rogers, *War Cruel and Sharp*, p. 253, take this to mean that du Boys and his garrison suffered heavy losses in the fighting, but our reading of the document suggests a more general meaning, and that du Boys was simply being commended for good service.
3 Burne, p. 150. Some of the ramparts of the medieval Pont de l'Arche can still be seen.
4 Burne, pp. 150–1.
5 On modern maps, listed simply as le Vaudreuil.
6 Charpillon, vol. 3, p. 431.
7 Ibid., pp. 612–17.

8 Wynkeley, in Murimuth, p. 363.

9 Edward, in Barber, *Life and Campaigns*, p. 21; Wynkeley, in Murimuth, p. 363.

10 Although the royal palace, if burned, cannot have been too badly damaged; only a few years later, Jean, Duc de Normandie was spending sizeable sums on decorative wall paintings for the palace, Charpillon, vol. 3, p. 613.

11 *Chronographia Regum Francorum*, p. 229; this figure may be an exaggeration, as almost certainly is the subsequent statement that a number of the citizens of the town were killed.

12 The English chroniclers sometimes confuse Gaillon with La Roche Guyon, which was not in fact attacked until the following day. Froissart goes so far as to confuse it with Gisors, many miles away.

13 Cotton MS Cleopatra D.vii, fol. 179, quoted in Baker, p. 253, maintains this battle took place at Longueville, and this has been followed by some modern historians, notably Sumption, p. 515. However, Viard, 'Le Campagne de juillet–août', p. 42, questions this and believes that the action described in the Cotton MS was the taking of Gaillon. Viard notes that there is no evidence of a castle at Longueville, and the meticulous history of Vernon by Edmond Meyer describes the villages of the Longueville district but makes no mention of a castle (Edmond Meyer, *Histoire de Vernon*, Les Andelys, 1874, vol. 1, p. 50). The problem stems in part from the fact that the reliable *Acta Bellicosa* is missing several pages of manuscript at this point, and other sources confuse locations with alarming regularity; see previous note.

14 Cotton MS for details of the battle and its aftermath, but see previous note.

15 Charpillon, vol. 3, p. 847.

16 Ibid., also Meyer, *Histoire de Vernon*, vol. 1, p. 50.

17 Now St-Pierre d'Autils.

18 The mill was owned by the Sieur de la Harelle, who owned the nearby village of St-Just; an annual fee of six livres and a dish of fish were due. Charpillon, vol. 3, p. 799. Le Bel, p. 86, says that the bridge had been deliberately broken by the French, but this seems unlikely, as it would then have been impossible to reinforce the garrison on the south bank.

19 Or so suggests Deniflé, p. 39. The burning of the faubourgs is attested by the *Grandes Chroniques*, vol. 9, p. 274. Rogers, *War Cruel and Sharp*, p. 254, interprets this as meaning the town itself was burned, but this is not generally supported.

20 The Kitchen Account simply gives 'Longville' as the place of the night halt.

21 *Acta Bellicosa*, p. 35, which confirms that the cardinals returned to the army that night.

22 This is conjectural; but apart from sheer coincidence, we can think of no other reason why the cardinals should suddenly appear with an offer of peace, especially given Philippe's early bellicose attitude.

23 Or indeed, both motives were equally important. These motives are again conjectural, but some hypothesis is needed to explain the events of that night.

24 Sometimes also known as Edward du Boys; *Eulogium*, p. 208 describes him as a knight of new making.

25 Baker, p. 81, mentions the attack taking place at night; Viard, 'Le Campagne de juillet–août', p. 43, suggests that Ferrers's men set fire to the town in order to provide light for their attack on the castle, and this seems reasonable. *Acta Bellicosa* mentions that the initial assault was resisted, indicating the garrison were prepared when Ferrers attacked the castle.

26 *Acta Bellicosa*, p. 35.

27 Atte Wode is the only casualty mentioned, but, once again, deaths and injuries among the common soldiers are often not recorded.

28 *Calendar of Inquisitiones Post Mortem*, vol. 9, p. 17, no. 35 records the inquisition held concerning atte Wode's lands at Kinver and Stourton, both in Staffordshire, on 8 May 1347 at Kinver. His lands had been granted to him by Henry Mortimer. The jurors knew where he had died, but not the exact date. They also recorded that he left a daughter, said to be aged seven weeks at the time.

29 Viard, 'Le Campagne de juillet–août', p. 43; Froissart, vol. 4, pp. 421, 424.

30 *Acta Bellicosa*, p. 35, says that the vanguard of the French army was in and around Mantes, implying a force of several thousand men. *Grandes Chroniques*, vol. 9, p. 275, also says the town was well guarded.

31 *Grandes Chroniques*, vol. 9, p. 275, mentions that the two armies could often see each other clearly across the river, and in this area the river and floodplain are comparatively narrow.

32 Epône is given as the halting place in the Kitchen Account, but the *Acta Bellicosa*, p. 35, gives Aubergenville. The practice of dividing the army at the night halt had been adopted at many points on the campaign, and it seems reasonable to suggest that it was done here as well.

33 *Acta Bellicosa* indicates, though without saying so directly, that the attack on Meulan took place on the 11th. Alfred Burne, however (p. 151), suggests that the Meulan attack must have taken place on the 12th, and we follow this for several reasons. First, the march on the 11th was a long one and would have been further complicated by the passage around Mantes. It would have been late in the day for a full-scale attack on the Meulan bridge; a simple raiding party, such as that at La Roche Guyon the night before, would not be sufficient, as the attacking force would have to be able to take and hold the bridge against the full weight of the French army. Second, the march the following day, the 12th, is very short. This is consistent with the main body waiting on the outcome of the Meulan attack; if, however, the attack had already been carried out and failed, then Edward would have needed to move swiftly on to Poissy, the last remaining bridge.

34 The *Acta Bellicosa* and the letters of the English king and his officers remain remarkably sanguine at this point, showing no sign of worry or stress. But these were written some weeks after the events described here, and benefit from 20–20 hindsight.

35 *Acta Bellicosa* says that several leaders of the army were wounded but does not name them, suggesting that neither Northampton nor Warwick was among the injured; certainly both remained active throughout the rest of the campaign.

36 Wrottesley, 'Crécy and Calais from the public records', Collections for a *History of Staffordshire*, 1897, p. 165.

37 *Grandes Chroniques*, p. 275.

38 The *Acta Bellicosa* and later the king himself accuse the French of cowardice in not crossing the river to attack the English, conveniently forgetting that the broken bridge also barred the French from crossing as well. Rogers, *War Cruel and Sharp*, p. 254, believes the 'red flames' mentioned by *Acta Bellicosa* may in fact have been red banners the colour of fire, indicating that the English were willing to fight to the death, but we have followed the conventional interpretation. The *Chronique de St-Ouen*'s statement (cited in Rogers, p. 254) that the English here encountered and defeated a force from Amiens is most likely a confusion with the later incident at Poissy.

39 *Acta Bellicosa*, p. 36, maintains Paris was clearly visible from Bures.

40 A point made by Sumption, p. 517.

41 The author of the *Acta Bellicosa* maintains he had tears in his eyes, though how this author, travelling with the English army, could have known this is not clear.

42 *Acta Bellicosa*, pp. 36 7.

43 So says Froissart, pp. 420, 421 and 424, and this seems likely; it would have been difficult to have procured a beam of sufficient size and brought it into place in time for the battle in the afternoon.

44 Wynkeley says 1,000 horse and 2,000 foot, in Barker, *Life and Campaigns*, p. 19, but this may be an exaggeration. *Eulogium*, p. 209 and le Baker both say 300 men-at-arms but do not give numbers for the foot. *Acta Bellicosa* says there were 21 carts, but other sources mention 30 and 32.

45 *Chronique des Quatre Premiers Valois*, p. 15 gives the most detailed description of the French force.

46 The word 'ballista' is sometimes translated as 'mangonel', but mangonels were catapults that launched heavy stones by means of a vertical arm; the ballista, as noted, is in effect an oversized crossbow.

47 The dimensions of the beam are given by the *Acta Bellicosa*, p. 37; Wynkeley says several beams were in place, but this in no way detracts from the courage displayed by the English.

48 *Acta Bellicosa*, p. 37.

49 *Acta Bellicosa*, p. 37, from which much of the above account is drawn, says the French lost more than fifty men, but this may be a reference to men-at-arms only; Richard Wynkeley's estimate of 1,000 is surely too high. The total French loss was probably in the low hundreds. *Acta Bellicosa* says there were no English casualties, but again this probably should be interpreted as meaning that no one of gentle birth was killed.

50 *Grandes Chroniques*, vol. 9, p. 278.

51 *Acta Bellicosa*, p. 37, and le Baker, p. 81, note that the bridge was passable by nightfall on the 13th, but other sources, including Wynkeley and Edward himself, suggest that work carried on until the 15th. It is likely that by nightfall on the 13th the bridge would have been passable in an emergency, but not secure enough for the repeated passage of heavy wagons.

52 *Grandes Chroniques*, vol. 9, p. 275.

53 Froissart, pp. 420 and 432, mistakenly lists Boulogne as being among the places burned. Viard, 'Le Campagne de juillet–août', p. 38, contains a good analysis of the various accounts of this raid. The identification of Harcourt as the leader of the unit that burned St-Cloud comes from le Bel, p. 87, but should perhaps be used with caution, as pro-French chroniclers, who viewed Harcourt (rightly) as a traitor, are perhaps overly keen to blacken his name.

54 J. Favier, *La Guerre de Cent Ans*, Paris, 1980, pp. 106–7. Favier also says that plans were being made to abandon the districts on the left bank of the Seine and defend the line of the river. Sumption, p. 517, maintains that public order had broken down to the extent that Jean of Bohemia's men-at-arms were required to police the city; if so, the use of foreign troops to police the populace must have inflamed the situation still further.

55 *Grandes Chroniques*, vol. 9, p. 274.

56 *Chronique des Quatre Premiers Valois*, p. 15, lists the nobles assembled; it mistakenly includes the Comte de Flandres, but he was still in the north preparing to defend Picardy against Hugh Hastings and Henry of Flanders.

57 *Grandes Chroniques*, vol. 9, p. 278. The *Grandes Chroniques* goes on to say that eventually the story was taken seriously and it was then that the men of Amiens advanced to attack the bridge, but English sources including the reliable *Acta Bellicosa* place the attack of the Amienois on the afternoon of the previous day.

58 The Archbishop is also variously identified as the Bishop of Meaux and the Bishop of Melun; see Viard, 'Le Campagne de juillet–août', p. 747, for his likely identity.

59 *Historia Roffensis*, cited by Rogers, *War Cruel and Sharp*, p. 257. Neither the posturing of Philippe's letter nor the bombast of Edward's reply should be taken seriously; both, as Burne, p. 152, suggests, were probably meant for public relations purposes, Philippe's in particular to salvage his own reputation after a bad day.

60 According to the *Grandes Chroniques*, he indicated that he planned to move towards Montfort l'Amaury, nearly twenty miles to the south-west.

61 Le Bel, p. 87; *Chronique des Quatre Premiers Valois*, p. 15; *Grandes Chroniques*, vol. 9, p. 276

62 *Acta Bellicosa*, pp. 37–8.

63 15 and 16 August are both given as the dates when Philippe's army crossed Paris and assembled at Antony. Given the length of time it would have taken to march the full force through Paris and across the Seine, it is likely that at least

part of both days was required. It is possible, of course, that the full army was not marched to Antony and that some units at least remained at St-Denis.

64 Inferred, as there is no other way of accounting for the speed with which the French later moved north; see following chapter.

65 The robe is described by Froissart, p. 426; although not verified elsewhere, this detail seems entirely in keeping.

Chapter 8

Poissy to Airaines

We shall never be dictated to by you, nor will we accept a day and place for battle on the conditions which you have named.

Edward III to Philippe VI, 17 August 1346[1]

Wednesday 16 August

The morning of the 16th of August saw the French and allied army forming up outside the southern outskirts of Paris, near St-Germain-des-Près. In full battle order, banners flying and armour gleaming, they then marched four miles south past Argeuil and Bourg-la-Reine to take up positions around the village of Antony. Here they settled down to make camp, resting and preparing for the battle which they expected, in all apparent confidence, to come the following day. With hindsight, it is almost impossible to believe how Philippe and his commanders could have been so naïve. Even if Philippe himself was prepared to believe that Edward was marching south prepared to do battle, why did not some of his commanders, especially that great veteran soldier the King of Bohemia, alert him to alternative possibilities? The explanation of some French historians, that Philippe believed sincerely in the laws of chivalry and assumed his enemy did likewise, does not hold water; Philippe was a statesman, who had founded a dynasty and governed a fractious kingdom of unruly nobles through a combination of force, persuasion and bribery for nearly twenty years. His belief in the laws of chivalry was almost certainly no greater than that of his opponent. What is much more likely is that he fell into the trap so common among generals, of believing what he wanted to believe. He had laid his plans with care; that they could go wrong now was unthinkable. And so he waited for Edward to come and give him a battle.

But Edward was now thirty miles away. Early in the morning the trumpets had sounded and mustered the army for the march north. Officials of the royal household had been posted to protect the priory, and also rather peculiarly the new royal palace, while the old palace which had been the quarters of the Prince of Wales was set ablaze. The remainder of the town was also burned, and under the pall of smoke the army crossed the bridge in a long column of men, horses and wagons. The crossing took around three hours.[2] The men of the rearguard division paused to break the bridge behind them, tearing up the handiwork of the royal carpenters and consigning the products of several days of hard work to the brown waters of the Seine. It was unlikely that any pursuit would come through Poissy, but Edward's commanders were seldom less than thorough.

The pause at Poissy would have given ample opportunities to scout the roads to the north. Moving swiftly, the army crossed the flat marshy plain in the bend of the river and climbed the steep escarpment on the far side. Moving the wagons up this slope was a gruelling task, and would have occupied much of the remainder of the morning. On the high ground once again the army moved through the Bois de l'Hautil, the bend of the Seine to the left and the valley of another deep river, the Oise, on the right.[3] The vanguard reached Boisemont by around midday and the army pressed on, turning slightly east of north and possibly splitting into two columns to cross the small river Viosnel around Boissy. The strongly fortified town of Pontoise, which protected the crossings of the Oise and the direct route to St-Denis and Paris, lay about three miles to the east, but although the English army were following their usual practice of firing the villages and farmsteads they passed, they were moving swiftly and made no effort to attack strong places such as Pontoise.[4]

From Boissy they moved on through the afternoon across a broad plain, the current site of Pontoise airport, and at the end of the day climbed another fairly steep hill into the village of Grisy-les-Plâtres, concluding a march of just over fourteen miles.[5] Grisy commanded excellent views of the surrounding countryside, especially to the south and east, and any French pursuit would have been easily spotted. But the plain remained empty in the evening light; still no French troops were stirring north of

St-Denis. That evening the mood among the commanders must have been quietly congratulatory. The English were by no means out of the woods yet, and in particular food was now becoming a problem. A fair number of sheep had been rounded up, but supplies of other stocks were starting to run dangerously low. According to some sources, many of the soldiers were now eating meat only, lacking pottage or flour for bread.[6] But they had escaped from a dangerous trap, and so far as they knew the road north lay open.

Thursday 17 August

By Thursday morning the truth had finally dawned on the French commanders that they had been outwitted. At Antony, Philippe hurriedly assembled his army and rode back towards Paris, and it is easy to believe the statements of the French chroniclers that he was in a towering rage.[7] One of Philippe's weaknesses throughout his reign was a refusal to take responsibility for his own mistakes. Now, not for the first time and certainly not for the last, he claimed loudly that he had been betrayed; indeed, according to the *Grandes Chroniques*, he made this claim to anyone who would listen during his ride back through Paris. What other excuse could there be for the behaviour of the army, marching and countermarching for days while the enemy burned the suburbs of the capital and then slipped away without a blow being struck? The king had been made to look a fool, and that this might be his own fault was not a possibility to be contemplated, at least in public. The murmur of treason within the city redoubled; many Parisians, the *Grandes Chroniques* continued, had tears in their eyes. Angry and humiliated, Philippe brought his army back to St-Denis in the evening and resolved at once to give chase to the English army. There were strong forces north of the Somme, and Edward could still be trapped there.

But Edward was still pressing north, and Thursday saw another long and gruelling march. The first stage saw the army through the hilly country between Grisy-les-Plâtres and Hénonville, once again keeping to the high ground. At Hénonville there was a steep hill to descend in order to cross the small river Troësne. From here there was a choice of routes north: the more easterly road runs across a level plain through Villeneuve-les-Sablons and St-Crépin-Ibouvillers, while the western route briefly follows the Troësne to Ivry-le-Temple, past the imposing church and granges which had formerly belonged to the Knights Templar, and then north to Montherlant and Valdampierre through more rolling and wooded country. It is probable that both routes were used, with the vanguard under the Prince taking the more easterly road and the main body, rearguard and baggage train staying to the west.[8] Once again, each village was burned as the army passed.[9]

By nightfall the main body under the king had covered sixteen miles, and was encamped in and around the village of Auteuil, about six miles south of the city of Beauvais under the shadow of a long line of buttes stretching roughly north-west to south-east. The Prince's division had pushed on another two miles to the hamlet of Vessencourt, below another line of hills which separated the army from Beauvais. The strain of two days of hard marching, on top of the rigours of the earlier campaign, was beginning to tell. The boots of the foot soldiers were beginning to wear out, and the sickness and straggling that inevitably accompany long forced marches were beginning to reduce the strength of the English army.[10] And scouts reported that Beauvais itself, which lay directly in their line of march, was fortified and heavily defended.

For the moment, however, Edward felt reasonably secure, secure enough to fling another gesture of defiance at his adversary. He had never formally answered Philippe's challenge to meet him in battle, delivered by the Archbishop of Besançon at Poissy three days earlier (although, as we have seen, he must have sent a verbal message which Philippe construed as an answer). Now, in a manner that the French historian Jules Viard has described as 'plutôt ironiques', he composed his formal answer:

> *Philippe de Valois, we have read your letters by which you tell us that you wish to fight us and all our forces, between St-Germain-de-Près and Valgrail-de-les-Presor between Franconville and Pontoise on Thursday, Saturday, Sunday or Tuesday next, as long as we and our men do no damage, burning or robbery. On this we let it be known to you that with God's assurance and in the clear right which we have to the crown of France which you wrongfully hold, to our disinheritance against God and right, we have come without pride to our kingdom of France, making our way to you to put an end to the war. But although you could have a battle with us, you break down the bridges between you and us, so that we cannot come near you or cross the river Seine. When we came to Poissy and repaired the bridge there which you had broken, we*

stayed three days, waiting for you and the army which you had gathered. You could have come there from any direction, as you wished, and because we could not get you to give battle, we decided to continue further into our kingdom, to comfort our loyal friends and punish rebels, whom you wrongly claim as your subjects; and we wish to remain in our kingdom without leaving it to carry on the war to our advantage as best we can, to the damage of our adversaries. Therefore, if you wish (as your letters indicate) to do battle with us in order to spare those whom you call your subjects, let it now be known that at whatever hour you approach you will find us ready to meet you in the field, with God's help, which thing we most earnestly desire for the common good of Christendom, since you will not accept or offer any reasonable terms for peace. But we shall never be dictated to by you, not will we accept a day and place for battle on the conditions which you have named. Auteuil, 17 August 1346.[11]

It is a marvellous piece of bombast, and, of course, not entirely true; Edward's march up the Seine had been forced upon him. But it still reads very well, and is a good example of how Edward, in public at least, justified his participation in the war.

Friday 18 August

On the third day after leaving Poissy the English moved towards Beauvais, the first real obstacle they had encountered since crossing the Seine. Beauvais was a large and wealthy city at the junction of two small rivers, the Avelon and the Thérain. On the south and west it is protected by high hills with steeply sloping buttes, broken by the river Avelon, which flows through a gap in the hills between Goincourt and the abbey of St-Quentin. The passage around the city to the west followed this gap, crossing the Avelon near the abbey and the faubourg of St-Just. The passage to the east of the city is on flatter ground, though there are some marshes along the Thérain to the east of the city. It seems likely that Edward decided, in order to save time, to divide his forces and bypass the city on both flanks.

The Prince of Wales's division moved out from Vessencourt, up over the buttes and across the high ground beyond Frocourt to look down on the city. Beauvais was, and is, dominated by the awesome bulk of its thirteenth-century cathedral, one of the largest in Europe. The city also possessed strong walls, which were well manned under the direction of the elderly but resolute Bishop of Beauvais, Jean de Marigny; however, there was the usual clutch of unwalled faubourgs and abbeys, especially to the north and east. Under the command of the Prince and the two marshals, Warwick and Harcourt, the vanguard moved down towards the city, dividing in turn into three units to cover each of the gates of Beauvais.[12]

The operation was time-consuming, but passed off smoothly. A small force of Picard men-at-arms tried to challenge the English forces crossing the Avelon near St-Just, but were beaten off; the Picards lost a number of men killed and four knights were taken prisoner.[13] The only other contretemps was a dispute between the Prince of Wales and his father the king. The young prince felt his men were capable of taking the city, and asked permission to do so; almost certainly against the advice of the two marshals, who had their own orders direct from the king. The king refused sharply; he could ill afford the losses in manpower and time that such an assault would require. A battle with the French field army might still be imminent, the king reminded his son, and in that case every man would be needed. The Prince at this point seems to have gone into a sulk, and done little or nothing to restrain his men from entering and burning the faubourgs of Beauvais. St-Just was burned along with the nearby abbey of St-Quentin, despite the prohibition on destroying monastic buildings, and severe damage was also done to the Benedictine abbey of St-Gemer.[14] As the army began to pass north of the city another Benedictine abbey, that of St-Lucien, was also set on fire. This happened virtually under the nose of the king himself, who was passing St-Lucien with his entourage, and the arsonists were seen to emerge from the abbey buildings as smoke began to rise. Enraged at this flouting of his orders in front of his eyes, Edward ordered his men-at-arms to seize the culprits, and twenty of them were summarily hanged. Edward's frustration is understandable, but if this action was intended to restore discipline in the army, then it did not succeed.[15]

By early afternoon the passage around Beauvais had been achieved without further incident. Marigny had, wisely, decided to let the English pass rather than trying to challenge them again. The army moved up the line of the river Thérain to the north-west of Beauvais, and the main body halted at Troissereux, the king taking up his quarters in another abbey, having marched about thirteen miles: still a respectable distance given the delays around Beauvais. The Prince's vanguard division moved another three miles towards Milly, also on the river. The previous two nights had been spent at camps where water was not so plentiful, and a chance to take on water now was not to be missed. The plateau of southern Picardy lay ahead, and it was still many miles to the Somme. The river supplied plenty of fresh carp, roach and bream caught by the royal fisherman, which was welcome indeed as the supplies of salt cod and salmon and stockfish were getting low, and enough fish was taken to feed the royal household for a couple of days.

Although the day's march was shorter than on the two previous days, good progress had still been made. The army had advanced forty-three miles in three days, and Edward and his commanders must still have been confident that they were far ahead of the French army. They would have been alarmed had they known the truth. For on the evening of the 18th, as Edward and his men sat down to their fresh fish at Troissereux, the vanguard of the French army rode into Clermont-sur-Oise, fifteen miles *east* of Beauvais, after a heroic march of thirty-five miles from St-Denis.[16] This corps included the Bohemian and Luxembourg men-at-arms under their blind king,[17] who had driven his men full out to catch up with the English. In a single day's march, Jean of Bohemia had restored the balance of the campaign, and much of Edward's priceless advantage had been lost. From now on it would be a straight race. If Edward could win the Somme first and unite with the Flemings, he would have succeeded in his goals. If not, he would be trapped, just as he so nearly was at Paris.

Saturday 19 August

In the morning the trumpets sounded and the army assembled, breakfasted and resumed its march north. The Somme was now only a little over forty miles away, three days' march assuming there were no further delays or opposition. One point which remains unresolved is whether the English commanders had maps of this region, and if not, how they were finding their way. Certainly they were following a very precise course. One later historian, Alfred Burne, calculated that 'for no less than sixty-eight miles its halting places did not diverge as much as one and a half miles from a dead straight line, a straightness of march unparalleled in military history, so far as my knowledge goes'.[18] This straightness of march was greatly assisted by the fact that, unlike Normandy, where the land was divided into many small fields enclosed with hedgerows, open-field systems predominated in the Vexin and Picardy. Much of the land was given over to cereal crops, and harvest was now well under way; many of the fields through which the army passed were bare stubble, while others were covered in tall golden corn. The stalks of crops such as wheat, in particular, were much taller in the Middle Ages than at present, and a field of standing corn could easily conceal a man. Those fields that had been harvested, however, could be traversed more easily.

Once again the army divided, with one force moving a little west of north towards Marseille-le-Petit,[19] following roughly the line of the modern D901, the other following parallel tracks to the east through Sauqueuse. Once again, too, smoke and flames began to rise across the landscape. The hangings of the arsonists at St-Lucien clearly had no effect whatsoever, for the Cistercian abbey of Beaupré was among the places burned that morning.[20] Later in the morning, the eastern division of the army descended into the pretty valley of the Herperie and fell upon the small town of Oudeuil; it too was set in flames. A nearby castle was occupied only by the local seigneur and his family and household, and these sensibly surrendered and were left unmolested. Pressing on north, the army burned Marseille in the afternoon. The Prince of Wales's division halted at Grandvilliers, having made only about twelve miles, perhaps delayed at Oudeuil. Unusually, it was the king's division that pressed on further to Sommereux, having marched fourteen miles. Sommereux was another former commandery of the Knights Templars, with a fine church and other buildings; the church still remains in good condition today. That night the household dined on stockfish and on carp and bream fished out of the Therain the previous day.

After the gruelling march of the previous day, the French army slowed its pace, but was still marching faster than the English. From Clermont the French marched a little west of north also in the direction of Breteuil. The place of their night halt is not given, but was probably Breteuil or a little to the south of it, meaning a march of nearly twenty miles. From Breteuil to Grandvilliers is about seventeen miles by road across the flat Picard plain, and even less directly across country. This was a short enough distance for the scouts and foragers of each army to have been in touch with one other. The plumes of smoke from Oudeuil and Marseille would have been clearly visible to the marching French and Bohemians and Luxembourgeois, indicating the course their enemy was following. The gap between the two armies was closing steadily.

Sunday 20 August

Short of food, in worn-out shoes, numbers reduced by straggling and fatigue and fighting over a period of nearly six weeks, the English army set out on Sunday morning. Almost immediately the king's division came across the small castle of Dargies, to the right of their line of march. This seems to have been deserted, and it was occupied, looted and set ablaze. The king's division then pressed on in the direction of Poix-en-Picardie, coming down off the Picard plain into the valley of the river Selles.

Poix was an old town, overlooked by heights on both north and south. It was strongly walled, and there was a fortified castle inside the town. The men of the vanguard division, coming up from Grandvilliers, reached the town first and found it strongly defended. The seigneur of the town, Jean de Tyrel, was absent, having gone to the muster at Amiens, but the towns-people were manning the ramparts and ready to fight. Unable to resist a challenge, the men-at-arms and archers of the vanguard moved into attack the town from the south, anticipating yet more spoils.

Edward, spotting this move, at once sent officers of his household to restrain the attackers, telling them in no uncertain terms to leave Poix alone and get back onto the north road. Doubtless by now able to see the clouds of dust on the roads to the east and south-east announcing the presence of the enemy, he needed to keep his army moving towards the Somme. Reluctantly, the men of the vanguard broke off the attack – at least, until the royal serjeants had ridden away, whereupon they resumed their preparations for the assault. Again they were seen, and again the serjeants returned, issuing even more peremptory orders to get moving. For a second time, the troops broke off and began to move away from the town, only to return once again as soon as the serjeants had gone. By this time Edward himself was out of sight of the town, and the disobedient soldiery, now led by Oliver de Ghistels, a Flemish knight in English service,[21] commenced their attack in earnest.

The fighting that followed was particularly bloody. The townspeople shot arrows and threw heavy stones from the ramparts, but they were no match for the English archers, who shot dozens of arrows at any face that appeared on the battlements. A number of the defenders were killed or wounded, and, under cover of the arrows, foot soldiers and dismounted men-at-arms began to break down the gates. Improvised scaling ladders were also raised and the English began climbing onto the ramparts and cutting down those of the defenders that remained. As at Gaillon, when the defence finally broke the armed defenders were hunted down and killed, with no quarter given. Ghistels's men then assaulted the castle and quickly took it. Several women were found sheltering here, including Jean de Tyrel's sister Marie and his daughter Marguerite, and these were in imminent danger of rape until rescued by two English knights, who extricated them from the castle and took them away.[22] The women were later brought before the king, who spoke kindly to them and gave them safe-passage to the abbey of Corbie on the far side of Amiens. Meanwhile the town was looted and, according to the *Acta Bellicosa*, proved to be particularly well stocked with valuables, for many people from the countryside had brought their goods here for safe-keeping in advance of the army's arrival. In particular, a number of horses were taken. Finally, in time-honoured fashion, the departing troops set the ravaged town on fire.[23]

Meanwhile up on the plateau, the rest of the army was hurrying north. The two divisions had crossed paths again, and the vanguard was now marching a couple of miles to the east of the main body, each force able clearly to see the other across the open fields of the Picardy plain. By the fall of night they had made sixteen miles; the main body came to rest at Camps-en-Amienois, the vanguard just to the east at Molliens-Vidame. The Somme was less than ten miles away.

But the French were even closer. By the night of the 20th the advance elements of the French army had reached Nampty-Coppegueule, nine miles south-west of Amiens and about the same distance across country from the Prince of Wales's position at Molliens-Vidame. Philippe was angling his line of march slightly to the west of Amiens, possibly to be in a position to intercept the English should they make a sudden move towards the city itself. His own intention was to combine the troops he had brought from the south with those mustered at Amiens and the small army of the Count of Flanders, which had been watching events around Béthune but had now been ordered south to Abbeville. This combined force would give him a massive advantage in numbers over his enemy, and would also give him full control of the north bank of the river. If anything, this position was even more advantageous than that near Paris. Part of the French army would hold the Somme crossings, while the rest forced Edward west towards the sea. Edward's options for retreat were severely limited, and it would be an easy matter for the French to trap the English between the Somme, the sea and their own men-at-arms. Suddenly, things were looking very rosy for King Philippe.

Monday 21 August

In contrast, by Monday morning the English position was looking increasingly bleak. There were a number of crossings over the Somme between Amiens and Abbeville, at – from west to east – Pont-Remy, Long, Longpré, Hangest and Picquigny. There were also bridges at Amiens and Abbeville, of course, but both these towns were held by strong forces of the enemy, the Picard men-at-arms and levies at the former, and the advance elements of the Count of Flanders's force at the latter. By now, Edward's scouts would have informed him that the other four bridges were also guarded by enemy troops.

The Somme crossing presented different problems from the crossing of the Seine. Today the Somme valley is largely open fields or woodland; the river has been canalised, at least below Abbeville, and the land has been drained. In 1346 the valley was a floodplain, inundated at high tide and either shallow water or marshland at low tide, as far upriver as Amiens. The valley, often up to a mile wide, was spanned by long causeways at the places mentioned above, with bridges over the channel of the Somme itself. Even a small force could block these causeways quite effectively, and the terrain also meant that it was difficult for either the English men-at-arms to mass for a charge, or for the archers to be deployed in sufficient numbers to shoot down the defenders.

Of all this, Edward and his commanders would have been aware. After the long march across Picardy, they were once again approaching familiar territory. Abbeville was the capital of the County of Ponthieu, the property of the king's mother and, until nine years ago, in English hands. Some of the English nobles knew the county, and Bartholomew Burghersh had served there as seneschal for a time. The geography of the area was known to them, as were the problems it created.

The crossings of the Somme could not be taken in a sudden rush by a small group of men, but a determined effort to force them ought to succeed. Edward rightly judged that, having achieved his first objective of catching Edward's force, Philippe would now slow down and proceed more methodically. The French too would need to rest and reorganise after their rapid march north, and Edward could calculate on having at least a couple of days' grace before Philippe moved against the English in force. Accordingly, after four days of forced marches, Edward moved his tired army forward only a short distance. The immediate destination was Airaines, six miles to the north of Camps-en-Amienois and Molliens-Vidame. Orders were accordingly given, and the army set off across the plain.

They had not gone far before they were aware of growing resistance around them. Encouraged by the near presence of their king and his army to the east, the local knights and people, those that had not already mustered at Amiens, began gathering and harassing the English army as it passed. Small parties of French troops began to hang on the English flanks, waiting for the chance to pick off stragglers or ambush foraging parties. In mid-morning one sizeable force began to menace the rearguard, and that division's commanders, Durham and Arundel, resolved to teach the enemy a lesson. Hugh Despenser and the Earl of Suffolk, Robert Ufford, were sent with a strong force of men-at-arms and archers to drive the enemy off. Rather than retreating, the French contingent chose to fight. This was a mistake: the scratch French force was never going to be a match for the battle-hardened English, and the French were quickly routed. More than two hundred French were killed, and sixty men-at-arms were taken prisoner.[24] The latter must have been something of an embarrassment for an army that was increasingly finding it difficult to feed itself, and it is likely that, as at La Roche Guyon, the prisoners promised to pay ransoms and were then sent away on parole.

By early afternoon the army was marching into Airaines.[25] No resistance was offered here, and it is probable that the town had been evacuated; the fate of Poix would have been known by now.[26] Jean de Croï, the seigneur, was with the army at Amiens. There was a large and wealthy priory on the high ground to the south-west, and also a sizeable castle to the west of the town, a little way north of the priory. The priory and church and parts of some later fortifications remain; the town itself was virtually demolished during three days of fighting in 1940 when a battalion of Senegalese and Congolese *tirailleurs* attempted to stop the advance of a German panzer division backed by dive-bombers. Enough remains, however, to see that Airaines had been in the fourteenth century a prosperous market town, situated at an important crossroads. From the English perspective, it offered a commanding view out over the plains towards the Somme. This plain was clear of enemy troops; Edward was indeed going to get his day's grace in which to attempt to force the crossings of the Somme. His commanders began making their preparations accordingly.

Almost immediately on arrival in Airaines, however, there was another alarm. A strong force of Bohemian men-at-arms and light cavalry swept in from the east and charged into one English contingent as it was making camp near the town. The English fought hard, but were being beaten down, and it was only the timely arrival of a strong force of mounted men-at-arms under the Earl of Northampton that rescued the situation. There was a short sharp fight before the Bohemians broke off and retreated towards Amiens. Northampton pursued them for several miles over the fields towards the city, but the Bohemians were better mounted and most made good their escape. Northampton took eight prisoners and killed another twelve, a reasonable exchange for the loss of Thomas Talbot, a man-at-arms in Robert Dalton's retinue, who was captured. The circumstances are not clear, but it is most likely that Talbot became separated from his own force and was forced to surrender.[27]

On the same afternoon, the main body of Bohemians and Luxembourgeois rode into Amiens and made rendezvous with the Picard troops already mustered there. Without halting, Jean of Bohemia turned his troops west and began marching them down the north bank of the river, strong detachments breaking off to reinforce the guards at each bridge. Unbeknown to them, when the English attacked the bridges the following day, they would face not local Picard levies, but veteran troops led by one of Europe's most experienced and admired commanders.

Notes

1 Quoted in *Acta Bellicosa*, p. 39.
2 Based on a rough calculation of how long it would have taken the army to pass over the bridge, assuming that the latter was approximately its present width. The *Grandes Chroniques*, vol. 9, p. 279, says the king himself left Poissy in mid-morning.

3 We have assumed this route based on a study of the ground. The alternative route, which seems to have been the one on which Lt.-Col. Burne based his calculations of the march distance, follows the banks of the Seine to the entrance of the Oise, then up the west bank of the Oise towards Cergy, and then due north. This would have been both a longer and more dangerous route, however; the road along the Oise is hemmed in by the river on one side and steep banks on the other, and would have been an ideal place for an ambush. It would also have taken the army very close to the strong town of Pontoise, another danger spot. Assuming that the English used the three days at Poissy to scout, the route up the centre of the bend to Boisemont looks the most inherently probable. The march times are our calculations.

4 According to Giovanni Villani (*Historia Universalis*, ed. L.A. Muratori, *Rerum Italicarum Scriptores XIII*, 1728, p. 947), the English did attack and burn Pontoise, but the description so closely mirrors the attack on Poix some days later that it is tempting to believe that the Florentine chronicler has confused the two. Neither contemporary accounts such as the *Acta Bellicosa* nor local sources in Pontoise note any attack at this time, although in a later edition Froissart says the faubourgs of Pontoise were burned.

5 Burne, p. 154, says sixteen miles, but his calculations may be based on a slightly different route (see note above).

6 Le Muisist, pp. 158–9; Viard, 'Le Campagne de juillet–août', p. 53.

7 *Grandes Chroniques*, vol. 9, p. 274, quoted in Rogers, *The Wars of Edward III*, p. 128.

8 This certainly was the pattern used over the next few days, with the vanguard marching to the east, nearest the point of danger, and the main body following a parallel route a few miles west, ready to reinforce the vanguard if it was heavily attacked.

9 Burne, p. 154, suggests that Edward may have reined in his men at this point and prevented plundering and burning, but this is not supported by either the chronicles or eyewitness accounts such as the *Acta Bellicosa*. However, although considerable destruction was done during the march north through the Vexin, some accounts appear to be exaggerated. In the third edition of his chronicle, Froissart suggests that places as far apart as Beaumont-sur-Oise and Gisors, many miles from the line of march, were burned; his source for this is probably the *Bourgeois de Valenciennes*, p. 494, which maintains that all the Vexin was burned and ravaged.

10 Villani, p. 947.

11 As quoted in the *Acta Bellicosa*, pp. 38–9. Some confusion has resulted from the fact that a near-identical copy of this letter is contained in the Patent Rolls (*CPR 1345–48*, pp. 516–17) and dated 15 August. Rogers, *War Cruel and Sharp*, p. 260, suggests 15 August may indeed be the correct date, and the letter was written and enrolled at the hamlet of Auteuil fifteen miles south-west of Poissy, very near to Montfort l'Amaury, where Edward told the Archbishop

of Besançon he intended to go; Rogers goes on to suggest that Edward may well have moved part of his army out of Poissy on the 15th in order to confront Philippe. It is an ingenious theory, and fits with Rogers's own view of Edward's motives and actions, but there are some problems. The distance from Auteuil in Île-de-France to Poissy is such that long marches would have been required on the 14th and 15th, which is inconsistent with contemporary accounts from the English army – including Edward's own letter – that he spent the three days at Poissy. In military terms, moving this far from the vital bridge also makes little sense. Viard's alternative suggestion, that the date in the Patent Rolls is wrong, is simpler and more sensible; dating mistakes in the Patent Rolls are rare but not unknown.

12 This last detail comes from Froissart, pp. 428 and 430, but seems a reasonable method of masking the city while the army passed by.

13 Froissart, p. 428. These men, like those who fought at Poissy, are described as being from Amiens, but as Amiens appears to have been the central muster point, they may in fact have come from anywhere in Picardy. Sumption, p. 520, mentions a conflict between the English vanguard and French troops near Vessencourt; this seems less likely, as Vessencourt is a long way from Beauvais and had, as Sumption rightly says, nothing to make it worth defending.

14 Denifle, p. 41; Froissart also mentions the burning of two abbeys, new edition, p. 390.

15 St-Lucien is called St-Messaen by Froissart, who erroneously states that the king stayed the night there.

16 Le Muisit, pp. 158–9.

17 Inferred because they were the first force to make contact with the English: see below. According to some accounts, Philippe himself was also at Clermont.

18 Burne, p. 154.

19 Now Marseille-en-Beauvaisis.

20 Denifle, p. 41.

21 According to the *Bourgeois de Valenciennes*, vol. 5, p. 472, which gives the name as Olifar de Ghistelles; Froissart names the commanders as Thomas Holland and Reginald Cobham, but it seems very unlikely that two senior and experienced captains would be involved in an act of disobedience on this scale. Ghistels had been in English service since at least 1345, see Barber, *Edward, Prince of Wales*, p. 254.

22 Froissart (pp. 431 and 433) names their rescuers as John Chandos and Reginald Basset. He also says the two women were Tyrel's daughters, whom he names as Marie and Jeanne; however, Tyrel only had one daughter, and Marie was the name of his sister. It should be added that this incident is unsupported by any other source, but we have left this in the narrative on the grounds that this sort of incident must have happened many times, here and in other places.

23 The reconstruction of events at Poix is rendered more than usually complicated by the fact that none of the sources agrees with the others. We have largely

followed the *Acta Bellicosa*, with some elements from Froissart and the *Bourgeois de Valenciennes*. Michael Northburgh thought it was the rearguard that had attacked the town, and it is quite possible that troops from the rearguard joined in as the army streamed past. Froissart muddies the waters by saying the army spent the night at Poix, and the fighting broke out the following morning when the townspeople refused to pay a ransom demanded by the army; however, other sources agree that the army spent the night well to the north of Poix.

24 Figures given by Northburgh, p. 22. According to Villani, Philippe had been sending messengers through the region urging people to resist by breaking down bridges and hampering the passage of the army.

25 The usually reliable Kitchen Account lists Acheux as the place where the army halted, and then simply says 'ibidem' for the next few days. It is generally accepted that this is an error, possibly made when the enrolled account was being copied, and that the next two nights were spent at Airaines, with the army moving to Acheux on the 23rd.

26 *Eulogium*, p. 209, says the inhabitants, terrified by the fate of Poix, surrendered, and so the town was not burned.

27 Northburgh, p. 22. Talbot clearly survived the fight and was probably back with the English army before Calais on 4 September, when he received a general pardon for good service; he may well have been exchanged for one of Jean of Bohemia's men captured in the same skirmish.

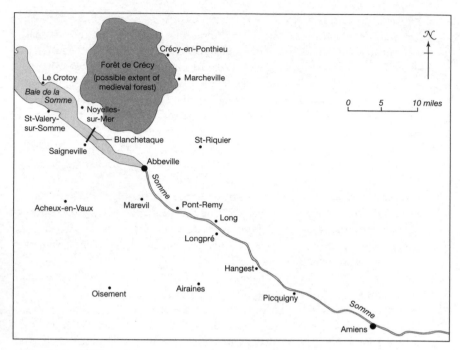

Map 5 The Valley of the Somme.

Chapter 9

The Somme

The King of England was very pensive; he ordered mass before sunrise, and his trumpets to sound for decamping.

Jean Froissart

Tuesday 22 August

The situation, as Lieutenant-Colonel Burne remarks with some under-statement, 'was becoming exciting'.[1] For both kings, a great deal was now at stake, and everything depended on whether the English could force a passage of the Somme. To this end, Edward detailed a strong force under his two marshals, the Earl of Warwick and Godefroi d'Harcourt, to reconnoitre the river and seize a passage if at all possible. His main force, however, he held back at Airaines, partly to rest the troops and partly to avoid being trapped against the river should the French main body choose to advance towards him. This was a bold move, given how close the French army was and how large it had now become; but no matter what other faults he may have possessed, Edward had no shortage of nerve.

While the king waited in Airaines, Warwick and Harcourt with 1,000 men-at-arms and 2,000 mounted archers rode out at dawn to try the river crossings. They rode first to Pont-Remy, six miles to the north-west. Descending steep banks near Liercourt, they found a mile-wide stretch of marshland traversed by a causeway. On the far side of the valley flowed the main stream of the Somme, spanned by a bridge which led into the village of Pont-Remy on the north bank. The bridge had been fortified, probably with temporary barricades of rubble and wood, and was well guarded, the local levies reinforced by troops of the King of Bohemia and also those of Jean of Hainault, who had joined the king on the north bank.

The situation must have looked hopeless, but Warwick and Harcourt were determined to try. Dismounting their men, they advanced up the causeway on foot, the men-at-arms covered by the archers. As they approached the bridge they were shot at with crossbows and at once began to suffer casualties. The archers shot back, but too few of them could deploy on the causeway for their arrows to make any real difference, and although the enemy suffered too, they held their ground. Retiring, Warwick and Harcourt regrouped and attacked again, and were again repulsed. It was mid-morning before they finally accepted defeat and retired to the south bank, having suffered heavy losses and gained nothing.[2]

Remounting, the English force turned south-east, following the line of the Somme to the small town of Fontaine-sur-Somme, two miles away. This was unwalled and deserted.[3] Still nursing their wounds, the English fired the town and moved swiftly on towards Longpré. There must have been an unpleasant reminder of earlier days of the campaign at this point, for as Warwick and Harcourt pushed up the river on the south bank, Hainault and the King of Bohemia tracked them along the north shore. Two miles beyond Fontaines was another causeway and bridge leading to the town of Long on the north shore, but this was heavily defended and the bridge broken down; any attack here would be hopeless.[4]

Next came Longpré, another small town on the south bank at the confluence of the river Airaines with the Somme. Like Fontaines, the town was unwalled, and it and a nearby college of canons were burned as well. Just east of the town lay another causeway and bridge, leading to L'Etoile on the north bank; the causeway was much longer than at Pont-Remy, and the ground even more marshy and difficult. Another strong force of Picards, Hainaulters and Bohemians was waiting on the far side. This time the marshals withdrew without attempting the assault.[5] The blind king was matching their every move.

The day was wearing on, and leaving Longpré still burning behind them, they rode on to the next bridge at Hangest, four and a half miles further on. Although the valley here was narrower, the bridge had been broken and the north bank was defended. Meanwhile, scouts reported that the town of Picquigny, five miles on, was both fortified and heavily defended. Jean de Picquigny, the local seigneur, was an experienced captain, and he could call upon powerful reinforcements, for Amiens, the central base of the French army, was only eight miles further on. To attack Picquigny would be folly of an extreme nature. Warwick had done his best; he had tried five crossings and had failed at all five, but he could hardly be blamed for this. He gave the order to retreat, and late in the day his force returned to the main camp at Airaines, exhausted after a battle lasting several hours and a journey of over thirty miles.[6]

Much had depended on the English succeeding in finding a crossing. Now only two possibilities remained. The first was an assault on Abbeville itself. This would be very risky, for if the French army fell on the English rear while it was attacking the town to its front, the English would be caught between two fires and in all likelihood destroyed. However, a sudden, swift *coup de main* might succeed. The only other possibility was a ford that was rumoured to exist across the tidal marshes downriver from Abbeville. Several men in the English army knew of this ford, but its whereabouts were apparently uncertain.[7]

Dinner was mutton, poultry and cheese, with mustard, vinegar and pickled vegetables. In a pensive mood, as Froissart says, Edward gave his orders for the following morning. Time was running out; the French could not be expected to wait around Amiens for much longer. The main body would proceed due west into the county of Vimeu towards Oisemont, hopefully to draw the enemy's attention away from the river and make Philippe think Edward had abandoned the attempted crossing and was now attempting to escape down the coast.[8] Meanwhile, the two tireless marshals would descend swiftly on Abbeville and hope to carry it in a rapid assault. Edward himself would accompany them; if the attempt succeeded, the main body would divert immediately towards the town and cross the river with all speed.

* * *

Edward's assumptions about his enemy were correct. Philippe had entered Amiens and mustered his forces, and although the army was badly disordered by the rapid march north and some contingents of foot soldiers were still en route, he still had 12,000 men-at-arms at his disposal on both sides of the river, and a large body of foot soldiers including 6,000 Genoese crossbowmen from the contingents of Doria and Grimaldi, commanded now by Ottone Doria in person. Anticipating Edward's intentions almost exactly, he sent a strong contingent of men-at-arms and crossbowmen to Abbeville to reinforce the townspeople, where the redoubtable mayor of the commune, Collard-en-Ver, was preparing the resistance. Another, even stronger force, 1,000 men-at-arms and 3,000 foot including several hundred crossbowmen under the command of a reliable captain, the Burgundian Godemar de Fay, was sent further downriver to guard the north shore of the Somme estuary. With better information than Edward, Philippe not only knew of the existence of a ford called the Blanchetaque, but knew its precise location. Fay's men were an insurance policy; should the English find the ford, they would be unable to cross.[9] Meanwhile, he ordered his main army, or such of it as he could collect, to advance in the morning on the English position at Airaines and begin the task of slowly driving Edward westward to the sea. Sooner or later, he reasoned, the English king would have two choices: give battle on highly unfavourable terms, or starve.[10]

* * *

And fifty miles to the north, matters were going from bad to worse. The Anglo-Flemish siege of Béthune had never made much progress, and the enterprising commander of the garrison, Godefroi d'Ennequin, had made it clear that he would stand firm. Of recent days the besiegers had grown idle, and Ennequin saw that their vigilance over the town was relaxing. Accordingly, he resolved on a sortie. At dawn that Tuesday he led a strong force from the garrison out of the town gates and fell on the still sleeping enemy camp. Chaos ensued, with Ennequin's raiders burning tents and wagons and killing indiscriminately, then rushing back to the safety of the town before the besiegers could organise themselves. His bold raid had an immediate impact. Morale among the besiegers plummeted still further, and despite the remonstrances of Hugh Hastings, the Flemish commanders began to talk openly of going home. Desperate, knowing that Edward's army was drawing near, Hastings persuaded them to stay for a few more days, perhaps hoping that if they received news that Edward had crossed the Somme and was drawing near, they would stay in the field.

Wednesday 23 August

At dawn next morning the English royal household heard mass, and then the trumpets sounded and the army began to move. Once again Warwick and Harcourt rode north-west, this time skirting the bloody causeway at Pont-Remy and making directly for Abbeville. The marshals rode into the village of Mareuil on the south bank, a couple of miles south-east of the town, and while the archers burned the village, castle and Benedictine priory – no one was bothering about the destruction of ecclesiastical property any more – Edward with an escort of two hundred men-at-arms of his household rode on to the heights of Mont Caubert, from whence he could look down at the capital of his former county, a mile to the north.

Things could have been worse; the valley narrows a little at Abbeville and is partly straddled by a tongue of higher ground reaching nearly to the town. There was no need to approach along a narrow causeway. However, the town was heavily walled and fortified. The burgesses of Abbeville had, with great prudence, spent much money and effort on fortifications over the past few years, and even though the walls were still weak in places, the town would be a tough nut to crack. It could be carried by a *coup de main* only if the defenders were lax and off their guard, and this they clearly were not.[11] Indeed, even as Edward and his men watched, a strong force issued from the city, led by the mayor, Collard-en-Ver, and made straight for the heights to drive him off. Outnumbered, the king withdrew swiftly towards Mareuil, and Warwick and Harcourt hastened to meet him. Now it was Collard's turn to withdraw, and he retired on the town harried by the English horsemen. Both sides suffered losses, but Collard regained the gates in the face of the English pursuit – a difficult feat, as we shall shortly see – and as the leading English approached the city they could see it was well defended and impregnable.

Edward's pensive mood of the previous evening must have deepened. Recalling his marshals, he withdrew his force to the south-west to rejoin the rest of the army. The main body, meanwhile, had marched the eight miles to Oisemont. They had moved swiftly, for scouts had reported the French were on the move from Amiens. Some baggage and food had to be abandoned in the camp at Airaines, a sure sign that the English were in a hurry. As noted, the royal household seemed to be able to find sufficient supplies of beef and mutton to maintain a table, but the army itself was getting very hungry indeed; the bread had now given out completely and most of the men were living on meat and fruit. While this might appeal to followers of the Atkins diet today, it was not sufficient for men who were marching and fighting for many hours a day.

And at Oisemont the English found their way barred once again. An emergency muster had been called for the county of Vimeu, into which the English army was now venturing, and this had assembled at Oisemont under the command of a veteran banneret, the Seigneur de Boubert, whose own lands lay about fifteen miles to the north-west, not far from St-Valery. Reinforcements had come from the townspeople of Oisemont itself, and from several other minor nobles of Picardy and Upper Normandy. The Seigneur de Brimeux, whose cousin had died a few weeks earlier at Caen, was with the force, and other nobles included the Seigneurs de Saines, de Louville and de Sempy.[12] Numbers are not known, but the total force must have been at least several hundred men, possibly as many as a thousand; but it had been hastily raised and was probably badly armed. Foolishly, Boubert chose to wait for the enemy in the open field rather than behind Oisemont's walls.

His men were no match for the English army, which, upon seeing this force drawn up in the fields outside Oisemont, moved straight in to the attack. The French, outnumbered, broke at first contact and fled for the safety of Oisemont. The gates opened to receive the fugitives, and then occurred one of those scenes which are all too common in medieval warfare: an army routed in the field, fleeing for the shelter of a fortified place, with hundreds of men struggling to get through a narrow gate, jammed against each other in panic, some of the injured slipping and being trampled by their comrades; and meanwhile, at the rear of the press, enemy men-at-arms leaning down from their horses and killing. Boubert's men were slaughtered; he himself was caught and forced to surrender to John Chandos, and Louville and Sempy were captured as well. They were the lucky ones. The English men-at-arms and archers cut their way through the press of the fleeing French, stormed the gate before it could be shut, and turned on the town itself. As at Poix, they killed every man they found, hunting the survivors through streets which were already beginning to burn. A great cloud of smoke lifted into the sky, marking with unerring accuracy the position of the English army.[13]

* * *

At about the same time, King Philippe entered Airaines, surveying the abandoned baggage of the English. According to legend, the English had left food prepared for their midday meal, abandoned in their hasty withdrawal, and so 'the French ate the food the English had prepared for them'.[14] Airaines itself had not been burned; the promise made to the townspeople had, unusually, been respected.[15] Seeing this and the smoke rising in the west, Philippe realised that his strategy was on its way to being fulfilled. The Somme was blocked, thoroughly, and Edward was being forced west. Philippe's own army was still disordered, but he had time on his side.[16] He ordered a halt at Airaines while his marshals, Charles de Montmorency and Robert de St-Venant, reordered his troops. He may even have planned to halt for the night at Airaines, but then late in the day his scouts reported that the English army had not continued west from Oisemont, but had instead turned north-west in the direction of St-Valery. Clearly, Edward had not yet given up on the possibility of crossing the Somme, and so Philippe marched on to Abbeville.[17]

* * *

North of the Somme, Godemar de Fay's four thousand marched past Abbeville, watching the flames of burning Mareuil on the south bank. Later, too, they saw the smoke of Oisemont in the distance. Their orders were not to get involved in the fighting on the south bank, but to proceed to the Blanchetaque. While Philippe bottled up the English south of the river, Fay would be the cork in the bottle, preventing them from crossing the ford. He had under his command a strong force of men-at-arms, several hundred Genoese crossbowmen, and local levies from other towns in the area, including Abbeville and St-Riquier, and also Le Crotoy, Rue and Montreuil, the latter three of which lay to the west and north.[18] This force, it was deemed, was more than ample to prevent the English from crossing the long tidal ford.

* * *

At Oisemont, the main army, under the command of the Prince of Wales and Northampton in the king's absence, received new orders. The attack on Abbeville had failed; the attempt on the ford would have to be made. A raiding party was detached to burn the small town of Senarpont, five miles to the south on the river Bresle, to continue the illusion that the English were moving south and west.[19] The main body of the army turned north-west, and some time in the afternoon made rendezvous with the king and the marshals, who had turned south-west after leaving Abbeville.[20] The main body halted at the pretty village of Acheux, while a smaller raiding force under Godefroi d'Harcourt rode on to reconnoitre. Lame or not, the marshal was indefatigable; he had already ridden around twenty-five miles and fought one action, and now he rode on to the north-west, probably passing through Boubert and the nearby village of Mons-en-Vimeu as he did so, and late in the day approached the town of St-Valéry-sur-Somme, on the south bank of the Somme estuary where it opens out into the sea.

St-Valéry, the capital of the county of Vimeu, was an important port. With its smaller sister town of Le Crotoy, almost immediately opposite on the north bank a couple of miles away, St-Valéry controlled the mouth of the Somme and river commerce to and from Abbeville and Amiens further inland. The town had been a major port for centuries. It was at St-Valéry that William the Conqueror had mustered his Norman army for the invasion of England, and it was from the estuary of the Somme that his fleet had sailed in the autumn of 1066. The town sat on a low eminence overlooking the river and the coastal marshes and plains, well fortified, dominated by its castle and the church of its great Benedictine abbey. The walls were in good repair and the town garrison had recently been reinforced by a strong force from Abbeville under Guy, Comte de St-Pol, and Jean de Huy. Harcourt's tired men could do little against them. There was a brief skirmish outside the walls, but the French withdrew into the town in good order, and Harcourt pulled back. Night was falling when the lame marshal returned to camp, having ridden over forty miles that day.

At Acheux, the army was eating its meagre rations and preparing for the morning. It was Wednesday, a meatless day, and the stocks of preserved fish were fast dwindling; the little stream that runs through Acheux was too small, especially at the end of a dry summer, to offer any chance of augmenting this with fresh fish. The royal household dined off four salt cod, three salt salmon, six stockfish and a variety of eels of various sizes, a diet that was not only growing tiresome but somewhat thin. However, Edward and his commanders may well have reflected that unless they could ford the river tomorrow, the issue of food stocks would soon become redundant.

That there was a ford called the Blanchetaque, or 'white spot', across the estuary below Abbeville was no secret. The existence of the ford was known to locals, and it may even have been used to drive cattle from one side of the river to the other.[21] The origin of the name seems to come from the pale stone which marked the line of the ford and provided a hard bottom along which livestock and wagons could be transported; according to Froissart, the bottom was hard gravel and white stones.[22] It is not clear whether the ford itself was a natural feature such as stone outcrop, or a man-made roadway. The *Histoire d'Abbeville* opts for the former, noting that a similar outcrop could still be seen at Le Crotoy 150 years ago.[23] The narrowness and straightness of the ford might suggest the latter, but when or for what purpose such a roadway might have been built is unclear.[24] The theory that it was a Roman road, built when landforms were different and the estuary drier, is an intriguing piece of speculation and no more unlikely than any other theory, but is unproven.

Whatever its nature, the Blanchetaque existed, spanning the estuary from the village of Saigneville to the north bank of the river a mile west of the modern hamlet of Le Port.[25] To get an impression of what the estuary looked like in the fourteenth century, one need only go a few miles towards the sea, to Noyelles or St-Valery, and look out across the mussel beds at the vast expanse of shallow water, sand and mud, to see the nature of the barrier faced by the English army. The ford was passable only at low tide, and then only for a space of a few hours. The canal and a low dike further down the estuary have drained the estuary, which is now green farmland, and today it is possible to drive or walk most of the track followed by the ford, but there is no bridge over the Canal Maritime d'Abbeville, which here runs down the middle of the estuary from Abbeville to St-Valery.

The question of 'who knew about the Blanchetaque' is one that continues to vex historians. Several possible informants have been identified. Ponthieu, on the north bank of the river, had been in English hands until 1337; Englishmen had visited the county and even lived there, and were familiar with its geography. One unnamed soldier in the ranks of the English army knew the area particularly well; originally from Ruston near Nafferton in north Yorkshire, he had lived in Ponthieu for sixteen years. The chronicler of the abbey of Meaux, who seems to have had a reliable source, says that it was this Yorkshireman who informed the king about the ford.[26] It has also been suggested that a Flemish esquire, again unnamed, in the service of Olivier de Ghistels knew the area and knew about the ford.[27] There are other possibilities too; Bartholomew Burghersh, the Prince of Wales's tutor, had been seneschal of Ponthieu for some years, and although he was probably not a frequent visitor, others of his household may have been. Godefroi d'Harcourt's nephew Jean, then with the French army at Abbeville, was married to the daughter of the Countess of Aumale, whose lands were nearby, so it is just possible that Harcourt was familiar with the region.[28] And Edward himself had visited the county in his youth.

The most popular and enduring story, however, is that the existence and location of the Blanchetaque were betrayed to the English by a French soldier. After halting for the night on the 23rd, Edward sent for the prisoners taken at Oisemont. Boubert and the other knights were questioned first and asked if any knew the location of a safe passage over the Somme. They refused to cooperate; one can imagine they did so quite indignantly. Then the ordinary men-at-arms and foot soldiers were interrogated, often quite sharply; rewards were offered to those who would provide information, threats were made if they refused to help. Finally one man, a common soldier named Gobin Agace from the nearby village of Mons-en-Vimeu, agreed to give information in exchange for his freedom and 100 gold *écus*, a small fortune for a man of his position. This must have been particularly galling for the captured French commander, Boubert, for Mons was in his seigneurie and Agace was in all likelihood one of his retinue. Under further questioning, Gobin Agace revealed the existence and location of the ford, and even offered to guide the English army there. His name became synonymous with treason in French history.

Thus the story goes, as it is related by Jean le Bel, and afterwards with certain embellishments by Jean Froissart and many others. It suited the French at the time to believe this, for, as we have seen, Philippe VI was a suspicious man who tended to see treason where it suited him; somehow he seemed to find it more comforting to believe that his failures were the result of betrayal by others rather than his own mistakes. The *Grandes Chroniques*, whose author was usually loyal to Philippe, hints darkly that while Edward was at Airaines, he was warned of the approach of Philippe's army by letters from traitors within the French court; other disasters are often ascribed to treason.[29] But doubts must exist as to whether Agace was solely responsible for what followed. As noted above, some in the English army knew of the existence of the ford, and Edward's line of questioning, asking if anyone knew the location of a ford or other way across the river, suggests he was not simply groping in the dark but had a fair idea that such a passage already existed.

But if the English knew the ford existed, did they necessarily know where it was? It has been suggested that the location of the ford was fairly clearly marked and the English ought to have been able to find it unaided;[30] but time was of the essence, and even a short delay in finding the ford might well prove to be fatal. So the Agace story, or a version of it, may in part be true; the information that earned him his freedom, a purse of gold and everlasting infamy, was not the existence of the ford, but its precise location. According to Jean le Bel, he was also able to tell the king that low tide would be in the middle of the following morning, meaning the English could work out a schedule for their march. This knowledge gave the English commanders an advantage: rather than searching for the ford in the morning, they could now march directly to it and begin crossing immediately at low tide.

The fall of night, then, brought some relief to Edward and his captains. They knew their course the following morning, and knew that a chance of escape from the French trap had been offered them. What they did not yet know was that Godemar de Fay and 4,000 men sat waiting for them at the north end of the ford.

Thursday 24 August

The trumpets sounded at first light.[31] In the village of Acheux and in the fields around it, the weary army rose to its feet and began striking camp. No fires were lit; time was now of the essence and meals would have to wait. Swiftly, the Prince of Wales's division moved out on the road to the north towards the river six miles distant, followed by the king's division, the baggage train and Durham and Arundel with the rearguard. Scouts deployed eastward into the sunrise, checking the roads for signs of the French.

This was the moment of greatest peril. The entire army needed to be assembled on the river bank by low tide in order to make the crossing as quickly as possible. Failure would result in their being pinned against an impassable ford with the French advancing in strength from the east. The atmosphere on that final approach to the Somme must have been tense indeed. From Acheux the army moved in the dawn light north to Quesnoy-le-Montant, from where they could see the estuary of the Somme opening out before them, and then followed the dusty roads through the cornfields and pasturelands towards the river, where they descended a steep path through hills overlooking the Somme towards Saigneville.

Sunrise, on St Bartholomew's Day. It was then five o'clock in the morning.[32] The Prince's advance units rode or marched down into Saigneville. The village itself sat on a low bank above the river, perhaps thirty feet high. From the edge of the village, the Prince's men looked out over a wide estuary, a mile and a half across, of flowing water interspersed with patches of marsh.[33] On the north shore the land rose up steeply, a green bank 150 feet in height. To the west the river broadened to meet the sea. St-Valéry, that had repulsed Harcourt the previous afternoon, stood clearly visible on the south bank five miles away, while opposite it was the little port of Le Crotoy, where, if all had gone to plan, reinforcements and supplies would have been waiting. The water was flowing west, indicating that the tide was receding, but it was still too deep to cross. And as the light grew stronger, the English could see on the far bank the glint of metal and the bright colours of banners and coats of arms. The enemy was waiting for them.

There were no other options now. More and more English troops came in from the south, piling up in a dense body around Saigneville. The eastern and southern roads were blocked by the French army, to the west lay the sea. The English would have to force a crossing. The sun rose into the sky. On the north bank, Godemar de Fay's four thousand continued to wait and watch. Then scouts rode in with news that French troops were moving west from Abbeville along the south bank of the Somme, straight for their own position.

*   *   *

Philippe of France was manoeuvring into position to trap his enemy at long last. Saigneville was only six miles from Abbeville; all Philippe had to do was march west, driving the English before him. From Saigneville, Edward could only go a few more miles to the west before he was up against the heavily defended bulwark of St-Valéry, and the sea and the salt marshes beyond that. Or if Edward chose to attempt the crossing, he would be held in mid-river by Fay's strong force on the north bank, while he occupied the south bank; the English would be trapped in mid-river with the tide rising. To the two earlier options Philippe planned to present to the English, starve or fight, he could add a third: drown.

And so, carefully and deliberately, he marched the greater portion of his army out of Abbeville along the south bank of the river towards Saigneville. But he was too careful, and too deliberate; and too late. Once again believing victory in his grasp, he was moving too slowly. Had he marched at first light, as Edward had done, he would have reached the ford about the same time as the English. But he had been bedevilled in the past by confused marching arrangements which left his army disordered, and this time he intended to make no mistakes.[34] And so it was that by the time the English began to cross the Blanchetaque, the leading men-at-arms of the French vanguard were still several miles away.

* * *

By mid-morning the water along the path of the ford was only knee-deep, although there were dangerous marshes to either side. The order to advance came down; horsemen climbed into their saddles and archers strung their bows, and the leading companies moved down to the riverbank.

The honour of leading the attack fell to Hugh Despenser.[35] No one knows whether he was singled out for the post, or whether he asked for it, perhaps as a matter of honour or to prove his valour. The company under his command consisted of several hundred archers and a force of men-at-arms. The archers took the lead, filing along the ford with their bows held up out of the water and the men-at-arms splashing along in column behind them. As Despenser's men moved slowly out into the river, other companies moved into column behind them. Soon the bulk of the vanguard was strung out in a long column across the ford, while the other two divisions waited and heard more reports of the French closing in from the east. The leading French troops were now only a few miles away.

It was not the French behind, but those in front on whom Despenser's men were focused. A mile and a half is a long way when wading through knee-deep or waist-deep water, and during the three-quarters of an hour it took Despenser's men to cross the ford, they would have had plenty of time to see the opposition: Genoese crossbowmen lined up along the foreshore, other foot soldiers and a group of several hundred men-at-arms on the steep bank behind them.

It was while they were in this position, helpless and slow-moving, their bows held up out of the water, that the Genoese began to shoot. With the advantage of height, they could outrange the longbowmen, who were also hampered by the water. Crossbow quarrels flew among the wading men, sometimes splashing into the water, sometimes finding their targets. One after another, Despenser's men died, killed by the bolts or falling wounded and helpless and drowning in the tidal waters. But still they came on.

The north bank was very near now, and the crossbow bolts were doing greater execution. But the water was shoaling too, and now in the shallows Despenser's men could finally bring their bows down to the ready, draw arrows from their quivers, nock and shoot back at their tormentors. Once again, the rate of fire of the longbow began to tell, even though the Genoese may have outnumbered Despenser's archers. They gave ground, bodies littering the foreshore, and the English archers gained solid ground and moved aside to let Despenser's men-at-arms come plunging up out of the water and ride ashore. In reply, Godemar de Fay's men came charging down upon them, the steepness of the slope adding to their impetus, attacking both Despenser's horsemen and the archers and seeking to push them back into the river.

It was a bloody fight, and it lasted for some time. Some of the French gained the river and even rode out into the water, fighting with the English still in the ford. A knight of the king's retinue, the Yorkshireman Thomas Colville of Bukdensike, Yearsley, was particularly prominent, fighting hard with one French opponent whom he eventually drove off.[36] But the English had the advantage of numbers, and were fighting also with a ferocity born of desperation. If they did not get ashore quickly, they would be trapped in the middle of the river, and by now the tide had also begun to rise. More contingents of men-at-arms piled in, Warwick, Reginald Cobham, Northampton himself as ever near the point of greatest danger. Sheer weight of numbers pushed Fay's men back up the slope. The French losses began to mount. In the end they broke and fled, some streaming back towards Abbeville with Warwick's men in hot pursuit and cutting down the slower of the fugitives, others pursued towards Noyelles by Despenser's troops, still streaming seawater and blood.

On the south bank the final crisis had come. Much of the army was still around Saigneville, and the first French troops, Bohemian light cavalry, were closing fast. Edward took a decision, and ordered the entire army into the river. The wagons and horses would cross by the causeway; the foot soldiers simply floundered into the water and began to wade through the mud and reeds. The water was deep and the ground treacherous, and despite the king's later assertion that they crossed safely, it is not improbable that a few men drowned. The king's division crossed, reaching the corpse-littered slope on the far side, and Durham and Arundel hustled their men into the water, which by now must have been up to their necks in places.[37] The baggage train was strung out across the causeway, guarded by men-at-arms; only a few wagons remained on the south shore.

The Bohemian light cavalry could now be seen streaming down the south bank from the west, and the first of these charged into Saigneville, slaughtering the drivers of the few wagons still remaining, and then watching impotently as their enemy made their escape. At least part of the English army was still in the river, but the Bohemians were not strong enough to attack them, and in any case the tide was rising. Messengers were sent to the French king, informing him of his failure. Incredibly, to everyone involved, the English had escaped.

* * *

The crossing of the Blanchetaque by Edward's army has rightly been described as one of the most astonishing military feats of all time. Lieutenant-Colonel Burne, himself a decorated army officer, comments that 'there have been few feats of arms so astonishingly successful against odds in the whole of our proud military history', and the barrister and historian Jonathan Sumption calls it 'a remarkable feat of arms'.[38] Contemporary chroniclers, even those who do not give much detail about the rest of the campaign, all mention this incident, showing that it made a deep impression at the time. Most of the contemporary English accounts reflect a kind of stunned disbelief that they had actually got away with it. And rightly so. Fording a broad tidal estuary would have been a difficult and painstaking operation even without opposition. And Godemar de Fay's blocking force was a strong one and enjoyed immense advantages of position. Only the sheer courage and fighting ability of Despenser's men had made the crossing possible.

The crossing of the Blanchetaque was more, however, than just a feat of courage. It had also completely changed the strategic picture yet again. The cork had been forced out of the bottle, and the English army was now where Philippe's plans said it should not have been: on the north side of the river. The chroniclers suggest that he was close to despair when he ordered his great army to turn around and begin marching back to Abbeville. The Blanchetaque crossing would not be viable until low tide in the evening, and in any case the period of low tide was probably too short to permit Philippe's much larger force to cross in safety; moreover, if the English chose to dispute the passage, there was little chance that the French could replicate the earlier feat of arms.[39] So it was back to Abbeville, to cross in safety through the town; only to find that the town's dilapidated bridges had become seriously weakened by the passage of so many men and horses, and needed repairs before they could be safely used again.[40] It was evening before Philippe returned to Abbeville. The mood in the French camp was bleak, and accusations of incompetence and worse began to be hurled at the unfortunate Godemar de Fay.[41]

As for the English, their relief can be imagined. Jean le Bel speaks of the joy in the hearts of the English as they realised they had reached safety and suggests they regarded the crossing as a miracle.[42] However, they were not so overcome with delight as to ignore the realities of war. De Fay's men had broken, with part of the force fleeing east towards Abbeville and the remainder, particularly the levies from Rue and Montreuil and Le Crotoy, to the north. These latter eventually rallied at Sailly-Bray, three or four miles to the north; Fay himself may have been with them, although he is said to have been seriously wounded during the fighting at the Blanchetaque.[43] Those Frenchmen making for the shelter of Abbeville were pursued by Warwick's mounted men-at-arms, who rode among the fleeing foot soldiers for a distance of three miles and cut them down ruthlessly; some accounts say the fugitives were chased all the way to the gates of Abbeville. English losses in the fighting at the Blanchetaque are not recorded, but probably numbered several hundred, many killed by crossbows while still in the water and others simply drowned. French losses were in the order of two thousand killed and captured, mostly during this pursuit.[44]

While Warwick continued the slaughter of the hapless levies from Abbeville and St-Riquier, the main body swung north-west towards the town of Noyelles, some two miles away. Noyelles was the home of Catherine,

Countess of Aumale, the widow of Jean de Castille-Ponthieu, Comte d'Aumale and Seigneur of Noyelles. The countess's family connections were even more complicated than usual. Her daughter, Blanche of Castile, was married to the younger Jean d'Harcourt, son of the Comte d'Harcourt and currently serving with his father in the French army; and, of course, the nephew of Godefroi d'Harcourt, marshal of the English army. Catherine herself was the sister of Robert, Comte d'Artois, the rebel who had joined the English at the outset of the war and later been killed in Brittany.[45] She herself had no love for Philippe de Valois, and had earlier attempted to resist the entry of French troops into Noyelles. Now she had to watch as the English vanguard, their blood still up from the crossing of the Blanchetaque, stormed into the town and looted and burned in swift fury before pushing on west towards Le Crotoy.[46] The Countess herself was later able to surrender, calling on Godefroi d'Harcourt to intercede for her, and her castle and household were placed under protection.

Brushing aside Fay's forces at Sailly-Bray in a quick skirmish,[47] the main body now turned east, towards the Forêt de Crécy, leaving a strong party to watch the Blanchetaque in case the French should attempt a crossing at the evening low tide.[48] A raiding party moved out to the north along the edge of the coastal marshes to burn the town of Rue, some eight miles away, and another stronger force under Hugh Despenser went west along the north shore of the Somme estuary towards Le Crotoy three miles away, now virtually isolated by the high tide. The little port was well fortified and defended by 400 men including a number of Genoese crossbowmen, but Despenser's men took it in a furious assault, massacring the defenders and plundering and burning the town. At both Rue and Le Crotoy, the raiding parties were under orders to seize all the food stocks they could find, and at Le Crotoy they struck it lucky: there were several ships in the harbour from La Rochelle and other ports, laden with wine from Poitou and Gascony, while in the town itself there were numbers of sheep and cattle, driven in for safety from the mainland.[49] Herding the cattle and carrying as much of the wine as possible, Despenser's men rode east towards the main army, which by late afternoon had withdrawn east of Noyelles and was waiting on the edge of the forest, not far from the river, able to either return and defend the Blanchetaque in event of an enemy crossing, or move north into the forest should a threat materialise in the direction of Abbeville.[50] Exhausted after yet another day of hard marching and fighting, the army made watchful camp in the open fields, deploying scouts southward towards Abbeville, but there was no sign of enemy movement northwards. The supplies taken at Le Crotoy provided sustenance for one decent meal, at least, and the royal household dined on captured beef and mutton along with some of the last of its stocks of poultry.

*   *   *

In the north, the end had finally come for Hugh Hastings's ill-starred expedition. The quarrelling among the English and Flemish commanders reached a crescendo, and spread to their men. There was a pitched battle between the men of Bruges and another contingent, who resented the influence of Bruges. In the end Hastings was forced to give in and consent to a retreat. At the same time as the English were crossing the Blanchetaque, the Flemings were setting fire to their siege engines in the lines around Béthune. Later in the day, the Flemish army began withdrawing slowly to the north, back towards its home territory. Hastings was able to send off a messenger with orders to find the king, assuming he had crossed the Somme, and give him the news; more than this he could not do.[51]

Friday 25 August

On Friday morning the English army marched north and east towards the town of Crécy-en-Ponthieu.

The Forêt de Crécy remains a substantial area of dense woodland. In the fourteenth century it was larger still, probably extending several miles south of its current extent around the village of Forest-l'Abbaye, nearly to the north bank of the Somme. Although the current forest has some modern plantations of conifers, much of the original forest remains, mostly oak and beech. This was not a wild land: it was a managed forest, its trees harvested for building timbers and coppice wood, and it would have been penetrated by a number of tracks. In particular a fairly good road, a 'chemin vert' or forest road, ran from Noyelles through Forest-l'Abbaye to the north side of the forest, emerging at Crécy.

Crossing through this dense woodland was an operation not without peril. Such woodlands were good places for ambush, and the possibility existed that a small French force could block the passage while the main French army came up from the rear, trapping the English between two

fires. But English confidence was high once more, and Edward and his commanders took a calculated risk that the French had not yet stirred out of
Abbeville. Cautiously, they made their way along the forest road towards
Crécy in a long column.[52] Meanwhile the senior commanders, Northampton, Warwick and Harcourt, and some of the other most experienced
captains, including the veteran Reginald Cobham, 'vaillant chevalier
durement' as Froissart calls him,[53] and also Richard Stafford and Robert
Ufford, the Earl of Suffolk, rode ahead. Emerging from the north-east
edge of the forest, they rode down the slope towards the little river
Maye, through the streets of Crécy itself, and up onto the high ridge
beyond.

They found a battlefield that might have been tailor-made for their
purposes (see Map 6). Between Crécy and the hamlet of Wadicourt about
a mile and a quarter away runs a long high ridge, sloping down into the
valley of the Maye. The gradient of the hill is steep but not excessively so;
it would not deter mounted men from riding up it, but it would slow their
pace and take some of the impetus out of a charge. At the bottom of the
slope is a valley, later known as the Vallée aux Clercs; on the south-eastern
side the ground slopes up again towards a series of four villages, Estrées-
lès-Crécy, Fontaine-sur Maye (as its name suggests, at the headwaters of
the river Maye), Froyelles and Marcheville. Beyond these lay the ancient high
road running from Abbeville to Hesdin. At the right, or south-western end
of the ridge, which was surmounted by a windmill, the hill falls steeply
towards Crécy itself and then the Maye, with the forest beginning on the
far side of the river. On the left, or north-eastern end of the ridge, Wadicourt
sits on a high point of ground commanding views not only to the south
but also to the east and north, looking down into the valley of the Authie.
To the rear is another patch of dense woodland, today known as the Bois
de Crécy-Grange, which again covered a considerably larger area than it
does today. The whole is 'favorable à l'organisation d'une position défensive',
as the modern guide has it, and resembles in many respects the fields of
victory in earlier campaigns such as Halidon Hill.[54]

So favourable indeed was the position that it is quite likely that it was
already known to the English commanders, and they had marched from
the Blanchetaque with this position in mind. As noted earlier, a number of
men in the English army were familiar with Ponthieu; some had even lived
there. Both during the planning of the campaign and during the most

recent stages of the march, that local knowledge would have been discussed. The ridge between Crécy and Wadicourt is one of the most prominent features of this part of Ponthieu; as noted, from Wadicourt there is an extensive panorama across the valleys of the Authie and the Maye. There is no indication in any of the English sources that there was any prior knowledge of the Crécy position; but if we accept that they did have some prior knowledge of the Blanchetaque, it is not at all unreasonable to assume that at least the basic outlines of the Crécy position were known.

That the English deliberately chose to march to Crécy is indicated by the line of march. After crossing the Blanchetaque and taking Noyelles, the army could easily have moved north, skirting the marshes around Rue and making for Montreuil, the ancient capital of Ponthieu. Instead, they moved back inland, diagonally across the front of the enemy army at Abbeville, and taking up a position close to one of the main north roads out of the town, that leading to Hesdin. The march to Crécy indicates that after days of running, the English army had chosen now to turn and fight; and that having made that decision, the commanders had also chosen to make their stand at Crécy.

Why fight? Why not keep running? Edward's speech, at least as it is put into his mouth by Froissart, is that Ponthieu was rightfully English territory; it was the land of his lady mother, and he was resolved to defend it. This may well have served as a useful temporary justification, but is hardly relevant given that Edward was claiming to be king of all France; there was nothing to make Ponthieu more worth defending than any other part of it (and the fact that his army had just plundered and burned three of Ponthieu's towns does not suggest his attachment to the county was particularly deep).[55] More likely is the view expressed by the French historian Jules Viard, who believes that Edward's army was increasingly incapable of eluding its enemy.[56] Hungry men with worn-out shoes could not go on much longer; although the provisions taken at Le Crotoy had solved the immediate food crisis, these would soon be exhausted. There would be no help from the Flemings, for, as Jonathan Sumption believes, by the afternoon of the 25th Edward was probably aware that Hastings and Henry of Flanders had begun to retreat.[57] Behind the English lay yet another difficult obstacle, the Authie, which once again ran through a broad valley full of marshes and would take time and effort to cross, and could prove as dangerous as the Somme should the French once again launch a strong pursuit.[58] The position at Crécy offered the English the best chance they were likely to get for some time. Although Edward believed himself to be outnumbered by the enemy by six to one (the real figure was more like four to one, including all the various scattered contingents of the French army),[59] he also knew his own army's strengths – and his enemy's weaknesses. By using the terrain skilfully, he could negate at least some of the enemy's advantage of numbers.

And so Edward gave his orders. The army halted inside the forest, which would conceal them from enemy scouts.[60] The rest of the day would be spent in preparing for battle. In the shelter of the woods, tired men mended plate armour and chainmail, sharpened weapons, restrung bows and checked the fletchings on tens of thousands of arrows. The commanders continued to survey the ground, and, with time in hand, worked out in detail the positions each unit would occupy. The division of the Prince of Wales would occupy the right of the line, the post of honour nearest the enemy; Durham and Arundel's division would be on his left; the king himself would command the reserve.

All through the afternoon scouts watched the approaches to Abbeville, waiting for the French to stir. There was no move, although the scouts may well have seen French scouts moving out on a similar mission. The afternoon of the 25th of August wore on and the English were able to make their preparations calmly and quietly. In the evening the army ate the last of its provisions from Le Crotoy, and the low level of food stocks can be judged by the fact that the royal household that day consumed four salt cod, two and a half salt salmon, six stockfish, four large eels, half a hundredweight of pimpernels, three pike, two carp and a quantity of whale meat – a far cry from the meals of early in the campaign. Later, Edward issued further orders. At dawn the following morning, the trumpets would sound and the army would march to the field and take up its positions for battle. That he was confident the French would come seems evident from almost every source; indeed, such was his confidence that Alfred Burne, echoing the earlier suspicions of the *Grandes Chroniques*, wonders if there was after all a traitor in the French camp.[61] Although the possibility cannot be discounted, it is more likely that Edward simply knew his enemy. Twice balked, twice humiliated, Philippe would not refuse another challenge. That he would march next day in pursuit of the English could be regarded as certain. The only difference was that this time the English were standing still and waiting for him.

* * *

In Abbeville, the French army spent yet another day in sorting itself out after the marching and counter-marching of recent days. While the notables took up quarters in the towns of Abbeville and St-Riquier, the common men-at-arms and foot soldiers camped around the towns and along the banks of the Somme. The army was now vastly larger than that which Edward had first faced across the Seine. The Normans and Genoese had been augmented by contingents from the Île-de-France, Lorraine, the Majorcan territory on the mainland, Blois, Auxerre and the Auvergne, Picardy and Flanders. Loyal Flemings and Hainaulters had ridden in with Louis de Nevers, Count of Flanders. Jean of Bohemia had brought both his own Bohemians and Luxembourgeois, and also allies such as the Count of Salm. Other powerful contingents were still on the way; Louis of Vaud's Savoyards, after weeks of marching, were now close by. More contingents of foot soldiers, many of them levied from ecclesiastical lands and led by their archbishops and bishops, were also arriving on the south bank of the Somme. All in all, the army assembling around Abbeville numbered probably a little over 40,000 men, although some of these were still on their way north and had not yet joined the main body.[62]

While the army assembled once more, the two French marshals, Charles de Montmorency and Robert de St-Venant, sent out scouts to the west and north. To the west they saw the smoke rising from the ruins of Noyelles and Le Crotoy, indicating that the enemy had been active there, but none seems to have ventured as far as either town to verify this. More scouts rode north along the Hesdin road and returned in the evening, having seen small parties of the enemy in the fields near Crécy-en-Ponthieu, to the north of the Forêt de Crécy.[63] Little importance was attached to this discovery, and Philippe continued to believe that Edward was still at Noyelles and Le Crotoy and preparing to retreat north. He gave his own orders; at dawn the army would march west to Noyelles, find the trail of the retreating English and then begin again the task of overhauling and trapping them.

The 25th was the feast day of St Louis, and Philippe, who had taken up quarters at the Benedictine abbey of St-Pierre in Abbeville, entertained his nobles to dinner. As it was Friday, the assembled nobles dined on fish, although their meal was undoubtedly rather better prepared and the fish more carefully dressed than in the tents in the woods near Crécy. The date was hardly an auspicious one: Louis IX of France had been a supremely good and pious man and an able administrator, but as a soldier he was a disaster. His first expedition to the Middle East had ended in the destruction of his entire army and his own captivity in the hands of the Mamlûk rulers of Egypt; his second, to Tunis in 1270–1, had resulted in his own death. Whether any of the assembled nobles was tactless enough to remark on this is not known.

It was, say the chroniclers, a glittering company. Four kings sat down to dinner that night: Philippe of France, Jean of Bohemia, Charles, King of the Romans and Jaume of Majorca. Other great princes included Philippe's brother, the Comte d'Alençon, his nephew the Comte de Blois and the latter's brother-in-law the Duc de Lorraine. The Counts of Flanders, Namur and Salm, leaders of contingents from the Low Countries, rubbed shoulders with the Comte d'Aumale, whose mother's town had just been burned by the English, and the Counts of Boulogne, Sancerre and Auxerre. The princes of the church were there in force as well, including the Archbishops of Rouen and Sens and the Bishop of Laon, all of whom had set aside pastoral duties to lead their contingents into battle. It was, says Froissart, a 'grand recreation et grand parlement d'armes'.[64]

Undoubtedly sensing the frictions within this polyglot, multinational army, and as ever unsure of his own authority, King Philippe urged the nobles to remain always in covenant with each other and to trust one another. Whatever differences existed between them should be put aside; what mattered now was unity. It was a brave hope, and a vain one. On the morrow, the commanders of the French army would behave as they always behaved: exactly as they wished.[65]

Notes

1 Burne, p. 156.
2 Froissart, vol. 5, pp. 2–6; le Bel, pp. 96–7; Le Muisit, p. 159. Sumption, p. 521, says the English took heavy casualties. Given the nature of the fighting this is likely, and it is extremely unlikely that anything else would have forced Warwick and Harcourt to break off, given the increasingly tense situation.

3 There does not appear to have been a crossing at Fontaines, though a road does lead across the valley today.

4 Many sources say the English force went to Long, but this is clearly a convenient shorthand, as Long is on the wrong side of the river.

5 Froissart says the two bridges were well guarded; he is presumably referring to the bridges of Longpré and Long, which are not more than two miles apart.

6 Froissart mentions Picquigny, but does not note any attack, leading us to conclude that the town was scouted but not directly approached. He does not mention Hangest, but the *Chronique Normande*, p. 79, does. The *Chronique* suggests that the approach to Hangest took place before the battle at Pont-Remy, in effect a reverse itinerary to the one we describe. However, it seems inherently probable that the English would attack Pont-Remy first, as it was farthest from the French army.

7 Ghistels's esquire, the Yorkshireman: see Barber, *Life and Campaigns*. Others with experience of Ponthieu may have known as well. Bartholomew Burghersh had served as seneschal of Ponthieu, though it is not known how often he visited the county, and Edward himself had visited the county in his youth.

8 That Edward's march on Oisemont was a ruse is accepted by both Viard, 'Le Campagne de juillet–août', p. 58 and Burne, p. 157. He may not have known that yet more French troops were mustering there.

9 The *Chronique de St-Ouen* quoted in Rogers, *War Cruel and Sharp*, p. 363, suggests that Fay was not guarding the ford specifically, but was merely tracking the English line of march. However, the English force would not have been visible to Fay's men, and it is much more likely that, as modern historians accept, he was sent specifically to guard the ford.

10 A point nicely made by Froissart, p. 3.

11 Footnote by Viard in le Bel, p. 94; *Histoire d'Abbeville*, p. 195.

12 The names are given by Froissart, with the usual caveat.

13 Froissart, pp. 10–11; *Histoire d'Abbeville*, p. 196.

14 *Grandes Chroniques*, vol. 9, p. 281. It is a commonly repeated legend, but given that the English had been preparing to march the night before and the last troops were probably out of the town by mid-morning, it is hard to understand who was cooking what for whom.

15 Although the Comtesse de Dreux, who had lands in the area, later complained of damage done by the French troops; see editor's footnote in le Bel, p. 91.

16 The continuing disorder of the French army is commented on by Viard, 'Le Campagne de juillet–août', p. 94 in his notes on le Bel, suggesting Philippe was still waiting on contingents coming up from the south, the Savoyards in particular.

17 Froissart says that Philippe spent the night at Airaines, but also says that Edward stopped that night at Oisemont; in both cases he is incorrect.

18 Figures for Fay's force range from 1,200 (*Chronique Normande*) to 12,000 (Froissart). Of eyewitnesses, Richard Wynkeley thought Fay had 1,000 horse and 5,000 foot and Northburgh thought 500 men-at-arms and 3,000 foot;

the king himself merely says they were 'a large number'. *Chronique Normande*, p. 79; Froissart, vol. 5, p. 14; Murimuth, pp. 21–6; Barber, *Life and Campaigns*, p. 22.

19 Froissart, p. x, claimed that Aumale, eight miles south of Senarpont, was also burned, but Viard, 'Le Campagne de juillet–août', p. 58, thinks this may be a confusion with the village of Aumâtre, part way between Oisemont and Senarpont.

20 All this is inferred, but if the king and the marshals had ridden directly to Oisemont and then gone on with the army to Acheux, they would have covered a minimum of thirty-two miles that day; a rendezvous, possibly even at Acheux itself, seems much more likely.

21 According to the *Chronicle of St-Ouen*, cited by Rogers, *War Cruel and Sharp*, p. 263.

22 See Froissart, new version vol. 1, pp. 391–5 and vol. 2, pp. 1–11, for a long account of this episode; also le Bel, p. 96, *Histoire d'Abbeville*, p. 197.

23 *Histoire d'Abbeville*, p. 197.

24 Barber, *Edward, Prince of Wales*, p. 61, also refers to the ford as a chalk outcrop in the riverbed. Alfred Burne, pp. 158–9, appears to prefer the causeway theory. An eyewitness, Richard Wynkeley, says that the local people were accustomed to crossing in groups of no more than ten (presumably meaning ten abreast), and le Bel says the track could be crossed by twelve men marching abreast, in Barber, p. 19, le Bel, p. 96.

25 Viard, 'Le Campagne de juillet–août', believes Le Port was the northern terminus, but we have followed Burne, p. 158.

26 *Meaux Chronicle*, p. 57, see also Barber, *Edward, Prince of Wales*, p. 61.

27 *Bourgeois de Valenciennes*, cited in Froissart, p. 472, who gives a long and colourful story of the esquire giving this information to the king and then leading the army to the ford for the next morning. If true, some explanation of why the esquire kept this information to himself for so long is surely required.

28 A point made by Rogers, *War Cruel and Sharp*, p. 235, though such family connections do not necessarily mean Harcourt was familiar with the area.

29 *Grandes Chroniques*, vol. 9, p. 281.

30 Most recently by Rogers, *War Cruel and Sharp*, p. 263.

31 Froissart says the trumpets roused the camp at midnight, but as he has the army starting at Oisemont, this can be disregarded.

32 Viard, 'Le Campagne de juillet–août', p. 62, has calculated that the sun rose at 4.56 a.m.

33 Burne, p. 158, initially gives the distance as 2,000 yards, but corrects himself on the following page.

34 Viard, 'Le Campagne de juillet–août', p. 64, believes it was Philippe's intention to trap the English in the river, presumably to let them drown. We have inferred the motive for Philippe's slow departure from Abbeville from his behaviour in similar situations, notably the previous day at Airaines.

35 Wynkeley suggests that the attack was led by Cobham and Warwick, and they were undoubtedly prominent, as was Northampton. Why Despenser commanded the leading unit is not clear, as for much of the campaign he served in Arundel and Durham's division; it is probable that he volunteered for this, the post of honour. Though an experienced and loyal commander, Despenser may still have lived under the shadow of the infamy of his father and grandfather, the corrupt favourites of Edward II; a feat of arms such as this would surely have redressed the balance in terms of public perception.

36 *Eulogium*, p. 210, *Chronicon a Monacho Sancti Albani*, p. 22 and *Chronicon Henrici Knighton*, vol. 2, p. 102 all mention Colville. *Anonimalle*, p. 22, seems to suggest the incident happened after the crossing of the river, but *Eulogium* mentions jousting in the water.

37 Edward later asserted that the army had crossed a thousand abreast, completing the crossing in an hour and a half; an impossibility if the entire force had to file in columns across the causeway. Richard Wynkeley confirms this, adding that the locals who knew the place were greatly amazed. The decision to simply wade into the river, which could have been disastrous, must have been forced on the king by the news that the Bohemians were closing in.

38 Sumption, p. 524.

39 Legend has it that following the Blanchetaque crossing, Edward challenged Philippe to cross the river and fight him, offering him free passage, but Philippe refused. How this challenge was delivered across a mile and a half of water is not clear, and this is probably a later embellishment.

40 *Histoire d'Abbeville*, p. 199.

41 The *Chronique Normande*, doubtless repeating a rumour of the time, suggested that Fay had abandoned the field while his men were still fighting, in effect deserting them, p. 79. The *Chronographia Regum Francorum*, p. 320, accuses Fay of incompetence. These continued to be the standard views of Fay for many generations, until his reputation was partially rescued by Chateaubriand (see *Histoire d'Abbeville*, pp. 197–8). Contemporary English sources, on the other hand, indicate that the resistance put up by Fay and his men was very strong.

42 Le Bel, p. 98.

43 *Histoire d'Abbeville*, p. 199.

44 The figure of 2,000 is most common, for example, Wynkeley, p. 19, *Chronicon a Monacho Sancti Albani*, p. 22. Le Muisit, p. 160, says more than 1,000; the *Bourgeois de Valenciennes*, p. 472, puts the figure as high as 3,000.

45 Sometimes erroneously referred to as the daughter of the Comte d'Artois; see Viard, 'Le Campagne de juillet–août', p. 64. The *Bourgeois de Valenciennes* gets rather muddled at this point, and places the Countess as fighting with Fay's force in defence of the Blanchetaque and being captured by the English: see Froissart, vol. 9, p. 472.

46 Le Bel, p. 98, thought – quite logically – that Noyelles had been spared on account of the Countess's relationship to Godefroi d'Harcourt, but in a footnote, Viard, 'Le Campagne de juillet–août', cites letters from the Countess in 1347 indicating that the town was burned, and only the nearby castle was spared.

47 *Histoire d'Abbeville*, p. 197.

48 According to Froissart, Fay eventually rejoined the main body at St-Riquier, where he was the following evening.

49 Despenser's attack on Le Crotoy and its outcome is described in detail in le Bel, p. 96 and after him Froissart, pp. 22–4; see also *Chronicon a Monacho Sancti Albani*, p. 22.

50 The exact halting place is an assumption; the Kitchen Account gives the place of the night halt as 'under the Forest of Crécy'. Edward's own letter to Thomas Lucy shows his concern that the enemy might ford the Blanchetaque in his rear, and watch was kept on the ford until after low tide the following morning. Baker believes the king stayed on the river bank near the Blanchetaque until the evening of the 25th: see p. 81, but this is unlikely.

51 Sumption believes the news of the Flemish withdrawal reached Edward shortly after it happened, and played a role in his decision to stand and fight in Ponthieu.

52 It has been suggested that the English, rather than risk the forest crossing, instead skirted the forest, passing by way of Lamotte-Buleux and Canchy; but as the wooded area extended much further south than at present, this road too would require a passage through the forest and there was nothing to be gained. If we assume that the English were making for Crécy specifically, then the Noyelles road is the more logical.

53 Froissart, ed. Lettenhove, vol. 5, p. 25.

54 Colonel Pierson, 'La Bataille de Crécy', Crécy, n.d., p. 3.

55 The three being Noyelles, Le Crotoy and Rue, which are mentioned in several contemporary sources. The suggestion in some chronicles that St-Riquier was also burned is almost certainly an error: St-Riquier, to the north-east of Abbeville, was one of the major concentration points for the French army.

56 Viard, 'Le Campagne de juillet–août', p. 64.

57 Sumption, p. 524.

58 Viard, 'Le Campagne de juillet–août', p. 64; a point made at the time by the chronicler Villani, vol. 13, p. 947.

59 Froissart, first redaction, ed. Lettenhove, vol. 5, pp. 24–7; later redactions increase this to eight to one.

60 Edward did not, as Froissart suggests, march his whole army onto the battlefield on the 25th. The letters of Edward himself, as well as those of Northburgh and Wynkeley and the records of the Kitchen Account, are categorical that the army spent the night inside the forest. This was sensible, as it concealed the army's position from the French.

61 Burne, p. 126.
62 There is some controversy over the size of the French army: see Appendix.
63 Froissart, pp. 27–8, says that the scouts discovered the full English army already in position. But, as above, Froissart's timing is off and the English force was still inside the forest. What the scouts saw was probably the marshals and other commanders surveying the field.
64 Froissart, pp. 27–9.
65 Froissart, pp. 27–9. The English translation of this passage is rather free: 'the king intreated them after supper that they would always remain in friendship with each other; that they would be friends without jealousy, and courteous without pride.' See Froissart, *Chronicles of England, France and Spain*, ed. T. Johnes, London, 1896.

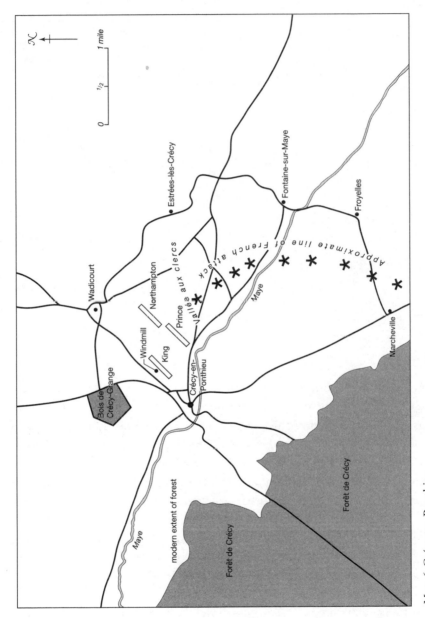

Map 6 Crécy-en-Ponthieu.

Chapter 10

Crécy-en-Ponthieu

Kill these scoundrels, for they bring shame upon us!

Charles d'Alençon

Let the boy win his spurs.

Edward III

Saturday 26 August

Morning

The trumpets sounded early in the English camp in the Forêt de Crécy, echoing among the trees. The previous night the king had gone to pray before his travelling altar, remaining there until nearly midnight, and doubtless others had done the same.[1] The commanders had rested for a few hours, and then in the cold light of dawn roused their men. The members of the royal household and the senior nobles gathered to hear mass said by the Bishop of Durham, Thomas Hatfield,[2] and to take communion. And then camp was struck and the army began moving north-east through the woods. In the morning light the English army filed slowly down the slope to the Maye, forded the little river around the town of Crécy, and climbed up onto the ridge beyond.

Quietly and efficiently, they made their dispositions. The army would fight in the same three battalions in which it had been organised all through the campaign, though some men seem to have been switched from one battalion to another to ensure a balanced force. The ground had already been chosen by the commanders the previous day, and preliminary positions marked. Now, with great care, they posted their men. Although the ridge was long, it was not necessary to cover the whole of it. The French could be expected to come from the south-east, where the Abbeville–Hesdin road emerged from beyond the forest and ran along the high ground above the villages of Marcheville and Froyelles. Assuming that the French moved straight into the attack from this direction, they would cross the Maye somewhere below Fontaines and move straight towards the south-western end of the ridge. The vanguard division was accordingly posted here, its right flank covered by the steep western slope of the ridge and the town, its left partially protected by a series of steeper contours, the remnants of ancient cultivation terraces known as *radaillons*.[3] The English commanders believed – correctly as it turned out – that the terrain would tend naturally to channel the French attack towards the face of the vanguard division, and the natural instincts and aggression of the French men-at-arms would do the rest.

The brunt of the attack would therefore fall on the vanguard, and it was here that many of the best and most experienced men were placed. Once again the Prince of Wales had the command, but as before he was in the care of the two marshals, Godefroi d'Harcourt and Thomas Beauchamp, Earl of Warwick.[4] Other veterans with this division included Reginald Cobham, one of the heroes of the Blanchetaque, the prince's tutor Bartholomew Burghersh, and Richard Stafford and Thomas Holland, the latter still nursing his wounds from Gaillon two weeks earlier. There were young firebrands too, including the dashing James Audley and the younger Bartholomew Burghersh. Thomas Daniel and Richard FitzSimon were there, the latter carrying the Prince of Wales's dragon standard. The Earl of Oxford, the Lords Latimer and Bourchier, Thomas Clifford and Richard Neuville were among others posted there.

The vanguard was also reinforced from the other divisions, so that it was now the largest of the three. Fifteen thousand men had landed at St-Vaast, but battle casualties at Caen, Gaillon, Meulan, Poissy, Pont-Remy, Oisemont and the Blanchetaque had probably accounted for between 1,500 and 2,000 of these. Others had returned home at the end of July, and natural wastage through illness, straggling and desertion had reduced the numbers of the remainder to about 10,000, including non-combatants. Of this force, the Prince had under his command 800 men-at-arms, 2,000 archers and 1,000 foot soldiers including Welsh spearmen and 'brigands'.[5]

These latter were probably dismounted hobelars, made conspicuous by their quilted jackets or brigandines (although, given their plundering habits on the campaign to date, the modern meaning of the word might apply equally well). According to the now standard English tactical doctrine, every man of the division dismounted and the horses were sent away to the rear. The men-at-arms, spearmen and hobelars formed up in a dense line facing down the hill, while the archers were posted on their flanks. According to Froissart, the formation of the archers was like that of the teeth of a 'herce' or harrow, and generations of historians since have expended gallons of ink in trying to understand what the chronicler meant: hugely intricate sawtooth formations have been projected, and people have gone so far as to examine manuscript illustrations of harrows and hypothesise formations based on their shape. As usual, the simplest explanation, that given by Alfred Burne, is almost certainly the right one. The archers formed up in two solid triangular wedges of about 1,000 men each, with one wedge positioned on the right flank of the line of men-at-arms, and the other on the left.[6] Except at very close range, the longbow does not shoot on a flat trajectory, meaning the men at the rear can nearly always shoot over the heads of those in front, and in this case the slope of the hill meant that those at the rear were higher and could clearly see and shoot at their enemy.

This formation had a simple, deadly purpose. Enemy cavalry charging at the wedges of archers would tend to shy away from the arrows coming straight into their faces, just as in later centuries French cavalry attacking the squares of British infantry at Waterloo would part to go around the infantry rather than charging straight into them. To encourage this process still further, the archers dug dozens of small pits, a foot square and a foot deep, so Geoffrey le Baker tells us, in front of their formation.[7] This tactic too had been adopted at Morlaix in 1342 (and before that, had been used with great effect against the English by the Scots at Bannockburn in 1314). The front line of charging horses would stumble or fall when stepping in these, causing confusion and forcing the rear ranks to veer around them. By one means or another – the slope of the ground, the pitfalls, the hail of arrows – the French would be remorselessly channelled towards the face of the formation of dismounted men-at-arms and spearmen. And there, disorganised by the uphill charge and the arrows, they would be held in hand-to-hand combat, while the archers continued a deadly crossfire, shooting into the flanks of the enemy at close range.[8] The ground in front of the men-at-arms and between the two wedges of archers would become, in modern parlance, a killing ground.

It was a tried and tested formation. It had worked for Edward Balliol and Gilbert d'Umfraville at Dupplin Moor, and it had worked spectacularly well at Halidon Hill. It had worked too at Morlaix, after many anxious moments when the English archers had nearly run out of arrows. It ought to work here too; until one remembered the size of the enemy force now mustered around Abbeville, and that the English army was tired and short of food. It is not surprising, therefore, that the mood in the English army remained sober, and perhaps more than usually religious.[9]

To the left and a little refused – that is, behind the line of the vanguard – was the old rearguard division, under the command of the Bishop of Durham and the Earl of Arundel. This division's role was intended to be twofold: to guard the left flank of the vanguard in case any French troops should force their way up over the terraced *radaillons*, but, more crucially, to reinforce the Prince's division should it be hard pressed. This immediate reserve force consisted of a further 1,200 archers and 500 men-at-arms. Northampton had posted himself here so as to be better able to direct the battle, and there was also a solid core of experienced fighting men including the Earl of Suffolk, Ralph Basset of Sapcote, Lewis Tufton, John Sully and Robert Colville.[10] Because this unit might well have to fight to its front as well as reinforcing the Prince, it was formed up in a smaller version of the formation described above, with the men-at-arms in the centre and two wedges of 600 archers, one on each wing. The right-hand wedge was within bowshot of the Prince's division, and could probably shoot at long range at enemy troops attacking the latter.

The third division remained under the command of the king himself, formed up just in front of the windmill. Details of this division are sketchy, but it included about 2,000 archers and 700 men-at-arms, including the king's retinue and household serjeants. Here on the highest point of the position flew the quartered leopards and lilies of the king's own banner. Finally, the army's wagons were taken a little way to the rear and formed into a large park, a hollow formation with the wagons positioned nose to tail, a solid barricade with only a single gate allowing entrance. The wagons may have been further protected by a barricade of sharpened wooden stakes, cut in the nearby woodland of the Bois de Crécy-Grange.[11] Inside this barricade went most of the non-combatants of the army: clerks, farriers, grooms, kitchen servants of the royal household and others, and here too went the thousands of horses, knightly destriers and humble carthorses all herded in together. A few people remained outside, however. The wagons nearest the army were those that carried the reserve supplies of arrows, and pageboys and other servants remained in readiness to run bundles of arrows forward to the men in the front lines to replenish their supplies.[12]

One final refinement, not seen in previous battles, was now added. The three bombards were unloaded from their wagons and carried, with supplies of powder and stone shot, to a position on the slope somewhere near the Prince of Wales's division, and emplaced so as to face down the hill. Inaccurate and slow to reload, they would not do much real damage to the enemy, but their psychological impact might be rather greater. Neither army had used these weapons in the field before, and many French, especially the inexperienced levies from the northern provinces, would never have seen one or heard one fired. That Edward was prepared to employ them now suggests that he was searching for every ounce of advantage he could find to counteract his enemy's overwhelming numbers.[13]

The English tactical plan, then, was a simple one, based on previous successes. The attacking French would be 'encouraged' to attack the dismounted English men-at-arms of the vanguard, and would be shot to pieces by the archers, and bombards, as they did so. Northampton would protect the dangerous left flank of the Prince's division and stand by to provide reinforcements if needed. The king's division would be ready to reinforce either of the other divisions if disaster threatened. If the very worst happened and the *furor franciscus* rolled over both front-line divisions, those behind could escape into the wagon park or the Bois de Crécy-Grange where the French mounted troops could not pursue, and there make a new stand much as Northampton had done at Morlaix; in which case something might still be salvaged from the wreckage.

By midday the troops were in position. The pitfalls had been dug, the archers had checked their fields of fire and arranged their supplies of arrows, probably through the simple expedient of sticking them point first into the ground in front of them (a simpler and faster method of reloading than drawing from a quiver slung at the belt or back). The standard issue of twenty-four arrows had probably been augmented to thirty-six or forty-eight each, which would give each man three or four minutes sustained shooting before new supplies would be required.[14] When all was ready,

Edward himself inspected the positions and the army. According to Froissart he had not yet put on his armour, and was dressed in a green and gold pourpoint and carried a white baton in his hand, riding on a white palfrey, or riding horse (presumably one of the few not yet sent to the safety of the wagon park).[15] He was accompanied by the two marshals, and probably also by the Constable. Quietly, he exhorted each man to do his duty and to remain in position until otherwise ordered. No one was to break ranks or go out to rob the dead, and anyone caught doing so was to be punished by death or mutilation. In particular, Edward ordered that no prisoners should be taken in the coming fight. This was not due to any desire to exterminate his enemies, but rather to the need to force his men to concentrate on winning the battle, not on personal enrichment. Every effort must be devoted to defeating the French, and that meant staying in position and killing as many of the enemy as possible, as quickly as possible. Chivalric convention could go hang; at this stage, victory was all that mattered. It is worth noting that the French army had received identical orders.

After touring all three divisions, the king ordered his army to eat and fortify themselves for the coming battle. It is not known what food remained, but the accounts of the royal kitchen for that day record the consumption of nothing more than some pease pottage and onions. Edward himself now put on his armour, though he left off his bascinet, and conferred with the Prince of Wales and his senior commanders, giving last-minute instructions. To his sixteen-year-old son he offered further words of encouragement, instructing him to do his duty and to trust that God would give the day to the English. The Prince bowed and kissed his father's hand and then strode off to take up his command. The king then quietly called for four knights, Bartholomew Burghersh, John Chandos, James Audley and William Penniel, and instructed them to take special care of the Prince and guard him well. These four then rejoined the Prince and took up their positions around him.[16]

Now there was nothing to do but wait. The day was hot and muggy, and the troops were ordered to sit down and rest.[17] The archers sat, surrounded by small forests of arrows stuck into the earth, bows resting on the ground beside them. The men-at-arms and spearmen sat or sprawled on the slope, sweating in their armour, holding the kinds of conversations that men have just before a desperate battle. Over the whole army, an atmosphere of order prevailed.[18] Edward and his commanders had been meticulous in their preparation. They sat, waiting, banners flapping idly overhead in the humid air; and thus it was that the first French scouts, riding up the Abbeville road past Marcheville, found them in the early afternoon.

* * *

The contrast between the calm and order along the ridge and the ever-spiralling chaos a few miles to the south could not have been much greater.

In Abbeville, the trumpets had sounded at dawn. King Philippe and his nobles attended mass in the church of the abbey of St-Pierre,[19] and then the king and his marshals, St-Venant and Montmorency, began the laborious task of assembling the army. Troops were spread out all across the fields between Abbeville and St-Riquier, and some units, notably Louis of Vaud's corps from Savoy, were still south of the Somme. If all these contingents were added together, including the Savoyards, Philippe probably had about 40,000 men at his disposal.[20] The polyglot army, speaking several dialects of French, Occitan, Italian, Flemish, Luxemburgisch, German and Czech, was led by lords who were becoming increasingly fractious and resentful, of the king and of each other. The homily at supper the night before seems to have had little effect, and Philippe continued his increasingly desperate attempts to bind the *grands seigneurs* more closely to him and force them to forget their own private quarrels. Grand gestures were made and gifts given in hopes of creating loyalty, rather like desperate parents bribing spoiled children with sweets. A handsome black horse was given to John of Hainault, who until so recently had espoused the English cause. Hainault swiftly passed it on to his standard bearer, the veteran knight Thierry de Sencelles, possibly as a grand gesture of his own, more likely because he was a better judge of horseflesh than his king.[21] As events would show, even Philippe's generous gestures had a habit of going awry.

Philippe and the marshals apparently intended that the men-at-arms should fight in three divisions, the first under Jean of Bohemia, the second under the king's quarrelsome brother, Charles de Valois, Comte d'Alençon, and the third under the king himself. This was to be the *battle* order; but these three divisions, which would have numbered about 4,000 men-at-arms apiece, were too cumbersome to march all together, so the *march* order would consist of eight or nine smaller divisions. Upon approaching the enemy, these would then form up into battle order, combining into the three larger divisions noted above.[22] The whole would be screened by Ottone Doria's Genoese crossbowmen and marines, numbering about 5,000.[23] To the rear would follow the great mass of foot soldiers, levies from the communes and rural districts, inexperienced and poorly disciplined troops who would hopefully not be called upon to do any real fighting.

The vanguard led off soon after sunrise. Bohemia led his own men in company with the contingents of his son, the King of the Romans, and probably also the Count of Salm and his men from Liège. So great was the press of men and horses and wagons, however, that each contingent had to wait its turn before taking to the road, and by midday many units were still standing around Abbeville, waiting for the roads to clear. The direction of march was west, along the north bank of the Somme. Apparently still believing that the English had moved north from Noyelles, Philippe intended to march to Noyelles himself, pick up the English trail, and then follow his enemy north towards Rue. There were still some formidable obstacles in the English path, notably the marshes at the mouth of the Authie and then more marshes a few miles further north at the mouth of the Canche, the crossings of the latter protected by the strong town of Montreuil. Further chances to trap the English might well come. Apparently ignoring the rumours of English activity north of the Forêt de Crécy, and also the advice of the King of Bohemia, who felt sure that Edward would stand and fight, Philippe continued to believe what he wanted to believe, that the enemy was retreating north.[24] It was probably one of the French marshals who ordered scouts to ride out to the right of the line of march and scout once again the area around Marchemont, nine miles north-west of Abbeville on the east side of the forest.

Onward the army marched, through the heat of a late August morning. Fully armoured men-at-arms sweltered in the saddle. The Genoese, encumbered with quilted brigandines, heavy wooden and steel crossbows, metal winding ratchets and quivers full of steel-tipped iron bolts, marched doggedly through the dust, doubtless thankful that at least their pavises, the heavy wooden shields behind which they sheltered when in battle, were being carried along by wagons in the rear. The wagons themselves trundled slowly down the choked roads, and after them came the weary men of the communes, marching unenthusiastically in the clouds of dust kicked up by the thousands of horses ahead of them. By midday the vanguard was nearing Noyelles, six miles west of Abbeville, and scouts were reporting no sign of the enemy. This was not a surprise. It had been nearly forty-eight hours since Edward's men had taken and burned the town, and they were likely now to be well to the north. The French commanders were probably beginning to think about halting for the midday meal, to water the horses in the Somme and allow the men to rest, when the scouts from the north returned to the main body. Their news was startling. The English were not retreating north; they were drawn up in order of battle, waiting on a hillside north of the Forêt de Crécy, only about ten miles north of Abbeville.

Jean of Bohemia had been right: Edward had stopped running at last, and was now prepared to stand and fight. A wise commander at this point would have seen that there was no longer a need for haste, and would have acted deliberately. He would have rested and fed his men, and then marched them in good order towards the enemy position. But something in Philippe seems to have snapped at this point. He had been humiliated too many times by his clever enemy, who had always slipped through the net just when it seemed to be drawing tight. Now Edward wanted a fight; so, he should have one. Instead of halting, he ordered the army to march towards the enemy and concentrate around Marchemont on the eastern edge of the forest. And instead of proceeding in column, he ordered the army to turn right in echelon; that is, instead of each contingent following the one in front of it, all would turn right at once and proceed roughly in line abreast towards the concentration point.[25]

All along the line of march, from Noyelles to Abbeville, French troops turned and began making north down minor roads and across the open fields. Almost immediately, the order of march began to break down. The order to turn could only be passed by messengers on horseback, and Montmorency and St-Venant and their under-marshals could not be every-where at once. Inevitably some troops got the order before others; an hour or more may have passed before the order was relayed to every contingent in the army. Even worse, however, was the attitude of the French nobles themselves. The *grands seigneurs*, eager for battle, began to hurry towards the enemy without thought of the march order, each determined to get to grips with the enemy as soon as possible. Analysing events afterwards, the chronicler Jean le Bel concluded that the French army was ruled that day by pride and envy rather than military discipline, and it is hard to disagree with him.[26]

Order disappeared into chaos, and every contingent simply marched towards its destination without thought for the others. Congestion built up as the army moved north, with too many contingents trying to march down the same tracks. The wagon train fell behind, and the foot soldiers of the communes remained stranded to the rear. Units that were supposed to fight together lost touch with each other. Bohemia, who had been supposed to lead the vanguard, now found himself well to the rear, and had lost touch with even his son's contingent. Instead, Charles d'Alençon hurried to take the lead, eager to grab glory for himself. By some chance, however, Ottone Doria's Genoese got onto the road ahead of him. The king's brother was furious at this, but at least Doria's men were in the right position, which was more than could be said for most of the rest of the army.[27]

One question which continues to puzzle is: what were the French marshals doing? The task of the marshal, in a medieval army, was to command the men-at-arms – the main fighting arm of the French army, in particular – and ensure that they obeyed orders, kept formation and marched and fought in a disciplined manner. (The overall conduct of the army as a whole was the responsibility of the Constable, but the Constable of France was currently languishing in an English prison, and no replacement, even a temporary one, seems to have been appointed.) On the English side, we have seen throughout the campaign how the marshals, Warwick and Harcourt, were constantly active, usually at or near the front of the army, continually leading their men and setting an example to the others. They exercised leadership, and the other nobles and men-at-arms followed them without hesitation. But whenever we see Montmorency and St-Venant, they are always near the king. They issue orders, which are presumably delivered through their deputies, but they do not lead. They themselves seem to have no understanding of what is happening in the field. From this distance, it is impossible to know whether the fault lay with the marshals themselves, who did not know their duties and were incompetent, or with King Philippe, who tended to like to keep his close advisors and councillors close by him. But either way, the lack of a Constable and the failure of the marshals meant that the naturally independent and undisciplined noble leaders of the army were virtually free from control.

Instead of sending the marshals forward to survey the English position, Philippe sent four knights. To be fair, these were experienced men: John of Hainault was a veteran of many campaigns, as was Miles de Noyers, Philippe's standard-bearer, whose father had been a marshal and was a contemporary of Robert Bertrand. Henri le Moine of Basel was a veteran of many wars and an old companion in arms of the King of Bohemia.[28] His presence when the king gave his orders must have been coincidental, for although a vassal of the Duc de Lorraine, he was presently in the retinue of his friend King Jean. The fourth member of the group, Olivier d'Aubigny, Seigneur d'Aubigny and Coudray-Macouart, was also an experienced soldier, a member of an up-and-coming family and a member of the royal household.[29] The four knights set off on their reconnaissance, but they had to force their way through the increasingly chaotic press of marching men and horses, and it took them some time to reach Marcheville.

Early afternoon

The day wore on and a few clouds began to build up; as often happens in southern England and northern France, especially near the coasts, a hot muggy day was clearly going to end with a shower of rain. Sitting on the hillside beneath their banners, the English army could see dust rising far to the south, and, as time passed, the tramp of many thousands of feet and hooves became an audible murmur. Scouts kept in touch with the enemy progress, and there may have been some skirmishes; one English esquire was killed during the course of the afternoon, and it is possible that he was a member of a reconnaissance party that got too close to the enemy.[30]

By mid-afternoon the enemy were getting distinctly closer. Then a party of horsemen came into sight, riding up the Abbeville–Hesdin road and passing beyond Marcheville. Several had bright surcoats and shields, indicating they were knights. The party stood and surveyed the English ranks, then turned and withdrew back down the road. No one in the English army could now be in doubt; the French knew where they were, and knew their numbers and dispositions.

Another couple of hours passed. The clouds were thicker now, and rooks in the nearby woods, sensing a change in the weather, began to chatter.[31] Rain was imminent, and a few of the English archers, thinking erroneously that the water might cause their bowstrings to stretch, unstrung their bows and put the coiled strings under their caps to keep them dry.[32] However, they quickly had to restring them. The scouts had reported that the enemy were now very near, and now suddenly they were visible, the first columns of men on foot moving up past Marcheville and Froyelles and then deploying over the fields towards the English army. There were four or five thousand of them, and experienced soldiers among the English recognised them as Genoese crossbowmen and marines.[33] Behind these came the first glittering columns of mounted men-at-arms, shields and banners a riot of colour. Orders were passed down the English ranks, and there was a ripple of motion as the army rose to its feet and stood in position, calmly waiting for the enemy.

* * *

Henri le Moine and his companions had been impressed by what they saw. The English were clearly preparing for a fight, and were in a good position. The French army had marched for hours, and the men were tired and hungry. It was clear to le Moyne and the others that the army needed to stop, rest and reorganise; a hard fight was about to come, and it was essential that the men be fresh. Passing down the road to find the king, they took it on themselves to order the commanders of each contingent they passed to halt until further orders were received. It seems likely that Doria, himself an experienced soldier and well aware of the fatigue of his men, obeyed the order, but Alençon, pushing hard behind him, did not, and the Genoese were forced to keep moving or be trampled.[34] The bad blood between the commanders of the two leading contingents increased.

It was late in the day when le Moine and his companions found the king. Le Moine, who appears to have acted as spokesman for the other three, gave his report, describing accurately the position and numbers of the English. At the conclusion, Philippe asked for his advice: how should the French army respond? Le Moine hesitated, apparently reluctant to speak; probably he was worried that the advice he was about to give would not be well received. Finally he spoke, and gave his opinion that to attempt a battle that day was a mistake. Time was wearing on, men and horses were becoming fatigued, and he had seen for himself that the army was badly disordered. The army should halt and make camp for the night, giving the men a chance to eat and rest. In the morning, properly arrayed, they could march against the enemy a short distance away.[35]

This was sound advice, and, unusually for him, Philippe took it. He is sometimes portrayed as being in a fury and ordering his men to press on and attack the English regardless,[36] but Jean le Bel and Jean Froissart, whose informants were in the royal household and present at this meeting, are adamant that Philippe then ordered the army to halt. Le Moine went back to join the King of Bohemia, satisfied that he had done his best. Messengers were despatched with new orders, informing the commanders of the change of plans: the leading units were to withdraw a little way and the army would make camp for the night. But the poor command and control systems of the French army, coupled with the breakdown of the march order, meant that halting the army had now become quite literally impossible. The locations of many contingents were no longer known. As the army converged towards Marcheville, the columns on the left flank were being forced eastward by the forest, and the congestion and chaos increased. And when commanders were found, many of the proud and haughty seigneurs deliberately refused to obey orders. They had come to fight the English, and they were going to do so. Other nobles, seeing their rivals still going forward, did likewise lest they be left out of the fight. Those like Doria who may have wished to halt could not do so, for to halt was to risk being overrun by the press of men coming up from behind. And so, propelled by pride and envy and folly and its own momentum, the disorganised mass of the French army swept on to the north, towards where the English, disciplined and calm, awaited them.[37]

Late afternoon

The original French tactical plan had been a simple one. Doria's crossbowmen would advance and shoot down as many of the English as possible, disordering their ranks and weakening their force, and would then move aside to let the first division of men-at-arms charge home. If this failed to break the English, subsequent French divisions would then attack, using the battering-ram force of a mass of armoured horsemen to break up the enemy force and destroy it.

In no happy frame of mind, Ottone Doria began deploying his crossbowmen and marines north-west of Froyelles. He was aware that Alençon, pressing behind him, was growing increasingly impatient and anxious to be at the enemy. His own men were reluctant, complaining that they were tired and had not eaten all day, and that their pavises and reserves of ammunition were still in the wagons far to the rear. To add to his problems it had begun to rain, and some of his men were arguing that the rain would cause the twisted rawhide strings of their crossbows to stretch and render the weapons useless. This latter was not a genuine grievance, for it was not raining hard and it would take prolongued soaking to cause the strings to stretch in this manner, but it is easy to imagine the grumbling of soldiers who have marched too far and are looking for any excuse to call a halt.[38]

Listening to his men, Doria went to Alençon and asked for a halt, to give his men a few minutes to rest before going into battle. Alençon refused, swearing at Doria and calling him and his men 'canailles' and 'ribaudailles' (literally, scoundrels and debauched men, but almost certainly with other connotations). Doria, who came from a prouder and longer lineage than any Valois, almost certainly replied in kind. Tempers flared in the drizzle, but Doria returned to his men and gave the order to march.

Up on the ridge the rain had ceased. The clouds were clearing, and in a few minutes the sun was shining once more, low in the west now, shining on the backs of the English and illuminating the faces of the Genoese advancing towards them. Their formation alone was about half the size of the entire English army, and pressing hard behind them came hundreds of mounted men-at-arms, with still more pouring up the road from the south and swinging left into the fields towards the English position, banners and pennons waving, shields bright in the sun. The English army waited, silent and still, watching as the Genoese crossed the line of the Maye and marched on across the little valley towards the slope.

All at once the Genoese formation halted. Looking up at the English, the five thousand men shouted in unison; some blew trumpets, others leaped into the air.[39] Their war cry was doubtless intended to frighten the English, but it had no effect whatsoever: the English ranks remained immovable. The Genoese then resumed their march, and a few moments later halted again and delivered a second war cry. A third time the performance was repeated, and now the Genoese were at the base of the slope. They halted again, raised their crosswbows and, on command from their leaders, began to shoot.

The noise of several thousand steel-sprung crossbows being shot nearly at once must have been considerable, and for a brief moment the air between the two armies was blurred by the flight of the short black bolts. Had these struck the waiting archers, they would have done considerable execution.

But, partly blinded by the setting sun in their eyes and deceived by the slope of the hill, the Genoese misjudged the range,[40] and the entire salvo of bolts ploughed harmlessly into the earth in front of the English position. Hurriedly, the Genoese knelt to reload, winding back their bowstrings and preparing to fit a second bolt. Many never completed their task.

Instead there came a sound like a thunderclap, and up on the hillside there was a bright flash of flame and a gush of smoke. Stone shot, fired by the three bombards, hurtled through the Genoese ranks. Few if any men were killed or injured, but the already wavering crossbowmen hesitated still further in the face of this new menace. And as they stood, up on the ridge an order was given and the archers of the Prince of Wales's division planted their front feet and raised their bows. Two thousand bows raised to an angle of forty-five degrees and then bent into graceful crescents against the sky. A moment of pause to sight, and then came the *whack* of released bowstrings and the arrows soared in a cloud, and fell among the Genoese.

The effect was instantaneous and horrendous. The shower of arrows that descended was compared by some chroniclers of the time to a snow-storm or hailstorm; but here, every snowflake or hailstone was a bringer of death. Shooting into the dense Genoese formation, the archers could scarcely miss, even at long range. The quilted jackets of the crossbowmen were no defence; without their heavy wooden pavises, they might as well have been naked. They died in scores, then hundreds, and the arrows continued to fall without respite, the archers nocking and drawing and releasing while their previous shots were still in the air. It was, quite simply, a slaughter, and the Genoese took the only recourse left to them; they turned, some throwing their crossbows away so as not to impede themselves, and began to run towards the rear.[41]

They were met by a foe every bit as implacable as the one they had just faced. Charles d'Alençon watched the Genoese flee towards him, and his fury finally boiled over. Drawing his sword, he shouted to his men to kill the Genoese. They have betrayed us, he raged, and brought shame upon us, and now they block our own path so we cannot advance.[42] His men-at-arms seem to have needed little urging. The leading elements spurred their horses forward and began laying about them with their swords, killing many of the Genoese and driving the rest back towards the English. Some of the Genoese, in a despairing fury of their own, raised their cross-bows and began to shoot at the French men-at-arms, probably killing or wounding some before being cut down themselves. So intent were they on massacre that the French may not have realised they had moved forward into the range of the English archers, until the arrows began to fall once more.

As the French and Genoese hacked and shot at each other, the English archers killed both without discrimination. Horses and men both fell, knights and crossbowmen dying together until their bodies piled up in heaps 'like slaughtered pigs'.[43] Recoiling, the leading men-at-arms fell back out of range, and in this brief respite, the surviving Genoese managed to escape. One of them was Ottone Doria, gravely wounded – whether by an English arrow or a French sword is not known – and carried by his men. The battle was only a few minutes old, and already the slope below the English position was covered with hundreds of dead and wounded men and horses.[44] And as the French and Genoese withdrew, some of the Welsh and Cornish foot soldiers broke ranks and ran down the slope, moving among the bodies and killing those who remained alive with their daggers and spears and axes. This was contrary to the king's explicit orders, and he was reportedly furious when he heard of it; what measures he took are not known, but there are no further accounts of such indiscipline in the English ranks for the rest of the day.[45]

There was now a pause while Alençon's men regrouped. During the attack of the crossbowmen, most of his division had now arrived on the field, and he had been joined by Louis de Nevers, the Count of Flanders, and probably also by the Normans under Harcourt and Aumale. His own standard-bearer, the veteran knight Jacques d'Estracelles, had just arrived on the field, and in the afternoon heat the latter had removed his bascinet in order to breathe more freely. He rode up to his lord to find the latter ordering his men to attack. Estracelles was astounded; Alençon had perhaps two or three thousand men-at-arms assembled, but more were going to be needed. Should they not wait for the arrival of the king? But Alençon's blood was up, and he ordered Estracelles forward, telling the latter curtly to put on his bascinet and go. Estracelles had his own pride; he looked at his lord and said quietly that he would obey orders and put on his bascinet, but it would not be he who removed it.[46] Grimly, the standard-bearer prepared to lead the attack, knowing the arrows would fall most thickly around him.

In the valley, trumpets sounded, and Alençon's men began their charge. The air reverberated to the drumming of thousands of hooves. Sunlight sparkled silver on bascinets and armour, and lit up the bright colours of the shields and banners of the knights and nobles. Swiftly the armoured horsemen came on. Up on the ridge, the English stood immobile in their ranks and wedges; so far, they had not lost a single man. The pause following the defeat of the Genoese had given them time to replenish their stocks of arrows. They waited; and as the charging horsemen drew within range, once more they raised their bows and nocked and drew, and shot.

And once again the carnage began. At long range, the arrows arced high in the air and then plunged down at steep angles. Armoured men were comparatively safe, but unarmoured horses were not, and it was the horses the archers intended to maim or kill. They were shooting arrows with barbed hunting heads, that would stick in the flesh and could not be pulled out. Jean le Bel describes, not without horror, the results. Some horses fell, bringing their armoured riders crashing to earth. Others simply stopped in their tracks when they were hit, while still others tried to turn away from the enemy; some bucked or leaped in the air, maddened with pain. The screaming of hundreds of injured and dying horses can only be imagined. Any cohesion the French force had once had began to disintegrate as the horsemen struggled to control their mounts and keep their own momentum going, hampered as they now were by the slope and the corpses of men and horses that had fallen in the earlier attack. But still they came on, and still the arrows fell in clouds.

As the range closed and the trajectory flattened, the archers began firing arrows with bodkin points, steel chisels that struck with stunning force, punching through chainmail and weak points in armour even at a hundred yards' range. Now men began to fall from the saddle, shot through the body or the neck. Shields and banners were riddled with arrows. A constant din of noise could be heard, the terrible clash of steel arrowheads constantly impacting on armour and shield, and the even more terrible softer thuds of the same arrowheads hitting the bodies of horses and humans.

In the minute or so between the time they came into effective arrow range and the time they reached the English line, Alençon's men were hit by around 16,000 arrows.[47] Somewhere within that minute, Alençon himself died. It would be interesting to know if, in his final moments, he fully realised the disaster he had brought on himself and his country; from what we know of his temperament, it is unlikely.[48] Scores of other men fell, yet still the French came on. Closer to the English positions, more horses began going down as they stumbled into the pitfalls dug by the archers. Exactly as planned, the French shied away from the wedges of archers, coasting past them as Froissart puts it, and instead riding into the killing ground between the two wedges and in front of the foot soldiers and dismounted hobelars and men-at-arms.

Deluged with arrows, with men and horses going down every second, the French never faltered, and the *furor franciscus* struck the English line. The desperation of the fighting that followed can only be imagined. Bloody, with many men and horses wounded and half-mad with pain, the French hacked furiously at their opponents, undoubtedly knowing that if they failed they would have to retreat through that same murderous hail. The English for their part were equally desperate to hold on, knowing that a French breakthrough could very quickly turn the course of the battle. A solid core of French men-at-arms, led by Estracelles in some accounts, Louis of Flanders according to others, made straight for the distinctive figure of the Prince of Wales, standing in his surcoat quartered with the leopards of England and lilies of France, under the dragon standard of his principality. Here the fighting was heavy and bloody. The fury of the French quickly made itself felt. Several English knights and a number of foot soldiers were killed or injured. The Prince of Wales fought manfully, and Geoffrey le Baker presents a picture of him rushing into the fray, hamstringing horses and running men through with this sword,[49] but a charging French man-at-arms, possibly the Count of Flanders himself, knocked him to the ground. Other French horsemen converged on the scene. The Prince's standard-bearer, Richard FitzSimon, leaped to his rescue, throwing the dragon standard over the Prince's body and standing above him with sword gripped in both hands, fighting to protect his lord.[50]

It was, for the English, the most dangerous moment of the battle. Their formation had been penetrated; the Prince was down and his standard, the rallying symbol to which the medieval soldier attached so much value, had fallen. A few more minutes might well have seen the English front line break. One of the English knights of the vanguard, Thomas Norwich, broke away and ran back to the king's division, and a moment later was before the king himself, pleading for aid.[51]

The interview that followed has passed into English folklore. The Prince of Wales, said Norwich, was hard pressed and needed assistance. Is my son dead, demanded the king, or has he been captured? The answer was in the negative, though Norwich clearly thought that either event could not be long in coming. Then go back to your post, ordered the king, and do not return unless there is desperate need. As for the Prince of Wales, the honour of the day's victory will be his; let him therefore earn it. *Laissié l'enfant gaegnier ses esperons*, he concluded: let the boy win his spurs.[52]

Edward could probably afford to be blasé, because he would have seen what Norwich had not. Northampton, watching the progress of events from behind and to the left of the Prince's division, had seen how things were going, and sent Arundel with a substantial force of dismounted men-at-arms to reinforce the vanguard. Arriving on the run, Arundel and his men threw themselves into the fighting. This tipped the scales. One by one, the French were cut down. Nevers was dead, and so too was Jacques d'Estracelles, his grim prediction come true; it would be an English soldier who would unlace the bascinet from his dead body. Thomas Daniel, one of the heroes of Caen, forced his way through to the Prince and raised the standard once more, and the Prince himself rose to his feet, slightly wounded but perfectly able to continue.[53] Finally the French broke, their courage tried beyond measure, and they fled down the slope, pursued by vengeful arrows. It had been a close thing, perhaps closer than has sometimes been realised; but Northampton's timing and the fighting qualities of Arundel and the Prince of Wales himself and their men had held the line. Reorganising, tending to their wounded and their dead, replenishing arrows, the English waited for the next attack.

Evening

The fighting on the ridge above Crécy that day had a nightmarish quality about it. The images that come to us through the reports of those who were there and the chroniclers who wrote about it are often bloody and horrible: heaps of bodies of men and horses, wounded men being killed while they lay helpless, others trampled in the mud and suffocating, some even crushed to death by their colleagues pressed tightly around them. But over and above all this are two constant running themes: the order and discipline within the English ranks and the utter chaos which reigned amongst the French.

Some accounts of the battle, both contemporary and modern, have attempted to portray the French army as having at least a semblance of order about it. Some accounts speak gravely of the army forming up in three divisions, one commanded by Alençon, one by the King of Bohemia and one by King Philippe himself, and then advancing in orderly fashion to the attack. But most present a picture of pandemonium. The grand seigneurs who commanded the French army did not wait for one another, says Jean le Bel, but attacked in disorder, their contingents mixed together without any order whatsoever. By their pride and envy, he says, all was destroyed.[54] The *Grandes Chroniques* describes a scene of such utter chaos that Philippe himself was for a long time unable to get to the battlefield, so great was the press of disordered men in front of him.[55] Men did not join their banners or listen to orders, says Froissart, but simply threw themselves into the battle.[56] The English themselves seem to have watched with something close to amazement; the more experienced English knights saw at once that things had gone badly wrong for the French, and reckoned that unless they could pull together and reorganise, they stood little chance of winning.[57] Writing after the battle, the English poet Lawrence Minot believed that Philippe had thrown away his great army by failing to control it.[58]

Rather than forming up for battle, each contingent simply arrived on the battlefield and moved in to the attack. These new contingents were fatigued by their long march, disordered by passing through the press of men back along the roads to the south, and as they approached the battlefield, further disordered by having to push their way through the wreckage of previous contingents, the flotsam of riderless horses, wounded men struggling to find aid, men who had lost their commanders and were wandering aimlessly, commanders who had lost their men and were desperate to rally them – the usual scene in the rear areas of an army that is being defeated. Pressing forward, they came to the little valley and then the slope where the English stood, strewn with ever-increasing numbers of corpses. And they attacked, without order, without discipline, without coordination; without thought. They stood no chance whatsoever. Every attack was beaten back, every contingent that charged was shot to pieces by the archers.

Sometimes two or more contingents did join forces, but often only because of family or other ties of personal loyalty. Louis, Comte de Blois and Raoul, Duc de Lorraine, who were brothers-in-law, appear to have attacked together; it is probable that their contingents were marching near each other before the battle, and it would have been natural for the one to wait for the other before attacking. It did not matter; their hundreds of men-at-arms were not going to succeed where Alençon's thousands had failed. They did well, getting so close to the English line that Blois, his horse shot from under him, was killed by the Welsh spearmen rather than arrows. But the result was still the same: the attack was crushed, and Marie de Châtillon's husband and brother died within a few yards of each other on the bloody slopes.[59]

The apparent calm within the English ranks was probably deceptive. Among the archers, sweating in the evening heat, there was certainly a great deal of urgency. In the lulls in the fighting, after one attack had failed and been beaten back and the next was still pushing its way forward, men ran to and fro bringing up fresh stocks of arrows, either from the wagons or, probably increasingly as the day wore on, from the other divisions standing in reserve. Others may well have run onto the field to recover arrows that were embedded in the earth or in the bodies of the fallen; unless the shaft or fletchings are damaged, an arrow can be reused many times over. The archers themselves would rest their aching backs and arms and fingers, and probably boast to each other about their achievements so far. As each new attack developed they would stand to, and when the enemy came within range they would begin to shoot once more, not taking precise aim but simply loosing their arrows into the densely packed masses of horses and men, gradually lowering the trajectory until at fifty yards they were shooting nearly flat, driving their arrows through metal and flesh and bone. The English men-at-arms would stand tensely, gripping their weapons, wondering if this time the attackers would get through the arrows and charge home. Then the inevitable would happen: the French leaders would fall, the banners would go down and the attack would disintegrate into a mass of dead and dying men and horses, the survivors turning and falling back out of range of the arrows.

One of the most painful things for the English must have been watching as people they knew came up the slopes towards them. Among the English were many like Thomas Holland who had served in foreign lands, Prussia and Spain particularly, and there fought alongside French knights. They had been comrades, sometimes they had been friends. In an 'ordinary' battle it might have been possible to ransom these men and save their lives. Here, however, no mercy was being extended.

Standing on the ridge above Crécy, Godefroi d'Harcourt came face to face with the full consequences of his treason. In one of the first attacks of the day, possibly even that led by Alençon and Flanders, Jean, Comte de Harcourt led his Norman knights into battle. All that summer they had served France faithfully and well. Now they were plunged into the final battle. Harcourt himself led the way, red and gold colours distinct at the head of the charging force. His son Jean rode beside him; the young man's brother-in-law, Jean, Comte d'Aumale rode at the head of his own men along with them, and also in their number was Robert Bertrand, Vicomte de Longeville, eldest son of the lord of Bricquebec who had fought with such gallantry earlier in the campaign. Before Godefroi d'Harcourt's eyes, his brother died, shot down by the archers. Aumale died along with him, so did Bertrand.[60] Harcourt's son, Godefroi's nephew, was wounded and probably unhorsed, but survived. How many other former friends and neighbours of the lame marshal perished that afternoon is not known. There are reports that Harcourt tried to save his brother; if so, he failed.[61]

Some of the German knights serving with Edward's division to the rear watched with shock as the slaughter went on, and eventually one approached the king himself. Why was so much noble blood being shed? Was it not possible to take prisoners? If nothing else, a fortune in ransoms was being lost. The king rather tersely instructed them to obey his orders.[62] No one was to leave the ranks to take prisoners; there was too much at stake. In any case, it is not clear how the Germans expected to take prisoners in this kind of fighting. The arrows offered no quarter, and accepted no ransoms.

* * *

Watching an archer shoot on a summer's evening can be a pleasant thing. Drawing an arrow, the archer raises the bow vertically, gripped in his left hand, and nocks an arrow with the right. Sighting on the target, he draws steadily back until the bow describes a perfect arc and the bowstring and nock of the arrow are level with his ear. There is a moment of stillness, and then release; the bowstring cracks, the bow straightens and the arrow bounds away, arching upwards and then descending gently to its target. If the target is a paper bull's-eye pinned to a woven straw backing, the standard form of archery target, it strikes with a gentle thump. The movements of the archer are graceful; the bow and arrow are not snatched at, but drawn in a series of fluid movements. The bow itself is a seemingly delicate thing, and the arrows are slender wooden wands; only their gleaming point betrays their purpose and their power.

Imagine, however, that it is you that are the target, and the archer is shooting at you with intent to kill. The slender wands become three feet of feathered death, hissing through the air, clattering horribly on metal armour, ripping into unprotected flesh and organs. The speed of the arrows as they approach is unimaginable; the notion, fostered by Hollywood films, that men can leap aside to avoid flying arrows or strike them aside with swords, is simply ludicrous. Even at long range, their power is enough to dent full armour and make the wearer reel in the saddle. At fifty yards or less they are as deadly as bullets, the steel bodkin points biting easily through leather and quilted brigandines and chainmail, punching through even plate armour where it is thin or weak or badly made, piercing deep into horse flesh and human flesh, human bones and human brains.

And imagine further that there is not one archer but two thousand, and they are nocking and firing continuously, bows rising and falling in a steady rhythm, nock, draw, release, nock, draw, release. This is what the French men-at-arms charging at Crécy that evening had to face. As we noted above, at the height of each attack the English archers were shooting at a rate of around 16,000 arrows a minute; put another way, the attacking French faced nearly 300 arrows *per second* in their attempt to get to the English lines.

Yet, the French still came. Valour and pride of race were deep in their blood. They were the descendants of Charlemagne's paladins; their ancestors had fought with William the Conqueror, had crusaded against the infidel, had spread the fame of French arms across the Christian world and beyond. To retreat without striking a blow was the most shameful thing imaginable; better to die than to suffer dishonour. And so they came, and died.

The local Picard knights suffered terribly. Many had seen their homes and property burned in the past week, and revenge as well as honour may have been in their hearts. Their losses were proportionately high. Guy, Comte de St-Pol, the defender of St-Valery, was among the dead; Matthieu de Cayeux, whose home was in the county of Vimeu and who had fought under St-Pol's command, was also killed, and Jean d'Aumale died fighting alongside his brother-in-law Harcourt. The powerful baron Enguerrand de Coucy, whose lands had been ravaged by the English in 1340, was killed. Guillaume de Croï-Chanel, descendant of St Stephen of Hungary, died, although his cousin Jean de Croï, the lord of Airaines, survived, as did Jean de Picquigny.

The other contingents also suffered heavy losses. Jean de Châlons, Comte d'Auxerre, died at the head of his men, though his son who rode with him survived. Louis, Comte de Sancerre was killed, possibly in the same attack as Louis of Blois and Raoul of Lorraine. Jacques de Bourbon, the future Constable of France, was gravely wounded but managed to get his horse and himself off the field. The Vicomte de Thouars, brother of the Count of Flanders, was killed, probably in the same attack as the Count. From Champagne, Jean, Comte de Grandpré was killed, as was Bernard, Seigneur de Moreuil. The Comte de Blamont, whose lands lay near Metz, and his cousin Simon, Comte de Salm, were both killed, as were Thibault of Bar and the Vicomte of Ventadour. The list of great houses and noble names goes on and on.[63]

For one reason or another, many survived. In his letter home after the battle, Edward claimed King Jaume of Majorca as among the fallen, but this is an error; perhaps Edward himself saw someone else with a similar coat-of-arms go down. There is little mention made of the men of Majorca and Montpellier, and if they did attack it is likely that they did so more half-heartedly than their French comrades; their commitment to this war had never been terribly strong. The same was probably true of the King of Bohemia's son Charles, who was present only out of duty to his father and loyalty to his French friends; his calculating mind, however, was already looking towards a much larger future. But his men did attack with determination, and many died; Northburgh later said that there were six German counts and many minor barons and knights among the dead, and Froissart names the Count of Saarbrucken as one of them.[64] Peter Ursini, Count of Rožmberk and High Chamberlain of the Kingdom of Bohemia, was mortally wounded and died on 13 October.[65] But the King of the Romans was unharmed; at least for the moment. Others no doubt survived because they were towards the rear of their contingents and the bodies ahead of them absorbed the arrows.

Others survived through good fortune and the bravery of their friends. Thibault, Seigneur de Mathéfelon, had his horse shot from under him; this could be a sentence of death, for the men thrown to the ground were often trampled or suffocated by other horses coming up behind them, but Mathéfelon avoided this fate and managed to get off the field, unwounded and unharmed. Henri de Montfaucon, Count of Montbéliard, was similarly unhorsed but managed to escape.[66] Guillaume, Comte de Namur, also had his horse killed close to the English lines and would probably have been killed himself very soon after, but a contingent of men-at-arms under Louis de Juppeleu came to his rescue and pulled him off the stricken field. Froissart repeatedly tells us that many gallant deeds were done that day by the French, and we can see that this was true; braving the arrow-storm to go to the rescue of a comrade or friend required true and selfless courage, and men like Louis de Juppeleu deserve to be remembered.[67]

* * *

But it was all for naught. The French army was being comprehensively wrecked. Every contingent that attacked did so at ever more impossible odds, for by now the slope was churned to gory mud, watered not only by the earlier rain but by gallons of blood running from the corpses of men and horses. When Philippe of France finally reached the field of the battle he had not ordered and did not want, the sight that would have greeted his eyes resembled a medieval fresco depicting hell. The bodies of some of his finest seigneurs lay pierced with arrows, next to their horses. Many of the latter would have been still alive, kicking in their death throes or struggling to get up, unnerving the warhorses of the new arrivals. The cries of wounded men and horses filled the ears of Philippe and his household as they approached the field.

The battle was clearly lost. John of Hainault, who had ridden with the king all that day, urged him to withdraw. There were still sizeable French forces in the field which had not yet been commited. Let the king withdraw and rally these, and resume the attack in the morning. Others around the king seem to have concurred; this was, after all, very similar to the advice which le Moine had given several hours earlier. Since then the king had been trying to get forward to take command, but had been held up by the press of men and horses ahead of him.[68] Now, seeing the devastation of his army, he did not immediately reply to Hainault. Instead he rode forward, followed by the men of his household, Hainault, Charles de Montmorency, Robert de St-Venant, Edouard de Beaujeu, Olivier d'Aubigny, Edouard de Montfort, Jean de St-Dizier, and others, apparently looking for his brother, whom he hoped to still find fighting on the field. He had to ride quite a long way, down the slope into the valley, in order to see clearly in the failing light; and then he saw Alençon's banner, lying beside the body of Jacques d'Estracelles further up the slope, and the truth finally came home.

He attacked, of course; he had to. Neither his honour nor his crown would have survived the disgrace if he had turned and left the scene after so many of his men had died. And the attack disintegrated as so many before it had done. Robert de St-Venant, one of the marshals who should have prevented the disaster, died. Henri d'Uffalise, a Hainault knight in Montmorency's retinue, was killed along with many others. St-Dizier's horse was killed, but he escaped the field. Miles de Noyers, the standard-bearer, was a particular target as always, and the Oriflamme was riddled with flying arrows, which is probably what Richard Wynkeley meant when he said the standard was ripped to shreds.[69] Noyers's horse may also have been killed, for the English claimed they saw him fall, but he himself survived.

Philippe himself, easily recognisable, was the target of many arrows, for what English archer would not wish to claim that he had killed the usurping King of France? But Philippe's household protected him well; and, being king, he probably had better protective armour than many others. According to Froissart, the king's horse was killed and he was remounted by John of Hainault; but this detail may have been invented by Hainault himself. Richard Wynkeley is positive that Philippe was wounded in the face by an arrow,[70] and in other English chronicles this gradually transforms itself into a whole series of wounds in neck, body and leg, until the King of France must have resembled a pincushion. But if Philippe was wounded at all, it can have been no more than a scratch, for he went on to ride quite a number of miles in the days to come.[71]

A different fate befell Thierry de Sencelles, Hainault's banner-bearer who was mounted on the supposedly fine black horse that Philippe himself had given his master. In the midst of the charge the horse panicked and bolted, careering straight towards the enemy lines. Completely out of control, it carried the unfortunate Sencelles *between* the first two divisions of the English line, that is, between the wedge of archers on the left of the Prince of Wales's division and that on the right of Northampton's division. Amazingly, neither was killed. The Prince of Wales's archers were probably still too intent on the king to notice, and it is possible that by the time Sencelles was in range of Northampton's archers, they could not shoot without fear of hitting their own men. Having bolted completely through the English army, the horse then compounded its behaviour by throwing the unfortunate Sencelles into a ditch, where he lay injured and unable to rise. He was rescued by his page, who with great gallantry had followed his master through the enemy lines and helped him to his feet. Together the two men collected the banner and Sencelles limped off the battlefield to the north-east. Unable to find his lord, he and the page eventually made their way to Arras and then to Cambrai, and thence home.[72]

The attack ground to a halt, and Hainault and a little circle of men, including Montmorency, Beaujeu, Aubigny and Montfort, pulled Philippe from the field, Hainault himself at one point laying hands at the king's bridle to turn his horse. This is folly, Hainault urged; what purpose will you serve by throwing away your crown and your life, except to hand victory to your enemy? This time, possibly unnerved by what he had just been through, the king agreed. Collecting about sixty men-at-arms, all that remained of the royal household, Hainault and the others led their monarch away from the battle.

*　*　*

Back on the field, the last act of the tragedy was about to be played out.[73] Up past Marcheville and Froyelles the blind king of Bohemia came riding at the head of his men. They were a polyglot group of Bohemians, Germans, Luxembourgeois, French and others. In the circle around the king were the Swiss Henri le Moine, the Bohemian-German Heinrich von Klingenberg, the Czechs Henryk Rožmberk and Hron Jankovsti, Colin Petit de Maubuisson from Normandy, the Gascon Lambequin de Pé, Pierre d'Auvilliers from the Île-de-France, and the king's own illegitimate son, Jean de Luxembourg. Many were veterans of his earlier campaigns in France, Italy, Silesia and Prussia, united by their professionalism and their devotion to their master.

One glance would have told le Moine that the day was lost, and the king too must have known the truth, for he could hear the sounds of defeat and panic around him. Much of the army had disintegrated into little parties of men, sometimes only three or four; Jean le Bel describes them as wandering like lost men, searching for their lords and kinsmen, and Froissart says the sound of their desperate cries and calls reached even the English ranks.[74]

Jean asked le Moine the time, and was told it was sunset; he then asked how the battle was going, and le Moine described what he could see. The English archers were slaughtering the French, whose army was breaking up. Night was falling. There was, said le Moine, no chance of remedying the situation. This is a poor start for us, the king said drily, and he then asked after his son, the King of the Romans. No one could see him, but he was rumoured to be still alive, in another part of the field. In fact, by this point Charles too had probably retreated, following the example of King Philippe.[75]

What happened next has gone down in the legends of three nations. Prudence would have dictated that Bohemia should retire as well; but prudence had never been a salient feature of his personality. Various theories have been advanced as to why he did what he did: he was blind and growing old and had become tired of life; he was losing power in Bohemia to his restless, brilliant son and did not wish to die in obscurity; he had been a soldier all his life, and wished to die as he had lived; he felt that the defeat of the French was a stain on his own honour, and wished to wipe it clean. Some or even all of these explanations may be partly true. We shall never know.

Turning to his companions, Jean of Bohemia asked them to lead him forward so that he might, as Froissart puts it, strike one good blow with his sword. They agreed, and so that the blind king should not be separated from his escort, two of his friends, Henri le Moine and Heinrich von Klingenberg, looped their reins through his so that they could guide and control his horse. Then the trumpets sounded one last time, and the Bohemian contingent began to descend into the valley, pushing past the scattered remnants of the earlier contingents. The light was growing dim now and mist was beginning to rise, but there was still sufficient light for the English archers to see the large block of men-at-arms advancing slowly towards them. As the Bohemians began to climb the slope, the arrows descended once more. Hampered by the piles of corpses on the ground and by the blindness of their leader, who had to keep pace with the horses on either side, at times moving at little better than a walking pace, the Bohemians advanced into the holocaust.

Rožmberk was killed, and so was Jankovsti, whose grandfather had died fighting in Jean's service in the Tyrol fourteen years earlier. So too was Jean de Luxembourg, the king's bastard son. Petit and Auvilliers survived, and so probably did Lambequin de Pé. Thanks to force of numbers and the poor light, the Bohemians did get quite close to the English lines. Froissart, who claims to have had information from members of his household, says the king was seen three or four times during the advance, always going forward; and according to many accounts, he did get his chance to strike a blow with his sword. This may be a later fiction, designed to romanticise still further the death of one of Europe's most famous fighting men. It is much more likely that he died on the slope, sword in hand but unbloodied. When the English came out to survey the battlefield the following day they found the bodies of three horses, their bridles still looped together, and with them the bodies of the three men: Heinrich von Klingenberg, Henri le Moine and the blind king, Jean of Bohemia. He had indeed died as he had lived.[76]

Night

Night fell, heavy with mist and fog. There were a few more sporadic attacks, often by very small parties of men, which were easily beaten off.[77] For a time the English on the ridge could still hear men calling out in the valley below them, searching for lost friends and kinsmen. After dark some French men-at-arms did return cautiously to the battlefield and begin searching for survivors, but found none.[78] They would not have been able to get too close to the English position, however, for the latter, fearing a night attack, had kindled fires and lit torches to illuminate the field. The king ordered every man to remain in position. Strong as the attacks against them had been, they recognised that only part of Philippe's total force had been committed, and large numbers of men, including some strong contingents of men-at-arms, still remained out there in the night. They may also have been running short of arrows.[79]

Soon after the defeat of the Bohemian attack, the fifteenth since the battle began, Edward himself came down the hill from his post near the windmill and, coming to the vanguard, greeted his son. In the presence of a large number of his assembled men, the king loudly praised his son and proclaimed that the glory of the day's victory belonged solely to the Prince. The Prince modestly rejected this and replied that the victory was due to the king his father. Both men were, of course, playing a part; Edward was keen to establish his eldest son and heir as a war leader, and courtesy dictated that the Prince should honour his father and overlord. Nonetheless, there is much truth to Edward's views. The entire brunt of the French attack had been borne by the Prince of Wales's division, and they had behaved with great courage, skill and – most important of all – discipline, and everyone present recognised this. Not the least of the consequences of the battle were the establishment of the Prince of Wales's reputation as a warrior, and the further confirmation of the strength of the English tactical system based around the longbow. The combination of the two was to have potent consequences in the years to come, culminating ten years later in another day of English triumph and French disaster at Poitiers.

Rewards were also handed out to others who had distinguished themselves. Two knights, Alan la Zouche and John Delisle, were made bannerets.[80] Fifty others were knighted, including John Beauchamp, Guy Bryan, Peter de Braose, Henry Dengaigne, Thomas Lancaster, and John Ravensholme; they were also given annuities ranging from £20 to £40 a year, although Thomas Lancaster's annuity was larger, 100 marks (about £66).[81] Rewards were handed out to common soldiers as well. The Cheshire man Thomas Crue's brother had been injured in the first attack, and Thomas had helped him off the field and taken him to the hospital in the wagon park, remaining there to tend to his hurts; he did not rejoin his comrades until later in the evening, thus missing out on his share of the rewards.[82]

As the noise died down and it became clear that no new attack was imminent, the English began to relax a little. The men remained at their posts, and a small and hasty meal was prepared; the royal household ate the food of common soldiers that night, pease pottage with onions.[83] They ate in the field, still under arms, waiting and watching. The mood in the English ranks was one of sober rejoicing. They had always been confident that they could win, but a victory on this scale can hardly have been imagined. Le Bel says that they thanked God for their good fortune, but that there was also considerable jubilation.[84] Both are perfectly understandable. However, there was also an awareness that the affair might not yet be done. As noted, there were strong forces still arrayed against them, and much would depend on how quickly Philippe and his marshals could reassemble their army. The senior nobles then retired to their tents and rested as best they could, still in armour; the others slept in the open with strong guards posted, watching through the night as the fog swirled around their torches at the head of the corpse-strewn slope.

* * *

To the south and east of the battlefield, chaos still reigned. Those who had survived the battle made their way away from the field, towards Abbeville or further east to the more certain shelter of Amiens. Hundreds were wounded; hundreds were also on foot, having lost their horses. The wealthier knights and nobles who could afford remounts had doubtless found their servants by now and ridden away from the field, but the common men-at-arms had no option but to walk. As time passed and the fog grew thicker, many of these weary men simply stopped and went to sleep in copses of trees or under hedgerows.[85] Some of the contingents that had retained their cohesion also stopped and made camp; one such group included Charles of Luxembourg and his remaining men-at-arms.

And what of Philippe himself? For reasons which have never been fully explained, instead of retiring towards Abbeville, the king and his small escort set off to the north-east towards the castle of Labroye, which guarded the Abbeville–Hesdin road at the point where it crossed the river Authie some five miles from the battlefield. It was dark when they reached Labroye, and when they knocked at the gate they were greeted by the castellan, Jean Lessopier, who was unable to see clearly in the night and mist and demanded their identities. The king himself answered: 'Ouvrés, ouvrés, chastellain; c'est li infortunés rois de France.'[86] Supposedly recognising the king's voice, or at least being reassured as to their identity, Lessopier opened the gates. Here the king was able to rest and eat and drink – it may be supposed that he too had had nothing to eat since morning – and the party then set out for Amiens, twenty miles away, riding through the night and eventually reaching the city in the morning.[87]

Unimaginably, he had lost the battle; lost it so catastrophically that in the short term there was simply no possibility of recovery. Strong forces still remained in the field, but who was to lead them? Many of the greatest French nobles had died, the king's own brother and nephew among them. Others were wounded or scattered across the countryside, their whereabouts and fate unknown. A strong constable or marshal might have attempted to take charge, but Montmorency was not the right man for the job; and neither was Philippe himself. Throughout the night, the army continued to disintegrate. The foot soldiers who had advanced so laboriously from Abbeville in the wake of the men-at-arms received no orders and most camped in the open fields; their commanders, men like the Archbishop of Sens and the Grand Prior of the Knights Hospitaller, would have known from contact with men retreating from the front that a battle had been fought and the French had lost, but probably had little idea of the scale of the defeat. They certainly had no idea as to what they should do next.

What had gone wrong? The first failure had come early in the day, when Philippe had reacted too quickly to the news of Edward's whereabouts; instead of deploying his army methodically, he had simply marched every man to the scene as soon as possible. As a result, cohesion had broken down and the march order had been lost; only Alençon was able to muster a sizeable portion of his battle order. Then had come the failure to take le Moyne's advice and halt for the night to rest and reorganise. Opinion is divided on this issue, but the majority of contemporaries and modern historians agree that Philippe did wish to halt the army, but was unable to do so thanks to a combination of the loss of cohesion, inefficient command and control systems, incompetence on the part of his marshals, and the undeniable arrogance of his nobles. The failure of the Genoese to make any impact threw the French tactical plan into still further disarray. Last of all, that 'pride and envy' of which Jean le Bel wrote so bitterly translated itself on the battlefield into overwhelming arrogance and suicidal folly. It is impossible to avoid the conclusion that the French who attacked that day simply threw away their lives. Much of the blame must rest with Philippe, who failed to exercise leadership, and Montmorency and the dead St-Venant also failed in their duties. And if Charles d'Alençon had been a different man, or if it had been the King of Bohemia who had followed the Genoese onto the field, the outcome might perhaps have been different. In the final analysis, however, the French were defeated by an enemy who had everything they lacked: strong leadership, a sound tactical plan and an army that, by the standards of the Middle Ages, was efficient, disciplined and well ordered.

Notes

1 Froissart, p. 35.
2 This can be safely assumed; he would probably not have said mass on every morning of the campaign, but on such an important occasion one would normally expect the senior prelate to celebrate mass.

3 See Burne, pp. 170–1 for more on these. Although heavy ploughing has largely ironed out these terraces, some traces of them can still be seen today.

4 Murimuth, p. 246, places Northampton with this division as well. This is in Murimuth's own narrative, not the eyewitness letter of Richard Wynkeley which he cites elsewhere, and may not be accurate.

5 These figures come from the second redaction of Froissart, and as ever with this source are used with caution; but there are some reasons for assuming they may have been close to correct. In the second redaction Froissart tells us he has had access to senior English eyewitnesses, including John Chandos and Bartholomew Burghersh, and the figures given for this and the other two battles are both quite precise and quite low. His overall strength for the three divisions comes to 8,200 men; which, assuming another 1,500 non-combatants and guards with the wagons in the rear, results in a figure very close to our own estimate of 10,000. In the first redaction, he estimated the total English force at over 18,000, an estimate probably based on the very similar figure given by Jean le Bel, p. 105; in the third redaction, perhaps not trusting his own sources, he pushes the figure back up to 15,900. But both these figures are in excess of the force which landed in the first place! The figure in the second redaction, if not absolutely accurate, is probably fairly close to the real picture.

6 Burne, pp. 171–2; supported by the contemporary evidence of le Baker, p. 84.

7 Baker, p. 84.

8 Ibid.

9 Baker's statement that the English army fasted on the Saturday and called on the Mother of Christ to aid them is not strictly true – at least, not as far as the fasting was concerned – but probably accurately reflects the prevailing mood.

10 Suffolk is not mentioned in Froissart's list but is mentioned in the *Anonimalle Chronicle*, p. 22; however, this also includes the Earl of Huntingdon, William Clinton, who was still in England.

11 *Histoire d'Abbeville*, p. 201. The location of the wagon park has been controversial; Villani, p. 165, appears to suggest the wagons actually formed part of a barricade in the English front line, and this has been followed by some modern historians (Barber, *Edward, Prince of Wales*, p. 64; Sumption, p. 527). Given the function of the wagon park and the importance of keeping its contents safe, we doubt this. Other contemporary sources which mention the wagon park site it to the rear of the main English position; for example le Bel, p. 105; *Chronique Normande*, p. 81.

12 This is an assumption, not specifically mentioned in the contemporary accounts, but Burne feels sure it happened, and so do we. After the near-disaster at Morlaix, the need to ensure a steady supply of arrows to the front line must have become apparent, and Northampton does not strike us as the sort of man not to have learned from previous mistakes.

13 The presence of the cannon was long doubted, but is now generally accepted; see Burne, pp. 192–202 for a long summary of the evidence. Three is the number of cannon usually mentioned, although Sumption, p. 528, concludes that Edward had more than 100 firearms at Crécy; however, T.F. Tout, 'Firearms in England in the Fourteenth Century', pp. 239–40, concludes this is unlikely.

14 Suggested by Burne, p. 173; again, this seems a sensible and logical precaution.

15 Froissart, p. 34. That the king did conduct such a tour of inspection seems more than likely, though some of the details may have been invented.

16 Froissart, p. 36. Again the details may well have been invented at a later date, but as Chandos is one of Froissart's sources, the core of the story is likely to be accurate.

17 The heat is inferred by several references to men on both sides taking off their bascinets so that they could breathe more easily; the humidity is inferred by the rain that fell later in the afternoon.

18 Viard, 'Le Campagne de juillet–août', pp. 68 ff., repeatedly contrasts the order, discipline and calm of the English with the chaotic dispositions of the French.

19 *Histoire d'Abbeville*, p. 203, says the abbey was called St-Etienne.

20 There is still considerable debate over the overall size of the French army (see Appendix), although, as we shall see, the precise figure did not in the end really matter.

21 Froissart, p. 61.

22 Or so we think, for there seems no other way of making sense of the French formation. For more on this tricky subject, for which there are nearly as many opinions as historians, see Appendix.

23 Realistic assessments of their strength range from 4,000 to 6,000; see Appendix.

24 The *Bourgeois de Valenciennes*, p. 476, notes that Philippe's advisors believed the English would not dare risk a battle.

25 For the argument that the French army turned in echelon rather than continuing in column as described by French historians, see Appendix.

26 Le Bel, p. 102.

27 *Histoire d'Abbeville*, p. 206, notes that the friction between Doria and Alençon began before the army reached the battlefield, and there are hints of this too in Froissart and le Bel.

28 See J. Viard, 'Henri le Moine de Bâte a la Bataille de Crécy', *Bibliotheque de l'école de Chartes*, vol. 66, 1906, pp. 489–96.

29 The fourteenth-century Aubignys were of no relation to the Sieurs d'Aubigny who rose to prominence in the fifteenth and sixteenth centuries, and were of Scottish extraction.

30 Knighton (*Chronicon Henrici Knighton*, p. 38), when discussing English casualties says the esquire was killed before the battle. The source of his information is not known.

31 Froissart mentions the presence of *corbis*, which can be translated as either crows or rooks. The authors, who live opposite a rookery, can well attest to the behaviour and noise often made by rooks before a thunderstorm. The existence of the *corbis* at Crécy has often been doubted, not least because in later redactions Froissart hugely exaggerates both the numbers of the birds and their impact on those who heard them, but there seems no reason to believe the entire story is false. Froissart, pp. 46, 49.

32 Nangis, vol. 2, p. 202. In fact, as experienced archers would have known, wetting a hemp bowstring causes it to contract rather than expand; the only effect would have been to make the bows slightly more difficult to string, but presumably they were strung already. That does not mean this incident did not happen, however; the belief that wet bowstrings would stretch might be another in a long list of military superstitions that persist to this day. As late as the 1950s, unless compelled by dire emergency, ships of the United States Navy would not put to sea on a Friday!

33 Le Bel, p. 100, says Doria's force was composed of crossbowmen and *bedaux*, a term which Contamine, *Guerre, Etat et Societe*, p. 22, says is one of a number of alternative names for a foot soldier. The distinction between these and the crossbowmen suggests that at least some of Doria's corps were armed with spears or swords; conceivably these were present to protect the crossbowmen.

34 *Histoire d'Abbeville*, p. 206.

35 Le Bel, p. 101; Froissart, p. 37.

36 For example, in the *Grandes Chroniques*, p. 282. Most modern historians accept that Philippe wished to postpone the battle, but for an argument to the contrary see Rogers, *War Cruel and Sharp*, pp. 267–8.

37 Le Bel, p. 102; Viard, 'Le Campagne de juillet–août', p. 71.

38 For the attack of the Genoese, see le Bel, p. 102; *Chronique Normande*, p. 80; *Grandes Chroniques*, p. 282; Froissart, pp. 46–9; le Baker, p. 84; Villani, pp. 165–7; also *Histoire d'Abbeville*, pp. 206–7. The wetting of the bowstrings was a red herring, as confirmed by Viard, 'Le Campagne de juillet–août', pp. 74–5, and Burne, pp. 188–9. Viard goes so far as to doubt whether the rain happened at all, suggesting that chroniclers may have been referring to the 'rain of arrows'. Burne believes there was rain, but its effects have been exaggerated.

39 The trumpets are mentioned by the *Bourgeois de Valenciennes*, p. 477. The curious detail of leaping in the air comes from Froissart.

40 It was this, we believe, rather than any supposed wetting of the bowstrings, which caused the Genoese to shoot short.

41 Froissart, p. 49, maintains that some of the crossbowmen cut their own bowstrings; this seems rather pointless, and also would not have been easy to do.

42 Some chroniclers claim that King Philippe himself ordered the killing of the Genoese, but Philippe was still some distance from the battlefield; there may be

a confusion with a later incident in Amiens where Philippe reportedly ordered the execution of some Genoese for treason.

43 This image is courtesy of Jean le Bel, p. 203.

44 It is impossible to know for certain how many Genoese died; according to some accounts, they were all but wiped out. Casualties were certainly very heavy and probably ran into the thousands, but more may have escaped than is generally realised. Doria recovered from his wounds and was back commanding crossbowmen in French service the following year.

45 Froissart, p. 47.

46 *Histoire d'Abbeville*, p. 208.

47 Our calculation. 2,000 archers shooting a conservative twelve arrows a minute would shoot 24,000 arrows a minute, but we have reduced the figure on the grounds that not all archers would have been in range all of the time. That it would take the charging cavalry a minute to go from arrow range to first contact seems reasonable, given the obstacles, the nature of the slope and the disorder caused by wounded horses going out of control; unhindered, of course, the horsemen would have covered the ground much more quickly.

48 Alençon's death before the lines made contact is inferred from the fact that he disappears from view; Nevers and others are mentioned in the fighting that followed, but not he.

49 Le Baker, p. 84.

50 *Histoire d'Abbeville*, p. 209, mistakenly refers to the standard-bearer as Richard Beaumont. A legend persists that Nevers had briefly captured the Prince but was then forced to let him go.

51 Froissart, p. 57, suggests that the commanders of the vanguard sent Norwich, but they would have been familiar with the tactical plan; why not send for assistance from Northampton and Arundel, as originally intended? It is more likely that Norwich acted of his own accord.

52 Ibid. This is the story from the first redaction; later redactions vary in minor details.

53 Ibid., but note that no other account mentions this; the 'wound' may have been no more than bruises. The *Bourgeois de Valenciennes*, p. 376, says it was the Bishop of Durham who led the reinforcements.

54 Le Bel, p. 103.

55 *Grandes Chroniques*, p. 283.

56 Froissart, p. 57.

57 Ibid., p. 50. This comment appears in the fourth redaction; Chandos and Burghersh are the probable sources.

58 Ibid., p. 478.

59 Froissart seems to indicate that both Blois and Lorraine were surrounded and killed by English and Welsh foot soldiers (p. 56); another legend, noted by Lettenhove, p. 481 (from le Muisit), has it that Blois actually reached the

Prince of Wales's standard before being cut down, but this may be a confusion with the events of the first attack. The *Chronicle of St-Omer*, cited in Rogers, *War Cruel and Sharp*, p. 268, suggests that Blois deliberately dismounted and led his men on foot, but this seems very unlikely. The *Chronicle* also apparently confuses Louis of Blois with his brother Charles, who had been defeated by Northampton at Morlaix.

60 Thompson, in a footnote in le Bel, p. 262, says Aumale was only wounded, but this is contradicted elsewhere. Thompson also erroneously identifies Bertrand with his father the marshal.

61 Froissart, p. 63, is particularly emphatic that he has this story on good authority. English reports after the battle listed Harcourt and both his sons among the dead, but the younger Jean d'Harcourt definitely survived, though wounded. His being unhorsed might account for his being listed as a casualty; the English would have seen him fall, and assumed he had been killed, as happened in several other cases.

62 *Chronicle of St-Omer*, cited in Rogers, *War Cruel and Sharp*, p. 269.

63 A list of French nobles and knights was compiled after the battle by the English, but has not survived in full. The chronicles and other accounts, including Edward's and Michael Northburgh's letter after the battle, give long lists, which are not always accurate; some of those listed as killed, such as the Counts of Savoy and Artois, were not present at the battle.

64 Avesbury, p. 371; Froissart, p. 54.

65 Editor's note in Baker, p. 262. Ursini may be the 'Lord Rosenberg' who appears in some English casualty lists, and even possibly the 'Lord Rossingbergh' mentioned by Murimuth, p. 248, who he says was a member of King Philippe's household.

66 Mathéfelon is erroneously listed as a fatality in the *Eulogium*, p. 210; Montbéliard's name appears by error as a fatality in several accounts.

67 Froissart, p. 59.

68 Philippe's difficulties in getting to the field are described by le Bel, who thinks Philippe may never actually have reached the field; however, the English were positive he was there, and the casualties suffered by his household indicate that he was involved in fighting. See also Froissart, p. 62.

69 Murimuth, p. 217; it is Wynkeley who claims the standard-bearer was killed, a claim often repeated, but Noyers lived until 1368.

70 Ibid.

71 A point also made by Henri de Wailly, *Crécy: Anatomy of a Battle*, Poole, 1987, p. 81. *The Bourgeois de Valenciennes*, p. 477, says Hainault himself had a horse shot from under him, but may be confusing the two events. *Chronique Normande*, p. 81, says Philippe lost two horses and was in great pain.

72 Froissart adds the detail about their route home in the fourth redaction (p. 67).

73 Most accounts state that Bohemia attacked late in the day, and there is a strong suggestion that his attack took place after that of Philippe. However, some state his attack was carried out early in the battle, and this is supported by Viard, *Le Campagne*. See Appendix.

74 Le Bel, p. 169; Froissart, p. 66. The general impression from nearly all accounts is of an army that simply disintegrated rather than fleeing from the field; the *Chronicle of St-Omer* is almost unique in suggesting that the French fled in panic (see Rogers, *War Cruel and Sharp*, p. 269).

75 Froissart, p. 54, says Charles left the field when he saw that things were going badly, but, as noted above, he did not withdraw until a number of his men had been killed. The *Chronicle of St-Omer*, quoted by Rogers, *War Cruel and Sharp*, p. 169, says that Philippe made some attempt to rally the retreating French. It is possible, but it seems odd that none of the other, more detailed accounts of the battle mention this.

76 Froissart, p. 55. Froissart insists that the king was involved in hand-to-hand fighting, but adds that no one knows how he died. The English accounts give no details of his death, merely recording the fact of it. According to *Chronique de Flandres*, vol. 2, p. 44, the English found the king's body while he was still alive, and he was taken to King Edward's own tent and given the last rites before expiring; this is repeated in some Czech accounts, but there is no evidence to support this.

77 Le Bel, p. 103, says these attacks went on until midnight, but this may be an overstatement of the case. For the timing of the battle, see Appendix.

78 Le Bel, p. 104; Froissart, p. 66; *Bourgeois de Valenciennes*, p. 477.

79 *Eulogium*, p. 210.

80 Ibid., p. 211, which says they were made 'barons', but in the 1340s becoming a 'baron' was largely a matter of being summoned to attend Parliament; appointment as a banneret is more likely.

81 Ibid.; *CPR 1345–48*, p. 474.

82 *Register of Edward the Black Prince*, part 3, p. 413.

83 Edward's own letter says that the army remained in the field all night without food or drink (repeated in *Eulogium*, p. 211). The Kitchen Account shows that a small meal was taken, listing peas, onions and flour in small quantities, but no meat; it is possible that this refers to the midday meal. But even if the account refers to supper, this was certainly not the celebratory banquet that some later historians have represented it to be!

84 Le Bel, p. 106.

85 Ibid., p. 107.

86 Froissart, p. 64. In some English translations, this passage is rather curiously translated as, 'open, castellan, it is the fortune of France.'

87 Froissart and the *Grandes Chroniques*, p. 284, both give this version of events. It is likely that at least some of the party also changed horses at Labroye, as

their own mounts would have been fatigued and some injured. *Chronique Normande*, p. 82, and the *Bourgeois de Valenciennes*, p. 477, say that Philippe stayed the night at Labroye and then went to Doullens and from there to Amiens the following day. This may have been his route, but it seems unlikely that he would have stayed the night so close to the enemy with so small a force to defend himself unless he had to.

Chapter 11

Aftermath

The flower of the whole knighthood of France has been killed.

Richard Wynkeley

The morning of Sunday, 27 August found thick fog still hanging over the fields and forests of Ponthieu, with visibility in places down to only a hundred yards or so.[1] At first light a strong English force, 500 men-at-arms and 2,000 archers led by Northampton with Warwick and Suffolk as his lieutenants, went out to reconnoitre to the east and south-east.[2] Their purpose was to discover whether the French army was re-forming and preparing for another attack, a possibility which must have appeared fairly likely to the English commanders.

They found instead that the French were still utterly disorganised. Their first encounter was with a large body of men of the communes of Rouen and Beauvais, foot soldiers with a few men-at-arms. These, mistaking the English for their own troops in the fog, went forward to join them, only to be met with arrows and a charge by the English horsemen. The French broke and fled and the English pursued them through the misty fields and woods for several miles, hunting them down and killing them; according to le Bel, the English were like a wolf among sheep.[3] There followed a considerable slaughter, although many of the fugitives were able to escape under cover of the mist.

Further on Northampton encountered another sizeable force led by Guillaume de Melun, Archbishop of Sens, and Jean de Nanteuil, Grand

Prior of the Knights of St John in France. Froissart claims that these did not even know there had been a battle the day before, although this seems very unlikely given their proximity to the field, and goes on to suggest that they had received orders that the battle would not begin until Sunday. Perhaps they had received and acted upon Philippe's order the previous afternoon, and were now waiting for further orders.[4] They too were wholly unprepared, and broke at the first English attack, with the Grand Prior among the dead. Another Knight of St John, the Chevalier d'Amposte, recently returned from Rhodes where he had distinguished himself in fighting against the Turks, was also killed. Unlike the previous day, the English were now taking prisoners: a number of French men-at-arms surrendered, and so did a number of the prelates who were leading the contingent, including the Archbishop of Sens, Hugues de Vers, Abbot of Corbie and Bérenger de Montaigu, Archdeacon of Paris.[5]

Other smaller parties were also encountered, men who had retreated from the battlefield and then, exhausted, made camp in the middle of the fields. One such party included Charles of Luxembourg, the King of the Romans, and his household. Ambushed in the mist, they managed to break free and escape, but not before several men had been killed and Charles himself had been shot by an English archer. He remained in pain from this wound for many months after his return to Bohemia; according to Czech tradition, the spa at Karlsbad (Karlovy Vary) was developed by royal physicians seeking a cure for the king.[6]

Apart from these, the English met with no resistance. Here and there they encountered small parties of survivors from the previous day, exhausted hungry men who were only too happy to surrender if given the chance; many were not and were simply shot down or cut down in their tracks. French casualties that morning can only be guessed at. Writing soon after the battle, Michael Northburgh put the figure at 2,000, while King Edward estimated it at 4,000; among the chroniclers, the *Bourgeois de Valenciennes* estimated the French losses on the 27th as 6,000 and Froissart's initial figure (later much inflated) is 7,000.[7] A figure somewhere within that range is probably accurate; given the mist and chaos of the morning, it is unlikely that any more detailed calculation can be arrived at. Some believed the number of French killed on the 27th to have been greater than on the previous day. English casualties were very light, although two knights of Suffolk's retinue, James Haumville and Robert Tyfford, managed to get themselves captured by the French; possibly they became separated from the rest of the force in the fog.[8]

Around mid-morning Northampton returned to the English camp, and made his report to the king, who had just come from mass. The area was now clear of French troops, and the English were secure. The king now turned his attention to the French fallen. After the slaughter of the previous day, the decencies now had to be observed. The first task was to identify as many of the dead as possible. Reginald Cobham and Richard Stafford were given this task, with three heralds to help in the identification of coats of arms. Two clerks were also sent to make lists of the names of the fallen. The work must have been thoroughly unpleasant, for it meant shifting hundreds of bodies of men and horses, by now stiffened with rigor mortis. At midday Cobham and Stafford returned, confessing that they were unable to identify many of the bodies. More men were sent, including Thomas Holland, who knew some of the French and Germans, and Olivier de Ghistels, who would have known some of the Hainaulters and others from the Low Countries; others sent to help included Guy Bryan and Henry Percy. At one point the king himself came down to view the scene.[9]

They found, as Richard Wynkeley later said, that the flower of French knighthood had been killed. As well as the great nobles, eighty knights banneret had been killed and nearly 1,500 other knights and esquires. Michael Northburgh states the total of men-at-arms killed as 1,542; a list was clearly compiled at the time, but unfortunately does not survive. It is not clear whether this refers to men who bore arms, that is, had their own coats of arms; if it does, then the total number of men killed in the cavalry charges is likely to be a little higher, perhaps 2,000 in all.[10] Along with these lay the bodies of the Genoese crossbowmen who had been shot by the English archers or cut down by the French men-at-arms. No count was made of their dead, but 1,000 is a conservative figure and the total might be as high as 2,500. All in all, somewhere between 2,500 and 4,000 bodies lay on the field, along with the corpses of thousands of horses. The bodies of these almost certainly outnumbered those of the men. In cavalry charges, the ratio of deaths and injuries of horses to that of men is often as much as two to one.[11] The number of dead horses may well have exceeded 3,000.

These figures do not of course include the wounded, of whom there must have been many hundreds. Medieval medicine was not so primitive as many today believe, and many men like Jacques de Bourbon and the younger Jean d'Harcourt made full recoveries from their injuries. But medieval physicians had no remedies against infections and gangrene and some of these wounded men undoubtedly died in the days or weeks after the battle.

And of what of the English army's own losses? They were astonishingly light, so light that modern historians often refused to believe them. Writing from the French perspective, Jean le Bel estimated the English losses at fewer than 300 men-at-arms. The English writers put the figures at far fewer: Richard Wynkeley says of the men-at-arms that two knights and one esquire were killed, while, writing some time later, Knighton thought the figure was three knights and one esquire.[12] This fits with documentary evidence, such as *inquisitiones post mortem* (which by law were conducted in England whenever a tenant-in chief died), that three English men-at-arms died at Crécy. Emery Rokesley, who had been knighted only recently, was killed when he threw himself recklessly at the enemy; this may have happened during Arundel's counter-attack, for Rokesley was one of Arundel's followers. Richard Brent was a member of James Audley's retinue and was probably among those – like Audley himself – who were sent forward to reinforce the Prince's division at the start of the battle. John Coggeshall was the son of a knight from Suffolk.[13] The circumstances of the deaths of Brent and Coggeshall are not known, but it is almost certain that they were killed during Alençon's attack and the hand-to-hand fighting that followed. Numbers of ordinary soldiers and archers killed vary; Froissart says twenty and le Baker thirty, but again these figures seem low. But the total number of English dead is unlikely to be more than a couple of hundred, and probably substantially less. Again, there were also a number of wounded.

On the field, the disposal of the dead began. Four hundred men were detailed to dig pits and bury the common dead, the Genoese and others. This was not as callous as it seems, and it is highly likely that some sort of burial rites were conducted; there is no evidence that the English were anything other than scrupulously correct in the treatment of the fallen. In the August heat, the bodies needed to be interred as quickly as possible; the English army was already shifting camp a mile north to the fields around the hamlet of Watteglise, so as to put some distance between it and the field. A great mass of harness, banners, shields, weapons and armour was piled together and burned.[14] Presumably the dead horses were also disposed of, either by burying or cremation.

The men of rank were listed and their bodies disposed of with some care. Those of high station predictably received the best treatment. Godefroi d'Harcourt, with emotions that can only be guessed at, removed the bodies of his brother and the Comte d'Aumale and took them to the church at Crécy, where they were laid out in a chapel. Others were removed to the main camp. In the evening, with solemn ceremony, the body of King Jean of Bohemia was brought into the king's tent. The body was washed with warm water and wrapped in linen and then laid on a bier. The Bishop of Durham presided over his funeral mass, with the king and his earls and many others present.[15] The foragers had been active in the country round-about, and there was plenty of meat for dinner that night; then, it may be supposed, the army enjoyed its first truly quiet night for many weeks.

*　*　*

Gradually, some kind of order began returning to the French army, as all who could made their way to Amiens and began to reassemble. The full scale of the French losses began to sink in, and Philippe himself seems to have been plunged into a profound depression. Typically, he believed that his defeat was the result of betrayal. His first target was Godemar de Fay, the defeated commander at the Blanchetaque. Had Fay held the river, the English would have been trapped and Crécy would never have happened. Believing Fay had sold out to the English, Philippe demanded his execution. His advisors made him see reason: if the whole army could not prevail against the English, how could Fay have been expected to do so?[16] In the end Philippe relented, and Fay's life was spared; within a few years, he was holding military commands once more. Instead the king vented his fury on the surviving Genoese, ordering the execution of several, although he later relented when he understood fully the position in which they had been placed. He then dismissed Charles de Montmorency, the surviving marshal, and appointed Edouard de Beaujeu in his place. Montmorency appears to have taken this well, and he went on to give loyal service for many years; longer than Beaujeu, who was killed fighting the English in 1351.

Philippe's major problem was that his army was breaking up. Many contingents were now leaderless, and their first priority was to recover the bodies of their dead overlords and go home; some were already sending messengers to the English as early as Sunday. The foreign contingents too were itching to be off; even the loyal John of Hainault was anxious to return home, presumably in order to put his lands into a state of defence in the aftermath of the disaster. The King of the Romans, now wounded, wanted nothing more than to collect the body of his father and leave, and the King of Majorca too seems to have faded away.

Only one dependable body of men remained. Louis of Vaud's Savoyards had finally caught up with the main army, having first skirted the battlefield and been made aware of what had happened. They had withdrawn to Amiens, and were still prepared to take the field. Philippe ordered them to Montreuil, some miles north-west of the English position, a large fortified town on the river Canche. He may have had some vague hope of using the Savoyards to delay the enemy while he re-formed his army and came up in their rear; if so, the plan came to nothing. He lingered for some days at Amiens, but on 7 September went south to his palace at Pont-St-Maxence in the Oise; en route he met his son the Duc de Normandie, who had at last arrived with part of his army from the south. The work of reconstruction then began. By 1 October Philippe was mustering a new army in the north at Compiègne; but never again would he risk a full-scale pitched battle against the English.

* * *

On Monday 28 August, carrying with them the bodies of the noble and knightly dead, the English army marched north and down into the valley of the Authie, where they halted at the abbey of Valloire, a little way from the small town of Maintenay.[17] Heralds had arrived that morning from Amiens to ask for a three days' truce in order to allow for collection and burial of the dead; this was granted, and soon emissaries began arriving to take some of the bodies away. Charles d'Alençon's body was among those removed; he was later buried in a Dominican convent in Paris.[18] The bodies of Louis de Blois and Jean d'Harcourt were also removed and taken back to their homes. Servants of Charles of Luxembourg arrived to fetch the body of the King of Bohemia; his entrails were buried with all due ceremony at Valloire itself and the remains of the body, together with the bodies of fifty of his men-at-arms who had died with him, were escorted in solemn procession to Luxembourg, where the king was finally buried at the abbey of Munster, near Luxembourg city.[19] The remaining knights were buried at Valloire itself.

These ceremonies occupied most of the day, and the army camped that night at Valloire. The following day, the 29th, they moved only as far as Maintenay on the far side of the Authie. They may have spent the time continuing to forage and replenish food stocks; certainly the Kitchen Account shows a marked improvement in both the quality and quantity of food available in the royal household. Nine carcasses of beef and twenty of mutton were consumed that day, along with luxuries such as eggs, milk and cheese, which had not been available for some days.

On the 30th the campaign began again in earnest, and the army marched north to St-Josse, pillaging and plundering now on a wide scale without any hindrance. The towns of Vaubain and Serain were burned, and Hesdin was attacked and the town burned, although the great castle that had once belonged to Robert of Artois held out. So also did Montreuil, the ancient capital of Ponthieu, strongly walled and with its local garrison reinforced by Louis of Vaud and the troops from Savoy. There were some skirmishes between the English and the Savoyards, but the latter prudently withdrew into the town, leaving the English to pillage the suburbs. Further north the English burned Étaples and Neufchâtel and all the country around Boulogne; one party attacked Boulogne itself, but again its walls were too strong. On 3 September the army reached Wissant; and on the following day they marched down off the high ground and moved in on the important sea-port of Calais. This too was strongly defended by a resolute captain, Jean de Vienne, and it was clear the town could not be stormed. A siege was therefore begun, and Edward sent home for reinforcements. Bartholomew Burghersh, John Darcy and two others crossed the Channel by boat with letters from the king and others, and a few days later they were in Westminster reporting to the council that had been left to govern the kingdom in Edward's absence, and passing on his requests for more men and supplies in order to take Calais. This effort was disrupted a few weeks later in early October when David II of Scotland began, belatedly, to act on the wishes of his ally Philippe of France and raised an army to invade northern England. There was a sudden flurry of activity, and men were detached from the camp at Calais and sent north to meet the new threat, joining the hastily assembled English army under the command of William de la Zouche,

Archbishop of York. But the threat did not last long. On 17 October at Neville's Cross, just outside Durham, the Archbishop's army inflicted on the Scots a defeat just as severe as that at Halidon Hill thirteen years earlier. This time there was no escape for King David of Scotland: taken prisoner in the fighting by the Northumberland esquire John Coupland, he was sent away to captivity in the Tower of London. English arms had triumphed yet again.

With the beginning of the siege, our story comes to an end. The siege would drag on until the following summer when the garrison, on the verge of starvation, finally surrendered. By this time a number of the veterans of Crécy were dead. Many, like Maurice Berkeley, died of dysentery or through enemy action during the siege. Old age and infirmity probably claimed John Darcy, for whom the rigours of the campaign must have been a severe strain. Michael Poynings was murdered while trying to protect his niece from assault back in England.[20]

The capture of Calais would prove to be the most lasting achievement of the campaign, remaining in English hands for over two hundred years and proving to be of lasting value as both a trading centre and a base for launching further attacks on France. The invasion of Normandy, on the other hand, had little immediate effect apart from the devastation caused to towns and countryside. By the end of 1346, even Godefroi d'Harcourt had returned home to Normandy, receiving a pardon from King Philippe; to the evident anger of Edward, who at once confiscated the properties he had given Harcourt in England. But the lame ex-marshal did not remain peacefully at home for long; in the early 1350s the Norman revolt Edward had tried so long to foster finally erupted in full force and Harcourt 're-ratted', joining the rebels and going over to the English once more. He was killed in a skirmish in the Cotentin early in 1355.

The military consequences of the battle of Crécy have been discussed at length by other historians. There can be little doubt that, in the short term, it changed the direction of the war. Edward came out of the conflict with greatly enhanced prestige at home and abroad, while French stock sank. But the victory was not decisive; France was still strong and still capable of raising armies. One of the consequences of Crécy was thus to ensure that the war would drag on for many years. There would be more disasters and triumphs for both sides, finally culminating in the battle of Castillon in 1453. This was to be a Crécy in reverse, with disorganised

English men-at-arms attacking a strong French position and being cut down in their hundreds by bows and firearms. Soon after the battle, the last English possessions in Gascony finally surrendered to France; Philippe VI's goal had finally been achieved.

Undeniably, there was one man who did well out of the battle of Crécy. Many legends have sprung up around Edward of Woodstock, Prince of Wales. It is said that he took his crest of ostrich plumes and the motto 'Ich dien' from the dead King of Bohemia, as a mark of respect for the latter. It is a pretty story, but sadly there is no record of either device ever being associated with the kingdom of Bohemia or the Luxembourg dynasty. Similarly, the nickname 'Black Prince' was not bestowed until several centuries later, and the Prince did not wear black armour on the day of the battle. But what *did* happen was significant enough. In full view of the army, the Prince had been acknowledged by his father and the other commanders as playing a leading role in the victory. He had behaved with great personal courage; his division of the army, fewer than 4,000 men, had borne the whole brunt of the attack. His reputation had been established, and would continue to grow. Ten years later, aged twenty-six, he proved that the faith shown in him by his father was justified when he again, greatly against the odds, took on a French royal army and crushed it at Poitiers. This time the victory was even more stunning, and both the King of France and his son were brought back to England as the Prince's prisoners. He became one of the heroes of his age, a chivalric icon fully in the image of Jean of Bohemia; even many of his French enemies admired him personally, while deploring the atrocities committed by his armies. Even death was kind to his reputation: cancer claimed him two years before the death of his father, and the Prince was able to die a romantic military hero without ever being exposed to the sterner tests of kingship.

And if Crécy was the foundation of one reputation, it was the end of another. Jean of Bohemia's thirty-year career in arms had at last come to an end. Here too, it may be that death was kind to his reputation, rather than letting him sink into sightless obscurity. His death caught the imagination of his age, and for generations afterwards the story of the blind king riding into battle, his bridle lashed to that of his comrades, was told and retold by historians and novelists. It was a poignant moment, and it is fittingly commemorated. On the edge of the battlefield there stands a small stone cross, erected in the nineteenth century with funds raised in both France and Bohemia, and it bears a simple legend:

CETTE CROIX RAPELLE LA FIN HEROIQUE
DE JEAN DE LUXEMBOURG
ROI DE BOHEME
MORT POUR LA FRANCE
LE 26 AOÛT 1346

Notes

1 Le Bel, p. 107, says visibility was less than half an acre.
2 Northburgh, quoted in Avesbury, pp. 369 and 371, who misidentifies Suffolk as Norfolk; Froissart, ed. Lettenhove, pp. 70–1.
3 Le Bel, p. 107.
4 Froissart, pp. 70–1. That this contingent should be ignorant of the battle seems unlikely, given the number of French stragglers in the area.
5 Northburgh mistakenly claims the Archbishops of Rheims and Sens were both killed, but Thompson in his edition of le Baker says that Sens was taken prisoner along with the Abbot of Corbie, p. 262. Kervyn de Lettenhove is adamant that Rheims also survived, but does not indicate whether he was captured, p. 481. See Lettenhove also for the Archdeacon of Paris, who was later sold to the Abbey of Colchester. For the Chevalier d'Amposte, see Froissart, p. 72.
6 See E. Petiška, *Charles IV*, Prague: Martin, 1994. The source for this tradition is not known.
7 Northburgh in Avesbury, pp. 369 and 371; Edward, in Barber, *Life and Campaigns*, p. 22; *Bourgeois de Valenciennes* in Froissart, p. 471; Froissart, p. 71.
8 Wrottesley, G., 'Crécy and Calais from the public Records', Collections for a history of Staffordshire, 1897, p. 165.
9 The sending of additional men to help with the search is mentioned in the fourth redaction of Froissart, p. 76; the king's visit is mentioned by Baker, p. 85.
10 Northburgh refers to 1,542 'good men-at-arms', Avesbury pp. 369 and 371; King Edward refers to more than 1,500 knights and squires, not counting commoners and foot soldiers; Le Bel, p. 108, 1,200 knights and then 15,000 foot soldiers, but the latter figure is far too high. Geoffrey le Baker's figure of 3,000 French dead for both Saturday and Sunday must be regarded as the minimum possible figure. For a detailed discussion of the casualty figures for both sides, see Viard, 'Le Campagne de juillet–août', p. 81.
11 For example, the Light Brigade at Balaclava in 1854 lost 238 men killed, wounded or captured, but lost 475 horses.

12 Froissart also mentions three knights, but the *Eulogium* only mentions one, Rokesley; again, see Viard, 'Le Campagne de juillet–août', p. 81.

13 If so, this would fit Wynkeley's tally exactly. It is possible that other men-at-arms were killed, but if men of property had been killed we would expect to find their names among the *inquisitiones post mortem*.

14 Knighton, p. 39 for the move to Watteglise; *Bourgeois de Valenciennes*, in *Oeuvres de Froissart*, ed. Lettenhove, p. 482 for the burning of the detritus.

15 For Harcourt, see editor's footnote in Froissart, p. 482; for the King of Bohemia's funeral, Baker, p. 85.

16 Froissart, p. 80.

17 Many sources simply refer to the abbey as 'Maintenay', sometimes calling it a priory, but Thompson (in Baker, p. 262) positively identified it as Valloire.

18 Viard, 'Le Campagne de juillet–août', p. 82.

19 Ibid.

20 See Chapter 2.

Appendix

Reconstructing Crécy

Reconstructing the events of 26 August 1346 is a difficult task, and, unsurprisingly, historians have come to quite different interpretations of the evidence. For example, two of the best modern historians of the Hundred Years War, Alfred Burne and Jonathan Sumption, describing Philippe as marching out of Abbeville in the morning in almost opposite directions: Burne says he went west towards Noyelles, while Sumption says he went north-east towards St-Riquier. The original sources themselves are often equally confused, and in the years following the battle there was a steady accretion of the myth and exaggeration that so often accumulates around dramatic events. We have tried to deal with as much of the latter as possible, and to reconstruct events in a way that is both in accordance with the sources and logical and militarily probable. Doubtless we are in error on some points. The purpose of this appendix is to explain our thinking on some of the key issues.

Sources

One of the great frustrations for historians of the 1346 campaign is that easily the best primary source, the *Acta Bellicosa*, peters out a few days before the battle; the surviving manuscript is damaged and ends with the taking of Poix. Many questions about the fighting along the Somme and at Crécy itself could probably be answered were an intact manuscript ever to be discovered. Lacking such, we are forced to fall back on three eyewitness accounts, chronicles of varying reliability, and (mostly English) administrative documents.

Of the eyewitness accounts, that of King Edward in his letter to Sir Thomas Lucy is disappointingly vague. Michael Northburgh's letter tallies very closely with that of the king (indeed, he may have drafted the king's letter), and, while Richard Wynkeley gives a few more details, his account is still quite short. Alfred Burne suggests that as non-combatants, Northburgh and Wynkeley might well have been in the rear inside the wagon park and thus not seen the fighting; this is possible, but they would still have had access to direct eyewitnesses immediately after the battle. It is equally possible that they were with the king around the windmill, however.

Of the chroniclers, Geoffrey le Baker, Jean le Bel and Jean Froissart all had access to eyewitnesses. Baker's account is brief but vivid and full of detail, as is le Bel's. For the time being, at least, le Bel leaves off his usual dislike of Edward III and gives a valuable and dispassionate account of the battle. So too does Froissart, who used some of the same sources as le Bel (and often uses le Bel as a source). There has been a reappraisal of Froissart in recent years, and Alfred Burne's damning view that 'he is not reliable – no, not for a single statement – without corroboration from another source', is too harsh. Froissart *does* exaggerate, and in later redactions seems to fancy himself as a latter-day Livy, putting long fictional speeches into the mouths of his protagonists, but, if handled with care, there is still much of value to be gleaned from him. Other important chronicles include those of Avesbury and Murimuth, who also used the letters of Northburgh and Wynkeley; Villani, who may have had copies of the letters sent from London by Italian merchants, and probably also spoke to some Genoese survivors; and le Muisit, the *Bourgeois de Valenciennes* and the authors of the *Grandes Chroniques* and *Chronique Normande*, who were writing nearly contemporary with events, along with a number of minor sources. Administrative documents, especially from the English side, provide more information and often corroborate details from the chronicles, such as the low English casualty figures.

Time

The timing of events on the day of the battle has always been rather vague. King Edward says that the first sight of the enemy was late in the morning, the battle began in mid-afternoon and lasted until evening. Other accounts progressively advance the battle, with some claiming the fighting lasted until midnight. There is some difficulty in determining exactly when the fighting began and ended. Medieval men did not wear watches, and time was kept by canonical hours, such as prime (sunrise), nones (midday), vespers (sunset) and so on. Prime and vespers in particular change with the seasons, and in summer in some localities, at least, they were not held to occur precisely at sunrise or sunset, but generally in early morning or late evening. It is not possible to translate 'prime' as '6 a.m.', as some writers have done.

Our timings are based partly on the accounts of eyewitnesses and the more reliable chronicles, but we have weeded out evidence which is inconsistent. The idea that the fighting lasted until midnight, for instance, can be ruled out on the grounds of strong evidence that the fall of night was accompanied by a heavy fog. We have also tried to calculate distances and times of march for the French army in order to see if the latter fit with the times advanced by most authorities. Edward's timings appear to be early, but not unreasonably so. The first sight of the enemy in late morning might well be the arrival of the first French scouts, on or just before noon. These would have taken some time to find Philippe and report, and it could well have been mid-afternoon by the time le Moine and his party found the English. Given the time of sunset, 'mid-afternoon', when the Genoese and Alençon first appeared around Marcheville, could reasonably be as late as 4 p.m., and another hour might have passed before the Genoese closed in and the fighting began. That the battle lasted until after sunset is indicated by suggestions in some accounts that visibility was growing poor by the time of the last attack. Some accounts also suggest the final attack was made by moonlight, but this again is inconsistent with the evidence of fog.

The weather

Froissart's famous thunderstorm and flock of crows have excited much attention, and the French historian Jules Viard goes so far as to suggest that the storm did not happen; he postulates that the 'thunder' may have been the sound of the English cannon. Other accounts suggest there were only a few drops of rain, and certainly the amount of rain was probably much less than Froissart suggests. We should remember, however, that in late summer in north-western France, as in southern England, it is quite possible to have heavy localised showers, sometimes accompanied by thunder, that will drench one location and leave another a mile away quite dry.

The day was clearly a hot one, and probably fairly humid as well, as some men-at-arms including Estracelles and King Edward removed their bascinets in order to breathe more easily. This is quite consistent with an afternoon rain shower; we can imagine the day dawning clear, then clouds building up as humidity increases, a sudden shower late in the day, then the clouds quickly clearing and followed by a brilliant clear evening. The high humidity and heat might also result in localised fog, and the valleys of the Maye and the Authie were probably very conducive to fog, which burned off only slowly the next morning. This may not have been exactly how the weather developed, but the picture is both meteorologically logical and consistent with available evidence.

Numbers

We have assumed an English force of 10,000, with a wastage of about one-third since landing at St-Vaast due to battle casualties, those who returned at Caen, sickness, desertion and like causes. This does not seem unreasonable, though it should be noted that other historians of the campaign do not assume as high a rate of wastage. This is, however, consistent with other campaigns of the period where the wastage rate is known.

Estimates of the size of the French army range from the 12,000 of one French historian to the 200,000 given in some of the chronicles. Both figures are absurd if we take the total strength of the French into consideration. The combined strength of the troops gathered at Rouen and Paris combined with those mustered at Amiens, those of Louis of Nevers and the other foreign contingents could easily have topped 40,000; the foreign contingents alone totalled close to 20,000 (see Chapter 3). Even with natural wastage of their own, there seems no reason not to accept Alfred Burne's figure of 40,000 *if* the entire army had been mustered together.

And therein lies the rub. Whatever the size of the French army in total, no more than a fraction of that force was concentrated on the battlefield at any one time. The initial attack by Alençon and Doria might have seen 8,000–9,000 French and allied troops on the field, but the effect was rather spoiled when they began fighting each other. Thereafter, attacks were launched by contingents of men-at-arms ranging in strength from a few hundred to a few thousand. No matter how large and magnificent the French army, the breakdown of command and control early in the day meant the advantage of numbers could never be employed. Given this, even if Philippe by some miracle had mustered 200,000 men, it seems unlikely that the outcome would have been any different.

The French approach to the field

Historians are divided over this issue along national lines; French historians such as Viard assert that when Philippe marched out of Abbeville on the morning of the 26th he did not know Edward's precise location, and initially marched west towards Noyelles, turning back when he learned that Edward was waiting at Crécy. English historians (with the notable exception of Burne, who follows this view) assert that Philippe marched more or less straight to Crécy.

We found the former view to be on balance more probable. It is entirely likely that Philippe did not know the exact whereabouts of the English army, as the English sources state definitely that the army remained concealed within the forest until that morning, sending out only a small reconnaissance party the day before. And Philippe had convinced himself, against the advice of the King of Bohemia, that Edward would continue to retreat and would not stand and fight. Moving towards Noyelles to pick up the trail of the supposedly retreating English would therefore be logical. On a related note, Crécy is only about nine miles from Abbeville, and if the French army marched at dawn the vanguard would have begun to assemble in front of the English position by midday; this does not fit with the timings discussed above.

Upon receiving first news of Edward's position, Philippe turned his army towards the enemy and despatched the scouting party of le Moine and the other knights to scout the enemy position. It is sometimes assumed that the army marched in a single column, each unit following the other to the west and then back around to the east and north (for example, the poster of the battle produced by the Office de Tourisme in Crécy shows the army marching in a long S shape from Abbeville to the battle). However, we believe it much more likely that each contingent was ordered to turn in echelon as described in Chapter 10. This has the advantages of inherent military probability and making it easier to explain the chaotic state of the French as they approached the field.

A word needs to be added about our distinction between march order and battle order. Throughout the campaign the English army had made no distinction between the two, marching and fighting in three divisions. The French army, however, tended to be more divided on the march, probably because of its greater size. At Cassel in 1328, the French had marched to the field in eight or nine divisions, and according to Geoffrey le Baker they did so again at Crécy. The practice seems to have been to then halt and form up into the three divisions of the battle order. It would have been good practice, however, for the divisions of the march order to roughly correspond to the divisions of the battle order, so, to take a hypothetical example, if the march order was nine divisions, the first three would fight together in the leading division of the battle order. Similarly, the commander of the leading battle division would have been near the head of the column of march, the commander of the second division further back, and the commander of the third division towards the rear.

The three division commanders of the battle are usually agreed to have been Bohemia, Alençon and King Philippe. Philippe is usually agreed to have commanded the third division, though occasionally the second. There is dispute as to whether Bohemia or Alençon commanded the vanguard. Alençon is perfectly possible, as he was the king's brother, but we have opted for Bohemia on the grounds that (a) he was the most experienced battle commander in the French army, (b) he had commanded, if only by default, the vanguard on the march from Paris and led the fighting along the Somme, and (c) the sources just fractionally favour him over Alençon. So we believe Bohemia led the vanguard out of Abbeville that morning, and was intended to lead the first division on the field. Some accounts still claim he did so, but this is unlikely in the extreme (see below).

The turn to the north, however, threw the march order out of kilter. Jean le Bel and Froissart both paint graphic and realistic pictures of individual divisions of the march order forcing their way through as best they could, abandoning all discipline in their eagerness to get to the enemy. It may be accounted a small miracle that Doria's Genoese ended up where they should have been at the front; but Doria again was a veteran commander, and knew what was wanted of him (even if no one else did). Bohemia, who had advanced most of the way to Noyelles, would suddenly have found himself near the rear of this mad scramble.

The whereabouts of King Philippe also call for comment. Several accounts, including some French ones, place him on the field at the start of the action, and attribute to him the choleric rage that ordered the slaughter of the Genoese and the reckless series of charges. This is out of keeping with Philippe's character, and with his reaction a few hours earlier to the advice given by Henri le Moine. And how would Philippe have got so close to the field in such a short space of time? Jean le Bel argues that the press of men and horses was so great that Philippe may never have reached the field at all, and we could regard this as highly likely were it not for the facts that Froissart and the English eyewitnesses not only say he did finally reach the field but describe his actions in detail, and that a number of men close to him were killed. But the idea that he gave coherent orders which were obeyed by any part of his army after mid-afternoon can, we believe, be discounted.

Events in the French army on the afternoon of 26 August are very difficult to decipher; chaos usually is. We believe, however, that the most probable and likely cycle of events is that described in Chapter 10. After receiving news of the English presence at Crécy, the French army turned in unison to the north, quickly lost formation and discipline and became a disorganised mass. Alençon forced his way to the front, followed by others of the *grands seigneurs*, leaving the two kings further back in the army. By the time the first French contingents reached the English position, command and control had entirely failed. This is entirely consistent with what happened next.

Battle formations: English

Most sources agree on the English formation, apart from the debate about the deployment of the archers alluded to in Chapter 10. Some modern accounts assume the English were stretched all along the ridge from Crécy to Wadicourt, but this would have stretched the force very thin. The known French preference for frontal attacks also meant this was unlikely. Some modern sources indicate that the wagon park was part of the English front line, but this is probably the result of a mistake by Villani, who also indicates this; every other primary source that mentions the wagon park puts it well to the rear, which was consistent with other English tactical formations. The baggage train was still too necessary and valuable to risk its destruction. Otherwise, our description of the English formation follows most conventional accounts.

Battle formations: French

Was there one? It seems unlikely, at least after the first few minutes.

About the only thing on which all the sources are agreed is the opening passage of the battle. Doria's men formed up, with Alençon's crowding after them. When Doria's men retreated, Alençon's attacked them, then attacked the English with the results described.

Apart from this, all is confusion. Some chroniclers and later writers, including modern military historians, persist in the view that, on reaching the battlefield, the French formed up in three divisions of men-at-arms with the Genoese in front before they attacked. This has led to some notable absurdities: for example, in some accounts the King of Bohemia leads the first division and Alençon the second, yet Alençon attacks the Genoese. Presumably he would have had to charge through Bohemia's division to do so, yet this is never mentioned.

Altogether more likely is the picture of utter chaos that is described by le Bel, Froissart and others closer to events. Of the English eyewitnesses, Northburgh says only that the English scouts reported four large battalions of the enemy approaching in the afternoon; this does not have to represent the entire army. Wynkeley says three major assaults were made, but does not mention the enemy forming up in divisions on the field. Edward, who watched the entire event from his post near the windmill, does not even go this far, merely saying that the two armies came together.

We do not believe that, on this occasion, the French army did form up in three divisions, or any other coherent battle formation, following the first attack. The picture described by le Bel in particular, of each contingent forcing its way to the front and then attacking as soon as it sighted the enemy, is altogether more likely and entirely consistent with events.

How many attacks?

Wynkeley mentions three attacks; Geoffrey le Baker indicates there were fifteen attacks in all, but three major attacks when the French 'raised the general war cry'. King Edward says the enemy 'often rallied', suggesting a series of attacks, although we believe these are more likely to be attacks by fresh contingents coming onto the field rather than contingents which had already attacked rallying and returning to the fray. Froissart and le Bel do not even try to count the number of attacks launched. In absence of a better guide, we have taken le Baker's figure of fifteen (which suggests, however, that some of the nine divisions of the march order must themselves have fragmented in the chaos before the battle; this seems eminently likely). The three major attacks can be regarded as the assaults of the three largest contingents, those of Alençon, King Philippe and King Jean of Bohemia, while the others were by smaller contingents such as that of Blois and Lorraine. This also fits with the length of time the battle is said to have lasted. It is possible that later attacks were joined by survivors or stragglers from earlier contingents, but it seems unlikely that any major contingent would have rallied and returned to the fray. It is possible, of course, but given the high casualties, the loss of so many leaders and the shambles that existed in the French rear areas, it would have taken a superhuman effort to organise the remainder of a contingent of men-at-arms for a second charge at the English lines.

Apart from Alençon and Bohemia, we have made no attempt to determine in which order the various contingents launched their assaults. King Philippe, we may assume from the argument above, came fairly late, but was not last. Bohemia is often portrayed as being in the front line, but we doubt this. There is the question of his position in the march order; there is the alleged conversation that Froissart says he had with Henri le Moine, indicating that the battle was well advanced when Bohemia arrived; there are several accounts, and also a Czech tradition (based on what we do not know) that it was nearly dark when Bohemia attacked. This would place him among the last, if not absolutely the last, contingent to launch an attack; much later and darkness and fog stopped all activity.

The constant stream of attacks must have placed the English arrow supply under considerable strain, although it should be remembered that most attacks lasted only a few minutes and thus the archers were not shooting continuously. Even so, the forty-eight arrows which each man carried onto the field were good for only about four minutes of sustained shooting. The army seems to have carried an adequate number of arrows (see Chapter 3), but getting these from the wagon park to the archers in the front lines must have required a constant stream of men running to and fro carrying bundles of arrows. Fortunately, arrows have one great advantage over bullets; they are reusable, provided they have not been damaged. We can assume that in the lulls between attacks, some archers ran onto the field near their lines and collected spent arrows to be shot again. Whatever expedients were resorted to, they seem to have worked; unlike Morlaix, not until the very end of the battle is there any hint that the supply of arrows was running low.

Casualties

Apart from Northburgh's figure of 1,542, there are only vague estimates of French casualties. This is sometimes taken as the *total* of French casualties, but it seems clear that Northburgh is referring only to men who wore coats of arms. No count was made of the ordinary mounted serjeants, or the Genoese, who must have suffered terribly. Our figures are estimates, but we do not believe they are unreasonable ones.

There has been scepticism about the low number of English casualties noted by Wynkeley, but in absence of other evidence, we see no reason to doubt this. At Agincourt, there was much more prolongued hand-to-hand fighting but English casualties were similarly low.

Bibliography

Unprinted primary sources

Public Record Office:
E101
E159
E403
SC1/39
SC1/40
SC1/41

British Library:
Add. MS 38823
Harley 246
Harley 3968
Stowe 574

Printed primary sources

Acta Bellicosa, translated in Richard Barber (ed.), *The Life and Campaigns of the Black Prince*, Woodbridge, 1986.
Actes Normandes de la chambre des comptes sous Philippe VI de Valois, ed. L. Delisle, Paris, 1871.
Adam Murimuth, *Continuatio Chronicarum*, ed. E.M. Thompson, London, 1889 (cited as Murimuth).
Anonimalle Chronicle, 1331–1381, ed. V.H. Galbraith, Manchester, 1970.
Blondel, Robert, *Oeuvres de Robert Blondel*, ed. A. Héron, Rouen, 1891.
Bourgeois de Valenciennes, in Froissart, *Oeuvres*, ed. Kervyn de Lettenhove in vols 4 and 5.

Brut, or the Chronicle of England, ed. F.W.B. Brie, Early English Text Society, 1906–8.

Burghersh, Bartholomew, in Robert de Avesbury, *De Gestis Mirabilis Regis Edwardi Tertii*, ed. E.M. Thompson.

Calendar of Close Rolls (cited as *CCR*).

Calendar of Fine Rolls.

Calendar of Inquisitiones Post Mortem, vols 8 and 9.

Calendar of Patent Rolls (cited as *CPR*).

Chronicon a Monacho Sancti Albani, ed. E.M. Thompson, London, 1874.

Chronicon de Lanercost 1201–1346, ed. J. Stevenson, Edinburgh, 1839.

Chronicon Galfridi le Baker de Swynebroke, ed. E.M. Thompson, Oxford, 1889 (cited as Baker).

Chronicon Henrici Knighton, ed. J.F. Lumby, 2 vols, London, 1889–95.

Chronicon Monasterii de Melsa, London: Public Record Office, 1863–8 (cited as *Meaux Chronicle*).

Chronique de Flandres, Paris, 1838.

Chronique de Jean le Bel, ed. J. Viard and E. Déprez, Paris, 1905 (cited as le Bel).

Chronique de Pierre de Cochon

Chronique des Quatre Premiers Valois (1327–1393), ed. S. Luce, Paris, 1862.

Chronique de Richard Lescot, ed. J. Lemoine, Paris, 1896.

Chronique Normande du XIVe Siècle, ed. A. and E. Molinier, Paris, 1882.

Chronographia Regum Francorum, ed. H. Moranville, 3 vols, Paris, 1891–7.

Cronica di Giovanni Villani, Florence, 1823.

Eulogium Historiarum, ed. F.S. Haydon, London, 1863.

Froissart, Jean, *Chronicles of England, France and Spain and adjoining counties*, ed. T. Johnes, London, 1896.

Froissart, Jean, *Chroniques, Livre 1, le manuscrit d'Amiens*, ed. G.T. Dilke, vols 2 and 3, Geneva, 1992.

Froissart, Jean, *Oeuvres de Froissart*, ed. Kervyn de Lettenhove, vols 4 and 5, Brussels, 1937.

Gilles le Muisit, *Chronique et Annales*, ed. H. Lemaitre, Paris, 1906.

Gray, Thomas, *Scalacronica*, ed. H. Maxwell, Glasgow, 1907.

Guillaume de Nangis, *Chronique de Guillaume de Nangis.*

Les Grandes Chroniques de France, ed. J. Viard, vol. 9, Paris, 1887.

Hemingburgh, Walter of, *Chronicon*, ed. H.C. Hamilton, vol. 2, London, 1984–9.

Northburgh, M.: in Robert de Avesbury, *De Gestis Mirabilis Regis Edwardi Tertii*, ed. E.M. Thompson.

Register of Edward the Black Prince, 4 vols, London: Public Record Office, 1930–3.

Robert de Avesbury, *De Gestis Mirabilis Regis Edwardi Tertii*, ed. E.M. Thompson, Rolls Series, 1889 (cited as Avesbury).

Rotuli Parliamentorum.

Rymer's Foedera, ed. A. Clark *et al.*, London, 1816.

Viard, J., *Le Journaux du trésor de Philippe VI de Valois*, Paris, 1889.

Viard, J. and A. Vallée (eds), *Registres du Trésor des Chartes*, Paris, 1979–84.

Wrottesley, G., 'Crécy and Calais from the Public Records', Collections for a *History of Staffordshire*, 1897.

Wynkeley, R. in Richard Barber, *The Life and Campaigns of the Black Prince*, Woodbridge, 1986.

Secondary sources

Abulafia, D. (1994), *A Mediterranean Emporium: The Catalan Kingdom of Majorca*, Cambridge: Cambridge University Press.

Ainsworth, P.F. (1990), *Jean Froissart and the Fabric of History: Truth, Myth and Fiction in the Chroniques*, Oxford: Clarendon Press.

Allmand, C. (1988), *The Hundred Years War: England and France at War, c.1300–c.1450*, Cambridge: Cambridge University Press.

Ashby, E. (1996), 'Arrow Lethality: Part IV, The Physics of Arrow Penetration', www.tradgang.com/ashby/arrow%20lethality%20204.htm (19 July 2004).

Ayton, A. (1994), 'The English Army and the Normandy Campaign of 1346', in D. Bates and A. Curry (eds), *England and Normandy in the Middle Ages*, London: Hambledon.

Ayton, A. (1994), *Knights and Warhorses: Military Service and the English Aristocracy under Edward III*, Woodbridge: Boydell & Brewer.

Ayton, A. (2001), 'Sir Thomas Ughtred and the Edwardian Military Revolution', in J. Bothwell (ed.), *The Age of Edward III*, York: York Medieval Press, pp. 107–32.

Barber, R. (1978), *Edward, Prince of Wales and Aquitaine: A Biography of the Black Prince*, London: Allen Lane.

Barber, R., ed. (1986), *The Life and Campaigns of the Black Prince*, Woodbridge: Boydell & Brewer.

Bernardy, F. de (1961), *Princes of Monaco*, London: Arthur Barker.

Bilson, F. (1974), *Crossbows*, Newton Abbot: David & Charles.

Blair, C. (1958), *European Armour*, London: B.T. Batsford.

Bobková, L. (2002), 'The Royal Crown of Bohemia: A Central European Empire of the House of Luxembourg', in *The Czech State from the Hussite Wars to NATO Membership*, Prague: ELK, pp. 51–63.

Bois, G. (1984), *The Crisis of Feudalism: Economy and Society in Western Europe c.1300–1550*, Cambridge: Cambridge University Press.

Boitani, P. and Torti, A., eds (1983) *Literature in Fourteenth-Century England*, Cambridge: D.S. Brewer.

Bothwell, J. (2001), 'Edward III, the English Peerage and the 1337 Earls: Estate Redistribution in Fourteenth-Century England', in J. Bothwell (ed.), *The Age of Edward III*, York: York Medieval Press, pp. 13–34.

Boutell, C. (1907), *Arms and Armour in Antiquity and the Middle Ages*, London: Reeves & Turner; repr. Conshohocken, PA: Combined Books, 1996.

Burke, E. (1958), *The History of Archery*, London: Heinemann.

Burne, A.H. (1955), *The Crécy War: A Military History of the Hundred Years War from 1337 to the Peace of Bretigny, 1360*, London: Eyre & Spottiswoode; repr. London: Wordsworth, 1999.

Cazelles, R. (1947), *Jean l'Aveugle, Comte de Luxembourg, Roi de Bohême*, Paris: Tardy.

Cazelles, R. (1958), *La Société politique et la crise de royauté sous Philippe de Valois*, Paris: Tardy.

Chaplais, P., ed. (1954), *The War of Saint-Sardos (1323–1325): Gascon Correspondence and Diplomatic Documents*, London: Royal Historical Society.

Charpillon, M. (1868), *Dictionnaire historique de toutes les communes du département de l'Eure*, Les Andelys: Chez Delacroix.

Chaytor, H.J. (1933), *A History of Aragon and Catalonia*, London: Methuen.

Cleere, H., Crossley, D. and Worssam, B.C. (1985), *The Iron Industry of the Weald*, Cardiff: Merton Priory Press.

le Clerc, J. (1889), 'Philippe VI à la bataille de Crécy', *Bibliotheque l'école de Chartes*, pp. 295–7.

Clowes, W.L. (1897), *The Royal Navy: A History From the Earliest Times to the Present*, London: Sampson, Low & Co.

Collet, C., Leroux, P. and Marin, J.-Y. (1995), *Caen, cité médiéval, bilan d'archeologie et d'histoire*, Caen.

Contamine, P. (1972), *Guerre, état et société à la fin du Moyen Âge*, Paris: Mouton.

Contamine, P., ed. (1992), *Histoire Militaire de la France*, vol. 1, 'Des origines á 1715', Paris: PUF.

Contamine, P. (1994), 'The Norman "Nation" and the French "Nation" in the Fourteenth and Fifteenth Centuries', in D. Bates and A. Curry (eds), *England and Normandy in the Middle Ages*, London: Hambledon, pp. 215–34.

Cox, E.L. (1967), *The Green Count of Savoy*, Princeton: Princeton University Press.

Crossley, D.W., ed. (1983), *Medieval Industry*, London: Council for British Archaeology.

Curry, A. and Hughes, H., eds (1994), *Arms, Armies and Fortifications in the Hundred Years War*, Woodbridge: Boydell & Brewer.

Delisle, L. (1867) *Histoire du château et des sires de St-Sauveur-le-Vicomte*, Valognes.

Demangeon, A. (1905), *La Picardie*, Paris: Librairie Armand Colin.

Denholm Young, N. (1965), *History and Heraldry*, Oxford: Clarendon Press.

Denifle, P.H. (1899), *La Guerre de Cent Ans et la désolation des églises, monastères et hôpitaux en France*, Paris; repr. Brussels: Impression Anastaltique, 1965.

Deprez, E. (1902), *Les Preliminaires de la Guerre de Cent Ans, 1328–1342*, Paris: Thorin et fils.

DeVries, K. (1992), *Medieval Military Technology*, Peterborough, Ont.: Broadview.

Dufayard, C. (1922), *Histoire de Savoie*, Paris: Ancien Librairie Furne.

Dupont, G., ed. (1870–85), *Le Cotentin et ses Iles*, 4 vols, Caen.

Duseval, M.H. (1848), *Histoire de la Ville d'Amiens*, Amiens: Caron et Lambert.

Epstein, S.R. (1996), *Genoa and the Genoese, 958–1528*, Chapel Hill: University of North Carolina Press.

Estancelin, L. (1821), *Histoire des Comtes d'Eu*, Paris: Chez Delaunay.

Favier, J. (1980), *La Guerre de Cent Ans*, Paris: Fayard.

Fowler, K., ed. (1971), *The Hundred Years War*, London: Macmillan.

Fox-Davies, A.C. (1909), *A Complete Guide to Heraldry*, London; repr. New York: Bonanza, 1978.

Foy, T. (1980), *A Guide to Archery*, London: Pelham Books.

Fryde, E.B. (1947), 'Edward III's War Finance 1337–41: Transactions in Wool and Credit Operations', unpublished Oxford University D.Phil. thesis.

Fryde, E.B. (1967), 'Financial Resources of Edward III in the Netherlands, 1337–40', *Revue Belge de Philologie et d'Histoire*, XLV, pp. 146–7, 180–1.

Fryde, E.B. (1988), *William de la Pole: Merchant and King's Banker*, London: Hambledon.

Fryde, N. (1975), 'Edward III's Removal of his Ministers and Judges, 1340–1', *Bulletin of the Institute of Historical Research*, 47, pp. 149–61.

Fryde, N. (1978), 'A Medieval Robber Baron: Sir John Molyns of Stoke Poges, Buckinghamshire', in R. Hunnisett and J.B. Post (eds), *Medieval Legal Records Edited in Memory of C.A.F. Meekings*, London: Public Record Office, pp. 197–221.

Galbraith, V.H. (1982), *Kings and Chroniclers: Essays in English Medieval History*, London: Hambledon.

Ganiage, J., ed. (1987), *Histoire de Beauvais et du Beauvaisis*, Toulouse: Éditions Privat.

Gimpel, J. (1976), *The Medieval Machine: The Industrial Revolution of the Middle Ages*, London: Penguin.

Given-Wilson, C. (1986), *The Royal Household and the King's Affinity*, New Haven: Yale University Press.

Godfray, H. Marret (1891), *Documents relatif aux attaques sur les Îles de la Manche, 1338–45*, Jersey.

Grisel, C. and Niel, A. (n.d.), *Hommes et traditions populaires*, Amiens: Martelle Editions.

Guilmeth, A. (1842), *Histoire de la ville et des environs d'Elbeuf*, Rouen: Imprimerie de Berdalle de Lapommeraye.

Hardy, B.C. (1910), *Philippa of Hainault and her Times*, London: John Long.

Hardy, R. (1976), *Longbow: A Social and Military History*, Cambridge: Patrick Stephens.

Henneman, J.B. (1971), *Royal Taxation in the Fourteenth Century: The Development of War Financing, 1322–56*, Princeton: Princeton University Press.

Hulme, F.E. (1892), *History, Principles and Practice of Heraldry*, London: Swan Sonnenscheim.

Hyland, A. (1999), *The Horse in the Middle Ages*, Stroud: Alan Sutton.

Jones, T. (1980), *Chaucer's Knight: The Portrait of a Medieval Mercenary*, London: Eyre Methuen.

José, M. (1956), *La Maison de Savoie*, Paris: Éditions Albin Michel.

Keen, M. (1973), *England in the Later Middle Ages*, London: Methuen.

Keen, M. (1984), *Chivalry*, New Haven: Yale University Press.

Kooi, B.W. (1991), 'Archery and Mathematical Modelling', *Journal of the Society of Archer Antiquaries*, 34, pp. 21–9.

La Chavanne-Desbois, Ch. de (1866), *Dictionaire de la noblesse*, Paris.

Labande, L.-H. (1934), *Histoire de la Principauté de Monaco*, Paris: Auguste Picard.

Le Patourel, J. (1958), 'Edward III and the Kingdom of France', *History*, 43.

Le Patourel, J. (1971), 'The Origins of the Hundred Years War', in K. Fowler (ed.), *The Hundred Years War*, London: Macmillan.

Livingstone, M. (2003), 'The *Nonae*: The Records of the Taxation of the Ninth in England 1340–41', unpublished Ph.D. thesis, The Queen's University of Belfast.

Longman, C.J. and Walrond, H. (1884), *Archery*, London: Longmans, Green.

Longman, W. (1869), *The History of the Life and Times of Edward the Third*, London: Longmans, Green.

Louandre, F.C. (1844–5), *Histoire d'Abbeville*, 2 vols, Abbeville.

Lucas, H.S. (1929), *The Low Countries and the Hundred Years War, 1326–1347*, Ann Arbor: University of Michigan Press.

Lützow, F. von (1939), *Bohemia: An Historical Sketch*, London: J.M. Dent.

Markham, C.R. (1908), *The Story of Majorca and Minorca*, London: Smith, Elder.

Maskell, H.P. (1930), *The Soul of Picardy*, London: Ernest Benn.

McHardy, A.K. (2001), 'Some Reflections on Edward III's Use of Propaganda', in J. Bothwell (ed.), *The Age of Edward III*, York: York Medieval Press, pp. 171–92.

McKisack, M. (1959), *The Fourteenth Century 1307–1399*, Oxford: Oxford University Press.

McLane, B.W. (1988), *The 1341 Royal Inquest in Lincolnshire*, Lincoln Record Society, 78.

McNamee, C. (1997), *Wars of the Bruces*, East Linton: Tuckwell.

Metivier, H. (1862), *Monaco et ses princes*, La Flèche.

Meyer, E. (1874–5), *Histoire de Vernon*, Les Andelys: Chez Delacroix.

Miller, W. (1908), *The Latins in the Levant: A History of Frankish Greece (1204–1566)*, New York: Barnes & Noble.

Moisant, J. (1894), *Le Prince Noir en Aquitaine*, Paris.

Nicholas, N.H. (1832), *The Controversy Between Sir Richard Scrope and Sir Robert Grosvenor in the Court of Chivalry, AD MCCCLXXXV–MCCCXC*, London.

Nicolle, D. (2000), *Crécy 1346: Triumph of the Longbow*, London: Osprey.

Nicolle, D. (2000), *French Armies of the Hundred Years War*, London: Osprey.

Noble, P. (1992), 'The Perversion of an Ideal', in C. Harper-Bill and R. Harvey (eds), *Medieval Knighthood*, vol. 4, Woodbridge: Boydell & Brewer, pp. 177–86.

Oakeshott, R.E. (1961), *The Sword in the Age of Chivalry*, London: Lutterworth.

Oakeshott, R.E. (1962), *The Knight and his Horse*, London: Lutterworth.

Oman, C. (1924), *History of the Art of War in the Middle Ages*, London: Methuen.

Ormrod, W.M. (1990), *The Reign of Edward III: Crown and Political Society in England, 1327–1377*, London: Guild.

Ormrod, W.M. (1991), 'The Crown and the English Economy, 1290–1348', in B.M.S. Campbell (ed.), *Before the Black Death*, Manchester: Manchester University Press, table 5.1.

Ormrod, W.M. (1994), 'England, Normandy and the Beginnings of the Hundred Years War, 1259–1360', in D. Bates and A. Curry (eds), *England and Normandy in the Middle Ages*, London: Hambledon, pp. 197–214.

Packe, M. (1983), *King Edward III*, London: Routledge & Kegan Paul.

Payne-Gallwey, R. (1995), *The Book of the Crossbow*, London: Constable (expanded version of 1903 original).

Perrin, A. (1900), *Histoire de Savoie des origines à 1860*, Chambéry: Librairie-Lithographie A. Perrin.

Petiška, E. (1994), *Charles IV: The King from the Golden Cradle*, Prague: Martin.

Pierson, C. (n.d.), 'La Bataille de Crécy', Crécy-en-Ponthieu: Office de Tourisme.

Plaisse, A. (1994), *A travers le Cotentin: la grande chevauchée guerrière d'Édouard III en 1346*, Cherbourg: Éditions Isoète.

Plaisse, A. (1999), 'Cherbourg durant la guerre de Cent Ans', in *La Normandie dans la guerre de Cent Ans, 1346–1450*, Caen: Musée de Normandie.

Planhol, X. de (1994), *An Historical Geography of France*, trans. Janet Lloyd, Cambridge: Cambridge University Press.

Platt, C. (1973), *Medieval Southampton*, London: Routledge & Kegan Paul.

Polišenský, J.V. (1946), *History of Czechoslovakia in Outline*, Prague: Bohemia International.

Powicke, M. (1962), *Military Obligation in Medieval England*, Oxford: Clarendon Press.

Prestwich, M. (1980), *The Three Edwards: War and State in England 1272–1377*, London: Weidenfeld & Nicolson.

Prestwich, M. (1988), *Edward I*, New Haven, Connecticut: Yale University Press.

Prestwich, M. (1996), *Armies and Warfare in the Middle Ages: The English Experience*, New Haven: Yale University Press.

Rees, G. (1995), 'The Physics of Medieval Archery', *Physics Review*, January.

Robida, *Vielle France* (1890–3), 4 vols, Paris.

Rogers, C.J., ed. (1999), *The Wars of Edward III*, Woodbridge: Boydell & Brewer.

Rogers, C.J. (2000), *War Cruel and Sharp: English Strategy under Edward III*, Woodbridge: Boydell & Brewer.

Round, J.H. (1911), *The King's Serjeants and Officers of State*, London: James Nisbet.

Salzmann, L.F. (1923), *English Industries of the Middle Ages*, Oxford: Clarendon Press.

Sandret, L. (1866), *L'ancienne église de France, ou état des archévéches de France*, Paris.

Schaudel, L. (1921), *Les Comtes de Salm et l'Abbaye de Senonces aux XIIe et XIIIe siècles*, Nancy: Berger-Leurault.

Shneidman, J.L. (1970), *The Rise of the Aragonese–Catalan Empire, 1200–1350*, New York: New York University Press.

Stones, E.L.G. (1957), 'The Folvilles of Ashby-Folville, Leicestershire, and their Associates in Crime, 1326–1347', *Transactions of the Royal Historical Society*, vol. 7, pp. 117–36.

Sumption, J. (1990), *The Hundred Years War*, vol. 1, *Trial by Battle*, London: Faber & Faber.

Taylor, J. (1987), *English Historical Literature in the Fourteenth Century*, Oxford: Clarendon Press.

Tout, T.F. (1904), 'The Tactics of the Battles of Boroughbridge and Morlaix', *English Historical Review*, vol. 19, pp. 711–15; repr. in *The Collected Papers of Thomas Frederick Tout*, Manchester: Manchester University Press, 1934, vol. 2, pp. 221–5.

Tout, T.F. (1911), 'Firearms in England in the Fourteenth Century', *English Historical Review*, vol. 26, pp. 666–702; repr. in *The Collected Papers of Thomas Frederick Tout*, Manchester: Manchester University Press, 1934, vol. 2, pp. 233–75.

Tout, T.F. (1920), *Chapters in the Administrative History of Medieval England*, London: Longmans, Green.

Trebuten, G.-F. (1881), *Caen*, Caen: F. Le Blanc-Hardel.

Tuck, A. (1985), *Crown and Nobility 1272–1461*, Oxford: Oxford University Press.

Vaultier, M.F. (1843), *Histoire de la ville de Caen*, Caen: B. Mangel.

Viard, J. (1926), 'Le Campagne de juillet–août et la bataille de Crécy', *Le Moyen Age* (January–April), pp. 1–85.

Viard, J. (1913 and 1923), 'Itineraire de Philippe VI de Valois', *Bibliothèque de l'école de Chartes*.

Viard, J. (1906), 'Henri le Moine de Bale', *Bibliothèque l'école de Chartes*, vol. 66, pp. 489–96.

Vincens, M.E. (1842), *Histoire de la République de Gènes*, Paris: Chez Firmin Didot Frères.

Vivent, J. (1954), *La Guerre de Cent Ans*, Paris: Flammarion.

Wailly, H. de (1987), *Crécy: Anatomy of a Battle*, trans. A. Sookia and J. Sookia, Poole: Blandford Press.

Walmsley, J., ed. (1996), *Charters and Custumals of the Abbey of Holy Trinity, Caen*, part 2, *The French Estates*, Oxford: Oxford University Press.

Wentersdorf, K.P. (1979), 'The Clandestine Marriages of the Fair Maid of Kent', *Journal of Medieval History*, vol. 5, pp. 203–31.

Zurita, J. (1973), *Anales de la Corona de Aragon*, Zaragoza: Institución 'Fernando de Católico'.

Index

Edmund, Earl of Kent, 3
Edward I, 4, 10, 20, 22, 34, 54, 63
Edward II, 2, 3, 4, 21, 34, 54, 80
Edward III, 1–3, 4, 7, 11–12, 13–14, 15, 16,
 20, 21–2, 36, 41, 42, 61, 69–73, 84–99,
 109, 113, 113–17, 118, 126, 129, 130, 134,
 141, 143, 144, 145, 147, 148, 149, 150,
 151, 152, 153, 161, 162, 166, 170, 172,
 178–9, 183–400, 185–6, 188, 189–90, 198,
 199–200, 203, 210–11, 213, 215–6, 213,
 222, 228, 236, 238, 239, 240, 245, 259**,
 263, 279, 282, 297, 291–2, 302–3, 320,
 325–6, 331
Edward III, personal possessions, 91–2
Edward III, personal qualities, 21–3, 113–17,
 178–9, 183–4, 210, 216, 219–20
Edward III, relations with nobles, 21–2
Edward of Woodstock, Prince of Wales, 2, 22,
 39, 40, 42, 46, 109, 112, 114–15, 117, 123,
 143, 144, 152–3, 160–4, 171, 202, 204,
 208, 210–11, 213, 221, 231, 232–4, 235,
 251–2, 255–6, 263, 275, 278, 279, 288,
 291, 299–300, 302–3, 321
Elbeuf, 189–93, 197, 206
Eleanor of Aquitaine, Queen of England, 7
Eleanor of Castile, Queen of England, 10
Eliška, Queen of Bohemia, 81
Elizabeth, Countess of Ormond, 34
England, invasion of, 3–4, 173–4
English territories in France, 6–8
Ennequin, Godefroi d', 220, 248
Epône, 210
Erpingham, Robert, 39
esquires, 29, 39–40, 46, 49
Estates General, France, 75
Estracelles, Jacques d', 47, 289, 291, 292, 299,
 327
Estrées-les-Crécy, 263
Étaples, 319
Eure (river), 198–9, 201
exemptions from service, 85, 97

faggots, 89, 181
Falkirk, battle of, 54, 62
Fay, Godemar de, 47, 74, 84, 127, 248, 251,
 254, 256–61, 317
Fermanville, 121
Ferrars of Chartley, Robert, 206–7
Ferrers, Robert, 123
Ferrers, Thomas, 17
Fevre, Andrew le, 41, 88
Fevre, Katherine, 88
Fevre, Walter le, 59, 88
finance, English, 10–12, 42–3, 72–3
finance, French, 74–5

firearms, 58–9, 87–8
fish, 90, 112, 120, 122, 132, 145, 152, 165,
 172, 174–5, 185, 189, 204, 208–9, 221,
 234, 235, 265, 267
Fitzalan, Richard, Earl of Arundel, 16, 33, 36,
 38, 42, 47, 123, 144, 161, 181, 239, 255,
 258, 263, 277, 292
FitzSimon, Richard, 39, 275, 291
Fitzwaryne, Fulk, 38
Fitzwayne, William, 38
Flambard, Robert, 41
Flanders, 3, 12, 16, 22, 24, 58–9, 60–1, 70,
 72, 76, 83–4, 143, 185, 263
Flanders, Count of, 10, 237, 238
Flanders, Jeanne of, 13
Flemings, 24, 58–9, 60–1, 69, 143, 175, 177,
 210, 220, 248, 262, 263
fodder, 88–9, 18
Folkestone, 12, 115
Folville, John, 28, 29
Folville, Richard, 28, 29
Folville, Robert, 28, 29, 60
Fontaine-sur-Maye, 263, 274
Fontaine-sur-Somme, 246
Fontenay-le-Pesnil, 152–3
Fontenay-sur-Mer, 125, 129
food, 90–1, 93, 97, 98, 99, 112, 118, 120–1,
 122, 124, 125, 126, 132, 134, 143, 145,
 149, 152, 153, 165, 172, 174–5, 177, 178,
 179, 181, 182, 185, 186–7, 189, 191, 199,
 204, 208–9, 221, 230, 234, 235, 236, 247,
 249–50, 251, 252, 261–2, 265, 267, 303,
 319
food, shortage of, 236, 252, 261–2, 265
foot soldiers, 40–1, 51–9, 86, 87, 165, 289
foraging, 125, 126, 134, 145–6, 149, 152,
 153, 178, 179, 181
Forest of Dean, 44
Forêt de Rouvray, 190
Franconville, 219, 231
French crown, inheritance of, 8
French invasion plan, 173–4
French raids on England, 9, 11
French resistence to English invasion, 239
Freneuse, 204–5
Freshwater, Isle of Wight, 99
Fricamps, Friquet de, 127, 158, 164
Frocourt, 232
Froyelles, 263, 274, 285, 286, 300
Fuller of Dunwich, William, 41
furor franciscus, 60, 61, 278, 291
Fyncham, William, 41

Gaillon, 200, 201–2, 204, 206, 216, 275
Garderobe, Walter de la, 39

Index

Treaty of Corbeil, 5
Trier, 83
Troarn, 178–9
Troissereux, 233–4
Troyes, Chrétien de, 48
Trussel, John, 39
Trussel, William, 28–9
Tudor, John, 39
Tufton, Lewis, 277
Tybynton, John, 40
Tyfford, Robert, 314–15
Tyrel family, Seigneurs de Poix, 32
Tyrel, Jean de, Seigneur de Poix, 236
Tyrel, Marguerite de, 237
Tyrel, Marie de, 237

Uffalise, Henry d', 299
Ufford, Robert, Earl of Suffolk, 33, 36–7, 39,
    47, 96, 123, 239, 263, 277, 313
Ughtred, Thomas, 35, 122, 123
Umfraville, Gilbert d', 63, 277
Ursini, Peter, Count of Rožmberk, 83, 297,
    300–2
Utah Beach, 108, 110, 129

Vacognes, Guillaume de, 129
Valloire, abbey of, 318–19
Valognes, 123, 125–8
Valois, Marguerite de, 30
Vannes, 13–14, 36
Vatteville, 201
Vaubain, 319
Vaud, Louis, Count of, 79–80, 218, 280, 318
Vaureguard, 219, 231
Ventadour, Vicomte de, 297
Ventamiglia, 77
Verdun, Raoul de, 15, 134, 142, 180
Vere, John de, Earl of Oxford, 34, 123, 275
Vernon, 175–6, 200, 202, 203–5, 208, 209
Vernon, La Croix Saint-Leufroy, 203
Vers, Hughues de, 314
Vessencourt, 231, 232
Vexin, 235
Vienne, Jean de, 319
Vignoso, Simone, 77
Vimeu, 247, 252, 296
Vire (river), 131, 134, 141, 142, 144, 147

Wadicourt, 263, 264
wages, 86–7
Wales, 54, 62
Wallace, William, 62
Walton, Adam, 42
Warde, John la, 42
wardrobe, royal, 41–2, 92
Warewyk, Adam, 40
Warre, Roger de la, 3
Watenhoule, John, 95–6
water, shortage of, 187–8
Waterloo, 276
Watteglise, 316
Weald of Kent, 44
weapons, 43–59
weapons, hand-held, 47–9
weather, 325–6
Welsh foot soldiers, 184–5, 192
Wesenham, John, 73
West, Thomas, 38
Westminster, 93
Weston, Philip, 42
Weston, WIlliam, 41
Wetewang, William, 41, 93
Whet, Richard, 164
Whet, Robert, 40
William, Count of Hainault, 84
William I 'the Conqueror', King of England
    and Duke of Normandy, 6, 60, 161, 174,
    199, 252, 296
Winchelsea, 39, 177
Winchester, 12
Windsor tournament (1344), 2, 23
wine, 91, 97, 99
Wissant, 319
Wode, Edward atte, 3, 38, 206, 207
Wode, William atte, 42
Wrottesley, Hugh, 39
Wynkeley, Richard, 42, 93, 171, 177, 179,
    185–6, 199, 299, 315, 316
Wynnesbury, Nicholas, 42

Yarmouth, 99
Ypres, 83, 143, 185, 187

Zouche, Alan la, 303
Zouche, William la, Archbishop of York, 320

18